BANGLADESH

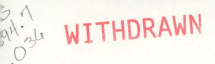

BANGLADESH
Biography of a Muslim Nation

Charles Peter O'Donnell

Westview Press / Boulder and London

Published in 1984 in the United States of America by Westview Press, Inc., 5500 Central Avenue, Boulder, Colorado 80301; Frederick A. Praeger, Publisher

Library of Congress Cataloging in Publication Data
O'Donnell, Charles Peter, 1904–
　Bangladesh: biography of a Muslim nation.
　Bibliography: p.
　Includes index.
　1. Bangladesh—Politics and government.　2. Bangladesh
—Economic conditions.　I. Title
DS394.7.036　　1984　　954.9′2　　83-23491
ISBN 0-86531-682-1

Printed and bound in the United States of America

10　　9　　8　　7　　6　　5　　4　　3　　2　　1

To Kay,
who lived in Bangladesh
and loves it and hopes for it as much as I
and to all the Americans
who have served in East Bengal, East Pakistan, and Bangladesh
and have left a part of themselves there

The National Anthem of Bangladesh

My Bengal of gold, I love you
Forever your skies, your air set my heart in tune
    as if it were a flute
In Spring, Oh mother mine, the fragrance from
    your mango-groves makes me wild with joy—
    Ah, what a thrill!
In Autumn, Oh mother mine,
    in the full-blossomed paddy fields,
I have seen spread all over—sweet smiles!
Ah, what a beauty, what shades, what an affection
    and what a tenderness!
What a quilt you have spread at the feet of
    banyan trees and along the banks of rivers!
Oh mother mine, words from your lips are like
    nectar in my ears!
    Ah, what a thrill!
If sadness, Oh mother mine, casts a gloom on your face,
    my eyes are filled with tears!

Original in Bengali by Rabindranath Tagore; translation by Professor Syed Ali Ahsan from *This is Bangladesh* (Dacca: Ministry of Information, People's Republic of Bangladesh, n.d.).

Contents

Illustrations

Preface

This life history of the Bangali nation concentrates its broad-brush treatment on Bangladesh's well-publicized political and economic development and on its less well-known physical, social, and cultural dimensions. As a history, it attempts to answer the questions of how the nation came to be independent and how it has fared since becoming a nation-state.

In the early sixties I served as the U.S. consul general in what was then East Pakistan and is now Bangladesh. I learned something of the spirit of the people and their difficult and stubborn problems. Since I left Dacca I have watched the people's successes, failures, and setbacks and their responses to Pakistani and Bangali governments.

The story of the Bangalis from the sixth century to the present is buried in the history of India and has yet to be fully retrieved. Historians have amply documented the Pakistan phase, but because the Bangali nation-state came into existence little more than a decade ago, its story, largely a record of current events, is incomplete and reflects only superficial analyses. Although the hindsight of a decade has helped to reveal the significance of many issues and made their interpretation easier, more complete data, scholarly analysis, and the vantage point of a larger time frame are needed before an authoritative history can be written.

To describe the people of the nation, past and present, I have used the term *Bangali* rather than the archaic *Bangalee* or the awkward adopted name, *Bangladeshi*. The word *Bengali* here refers both to the national language of the Bangalis and to the people of West Bengal, India, as well as their language. (The two languages are substantially the same.) The name of the new nation, originally written as two words, *Bangla Desh,* meaning "the land of the Bangalis," is now written as one word. Since the variant spellings of Bangali proper names would confuse readers, I have chosen one spelling and stayed with it, but I refer to important political figures by their informal (second) name as well as their formal name.

The Americans who served in the consulate general, the U.S. Information Service, the U.S. Agency for International Development, and the Peace Corps, as well as Americans employed by international agencies or U.S. firms and organizations, helped me prepare this portrait of the Bangalis and Bangladesh. The cooperation of my Foreign Service colleagues and the diplomatic representatives of other governments encouraged me to pursue this work. Because the story of the Bangalis attracted the attention of the world press, much of the information about recent developments there comes from articles and books by journalists as well as scholars. The Select Bibliography and Notes of this book are an acknowledgment of my debt to them.

I am grateful to Pakistani, Indian, and Bangali officials and private citizens for their hospitality and for my education in the affairs of the subcontinent. I greatly appreciate the assistance of the library staff of Loyola University of Chicago and in particular of Brother Michael Grace, S.J., in the preparation of this book. My gratitude also goes to Department of State officials for keeping me up to date. I am indebted to the editors of Westview Press. I owe particular thanks to Debra Patnaik of Oberlin College, Joel Wells of the Thomas More Association of Chicago, Gray Bream, Foreign Service colleague and former principal officer in Dacca, and my sons, Patrick and James, who lived in Dacca. I owe special thanks to my wife for her help, patience, and support.

Charles Peter O'Donnell

Introduction

A little more than a decade ago, the Bangali nation suddenly acquired the responsibilities of self-government. Democracy is a high-risk form of politics for this new, impoverished, and second-most-populous of the 42 Muslim nations. Limited experience with the complexities of the twentieth-century world makes the tasks of the Bangalis and their modernizing governments vastly more difficult than those faced by older democratic nations. And like many peoples before, they also have encountered the age-old political problem of translating their aspirations into workable policies and programs. Although their colonial experience taught them that rule by outsiders shuts down democracy, their government has yet to learn how to deal with political violence, partisanship, an erratic economy, a traditional society, overpopulation, the governments of neighboring nations, and its own mistakes.

The way in which the past evolved to fashion present-day Bangladesh constitutes the main theme of this "biography" and helps to explain the nation's problems, struggles, and progress.

The book opens by relating how the Bangali people developed into a national community when, after centuries of migrations, they came to live together in the delta region of the South Asian subcontinent and when, in the tenth century A.D., the Bengali language became their vernacular. By the thirteenth century, with the conversion of a majority to Islam, that community had evolved into a national society with a distinctive pattern of ethical, social, and economic life and an Islamic culture open to Hindu influence. From the thirteenth to the twentieth centuries the nonintervention of colonial rulers in their social and religious customs made it possible for the Muslim majority gradually to acquire social authority among the people of East Bengal.

One theme of the book is that centuries of colonial government protected Bangali traditional life but did not educate the nation in

1

self-rule. As members of the Mogul empire, the Bangalis retained the slow, nonpolitical rhythms of medieval agrarian existence. In the last years of the British Raj, however, two western-oriented political groups did emerge among the Muslims of the subcontinent. An aristocratic body, made up chiefly of non-Bangalis from what was to become West Pakistan, founded the Muslim League and led the movement for the separation of Pakistan from India. Bangali middle-class politicians living in Calcutta earned leading roles in local politics, independent of members of the Muslim League, and fought for a united Muslim Bengal. The joint decision of the Indian Congress party, the Muslim League, and the British government delivered the Bangalis of East Bengal to Pakistan.

Mounting Bangali opposition to Pakistan's quarter-of-a-century rule, nearly half of it under martial law or emergency laws, led to Bangali independence. During most of the first decade of the Pakistan era, the Bangali Muslim League, which supported a united Pakistan, controlled Bangali politics. The Awami (people's) League under the direction of H. S. Suhrawardy, along with other populist groups, denounced West Pakistan's domination of the agricultural Bangali economy and demanded political and economic parity with West Pakistan. Their campaign for provincial autonomy opposed the national integration programs of Pakistani presidents Ayub and Yahya. Students and public opinion repelled the attempts of the central government to establish a second language in addition to Bengali, and Bangali editors opposed press controls. Following a disastrous cyclone in 1970, the peasantry in a national election strongly supported Sheikh Mujibur (Mujib) Rahman, who had succeeded Suhrawardy as leader of the Awami League, and his party. Many Bangalis, however, voted for the opposition, an indication that a significant minority preferred Pakistani rule. Pakistani promises and concessions made over the years did not satisfy Bangali demands and ended with President Yahya's refusal to yield to Bangali demands for autonomy, which led to a declaration of Bangali independence. After a bitter nine-month war Bangali guerrillas and formidable contingents of Indian armed forces defeated the Pakistani army. Sheikh Mujib returned to Dacca from a prison in West Pakistan.

Another broad theme of the book is the turbulent years of Bangali independence, dominated by the charismatic figures of Sheikh Mujib and Ziaur Rahman. Both men had to deal with volatile political factions and with opposition from feuding military cliques. Violence sometimes broke out. Yet government programs rescued the economy from bankruptcy, improved the life of the people, and strengthened international relations. The gradual acceptance of social, political, and economic changes by the peasants served to keep the nation on an even keel.

For three and a half years, Sheikh Mujib and to a degree the Awami League directed the political life of the new nation. Under constant pressure from the opposition, factional strife within the party, and a critical press, however, Mujib's parliamentary government progressively splintered and public disorder intensified. The left importuned him to defend the government's socialist policies, religious fundamentalists pilloried his secularist stance, and a wide spectrum of opponents branded him pro-Indian. He had also to reply to charges of tolerating corruption among his officials and of poorly administering the affairs of government.

To halt the spreading disorder, Sheikh Mujib, then prime minister, convinced Parliament to change to a presidential government and to elect him president. He promptly formed a single party, BAKSAL (Bangladesh Peasants' and Workers' Awami League), to give himself personal control of public affairs. His authoritarian rule drew criticism from his outlawed political opponents, but it was politically ambitious military men that brought him down. He was assassinated by dissident officers of the regular army.

Mujib had accomplished many things for his people. He seriously addressed the nation's landownership problem, revived self-reliant programs in agriculture, and in a pragmatic spirit retained public industries while giving greater leeway to private enterprise. He obtained generous amounts of relief and reconstruction aid from Western nations and settled the nation's most urgent postwar differences with Pakistan and India.

Following the death of Sheikh Mujib and the collapse of later short-lived governments, General Ziaur (Zia) Rahman strode onto the political scene. Amid several bloody military coups, he restored a reasonable degree of public order as martial law administrator by alternating harsh and conciliatory treatment of the military. In 1978 he was elected president by a popular majority over more than a dozen opponents. He put together a coalition called the Bangladesh Nationalist party to manage the government and to contest in elections. When he turned his attention to economic matters, he expanded the role of private enterprise and decontrolled some public industries. He carried on a personal and highly publicized campaign to increase food production and accelerated rural programs to eliminate illiteracy and control population growth. During his administration the financial and political support of Western and Muslim nations and of international agencies increased. Political conflicts with India were blunted and economic relations generally improved. To keep his party coalition intact, however, he tolerated the distribution of political favors by his colleagues. He became an advocate for the armed forces; he indulged military retirees with cabinet posts and increased defense expenditures. His ruthless treatment of military rebels did not deter the rebels' fellow officers from assassinating him in 1981.

Fear that his assassination would provoke political chaos turned out to be exaggerated. Vice-president Abdus Sattar quickly invoked constitutional procedures that called for a presidential election. This and other actions mollified the opposition and produced a brief political calm. The 76-year-old Sattar was elected president in November 1981 over his Awami League rival by a large popular vote. In office, Sattar failed to resolve urgent economic problems, to hold the Nationalist party together, and to resist the determination of General H. M. Ershad, chief of the army, to take control of the government. On the eve of the eleventh anniversary of independence, the general forced the resignation of President Sattar, suspended the Constitution, and declared martial law. He announced that he had to take over because of widespread corruption in public life and "to save the country from crisis." He promised an eventual return to democracy but immediately named a five-man junta to rule the country.

As happens in new nations, Bangladesh's past soon caught up with its present. The prime divisive forces, violence and factionalism, disrupted the governing process and slowed down the economy. The Mujib and Zia regimes, as long as they lasted, had managed to hold the center together by spreading political favors but also by carrying out practical domestic and international programs. The two leaders' assassinations and the ascendancy of General Ershad brought the nation to a political crossroads that could lead to a return to democracy or to any of a number of types of authoritarian government, of long or short duration, Bangali or foreign. Democracy will not return unless the middle class does what it so far has not done—reconciles its political authority with an enhanced sense of responsibility for freedom, equality, and social justice.

Well known to be one of the poorest nations of the world, Bangladesh, like other poor nations, hardly shares in the well-being of the world's economies. In 1983, according to the World Bank, its per capita gross national product (GNP) was only $140 a year. Bangladesh is an example of the crying need for a world order in which rich and powerful democratic nations, if they wish to preserve the democratic way of life, attend more seriously to the problems of the developing nations, support their self-reliant programs, and seek a peace embracing all peoples.

CHAPTER 1

The Land and Its Resources

Tucked away in the northeast corner of the South Asian subcontinent, Bangladesh is the land where the Bangalis' social, cultural, economic, and political history has unfolded and where they are now confronting their present and future fortunes.

Although dwarfed by neighboring India, the 55,598-square-mile area of Bangladesh is somewhat larger than that of England and about the size of the U.S. states of Illinois or Wisconsin. It is larger than the state of Louisiana, but much of Bangladesh's terrain resembles Louisiana's delta region. Among the nations of the world Bangladesh ranks with the smaller states of Eastern Europe but has a greater area than many West African and Central American nations.

As history attests, the size of a nation is a measure of neither its problems nor its ability to cope with them. The modest size of Bangladesh does not make its problems easier to manage; instead, the problems are concentrated and more visible. Even Bangladesh's fertile soil and numerous rivers do not assure its prosperity or well-being; these resources need to be improved and utilized more efficiently.

Bangladesh's limited land, location on the subcontinent, climate, and other physical features have always influenced the mobility of the people, their social and economic pursuits, and their political actions.[1] Its location, separated from what was formerly West Pakistan by a thousand miles of northern India, figured in the Bangalis' break with their fellow Muslims.

Historians have used the name *Bengal* to describe the area of the Ganges-Brahmaputra valley that comprises present-day Bangladesh and India's West Bengal state as well as Assam state.

PHYSICAL FEATURES

A deltaic plain pierced by three great rivers—the Ganges, Brahmaputra (locally known as the Jamuna), and Meghna, whose waters rise in Nepal, China, and India, respectively—Bangladesh is bordered on two sides by hills and mountains, open on the west to the low country of the Indian Ganges, and open on the south to the Bay of Bengal. Immediately beyond its northeastern boundary, the Indian Shillong Plateau rises to 8,000 feet. The northwesterly thrust of the country nearly squeezes off India's state of West Bengal from the state of Assam and also separates India from the Plateau of Nepal and the high Himalayas. Mount Everest's summit is about 100 miles north of Bangladesh's northwestern tip. The Indian states of Assam and Tripura mark the northern and eastern boundaries. In the southeast the Chittagong Hills, rising some 2,000 to 3,000 feet, join the Burmese frontiers. The shoreline of Bangladesh along the Bay of Bengal extends 370 miles from a western projection of Burma to the beaches of West Bengal. Between these two points the low-lying land is cut by estuaries and tidal creeks. Fingers of land intermingled with islands of varying size stretch along this coast, formed by the three converging rivers as they empty into the Bay of Bengal.

One of the extraordinary forests of the world nestles in the southwest corner of the country. The Sunderban, a densely wooded tidal area of 2,000 square miles, reaching from the main river branch of the delta to the Indian border near Calcutta, is a network of inland islands through which a series of small rivers thread their way from the upper port of Chalna to the Bay of Bengal. A handful of people and thousands of wild animals, including the Bengal tiger and deer, live in this water-forest land.

Bangladesh is virtually surrounded by India. The two countries share a 1,500-mile-long border and have many of the same social, cultural, and economic problems.[2] Both are overpopulated and both have large peasant constituencies, significant minorities, and low standards of living. The closeness of the two countries troubles their political relationships. The hasty and incomplete boundary decisions of 1947 that separated East Bengal (East Pakistan) from India broke the economic and transportation links forged during the lifetime of British India. A 1974 pact between Bangladesh and India identified their disputed boundaries. Since then, technical border discussions relating to earlier land survey decisions have resolved most boundary disputes. In 1975 negotiations were also begun with India concerning mutual boundaries in the Bay of Bengal and conflicting oil exploration and marine resources claims in those waters.

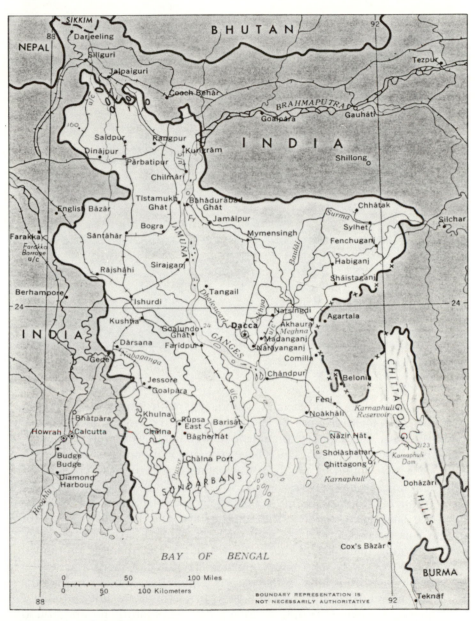

Map 1. Bangladesh

The Sunderban region.

Bangladesh's only other land boundary is with Burma; the common border runs for a distance of 120 miles along the ridges and rivers of the Burmese hill country. Boundary realignments were agreed on late in 1978. Bangladesh does not have a common boundary with Nepal, but the two countries are barely separated by a narrow corridor of Indian land 18 miles wide.

Travelers in Bengal several centuries ago paid tribute to the beauties of the land but complained about the heat and humidity. No doubt they missed the several delightful winter months of the dry season. The cooling influence of the high Himalayas and the Bay of Bengal gives the country a subtropical climate. The rainy, or monsoon, season normally lasts from June to the end of September. The spring months of March and April and the fall month of October are hot and sticky. From mid-November to mid-February the temperature hovers around 50° Fahrenheit or at higher but still comfortable levels.

The abundant rainfall prompted one of the political parties in East Bengal to use the umbrella to identify itself to illiterate voters. Although the average rainfall varies from 50 to 100 inches a year (200 inches in parts of Sylhet), the rains are welcomed for their cooling effect and their promise of good crops. The psychological uplift and the physical dangers of the monsoon are accurately described in Louis Bromfield's *The Rains Came.*

Nature has not always treated the Bangalis kindly. In recent years the beginning and end of the monsoon have often been followed by cyclones, some of them devastating.[3] The worst storms pack winds of 100 miles an hour or more that strike the shallow shore waters of the Bay of Bengal and whip up huge tidal waves. The angry waters rush across the land at heights of 5 to 20 feet, carrying away everything in their path.

The most devastating cyclone of the century occurred in November 1970. More than a quarter of a million persons lost their lives as wind and sea drove down on the islands and spits of land on the central shores of the Bay of Bengal. Eight other cyclones in the sixties caused extensive property damage and the loss of as many as 50,000 lives.

During the summer months one-third of the country is inundated by the overflowing rivers to depths of several feet—as much as 30 feet in low-lying areas. At the confluence of the three great rivers the monsoon flood creates a huge lake, interrupted only by trees and an occasional shelf of villages. When the waters gently cover the lowlands in a normal flood, large quantities of silt are deposited. The enriched soil produces two and even three crops a year. But downstream, flood waters pouring swiftly into the Bay of Bengal damage crops. During years of fast-flowing floods, 10 to 20 percent of annual yields are destroyed.

The rivers remain by far the most valuable natural resource of the nation, even though their water is shared with India, Nepal, and China.[4] According to Dr. Alan Berg of the World Bank staff, the groundwater under the Gangetic plain may be the greatest untapped reservoir in the world. Properly controlled use of this water, he believes, could increase agricultural production in the area by 400 percent.

The construction of the Farraka Barrage on the Ganges, inside India but close to the border of East Pakistan, became the subject of bitter controversies between Pakistan and India shortly after the Partition of 1947. The barrage diverted large quantities of Ganges water into its Hooghly River branch in order to flush out the silt that tends to accumulate in Calcutta Harbor. The diversion reduced the flow of the Ganges into East Pakistan, a flow that Pakistanis depended upon to irrigate thousands of acres. Sheikh Mujib's government reached an initial agreement with India permitting measured seasonal flows into Bangladesh. Similar agreements have been concluded between successive

Bangali and Indian governments, in spite of differences about the administration of the agreements and the amount of the scheduled flows. Bangladesh has benefited from the agreements, but of even greater concern now is its need for major flood control and hydroelectric projects on the Ganges and the Brahmaputra. These and alternative programs have been discussed among the Bangalis, Indians, and Nepalese but without resolution. A regional agricultural revolution could be achieved if disagreements among the governments were settled.

TRANSPORTATION

The economy of Bangladesh has benefited substantially from recent improvements in its transportation system, which had been in disarray because of long neglect and months of fighting in 1971, when the breakdown of transportation critically hampered agricultural production and distribution.[5]

The transportation system of the country is essential to its agricultural export economy, which relies heavily on cash crops for foreign exchange. The rivers, reaching into areas where the crops are grown, are the main highways of the system. Even at the lowest water levels there are 2,500 miles of waterways navigable by shallow-draft steamers plying five major river ports; in the rainy season the navigable miles nearly double.

The heavily traveled water route through Bangladesh from Calcutta and Assam—a distance of 350 miles—is one of the keys to regional economic development. The closure of the route during the Chinese-Indian border war of 1962 and the Indo-Pakistan war of 1965 prevented millions of tons of supplies from reaching India's northeastern states. Since independence the network has been open.

Riverboats provide cheap transportation for goods and people. Hundreds of small craft called country boats or sampans, propelled by manpower or motors, ply the country's streams. Small sampans equipped with one oar are far more numerous than the larger vessels, manned by a dozen or more oarsmen, that can transport as much as 35 tons of cargo. Thousands of passenger boats of varying sizes also traverse the river system.

The Bangladesh Shipping Corporation (which took over the shipping corporation of the central government of Pakistan in 1972) operates coasters and oceangoing vessels. The seagoing tradition of the Bangalis enables them to man the ships and save on part of the cost of their foreign trade.

The port of Chittagong was developed after Partition to manage the sea traffic of East Pakistan, much of which had been previously handled

Country boats (sampans).

by Calcutta. More recently, in order to export its principal foreign exchange goods—jute (a hard fiber), jute products (rug backing, bagging, etc.), and textiles—from a port closer to the growing areas and factories in Dacca and Khulna, the government of Pakistan opened a new port at Chalna, some distance from the Bay of Bengal. The government of Bangladesh is now constructing a more modern facility at Mangla, 20 miles downstream from Chalna.

Railroads and all-weather highways are difficult and expensive to build and maintain because of annual flooding and the high cost of construction materials. Railways and roads that have to be laid on the flood plain obstruct natural drainage and worsen the danger of serious floods. The railroads, most of them built 60 or more years ago, are still rudimentary. Hard-surfaced roads are lacking except between, in, and around the principal cities or near the tea estates.

Bangladesh inherited two railway systems from British India and East Pakistan: a meter-gauge road located east of the Brahmaputra, which serves the tea estates and the upland Brahmaputra valley and connects Dacca with the northeastern part of the country; and a broad-gauge road in southwestern Bangladesh, linked with an Indian West Bengal line, which ties Bangladesh to Calcutta and India's northwestern corridor. The railroads, originally built to connect British Bengal with the area north and east of East Bengal and to bring jute and other products to the Calcutta mills, have since Bangali independence been used to expand the internal Bangali economy and its foreign trade.

A national airline, Bangladesh Biman (Bangladesh Airlines), began service in March 1972. Pilots, navigators, and ground crews were recruited from among Bangali employees of Pakistan International Airlines and Bangali members of the Pakistani Air Force. Dacca and New Delhi promptly arranged for regular Dacca-to-Calcutta service. Bangladesh leased aircraft and bought planes for use in domestic and international flights. By 1981 Biman had significantly expanded its international routes. It now provides scheduled service to London, Europe, the Middle East, and South and Southeast Asia, as well as maintaining a network of routes within Bangladesh.

NATURAL RESOURCES

The presently known natural resources of the country are negligible, except for natural gas. Industrial expansion is thus restricted.

A basic resource deficiency is the nearly total absence of rock. Even the Chittagong Hills are composed of sand. Materials for housing, roads, and other construction are scarce and costly. In consequence, most of the people live in bamboo and grass huts, with or without imported tin roofs, which are symbols of affluence and influence in rural areas. Fortunately, bricks are readily made from the plentiful clayey soil; they are used to build small industrial plants and a limited number of houses. Open-air brick kilns, set up close to digging sites during the dry season, are a familiar sight around the larger cities and towns.

Extensive veins of coal are said to exist in North Bengal (the areas north and west of Dacca, especially the most northerly districts). All of the deposits so far discovered, however, are at such deep levels that mining would be prohibitively costly.

Efforts of U.S. and Soviet companies to find oil in the Chittagong region have been unsuccessful, but exploration continues.[6] Offshore areas in the Bay of Bengal have been explored by American and other foreign oil companies, but no oil has been found.

The construction of a nuclear power plant that had been planned by Pakistan was considered by the Mujib government but rejected as too expensive and threatening to the environment.[7] (The Ershad government has revived the plan.) In 1980 a French proposal to install an expensive nuclear reactor that would greatly increase energy supplies north of Dacca was accepted by the government of President Zia, provided other interested nations would help to assume the major financial burden of the installation.

If solar power technology could be developed as an economically feasible source of energy, it would be a great boon to the Bangalis, on whom the sun shines nearly year round.

Natural gas fields close to the earth's surface, estimated to contain 10 trillion cubic feet, are being exploited.[8] A fertilizer plant using gas from nearby fields was funded and built by the Japanese in the early sixties, with the help of American funds and expertise. The central government of Pakistan built a second fertilizer plant complex near Dacca. The Indo-Pakistan war and subsequent sabotage limited the two plants' production in recent years. The government of Bangladesh has built three more plants along the Chittagong coast. Since they have been in operation, the country has been able to export increasing quantities of fertilizer each year, adding to its foreign exchange earnings. Natural gas is soon to be substituted for diesel as a truck and heating fuel, in order to save on this expensive import.

INDUSTRY

Although industry contributed only 10 percent to the Bangali gross national product in 1980, its share in production had increased steadily since 1971.[9] Jute manufactures remain the chief product and commodity in trade. Other major industrial products include chemicals, textiles, and sugar. During the past decade the construction industry, using mostly imported cement and reinforcing rods produced at a Chittagong steel plant, has increased the number of commercial, industrial, and government buildings in Dacca and Chittagong. Forests, which cover about 15 percent of the area of the country, have since independence supplied expanding wood products industries, although they are not plentiful enough to supply wood for construction. The rivers and the Bay of Bengal abound in fish, which are mostly consumed domestically but are also exported.

Most organized industries were nationalized by President Mujib. Many tea estates and other state-owned industrial units were returned by President Zia and General Ershad to private ownership, and the nation's private sector is being enlarged with investments from Asian and Western companies.

AGRICULTURE

Nature has blessed the Bangalis with a bounty of land and water. About two-thirds of the area of the country—22.5 million acres—is under cultivation; the rivers embrace another million or more acres.[10] The fertile soil, sun, and water promise ample supplies of foodstuffs and cash crops. Yet only 20 or 30 percent of the capacity of the land is adequately used, according to Dr. Akter Hameed Khan, the organizer of a successful cooperative program at the eastern town of Comilla.

The inability of the nation's farms to grow sufficient rice (the staple of the people for centuries) and to feed the growing population has multiple causes. Among them are the inadequacy of water management, the lack of pest controls, and the slackness of the cooperative movement. Political and social obstacles to improvement have been equally serious. Not the least of them are infighting among politicians and the unwillingness of many of them to establish a fairer distribution of landholdings. The battle for provincial autonomy in the sixties, turmoil after independence, peasants' resistance to change, adverse weather conditions, and political corruption also slowed the growth of food production until the late seventies. Since then, a program encouraging peasant participation in new irrigation projects, aided by a succession of favorable monsoon seasons, has produced larger crops. The government's goal of self-sufficiency in foodstuffs by 1985 depends on good weather and a stable political climate. Meanwhile, food imports have been used to build granary stocks to meet future needs.

For decades to come the progress of the nation will be measured by its improvements in agriculture. Bangali leaders realize that, in addition to obtaining long-range foreign and local investments for projects like water management, they must somehow remake the farm economy into a network of self-reliant communities capable of producing larger quantities and greater varieties of food and other crops. Industrialization built around agriculture with foreign assistance holds the best promise of a more prosperous economy. For the next several generations the Bangali peasant, the producer of its life-sustaining food, its cash crops, and its granary stocks, is the keeper of the nation's fortunes.

CHAPTER 2

The Society and Its Problems

Until the middle of the present century traditional Bangali peasant society, although plagued by the usual adversities of life in small isolated villages, escaped the stresses of modern life. More recently, social issues such as the status of women, overpopulation, health, delivery systems, and the rise of urbanism have had some impact on the traditional ways of peasant society. Unenforced Pakistani family laws did not interfere with established custom. A Bangali middle class, which appeared earlier in this century, focused its attention on the economic and political problems created by Pakistani rule but paid little heed to social matters. The ruling middle class of independent Bangladesh has seriously addressed the nation's multiple social problems.

Significant differences between the societies and environments of Bangladesh and what was formerly West Pakistan help to explain Bangali independence. The Bangalis, separated from Pakistan by a thousand-mile stretch across northern India, live on the borders of Southeast Asia, while the Pakistanis are on the fringes of the Middle East. The semitropical wetlands of Bangladesh contrast sharply with arid Pakistan. Sixteen percent of the population of Bangladesh is Hindu, but Hindus account for less than 2 percent of Pakistan's population. Pakistan occupies an area seven times larger, but less populated, than greatly overpopulated Bangladesh. The Bangalis speak a different language than the languages of their compatriots and have been less favored economically and educationally.

THE PEASANTRY

Bangali society, like that of most developing countries, remains predominantly agricultural.[1] According to a 1961 census, rural areas

Jute harvesters.

(those with less than 5,000 persons) made up almost 95 percent of
East Pakistan and urban areas only 5.2 percent. More recent data,
calculated on different premises, showed that in 1980 about 90 percent
of Bangladesh's people depended on agriculture for their livelihood.
By 1981 the urban population had increased by 11 percent, but only
one city, Dacca, had a population of more than three million, and one
other, Chittagong, claimed more than one million.

The fundamental social unit, the extended family, is the social arbiter
of the peasantry. It educates its members in their rights and duties,
confirms their social and economic status, and preserves their religious
traditions. It protects the aged and, to the extent economic conditions
permit, gives job security to its members.

Bangali villages, all 68,000 of them, are small and close-knit communities. A typical village of 400 to 1,000 persons contains a number
of extended families. Among Hindus, the social status of the individual
depends on his or her membership in the family caste, and among
Muslims, Christians, and Buddhists, on citizenship in the village.

Although industrialization and technology have altered the lifestyles
of city dwellers, the influence of the extended family persists. Family
ties are important to the middle class as well as to lower-class urbanites.

Even individual breadwinners who move from rural areas to the cities cluster in familylike groups with others from their home districts.

The extended family has in recent years become unable to carry the increasing burden of its unemployed members, the victims of population pressures. Indeed, the massive problems resulting from the alarming increase of landless peasants and unemployed farm workers, thousands of whom have migrated to urban areas, have not yielded to any great extent to remedial actions by the government.

It was sometime after the Partition of 1947 that the extended family began to be affected by changes in the national socioeconomic structure. Three groups emerged: surplus-producing farmers, small or subsistence farmers, and landless or nearly landless farmers. The latter gradually produced a fourth group, made up of unemployed farm workers. The role of the "surplus" farmer became a subject of political debate during the Pakistan years. Surplus-producing farmers, owners of 5 to 33 or more acres, constitute a very small percentage of the peasantry and are the rich people of the nation. They gained their status when the legal authority of the zamindars (landlords and tax collectors) was abolished by the Bangalis in 1951, allowing the farmers to obtain reductions in taxes, or to evade them altogether, through their political connections. Many became moneylenders and increased their landholdings, sometimes beyond the maximum acreage permitted by the law. Most of the arrears in land revenue payments during the sixties are said by critics to have been owed by politically connected surplus farmers. Official data of the decade indicate that the number of landless farmers renting land from surplus farmers increased measurably. Demands for land reform began to be heard and were intensified by the pressure of rapid population growth on arable acreage, which had barely increased. In the 1970 election the votes of the poor and landless peasants contributed to the victory of the Awami League. Not long afterward charges were leveled that Awami Leaguers in Sheikh Mujib's government were using their positions to acquire substantial tracts of land. The charges weakened Mujib's regime and persisted under President Zia.

WOMEN

To Western observers the subordinate status of women is among the more obvious features of Bangali society.[2] Most Bangali women have only limited contacts with persons outside their families. An unmarried woman normally lives in the privacy of the family until an arranged marriage releases her to live in the seclusion of her husband's home, which she may share with other wives. Although some authorities hold that purdah (religious sanctions for the seclusion of women) is not sanctioned by the Koran, the practice took a firm hold in Bengal, perhaps because it is also a Hindu custom. Seclusion creates a society of shy women, unwilling and, after a time, unable to receive new ideas or to adapt to new ways of acting.

Changes in the status of women are, nonetheless, taking place, especially among a self-emancipated group of middle-class women whose social life is not unlike that of women in the West. More women are seeking a university education and becoming members of university faculties, and more of them are playing roles in political life as members of Parliament and the cabinet. Several Muslim women's organizations concern themselves with social welfare; Mother Teresa and her assistants have been welcomed.

Rounaq Jahan, a member of the political science department at the University of Dacca, is representative of this type of new woman. In an address to the Population Conference of Bucharest in 1974, she discussed the importance of rural women in developing countries. She noted that they constitute 70 to 90 percent of women in the world, that they are a dominant force in the subsistence economies in which they live, and that modernization has hardly touched them. Rural women, she said, should be lifted out of their "total immersion" in subsistence living and be given equal opportunities in education, employment (especially teaching, paramedical services, nutrition, etc.), and, above all, in the organization of women's cooperatives.

THE MIDDLE CLASS

A small Muslim Bangali middle class, representing less than 1 percent of the population, emerged as a political force prior to World War I in British India.[3] Under Pakistani rule, sharp differences split its professional, university-educated ranks, which included lawyers, jurists, bureaucrats, politicians, journalists, and landowners. The Awami League, critical of the central government's policies, led the opposition. The conservative Muslim League and fundamentalist religious parties supported the successive governments of Pakistan. After independence a similar alignment of parties acting alone or in uneasy coalitions vied with one another for popular acceptance. Their clashing ideological interests and personal ambitions sparked intense, even violent contests for power. The entrance of the military into the middle-class hierarchy during the early years of independence introduced a new virulence into partisan politics. Internal political struggles and a general scramble for control of portions of the national wealth continue today.

OVERPOPULATION

As long as the Bangalis were part of Pakistan, the size of their population was a matter of pride and an argument for greater representation in the National Assembly. Although they did not grow enough food to feed themselves, the supplements they received from abroad as part of aid to Pakistan partially alleviated the pressures of the food-population dilemma.

The population explosion, which began to attract attention in the fifties, has special importance for the Bangalis because of their limited living area.[4] Bangladesh is now the most densely populated area of its size in the world. The home of 90 million people (1982 estimate), it ranks ninth in population size among the world's nations. Population experts, who like to work with imaginery figures, point out that if the United States had the same density of population—1,400 people per square mile—it would have to house, feed, and clothe well over four billion people, that is, the population of the whole world. One does not need to be an expert to see that Bangladesh has a monumental population problem.

Since 1965 Bangladesh's annual population growth has been estimated at somewhere between 2 and 3 percent. Assuming a growth rate of 2.5 percent from 1980, more than 100 million people would live in Bangladesh by the year 1990—a density of 2,000 persons per square mile.

Whether this extrapolation is correct depends on many social variables, including changes in marriage customs and laws, a rise in the standard of living, and the acceptance of modern techniques of birth control. An estimate was made in 1980 that almost half the population was below the age of 15. Although longevity is barely rising, the youth of the population underscores the importance of measures to lower future population increases.

An abundance of evidence supports the view that overpopulation in Bangladesh is caused by its lifestyle and the rigidity of local customs. The high death rate among infants and children, reflected in an average life expectancy of about 47 years, has encouraged larger families among rural Bangalis. Additional children provide cheap labor for the peasant, who sees the solution of his problems in individual rather than social terms. Most girls marry at the time of puberty or soon afterward. Islamic law permits four marriages, and multiple marriages are common in Bangladesh, notwithstanding the fact that such arrangements can seldom be supported financially in an impoverished society. President Ayub tried with limited success to lower the number of Islamic marriages.[5] If the present government effectively extends the scope of that policy and also raises the marriage age, as proposed in the 1981 cabinet, society and the economy will benefit.

Undernourished societies like Bangladesh tend to produce more children than well-fed societies. Among Bangali Muslims this phenomenon may have been fortified by an instinctive desire to hold their lead in numbers over the Hindu population and all Bangali-speaking people, or to maintain a claim that the excess population of their country entitles them to migrate to less populated areas.

Religion, too, thwarts efforts to influence the birth rate, for traditional Islamic piety forbids birth control measures. Furthermore, purdah makes a woman in Bangali society a bearer of children and keeper of the household. These traditions, however, are slowly changing.

The Pakistani government's national birth control program, which began feebly in the late fifties, broke down in East Pakistan.[6] Peasant resistance to governmental controls and a lack of facilities and trained personnel were among the reasons for the failure of this initiative. In February 1972 the government of Bangladesh established a family planning association, including doctors and concerned women. Critics complained that the program was twenty-first on the list of the government's priorities. Later reorganizations of the cabinet included a minister of health and family planning.

Officials of international agencies and Bangali economists prevailed on the Mujib government to adopt family planning programs as an integral part of the Food for Work program. In 1975 several hundred rural health and family planning clinics disseminated birth control information. President Zia's government, urged by international agencies and aid-giving nations, further encouraged family planning. By the end of 1979 about 15 percent of Bangali families were said to practice birth control. By 1981 23,000 sterilizations had been performed. The president asked couples to limit their families to one child. Many Islamic religious leaders reportedly accepted these programs.

MIGRANTS

The government of India hastened the repatriation of Bangali refugees who fled to India in 1964 and 1971 and warned against Bangali attempts to migrate to West Bengal in 1978.[7] The indigenous people of contiguous Tripura and Assam, too, made it plain that they did not welcome Bangalis. Assamese students in 1980 staged months-long strikes in protest against the presence of Bangali migrants and settlers in their territory. Only the intervention of Mrs. Gandhi ended the strikes.

There is no likelihood that Burma would permit the immigration of Bangalis, even from among the tribal people of Burmese extraction living in the Chittagong Hill Tracts bordering Burma. In 1978, 200,000 Muslims were expelled from Burma into Bangladesh. Under a subsequent agreement between the two governments the Muslims, long-time residents of Burma, were repatriated.

The Bangalis, accustomed to a humid semitropical climate, did not feel at home in semiarid West Pakistan and found it difficult to converse with their neighbors. Thousands of them, who had been encouraged by the government of Pakistan to settle in the west, returned to Bangladesh under 1973 exchange arrangements. In the seventies and eighties, however, thousands of Bangalis took jobs in the arid OPEC countries. Well-paid employment made the desert an agreeable place to reside in, at least temporarily.

HEALTH

The short life expectancy of Bangalis, in 1978 officially estimated at only 47 years, is largely attributable to malnutrition and intestinal diseases.[8] Infant mortality, said to have been 237 per thousand in 1961, was at that time among the highest in the world. In 1974 the Bangali government claimed this figure had been halved. The life expectancy of peasant women is lower than that of men, because they receive less nutritious food and less adequate health care.

The existing health facilities and services cannot satisfactorily meet even the minimal needs of the people. The number of practicing doctors is small; in 1977 there were reported to be 9,350 physicians and surgeons. Good doctors are overwhelmed by the health problems they face. The government of President Zia inaugurated a training program for "barefoot doctors" to supplement the medical delivery system. Trained female nurses are few, partly because of religious opposition to the idea of nursing by women. Women doctors, on the other hand, although not numerous, have an important place in purdah society; Muslim women prefer them to male doctors.

Under Pakistani rule public hospitals were far below Western standards. In 1979 there were only 0.09 beds per 1,000 persons. Health services suffered severely during the 1971 war, during which a number of doctors and other medical personnel were killed. Since independence hospital facilities, located around the urban centers of the country, have nearly doubled.

The widespread practice of self-medication with proprietary drugs provides a living for many shopkeepers and foreign pharmaceutical firms and provides an irreducible minimum of health care. Information about the use of popular drugs is not available. Folk medicine, frowned upon by the medical professionals trained in the West, is used by large numbers of the Bangali poor.

The society and the economy are undermined by the low level of health in the population. Too many men and women, old in their thirties, have to concentrate on the task of keeping alive and have little energy left over to enjoy themselves and to contribute to their community. Not only do endemic diseases, especially cholera, persist in spite of recent, partially successful efforts to combat them, but also imbalances in the diet of the population seriously affect infants and women.

A nutrition survey of East Pakistan was undertaken between March 1962 and January 1964 by the Ministry of Health of the government of Pakistan, in collaboration with the University of Dacca and the Nutrition Section of the Office of International Research of the U.S. National Institutes of Health.[9] Published in May 1966, the survey showed that malnutrition affected the health and well-being of at least half the population of East Pakistan. Children, especially those of preschool age, and women of child-bearing age were the most severely affected; however, no age group escaped the effects of malnutrition. In a summary of its findings, the survey team concluded that the essentials of a good basic diet are available in the country but that the actual food intake of the persons surveyed was poorly balanced, especially in rural areas. Knowledge about the special nutrient requirements for young children and pregnant or lactating women was inadequately appreciated, so that even valuable nutritious food was not well distributed in the family. The best food was reserved for adult males, leaving women and children with the remains. The report proposed changes in the present dietary practices.

The principal authors of that report said recently that the situation they had described had not changed in any fundamental way; malnutrition among children and women is as alarming as ever. Although food production has increased substantially since 1964, population growth has limited general increases in food consumption. However, a 1981 study by a nutritional food science group at the University of Dacca reported that people were eating better than a decade ago. Yet malnutrition is widespread, infant mortality is very high, and the daily caloric intake of landless workers is below the recommended level.

HOUSING AND COMMUNITY PLANNING

Housing in rural and urban areas has deteriorated for decades, save in a few areas on the perimeter of Dacca, where public officials built and rented houses and apartments for middle-class families and for-

Low-cost housing, Dhaka (Dacca).

eigners.[10] The shanties in the slums and the thousands of squatters in large and small towns are conspicuous evidence of neglect and of the need for urgent attention to housing, although hard information about housing conditions is lacking.

The physical condition of the cities and towns gives visitors the impression of a country in trouble. According to an official estimate made in the sixties, only 30 percent of the population of the three largest cities, Dacca, Chittagong, and Khulna, had running water and a smaller percentage had sewage facilities when American engineering firms came in to install sewage and water systems in these cities.

During the 1971 war thousands of homes were destroyed in rural areas. In the immediate postwar period U.S. and European relief agencies contributed money and skills to the construction of new homes of much the same design and materials as the previous ones. Recent current and developmental budgets of the Dacca government increased funds for urban housing and planning.

THE CITIES

On the heels of independence, peasants fled from their war-torn villages into the larger cities.[11] Destructive floods and the influx of the rural unemployed added to the population explosion of these cities. The population of Dacca, around 700,000 in the mid-sixties, more than quadrupled in two decades. Similar increases occurred in the industrial city of Khulna and the port city of Chittagong.

The cities of Bangladesh more than ever dominate the nation's commercial and economic life and lead its cultural and political progress. Dacca, the capital city and perhaps the oldest city in the nation, is the focal point of Bangali life.[12] Located about 100 miles from the Bay of Bengal, it is relatively safe from the devastating cyclones that strike the bay and from the floods that inundate a large part of the country. The city, close to the center of population, serves as the hub of the nation's communication system. Because of its secure central position it stands at the crossroads of Bangali culture and politics.

CHAPTER 3

Bangali Culture

The use a nation and its government make of its culture, that is, its religion, language, education, science, and technology, contributes to the quality of its social and political life. However, political decisions about cultural matters may break or loosen the bonds of a community rather than unify its members. A 1952 and later martial law governments of Pakistan unwisely disregarded the Bangalis' attachment to their language when they attempted to introduce a second Islamic-oriented language, Urdu, in order to offset Hindu influences in Bangali culture. Moreover, government leaders did not pay sufficient attention to the need in East Pakistan for education and science and technology. And they sought diligently to control the independent Bangali press. Pakistanis who regarded Bangalis as a lesser people offended their pride and egalitarian spirit.

After independence the Bangali middle class, now guardians of the national culture, increased public expenditures for cultural programs, especially educational ones. Although longer spells of political stability will be required for Bangali literature and visual arts to flourish fully, science and technology have moved ahead with government help. The nation's lively press has maintained its democratic stance. Independence also made it possible for Bangalis to establish fruitful contacts with other Muslim nations and with non-Muslim cultures. However, the crucial relationship of religion to politics, as well as divergent economic concerns, incited domestic partisan differences and complicated relations with India. The problems the Bangalis encountered in reconciling their egalitarian spirit with the need for an orderly political authority are common among nations striving for democracy.

LANGUAGE

Bengali (Bangla), the language of virtually all of the people of Bangladesh, is the silken cord binding their culture and nationhood.[1] Derived from Sanskrit, it had established itself as the vernacular by the end of the tenth century. The virtual isolation of the Bangalis from the rest of the world until the seventeenth century confirmed its durability. Communication with their distant non-Bengali-speaking fellow Muslims in what became West Pakistan was exceedingly tenuous.

Bengali as the common language of the Muslim majority and the Hindu minority made relationships between the communities easier, even though the Bengali spoken by Muslims bears the marks of Islamic culture. Bengali speakers, aware that their tongue ranks eighth among world languages in number of speakers, are proud of its substantial literature, especially of its poetry.

Pakistan's rulers mistakenly believed that Urdu, a language identified with past Muslim ascendancy in India, would eventually be the lingua franca of Pakistan. They ignored census data that showed that Bengali was the native tongue of 98.47 percent, and Urdu for only 1.34 percent, of the population of East Pakistan. In all of Pakistan only 3.45 percent were native speakers of Urdu. The majority of West Pakistanis spoke Sindi, Pushtu, and Punjabi.

Presidents Ayub and Yahya tried unsuccessfully to persuade the Bangalis to learn Urdu as a second language and Urdu speakers to learn Bengali. But Urdu was the language of aristocratic Muslim leaders and of Muslim Biharis, migrants from India in the fifties, whom Bangalis regarded as wards of the central government. West Pakistanis had no reason to learn Bengali except to prepare themselves for civil posts in East Pakistan.

The Bengali language became a leading symbol of Bangali nationalism and emancipation. The first stamp issued by the Mujib government commemorated the death of two students killed by the police in language riots of the early fifties. The official organs of the political parties of Bangladesh are Bengali weeklies. Students' demands for more university instruction and textbooks in Bengali have been readily honored, and Bengali has been a compulsory subject in primary and secondary schools for years. After independence Bengali displaced English on street signs, auto license plates, and commercial names; it is increasingly used in government documents formerly published in English. The Constitution of 1972 made Bengali the state language. English, however, is used among educated Bangalis.

RELIGION AND POLITICS

The Bangali nation has always been a religious, ethical, and cultural community.[2] As an independent nation-state, its cultural and political life continues to be influenced by religion. Islam is the faith of more than 80 percent of the people and is officially recognized, making Bangladesh the third largest Islamic state in the world. Its Islamic heritage influences its relationships with Pakistan and other Muslim nations and distinguishes it culturally from secularist-Hindu India.

Islamic modes of life pervade Bangali society. Most peasants follow Islamic marriage customs; they call on Allah to give them better crops and children to till their fields. Mullahs (teachers) who live in the villages exert considerable authority as religious leaders. Sufism, a mystical Islamic movement that originated in the eighth century A.D., influences Bangali Muslims more than Muslims in other countries. Some ulema (Islamic scholars), traditionally opposed to the government's regulation of polygamy and divorce as well as its sponsorship of birth control measures, have in recent years softened their stand on population controls.

The Partition of British India in 1947 that divided Pakistan from India was a result of Muslims' insistence on a separate state where, as their leader, M. A. Jinnah, said, "they could rule according to their own code of life and according to their own cultural growth, tradition, and Islamic laws." Pakistani officials and their Bangali supporters feared India's military power and suspected India of planning to reassimilate Pakistan. Worried that the Hindu Bangali millions in East Pakistan endangered the unity of Pakistan, government leaders launched programs to counter Indian influence in the province. The campaign irritated Bangali opponents of the central government's social and economic policies, who held religious tolerance to be compatible with Islam.

After independence, however, Sheikh Mujib's policy of secularism intensified economic and political differences among political party members and leaders. President Zia's confirmation of the nation's Muslim identity permitted him to control party strife and proceed with modernizing programs. He continued Mujib's policy of religious freedom and cooperation with religious minorities.

Religion is a way of life in Bangladesh. All of its citizens belong to one of the world's religions.[3] Communal conflicts that have occurred between Muslim and Hindu communities are attributable less to religious passions than to social, personal, and political antagonisms.

The native Hindu minority in 1980 numbered about 13 million, or 15 percent of the population. During the first years of Pakistani rule, the Hindu community figured less and less prominently in national political life, and in the early fifties many Hindu leaders left for India. Only a handful of Hindu businessmen remained behind, along with millions of poor Hindu peasants. During the Ayub years the Hindu minority had virtually no political influence or representation. In the midst of communal turmoil in the sixties the Hindu community relied principally on Indian diplomatic representatives in Dacca for help. After independence the Hindu population cautiously reasserted itself in Bangladesh.

The Buddhist community in East Pakistan has a membership of about half a million. Buddhism was the religion of the Bangali people until the twelfth century, but today it is practiced only by the Burmese-speaking tribes of the Chittagong Hill Tracts. Their protests against private encroachments on their land and governmental neglect of their interests were frequently aired at provincial assemblies in the sixties. Since independence Buddhist political leaders have staunchly defended the interests of their people, with a moderate amount of success.

At the end of the seventies there were about 150,000 Christians in the country, a slight majority of them Roman Catholics. The Catholic population includes descendants of sixteenth-century Portuguese missionaries and their converts. Other missions, both Protestant and Catholic, were established during the lifetime of British India. U.S. and Australian Baptists and the British Oxfam mission serve the spiritual and material needs of their members. Most of the Garos, a tribal people, formerly animists (as other tribes continue to be), belong to various Christian churches. Scheduled-class (low-caste) Hindus, too, have become Christians. Proselytizing of Muslims is not permitted. Christian missionaries, in addition to ministering to the members of their faith, contribute relief supplies, aid in their distribution, and perform other social work, including health and educational services.

BASIC EDUCATION

John Kenneth Galbraith, in one of a series of lectures delivered at Indian universities while he was the U.S. ambassador in New Delhi, said, "Education is of high importance both as an object of immediate consumption and as a form of investment for future production. It is neither consumption nor investment, but both."[4] It is also an index of cultural and political vitality. Uneducated men and women, more often than not also poor, are culturally and politically deprived. A lack of education stalls technological programs and prevents people from improving their cultural resources and advancing in political freedom.

The people of East Pakistan were close to the bottom of the world's educational ladder. The 1961 census estimated that only 21.5 percent of the population older than five years was literate, that is, able to read with understanding a short statement on everyday life in any one of several languages. The rate of literacy in Bengali was reported as an even smaller percentage of the population. Only 31 percent as many women as men were literate—a reflection of the low status of women in this society, and a fact that limits the possibility of a rapid change in literacy rates. Literacy is normally acquired in school; in 1961 63 percent of the literates were in grades one through five. Although school attendance has increased, the adult literacy rate in 1975 was not much higher than it was several decades ago.

Measures to cope with adult illiteracy have had an effect, although a private U.S. foundation established in Dacca during the early fifties did not accomplish much. The Comilla Village Academy, which flourished in the next decade, conducted successful rural literacy programs using local mullahs. President Zia's government gave a high priority to adult literacy.

During the first ten years of its history East Pakistan received nominal amounts of financial aid for education. Expenditures for education in the fifties totaled approximately five rupees (just over one dollar) per capita, or half the meager educational expenditures of West Pakistan. Pakistan's five-year plan for 1965–69 did not fulfill its promise of more aid to the east. Although East Pakistan's provincial budget provided larger percentages for the operation and improvement of education than the budgets of many developing countries, the priority of education was low.

Teachers in the primary and secondary schools of East Pakistan were poorly paid and lacked adequate opportunities for advancement. Improvements in the quality of teaching through training institutes and other forms of in-service training, which did not begin until the sixties, barely improved teachers' morale.

Only about 30 percent of school-age children attended primary schools in 1960, the majority of them the first three grades. Lack of school buildings and a shortage of teachers have been cited as reasons for this situation. Thanks to increased expenditures by the government of Bangladesh, by 1980 65 percent of school-age children attended primary schools. Many rural parents still keep children out of school to work on the farm, at least part of the time. Secondary school attendance in 1960 was limited to a small percentage of teenage children, because education at this level was a provincial responsibility.

By 1980, however, 25 percent of these children were enrolled in public schools. Many secondary schools, originally financed by Hindu and Muslim zamindars, have operated for many years under religious auspices. Several of the private schools run by Christian religious communities are among the better educational institutions. The number of good privately supported Muslim secondary schools has increased. Nearly all of these institutions are now subsidized by the government, which controls their curricula.

During the 1971 war the Pakistani army is reported to have killed more than 1,000 teachers and destroyed thousands of school buildings. After independence the government appropriated millions for the relief and rehabilitation of the educational community. Many international organizations, foreign governments, and private groups helped to restore the educational system.

In each of its budgets up to 1982 the Dacca government allocated increasingly larger sums for education, especially for primary schools. Teachers benefited from the higher pay scales for government employees that were adopted in 1973. Between 1966 and 1975 the percentage of school-age children attending school increased from 47 to 73 percent, and in the same period the number of girls in attendance doubled. The enrollment in secondary schools tripled during those years. By 1976–77 there were 41,000 primary and 8,000 secondary schools in the country. Since 1977 current and developmental expenditures for education have steadily increased; they are the third largest current budget item.

HIGHER EDUCATION

The British founded the first university in the country at Dacca; five others were established under Pakistani rule. Their administration, course of instruction, and methods generally follow British models.[5]

The older universities of Dacca and Rajshahi, founded in 1921 and 1953 respectively, offer extensive programs and have large student bodies. The Agricultural University at Mymensingh and the University of Engineering and Technology, Dacca, date from 1961. The Jahangirnegar at Savar, just north of Dacca, dedicated in the spring of 1964, did not open until 1970. The sixth university, at Chittagong, enrolled its first students in 1966. By 1976 the total number of students in the universities was about 30,000, a number disproportionately small for the nation's population unless one remembers that university education in Bangladesh, as in Britain's Oxford and Cambridge, is largely restricted to the arts, sciences, and social studies.

The student bodies of the universities have been limited in order to increase funds for secondary schools and for technical and professional colleges, to keep a tighter control on student discipline, and to limit the number of unemployed and dissatisfied university graduates. In accordance with the British educational system, several hundred colleges affiliated with the universities offer specialized degrees in medicine, law, business, teacher training, music, and other subjects. More than 100,000 men and 13,000 women are enrolled. Below these levels, polytechnical schools offer specialized training in several fields.

The restrictive policies of the Pakistani government touched off student strikes and other forms of political agitation. At the University of Dacca throughout the sixties, professors and students emulated the political confrontations engaged in by the university students in Calcutta. Unwilling to return to their villages and despairing of finding the jobs for which their education had prepared them, students were readily recruited by political parties of the left, right, and center to carry out party chores or to agitate. The campuses were highly politicized during the governments of Presidents Ayub and Yahya. Nonetheless, the universities have produced many excellent graduates, and their facilities have contributed significantly to the intellectual life of the nation; many faculty members have joined the government.

With the savage killing of university professors, students, and other intelligentsia in Dacca and elsewhere by the Pakistani army in March 1971, the central government destroyed a source of political opposition. The provisional government of Bangladesh claimed that 280 intellectuals, including Hindu professors and Muslims identified with Bangali literary movements, were singled out for slaughter in Dacca and other parts of the country.

During the nine-month war for independence, the army at first closed the universities but soon reopened them under military control. Most of the students who attended during that period were affiliated with the fundamentalist Jamaat-i-Islam party. When Sheikh Mujib returned to Dacca he gave the universities civilian administration. Student political organizations were revived. As in the past, many students preferred to collaborate with radical elements in the government or its opposition. The Bangladesh Students' Union was supported by the anti-Mujib, pro-Chinese wing of the National Awami party led by Maulana Bhashani. The pro-Soviet faction of that party, however, allied itself with Mujib's Bangladesh Students' League. In July 1972 a group of students in Mujib's camp was attacked by members of a dissident student organization; more than 100 were injured. Months later, antigovernment students attacked the United States Information Office near Rajshahi University and firebombed the U.S. Information Library in Dacca. In order to combat student violence and opposition, Sheikh Mujib organized the Jubo (youth) League to support his policies. During General Zia's regime student agitation subsided as long as political party activity was suspended, but it resumed in 1983 under martial law.

THE ARTS

Under Pakistani rule the flowering of Bengali literature was adversely affected by the controversy over the use of Bengali as a state language.[6] Writers in Bengali were accused of being pro-Indian, and those who wrote in Bengali employing an Urduized script failed to win popular favor.

The great Bengali poet and dramatist, Nobel Prize winner Rabindranath Tagore (1861–1941), lived within the boundaries of present-day Bangladesh. His home near Khustia and the Indian border is a place revered by Bengali speakers. His song "My Golden Bengal" is the Bangalis' national anthem. Besides Tagore, the greatest Bengali poet was the Muslim Kazi Nazrul Islam (1893–1976). He wrote from 1919 until 1941, when he became insane. For him Bengali was a Muslim-Hindu tongue. He counseled Muslims and Hindus to use one another's legends and myths. Because he wrote and sang songs against British rule, most of his published works were proscribed by the British. His writings gave a fillip to the Muslim romantic spirit. The Bengali author Jasimuddin (1903–76) collected the traditional ballads of the Bangali countryside and made them a source of his own work. His stories evoke village life and the villagers' joys and sorrows.

As in other agricultural countries, the art and music of the Bangalis grew out of popular social and religious celebrations. Dancing and music native to Bengal thrives everywhere among the peasants, especially at the time of sowing and harvesting, the coming of the new year, and changes of season. The government added to the traditional holidays numerous commemorations of national events celebrated with songs, dances, and other forms of popular entertainment. In Dacca the Bulbul Academy of Fine Arts, the Nazrul Academy, and other organizations preserve the local traditions in music and art.

The Bangali, whether Hindu or Muslim, has a flair for painting and a deep love of nature, music, and the fields and villages. Under the direction of the late Zainul Abedin, famous for his hundred or more black and white sketches of the Calcutta famine of 1943, students in the art school (Shilpakala Academy) of the University of Dacca produced highly sophisticated examples of local art. Because Muslim artists find it difficult, if not impossible, to paint human faces because of the Islamic iconoclastic tradition, some of the Muslims in Abedin's classes turned with enthusiasm to contemporary abstract painting. Abedin, who died in August 1976, taught his students to portray the countryside in all of its quiet moments and colors. River and flood scenes, boat paintings, and village sketches were produced by his Muslim students and other artists. Hindu art students and artists, not bound by the Islamic tradition, did similar work but also depicted human features.

THE MEDIA

Newspapers have long been the preferred print media of literate Bangalis.[7] The modest circulation figures of the daily newpapers belie the actual readership. Although the ratio of newspaper circulation to the number of inhabitants is low, the number of readers of each copy is high. The quality and productiveness of the Bangali press has been surprisingly good, in spite of the fact that after Partition the press and publishing equipment in West Pakistan was far in advance of East Pakistan because of its greater access to capital for such enterprises.

Calcutta, prior to Partition, was the center of British, Hindu, and Muslim publishing and of newspapers in Bengali and English. The Dacca press had to start virtually from scratch in 1947. Until a newsprint plant was built near Khulna in the fifties, there was a serious shortage of newsprint. The plant, when built, served the needs of East and West Pakistan. Today it produces a surplus, which is chiefly exported to neighboring countries. The supply of newsprint in Bangladesh is ample.

In 1979, 30 dailies were published in five cities; those in Bengali had an estimated circulation of 300,000 copies, and four of the English dailies, 60,000 copies. More than 80 percent of the daily newspapers and half of all other publications are printed in Dacca. The concentration of the press in that city is due to the illiteracy and poverty of the countryside, to the lack of rapid transportation between the cities, towns, and villages, and, above all, to the political character of the newspapers. During the preindependence era as well as at the present time, the newspapers aligned themselves with political parties or factions headquartered in Dacca.

The political role of Bangali newspapers is illustrated by the history of one of the nation's major dailies. *Ittefaq*, a Bengali paper, in the sixties had the largest circulation of any daily in East Pakistan—35,000 copies. By 1979 its circulation was up to 140,000. Its editor, Taffazal Hussain, was a protégé of H. S. Suhrawardy, founder of the Awami League. *Ittefaq* could be said to have been the organ of the moderate wing of the Awami League. The newspaper was closed down several times during Ayub's administration, and Hussain served jail sentences for publishing allegedly subversive articles. The paper carried on a ferocious campaign against the Muslim League and kept up a drumfire of agitation over the issue of economic and political disparity. On the death of Hussain in the late sixties, his son, Anwar Hussain, became editor. After independence *Ittefaq* criticized Mujib's government for its corruption and its dependence on India. In 1975 the Mujib government took control of the paper, but Anwar Hussain regained ownership and control of the newspaper under Mujib's successors. *Ittefaq* maintains an independent stance in support of a democratic domestic policy and a strictly nonaligned foreign policy.

After independence the weeklies increased in numbers. They included organs of the Bangladesh Communist party, former Awami League periodicals, and a few specialized magazines on women and sports. *Huq Katha* continued publication under the ownership of Maulana Bhashani, head of the anti-Mujib wing of the National Awami party. Most of these periodicals, including the left-leaning *Holiday* (which was closed down for a time in June 1975), continue to appear.

Three wire services associated with Western and Soviet services supply news to the papers. In April 1975 Bangladesh joined 19 other countries in a pool run by Tanyug, the Yugoslav news agency.

Foreign newspapers and periodicals, of which the most important was the Calcutta *Statesman*, circulated in East Pakistan. The *Statesman* maintained a press representative in Dacca until he was forced to leave in the early sixties. A few Indian newspapers began circulating again in Bangladesh after independence.

The Mujib government reinstated a public information office to handle relations with the press, prepare semiweekly news digests, and assist its embassies in publishing newsletters for distribution abroad. In 1976 the Zia government created a press institute to provide in-service training for journalists. Abdus Salam, a highly regarded former editor of the *Bangladesh Observer*, was appointed director.

Mujib lifted the Pakistani government ban on highly popular Bengali films produced in India and encouraged their local production.

Successive Pakistani governments controlled newspapers and periodicals in both East and West Pakistan.[8] The Bangali press was kept on tenterhooks by the government's sporadic interventions. From time to time editors were jailed and the papers subjected to stringent regulations or closed down. A National Press Trust newspaper competed with dissident privately owned publications.

On its accession to power the Awami League acted as if it would be the guardian of press freedom. At the end of June 1972 the minister for information and broadcasting said in a radio statement that the government had no intention of setting up a government press or of interfering with the dissemination of the news by newspapers or periodicals. He reiterated the government's dedication to freedom of the press as a precondition for the establishment of democracy. But he also reminded the press, as had Mujib on other occasions, that it had the responsibility to create a positive public opinion by "constructive criticism."

The next year the government, more and more upset by rising violence and by stinging criticisms in the press, established press controls. President Zia relaxed the controls in 1980, but General Ershad reimposed them in 1982.

The government of Sheikh Mujibur Rahman took over the ownership and management of Pakistan's radio and television facilities.[9] Radio Bangladesh in 1971 maintained transmitters in six regions of the country. Its external service, begun in 1972, broadcast in eight languages by 1977. The Bangladesh Television Corporation, a former Pakistani body originally developed with Japanese assistance, operates from three locations in the country.

SCIENCE AND TECHNOLOGY

The scientific and technological work currently being done is insufficient for the country's needs, but the level of scientific studies and research is more advanced than in the great majority of developing countries.[10] The science departments of the universities of Dacca and Rajshahi are the focal points of scientific studies. The universities also engage in research and produce graduate students to carry on scientific work. The teaching staffs at these universities include personnel with excellent research qualifications and experience who were trained outside Bangladesh. Although in 1971 war seriously disrupted university life, the tradition of scientific studies has resumed.

Health research has been conducted by the Malaria Institute at Dacca and the nearby Cholera Laboratory, established by the Southeast Asia Treaty Organization (SEATO) and now financed by other international institutions.

The Jute Research Institute, which has been in existence for several decades, has never accomplished much. Since independence private groups concerned with expanding the export markets for jute, including the Bangladesh Mills Association and the International Jute Organization, have encouraged the development and sale of new jute products. The development of new uses for jute is essential if the nation's principal foreign exchange earner is to beat the heavy competition of synthetic bagging materials and bulk cargo carriers. Research on other farm products important to the peasant population goes on at the Agricultural University in the northern town of Mymensingh.

In 1977 the U.S. Agency for International Development (AID) financed the expansion of the Bangladesh Agricultural Research Institute, which was established in 1974 to improve the production of winter food crops such as wheat, legumes, oil seeds, and vegetables.

Laboratories doing research in industrial applications operate in several cities and at the University of Engineering and Technology, Dacca. A nuclear science training and research center began its work during the regime of President Ayub. Bangali students study nuclear sciences and technologies at schools in the United States and Britain.

CHAPTER 4

The Roots of the Bangali Nation and the Partition of 1947

The earliest story of the Bangalis—poor, egalitarian, imaginative, and independent; the Irish of Asia—was written by conquerers, missionaries, princely rulers, aristocrats, and peasants. By origin a mixture of Aryan, Dravidian, West Asian, Tibetan, and Burmese strains, the Bangalis lived on the periphery of the center of Indian and Chinese cultures. Their home on the soil-rich, well-watered plains of the Ganges and Brahmaputra made for a simple agrarian existence. Before and after the Christian era they were Buddhists and Hindus. In the twelfth century Muslim soldiers and Sufi missionaries from West Asia converted most of them to Islam. The pious Sufis, with their simple faith in Allah, found their greatest response among the untouchables, a majority among the Hindu population. The uncomplicated faith of Islam reinforced the untouchables' desire for social equality.

The Bengali language, which long before the conversions to Islam had become the common tongue of the people, helped to consolidate the religious faith of the Muslim majority as well as to establish lines of communication with the Hindu minority.

With the coming of the Muslim Akhbar to the Delhi throne in the sixteenth century, Bengal became part of the Mogul empire until the British took over.[1] Dacca was the chief city of Bengal for more than a century. The viceroy who represented the Delhi emperor in Dacca was either a member of the royal family or another important personage. Bengal, peaceful and prosperous, contributed to the stability of the Mogul throne. Although the land east of the Brahmaputra was physically

Baitul Mukarram Mosque, Dhaka (Dacca).

isolated from the rest of Bengal because of the difficulty of crossing that great river, the Moguls brought the eastern and western sectors of the country together under a common rule.

European interest in Bengal began with the Portuguese who, during the last quarter of the fifteenth century, established trading posts and Christian missions. They were soon displaced by the Dutch East India Company, which established commercial "factories" along the coast and indigo plantations on the shores of the Bangali Ganges. At the end of the seventeenth century the British secured themselves in Calcutta, by that time Bengal's largest, most important city. With the nearly concomitant decline of Mogul power, the British East India Company became the ruler of eastern India. Its hold on the area was confirmed when the British defeated the French at Plassey, a few miles north of Calcutta, in 1757. From that time on, the British were the masters of Bengal and the Ganges delta.

Muslim political influence in Bengal, according to Muslim historians, diminished with the ascendancy of Hindu zamindars, who had first become powerful under Mogul rule. Other historians attribute the Muslims' decline to the alliance of Hindu merchants with the East India Company.

AFTER THE MUTINY OF 1857

In 1857 Muslim and Hindu soldiers of the British East India Company were said to have been issued cartridges that had to be torn open using the teeth and that were smeared with pig and cow grease. The troops, most of whom were from Bengal, refused to load their rifles, revolted, and fought British troops for two years. British colonial policy in Bengal following the Mutiny of 1857 gave precedence to Hindus over Muslims.[2] In East Bengal, Hindus serving as agents of the British became effective and competent leaders of that community. The Hindus, quickly adapting themselves to British rule, outdistanced the Muslims in education, commerce, and government service. Muslim peasants stood aloof from the Western-oriented educational system established by the British and from the emerging Muslim middle class. The forward press of Hindus in East Bengal deprived the Muslims of valuable political experience and aroused their resentment.

While Calcutta was the hub of the British empire for nearly 200 years, the people of East Bengal lived an isolated rural existence, save for the presence of a handful of British civil servants, sent there to maintain law and order and assisted by Hindu lawyers, landlords, teachers, and clerks. East Bengal, an economic, social, and political backwater before the British took over, made slow progress under British rule. The production of jute, a profitable cash crop, overtook the production of indigo, but the principal occupation of the Bangalis was to grow enough food for themselves and to enjoy what few other things they had.

The barely perceptible pace of social and economic change in pre-Partition Bengal produced a long delay in the emergence of political movements but permitted the sociobiological forces at work to produce identifiable Muslim and Hindu communities. The census of 1951, taken a few years after Partition, showed a slight Muslim majority in all of Bengal and a preponderance of Muslims in what is now Bangladesh. Calcutta in West Bengal, at the time a city of more than three million with a large majority of Hindus, attracted the well-off and better educated professionals among Muslims as well as Hindus.

On the other hand, the majority of Muslims lived at or near the rice paddies and jute farms of East Bengal, where industry could hardly be said to exist. Food, clothing, and shelter were produced in the villages or locally. Manufacturers from Calcutta supplied the household utensils and the simple farming tools required by the peasants. Vehicles and other heavy equipment came from Britain.

After the development of rail and water transportation at the beginning of the nineteenth century, middle-class Muslim and Hindu families

Old Hindu temple, Jaydebpur.

living in East Bengal were able to maintain close contact with their relatives in Calcutta. The closer relationships accentuated family religious differences.

For centuries Hindus and Muslims in East Bengal had lived peacefully in the same or adjoining villages, each following their own way of life.[3] The social life of villagers was monitored by locally selected religious leaders, but their economic well-being was in the hands of zamindars (landlords) selected by the British government, for which they collected taxes. The land tenure system, known as the Permanent Settlement and established in March 1773 by Lord Cornwallis of Yorktown fame, fortified the hold of the zamindars, who were for the most part Hindus. For a century and a half they collected land taxes levied by the British on tenant farmers—the main source of Bengal's revenue. The zamindars, who retained 10 percent of their collections, invested their substantial income in the development of Calcutta and in the education of their children as businessmen, doctors, lawyers, and teachers. The Hindu landlords and the educated members of their families formed the elite of East Bengal and overshadowed its Muslim leaders until the 1920s.

THE DIVISION OF BENGAL

The administrative division of Bengal into east and west sectors, ordered by the British governor general, Lord Curzon, in 1905, stirred middle-class Muslim interest in home rule.[4] Lord Curzon decided to establish a new administrative capital at Dacca to govern a region that now includes Bangladesh and the Indian states of Tripura and Assam. He made this move because he thought that the territory under his jurisdiction had become too populous to administer as a single unit. He also believed that the interests of the Muslim majority in East Bengal had been neglected. His action delighted the local Muslims. During the administration of his immediate successor, Lord Minto, government offices were built and Dacca took on a lively air for the first time in centuries.

The Muslim League, founded in Dacca in 1906, a year after the division of Bengal, promised loyalty to the British Raj, abjured Muslim hostility toward other religious communities, frankly urged the advancement of Muslim political rights, and supported the separation of East from West Bengal.[5] Aga Khan III, leader of the Ismaili Muslims—an Islamic Shi'ite sect—was president of the league, and the league's secretaries were men from Aligargh University, the center of Muslim Urdu culture in British India. (The Dacca venue had been arranged by the Urdu-speaking nawab of Dacca and his Bangali followers.) In 1909 the league obtained from the British authorities the right to hold separate elections. This ruling gave Muslims the right to vote separately for candidates of their religious persuasion—an electoral system aimed at dividing British India into two religiously based political communities. The actions of the aristocratic league leaders represented initial steps toward a separate Muslim state.

Meanwhile, the Hindus in Bengal regarded Lord Curzon's establishment of a Muslim East Bengal as an unjustifiable restriction of their interests. They saw themselves outnumbered in the provincial legislatures of both East and West Bengal and launched a political drive against the "partition." Hindu commercial, landed, and professional groups living in Calcutta feared that the "partition" would threaten the city's shipping supremacy, if Chittagong was made a rival port. Hindu lawyers believed they would be displaced by Muslim attorneys. The Hindu Indian National Congress, a political propaganda organization, launched an acrimonious propaganda campaign against Lord Curzon's decision.

The congress had the support of a well-established Calcutta elite known as *bhadralok* (the respectable people), wealthy landowners, mostly upper-caste Bengali Hindus who at the turn of the century had assumed the mantle of ruling-class authority. They controlled the important political posts and patronage of the city. Opposed to British rule, they were incensed by the "partition" of Bengal.

In December 1911 Governor General Lord Hardinge, to appease Hindu wrath, reversed his predecessor's order and reunited East and West Bengal. Muslims in Bengal believed that the British had surrendered to Hindu pressures. A later British government, as if to compensate the Muslims, funded the establishment of the University of Dacca in 1921. Many Muslims of Bengal persisted in viewing the "partition" as the initial recognition of their autonomy.

The reunion of divided Bengal and the removal of the capital of British India from Calcutta to New Delhi during the following year quickened Muslim leaders' political consciousness and added to Indian determination, especially in Bengal, to force the British out of India.

Subsequent events in Bengal took place in Calcutta among the opposing economic and political interests of the Hindu elite and the Muslim and Hindu poor.[6] Muslim political leaders in Calcutta rose to positions of authority in what had been West Bengal. Two of the most prominent of them, Fazlul Huq, founder of the Peasants' and Workers' party, and H. S. Suhrawardy of the Muslim League, fought for Muslim rule in a "united Bengal" and stirred the political perceptions of the peasants of East Bengal.

Although Muslims represented only one-quarter of the population of Calcutta, from 1927 onward they managed, with the help of non-Hindu minorities, low-caste Hindus, and British citizens, to elect Muslims to top ministerial posts in the presidency of Bengal and to oust *bhadralok* leaders from the city government. In 1937 Fazlul Huq became the first minister of the presidency; in 1946 H. S. Suhrawardy took over the same office.

THE LAHORE RESOLUTION

At the Muslim League's 1940 conference in Lahore, Fazlul Huq, who had been persuaded to join the league by its president, Muhammad Ali Jinnah, was invited to introduce the principal resolution of the conference. Afterwards Bangalis cited the Lahore resolution in justification of their demand for provincial autonomy. The resolution read: "No constitutional plan would be workable in this country or acceptable to Muslims unless . . . the areas in which Muslims are numerically in the majority, as in the Northwest and Eastern zones which should be grouped in constituent States . . . shall be autonomous and sovereign."[7]

The Bangali view that the resolution aimed at autonomy for the Muslims of East Bengal was ignored by Jinnah in his announcement of 1944, which favored a single Muslim state, Pakistan, composed of six provinces: Sind, Baluchistan, North-West Frontier, Punjab, Bengal, and Assam. Assam, where the Muslims were in a minority, may have been included to remind the Bangalis of the "partition" when that area was under the jurisdiction of Dacca and to serve as a bargaining chip with the Indians and British. In 1946 a Muslim League meeting at New Delhi adopted a resolution demanding a unified Pakistan. It was said to "supercede" the Lahore resolution. This action implied that the Lahore resolution had in fact sanctioned the idea of Bangali autonomy.

Meanwhile Fazlul Huq and H. S. Suhrawardy rallied the Bangalis to the Muslim League cause, although Huq left the league in the forties and ran against it in the 1945–46 elections. Muslims in Bengal, unlike their coreligionists in the North-West Frontier, presented virtually no opposition to the idea of a Muslim state, perhaps because, independently of the league, they hoped for a united Bengal under Muslim rule.

BENGAL AND CALCUTTA

Muslims in the Bengal presidency of the forties were in a slight majority. Their political power had been whittled down, however, by the British communal award of 1932, which established representation in the provincial legislatures according to a formula and permitted the Muslims to win only a minority of 119 seats out of 250 in the Legislative Assembly. Eighty seats were reserved for Anglo-Indians, Indian Christians, Europeans, and respresentatives of interest groups—the majority of the latter were low-caste Hindus. Many of the 80 cooperated with the Muslim League rather than the Indian National Congress. In the general elections of 1946, the Muslim League won 113 seats and the congress 87. Suhrawardy, leader of the league, tried to form a coalition with the congress but failed. His ministry, which held office with the help of independent groups, remained precariously in power during a period of communal (Muslim-Hindu) riots until the Partition of 1947.

In March 1947 Suhrawardy again proposed a Muslim-Hindu coalition, this time to establish a united Bengal, separate from India, but the Indian National Congress would have none of it. Its members wanted control of Bengal as part of an independent India.[8]

On August 16, 1946, Direct Action Day, the leaders of the Muslim League told their followers to renounce all titles granted by the British government in token of their resentment of unfriendly British attitudes toward a separate Muslim state. On the eve of Direct Action Day, Suhrawardy declared that if power were transferred to the Indian

National Congress by the British, Bengal would declare its complete independence and set up a parallel government. In effect, he proposed to establish a Bengal government jointly controlled by Muslims and Hindus. The governance of Calcutta by Muslims was essential to his plan to unite East and West Bengal because Calcutta was the key to a united Bengal's trade and prosperity. But the Indian National Congress was in no way inclined to tolerate Muslim rule of the city's Hindu majority nor to accept a united Bengal, although Hindu radicals, opposed to the congress, approved the idea of such a union.

Suhrawardy told Lord Mountbatten, the British viceroy, that given sufficient time he could induce Bengal to remain united outside of Pakistan. The Hindu Bengali leader of the opposition, Kiran Shankar Roy, is reputed to have said that if the Muslim League gave up the idea of separate electorates in favor of joint electorates, to which Suhrawardy allegedly agreed, the unity of Bengal would be assured. The British governor, Sir Frederick Burrows, at one time favored joint Hindu-Muslim control of Calcutta, but later supported the British partition plan for two nations—Pakistan, including East Bengal, and India, including West Bengal.

The bloody encounter between Hindus and Muslims on Direct Action Day in Calcutta, vividly described in L. Moseley's *Last Days of the British Raj*, was an inauspicious prelude to the Partition of British India and a portent of Hindu-Muslim relations on the subcontinent. The carnage in Calcutta was matched in East Bengal. Communal massacres in the city were followed by outpourings of Muslims from India and Hindus from East Bengal.

"UNITED BENGAL" AND PAKISTAN

The original British cabinet plan for the transfer of power from Britain to India and Pakistan included an option for Bengal to decide on independence as a unit.[9] Pandit Nehru firmly opposed an independent Bengal on the grounds that it would lead to the balkanization of India. A revised program for Partition, worked out at Simla, reversed the cabinet plan and gave to certain provinces and parts of the provinces the option of voting for India or Pakistan without the alternative of independence. Suhrawardy, after conferring with Hindu Bengali political leaders, said he was hopeful of an agreement on a united Bengal. Mountbatten told the Muslim leader that an independent Bengal raised serious questions regarding Commonwealth membership. Moreover, he pointed out, Nehru was opposed to a united Bengal without close ties to a central Indian government. Suhrawardy later told Mountbatten that Roy had been unable to persuade members of the Indian National

Congress to vote for Bengal's independence. Suhrawardy suggested Calcutta be declared a jointly controlled city after Partition because he believed the congress might change its mind and support the idea of an independent Bengal. Sardar Patel, an Indian businessman and a leader of the congress, vetoed any proposal that would establish joint Muslim-Hindu control of Calcutta. Fazlul Huq and H. S. Suhrawardy thereupon supported the union of all Bengal in Pakistan.

On June 20, 1947, the Bengal Legislative Assembly met and in a 126-to-90 vote agreed that, if Bengal remained united, it should join Pakistan. Representatives of West Bengal's Hindu majority, however, voted 58 to 21 to partition the province between India and Pakistan. But in accordance with existing rules requiring majority Hindu support for legislative action, the vote of the assembly for a united Bengal as part of Pakistan was nullified.

When Nehru insisted that in any partition arrangements Bengal and the Punjab (a province of what was to become West Pakistan) be divided into two parts, leaving Muslims in control of East Bengal and Hindus in control of eastern Punjab, Jinnah agreed, remarking, "Better a moth-eaten Pakistan than no Pakistan at all." On August 15, 1947, hastened by atrocious internecine bloodletting in the Punjab and civil disorder in Bengal, India and Pakistan won their independence.

CHAPTER 5

Bangalis in Pakistan, 1947–65

With Partition, Pakistan made an easy legal transition to the status of a sovereign government. In departing India the British had thoughtfully arranged that the Government of India Act, passed by the London Parliament in 1935, should serve as the law of the land in Pakistan and India until new constitutions could be framed. The Indians took two and a half years to devise a fundamental law. Pakistan, unable to agree on a constitutional document, was ruled for nine years under Britain's colonial law; its first Constitution, adopted in 1956, lasted only two years.

Under the India Act of 1935, a governor general was the paramount legal authority in the province of East Bengal and in the western Pakistan provinces of Punjab, Sind, and North-West Frontier, as well as in nonautonomous areas. As the head of the central government the governor general appointed the governors of the provinces. However, during these nine years, the authority of the governor general was challenged by Pakistan's prime ministers and top bureaucrats and (less successfully) by the National Assembly elected by the provincial legislatures. The prime minister was selected by the dominant majority in the National Assembly.

In 1956 the first Constitution divided the country into East and West Pakistan (the two sections were popularly known as "wings"). The three provinces of West Pakistan were constituted as one unit for the purpose of representation in the National Assembly, and Baluchistan, also part of West Pakistan, was later made a fourth province, becoming part of the one unit. The prime minister elected by the National Assembly was the head of the government until General Ayub Khan assumed power as martial law administrator in October 1958.

PAKISTAN'S NATIONAL ASSEMBLY

The first legislative body of Pakistan, the National Assembly, was empowered to enact federal laws and to serve as a constitutional convention.[1] The colonialist procedure for selecting members of the assembly, detailed in the British government's plan for Partition, authorized elections by provincial legislatures, the members of which were elected by constituencies representing only 10 to 15 percent of the population.

East Bengal was awarded 44 seats in the 80-member assembly, a figure representative of its majority population. However, Jinnah filled four of East Bengal's seats with West Pakistanis. The Bangalis agreed to this self-effacing arrangement, probably in the hope of receiving other substantial benefits, including coveted government posts.

The oddly sorted representatives from East Bengal and western Pakistan in the first National Assembly could hardly be expected to accomplish great things. The membership from East Bengal consisted of Muslim and Hindu middle-class lawyers, and the delegation from western Pakistan was largely made up of wealthy Muslim landowners. Not only was the size of the body unrepresentative of a country of 80 million people; nearly half of the members did not attend its sessions regularly and 20 of the legislators were also members of central and provincial administrative agencies. All sessions of the assembly met in Karachi in western Pakistan, a thousand arduous miles west of Dacca.

The Muslim League, which could count on an absolute majority in the assembly, undermined Bangali bargaining power by questioning the loyalty of the 13 members from East Bengal (its Hindu population was about 10 million) who had opposed the establishment of Pakistan before Partition.[2] Their western Pakistani critics noted that the Hindus kept their families in India and sent money back to them through illegal channels. This argument had little weight in East Bengal, where a number of Muslim families, too, lived at least part time in India. On this count and others, the Bangalis' attitude toward their Hindu compatriots was appreciably more sympathetic than that of the Muslims in western Pakistan.

For the short time that Jinnah was alive (he died in September 1948), serious Bangali opposition in the assembly did not emerge, nor was it likely to, for Jinnah was a popular figure in all of Pakistan. Moreover, East Bengal at the outset depended on the Jinnah-controlled central government for administrative and other services. Personal factionalism in the provincial legislature of East Bengal created a political vacuum, which the central government and its civil servants readily filled. Jinnah, as governor general, had the power under the

India Act to appoint and remove provincial governors. Politicians in the provinces stood alertly in the wings, hoping to be chosen governor or appointed to a lucrative political post.

A basic political weakness of the government of East Bengal was its almost total lack of organizational personnel. When its ties to the Bengal presidency in Calcutta were abruptly broken at Partition, it lost 90 percent of its British and Indian civil servants. Only one Bangali among the several hundred former Indian bureaucrats came over to Pakistan. The administration and finances of the province were in a shambles. Bangali leadership in the first provincial legislatures was confused and ineffective.

BANGALIS' STRUGGLES FOR REPRESENTATION

Delay in achieving a national constitution meant that until 1956 the country was ruled by the central government operating from Karachi, first under Jinnah, then Liaquat Ali Khan, later Kwaja Nazimuddin (a conservative from East Bengal), and finally under a succession of other men, most of whom were dedicated to a united Pakistan.[3] Civil servants lent their weight to national integration programs.

Liaquat Ali Khan, in the hope of strengthening the Muslim League in East Bengal, cajoled Bangali politicians with jobs and the promise of greater influence at the Center, the seat of the government. Following the assassination of Liaquat Ali in 1949, Nurul Amin, a Bangali Muslim Leaguer, was appointed chief minister of East Bengal, and Kwaja Nazimuddin was promoted from that provincial post to serve at the Center as governor general of Pakistan and later as prime minister.

Factionalism soon disrupted the Bangali wing of the Muslim League. Nurul Amin cut his ties with Nazimuddin after the latter's tour of duty in Karachi. Nazimuddin alienated Amin when, on a visit to Dacca as prime minister in February 1952, he spoke on behalf of Urdu as a national language. The reaction of the students of Dacca University was instantaneous; fearing that Urdu would be imposed on them, they rioted. In the melee two students were killed. Amin, a Bangali speaker, had no sympathy for Nazimuddin's positions on Urdu nor a monolithic Pakistan. He believed it possible to reconcile Bangali "autonomy" with a united Pakistan. Nazimuddin was forced out of office in April 1953 by Governor General Ghulam Mohammad, a former top civil servant dissatisfied with the alleged inability of Nazimuddin to deal with the nation's problems.

The East Bengal Muslim League did not like what it had heard about a proposed 1954 constitutional document drafted by the Karachi government (but never published). It was known to propose a powerful executive and a Parliament with limited powers—a preview of President Ayub's presidential Constitution of 1962. Had Amin supported the document, he would have been accused of selling out to western Pakistani civil servants, chiefly Punjabis, advocates of a strong central executive. The Muslim League finally decided to oppose further action on the draft.

In order to deal with Bangali insistence on majority representation in the National Assembly, Amin met with Prime Minister Mohammad Ali Bogra, another conservative Bangali who had been chosen by Ghulam Mohammad, and with the chief ministers of the provinces, to work out favorable representation formulas. The prime minister proposed giving East Bengal 50 percent of the total vote in a bicameral national legislature and a Bangali majority in the lower house. Nurul Amin agreed to the compromise, but the former first minister of the Bengal presidency, Fazlul Huq, opposed it because he wanted more autonomy for the Bangalis and feared it would consolidate the power of the central government. The compromise plan was eventually rejected by the makers of the 1956 Constitution.

Mohammad Ali Bogra, prior to his selection as prime minister, had been Pakistan's ambassador to Washington. He soon turned his country's almost obsessive concern with domestic politics to foreign affairs, realizing that Pakistan could benefit from an American connection. Anxieties about the decision of the Russians to recognize Afghanistan's claim to a Pahktoonistan carved out of northern Pakistan encouraged Karachi to become an ally of the United States in the SEATO pact of September 1954 and a grateful recipient of military and economic aid. The pact increased Pakistan's rivalry with India and whetted the appetite of the Pakistani military for political power, with which they hoped to maintain the unity of Pakistan and recover Kashmir. The Partition had assigned Kashmir, with its Muslim majority, to India, angering Pakistani leaders who had demanded the inclusion of the territory in their country.

Mohammad Ali Bogra's apparent success in foreign affairs was not matched in domestic matters, where he might have been expected to help his fellow Bangalis. But he had no political base in western Pakistan and a limited one in East Bengal. He managed to hold on to power for 18 months.

PROVINCIAL ELECTIONS, 1954

The first election held in East Bengal brought Suhrawardy's newly organized Awami (people's) League together with Fazlul Huq's older Peasants' and Workers' party and other political groups, including communists, in a United Front against the Muslim League.[4] The Awami League, destined to be the leading political entity for the Bangalis during the following 20 years, grew out of a coalition formed by the astute middle-class lawyer from Calcutta, H. S. Suhrawardy, and the anti-Hindu leftist Maulana Bhashani. Suhrawardy dominated the league in its early years.

The Front won an overwhelming majority of seats in the 1954 provincial legislature. Nurul Amin's Muslim League had to be content with a meager ten seats. Fazlul Huq, as a member of the coalition, became the chief minister of East Bengal for the second time. The fine showing of the United Front convinced the politicians, civil servants, and the military at the Center that they had to constrain their Bangali foes.

Shortly after the election a labor strike in the Adamjee jute mill in Naranganj, a short distance south of Dacca, gave Karachi its chance to undermine the United Front. During the strike 400 persons were killed and 1,000 or more injured. The government concealed the fact that in large part the riot was a clash between Bengali- and Urdu-speaking Muslims (most of the latter had been driven out of India's Bihar state in 1951 by fanatical Hindus). The Adamjee family was said by Bangali critics to have given preferential treatment in hiring to the Biharis. The central government, with the help of a sympathetic press, attributed the violence to communist and Hindu influences. Fazlul Huq was ousted as chief minister for treasonable acts stemming from his alleged failure to halt the rioting.[5]

Fearing that the United Front victory and the disorders at the jute mill would lead to provincial autonomy, the Center also ousted the entire East Bengal cabinet and, under provisions of the India Act of 1935, installed Iskander Mirza, then defense minister, as governor of the North-West Frontier province.

In October 1954 it was the turn of the Muslim League Bangalis in the National Assembly, in combination with Pakistani anti-Punjabi politicians, to challenge the authority of the Center. Ghulam Mohammad, then governor general, construing their opposition to be tantamount to a coup, dissolved the assembly.

Dissension in East Bengal and conflicting political ambitions in western Pakistan provoked a political shift at the Center that appeared to be favorable to the Bangalis. Mohammad Ali Bogra's cabinet resigned and a new government was formed by Governor General Ghulam Mohammad. Chaudhuri Mohammad Ali, the candidate of the civil service, was named prime minister. Opposition leaders H. S. Suhrawardy and Dr. Khan Sahib of the North-West Frontier province, both of whom had been regarded as enemies of Pakistan, were included in the cabinet.

The prime minister, with their support, called up a Constituent Assembly to prepare and adopt a Constitution.

Provincial legislatures in June 1955 elected members to the Constituent Assembly. The Bangalis were awarded equal representation with western Pakistanis; the United Front, pledged to the advocacy of Bangali causes, represented East Bengal. During the assembly's sessions, Mirza was made governor general through a deal between the Muslim League and the United Front.

PAKISTAN'S FIRST CONSTITUTION

The National Assembly that adopted the Constitution of March 1956 refused to declare Pakistan an Islamic state but did require its chief executive, the president, to be a Muslim, a concession to the ulemas (orthodox Muslim theologians) and a strategem of political Muslims seeking to assert their country's independence of secular India.[6] The president was instructed to set up a commission to make recommendations for bringing existing laws into conformity with the injunctions of Islam.

The Constitution met the desires of the Bangalis for a parliamentary system. The president, elected by the Parliament, had to act in accordance with the advice of the cabinet, whose prime minister, as the head of the majority party in the National Assembly, was to be the effective leader of the nation. The Bangalis supported the system because it held out the hope that with equal representation in the assembly, one day they might have majority control of the Parliament and a decisive voice in national affairs. Under these circumstances they accepted the change in the name of the province from East Bengal to East Pakistan. Although the Constitution limited the authority of the provincial legislatures, Bangali leaders believed they could live with it.

The Bangalis might have gained more representation or a greater degree of home rule but for their factionalism. For example, the issue of whether to elect Hindu and Muslim members to the National Assembly with separate seats for each community or with joint electorates split the Bangali delegation. With the support of the Hindu Bangalis, H. S. Suhrawardy, leader of the Awami Leaguers, pleaded for a franchise based on joint constituencies. Fazlul Huq and his followers in the United Front voted with the Muslim League against joint electorates. Thus traditional and fundamentalist Muslim Bangalis challenged the "secularist" Awami Leaguers, and Fazlul Huq the leadership of Suhrawardy. A constitutional compromise procured a joint electorate for East Pakistan and separate electorates for West Pakistan.

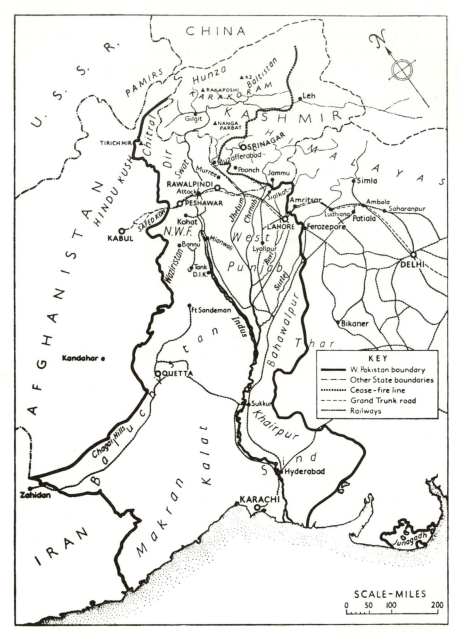

Map 2. West Pakistan (from Ian Stephens, *Pakistan* [New York: Frederick A. Praeger, 1963]). Reprinted by permission of Ernest Benn Ltd.

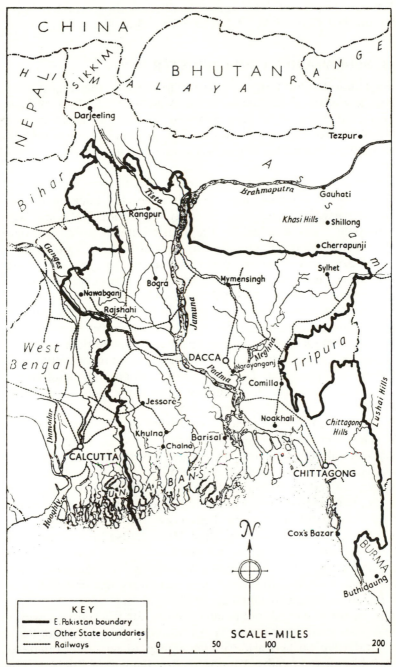

Map 3. East Pakistan (from Ian Stephens, *Pakistan* [New York: Frederick A. Praeger, 1963]). Reprinted by permission of Ernest Benn Ltd.

The Constitution of 1956 went into effect without popular approval, and Governor General Mirza became President Mirza.

H. S. SUHRAWARDY, PRIME MINISTER

The fading Muslim League won only ten seats in the August elections to the new National Assembly. Prime Minister Chaudhuri Mohammad Ali resigned because he was opposed in the legislative body by a coalition of East Pakistani parties and by members of a new Republican party of West Pakistanis, organized under the leadership of Dr. Khan Sahib.

Suhrawardy, chosen prime minister without the help of all the Bangalis, or, as it turned out, the whole-hearted backing of the Republican party, held his post for only 13 months.[7] His pro-Western foreign policy was attacked by the leftist Bangali politician Maulana Bhashani after the prime minister supported the Americans in the Suez crisis of 1956. His strenuous efforts to bring about greater provincial autonomy and his promise of more money for the development of East Pakistan were nullified by West Pakistani politics and politicians. Because President Mirza disliked a strong prime minister and wielded political power in his own right, his views eventually prevailed over those of Suhrawardy. Mirza's views of parliamentary government were clearly indicated in a radio broadcast in which he recommended the study of the American presidential system, which might be adapted to suit conditions in Pakistan. He wanted a presidency in order to establish what he called "controlled democracy."

Suhrawardy's downfall came about during a rift among West Pakistani politicians over the issue of the existing "One Unit" government for all of West Pakistan versus separate local governments for Sind, Punjab, Baluchistan, and the North-West Frontier. The Republicans, chiefly Punjabis, looked to Mirza instead of Suhrawardy to support their opposition to One Unit government. When Suhrawardy attacked the Republicans' stand on the One Unit issue, they withdrew their parliamentary support from him. President Mirza refused to call an election, the normal procedure in a parliamentary system when an existing government no longer commands a majority in the legislative chamber; Suhrawardy, the last of the Bangalis to head the government of Pakistan, was forced to resign in October 1957.

The record of Bangali politicians selected by the central government for top posts suggests that they were chosen to make a show of Pakistani unity and were pushed aside if they failed to win the confidence of West Pakistani politicians. For their part, Bangali politicians took on jobs at the Center in the hope of forging national policies that would favor Bangali interests. Most of them resigned when their efforts proved to be in vain or when they no longer satisfied those in control of the Center. Dissatisfaction with this in-and-out system increased Bangali hostility to the Center.

Several West Pakistanis succeeded Suhrawardy in the premiership. One of them, Firoz Khan Noon, a well-liked former governor of East Pakistan, managed to take on the prime minister's role when Bangali parties pledged themselves to him in return for a free hand in Bangali politics. Noon's short tenure was an uneasy one.

As if in concert, the ambitious President Mirza dismissed Fazlul Huq, Noon's appointee as governor of East Pakistan, and the provincial government in Dacca resigned because the newly organized leftist National Awami party, led by the Bangali Maulana Bhashani, withdrew its support. The National Awami party, which had split off from the Awami League, considered itself as much if not more of a people's party than the Awami League. The term *national* was intended to identify the party with Pakistani nationalism. Bangali factionalism was displaying its unruliness.

EAST PAKISTAN'S PROVINCIAL ASSEMBLY DEBACLE

As soon as President Mirza fixed the national election date for February 15, 1959, political leaders in East Pakistan began jockeying for position.[8] The Awami League, led by Suhrawardy, with a majority in the provincial assembly, maneuvered to get rid of the Speaker of the House, Abdul Hakim, a supporter of the Fazlul Huq group. In the midst of an assembly debate over seating Awami League members, the government, dominated by the Awami League majority, moved a no-confidence vote against the Speaker. A riot ensued as the Speaker ruled the motion out of order. In the scuffle, the Speaker left the assembly, but the majority repassed the no-confidence vote. A few days later the majority adopted a motion declaring the Speaker insane. Rioting resumed in the chamber; the deputy Speaker, serving as chairman, was clubbed and shortly afterwards died of his injuries.

The death of the deputy Speaker and the nearly simultaneous attempt of dissidents in West Pakistan to set up a separate state of Baluchistan caused President Mirza to abrogate the two-year-old Constitution. On October 7, 1958, he appointed General Ayub Khan as martial law administrator. Ayub lost no time in excoriating the politicians for lack of character. He pledged the restoration of democracy as soon as a more workable constitution could be adopted. Mirza described the provinces as on the verge of a bloody revolt and publicly accused Bhashani of high treason. Nothing came of the charge, however, because

Mirza was exiled to London by Ayub. According to one account, Ayub dismissed Mirza because "the armed services and the people demanded a clean break with the past." Ayub had begun his ten-year regime.

AYUB KHAN AND MARTIAL LAW

General Mohammad Ayub Khan, a Pathan, born in the North-West Frontier province during the first decade of this century, studied at Aligargh University and was a graduate of Sandhurst.[9] Commissioned in the British Indian army, he fought in Burma during World War II. In 1948 he held the first military command in Pakistan's East Bengal before being appointed a full general in 1951, at which time he became the commander in chief of the Pakistani army. Also during the fifties he served briefly as minister of defense. Following his selection as martial law administrator, he bestowed on himself the title of field marshal.

Although a Middle Eastern family man and devout Muslim, he preferred a western-style presidential constitution, favored modernized social customs, and supported religious tolerance. Well aware that he cut a fine British colonial-style soldierly figure, he enjoyed the pomp and circumstance of political power. His overriding concern as general and president was to preserve the unity of Pakistan.

Martial law, which remained in force from October 1958 to the promulgation of the Constitution of 1962, was overseen by General Ayub in the manner of a British viceroy of India, with the loyal support of the military and civil services.[10] The general's antipathy to political parties forced him to rely on bureaucrats for political support. The civil servants, as willing as Barkis to help run the country, thus increased their own political power.

Calling his regime "the revolution," Ayub proclaimed its purposes "to clean up the mess" and "to attack the problems of smuggling, black-marketing, and corruption." He first placed trusted military officers in charge of administrative affairs, but their unsophisticated efforts to free the nation of corruption promptly bogged down. Within a month martial law was eased; officers were removed from civilian duty, and the military courts that had been readied to enforce martial law were closed.

One of the early acts of the "revolutionary" regime was to jail its political enemies in East and West Pakistan. The government also took over the administration of the city of Karachi, the seat of the central government. The martial law organization strengthened earlier corrupt-practices laws, and special police forces were assigned to investigate and arrest government officials on charges of bribery, nepotism, and other forms of political corruption.

Ayub soon issued an "elective bodies disqualification ordinance," under which all former party politicians charged with misconduct, subversive activities, or actions contributing to political instability were disqualified from holding office until 1966. The precise number of politicians affected by the act was never made clear, but hundreds of them in both wings were prevented from carrying on public political campaigns.

During the early years of Ayub's rule extensive lists of political culprits appeared in the newspapers, many of them lower echelon civil servants. An Ayub order that high officials declare their assets as part of the anticorruption drive did not seem to have harmed any promising careers; no action was taken against any of them.

AYUB'S BASIC DEMOCRACY

In June 1951 Ayub decreed the establishment of "Basic Democracy"— a system designed, among other things, to replace what he despised as unworkable—political parties and the parliamentary form of government.[11] Basic Democracy provided a limited sort of public representation congenial to those who feared the political consequences of voting by illiterate majorities or the politics of bargaining. The structure of Basic Democracy resembled the government assemblies of the Union of Soviet Socialist Republics in that each consisted of a hierarchy of electoral bodies, the higher echelon representing the lower one. The government at the top was putatively connected with the people through an ascending chain of believers. The arrangement appealed to Ayub's sense of military discipline, order, and unity of command.

Basic Democracy, until its demise in 1969, comprised five levels of assemblies, each tier endowed with the authority to elect officials in the next highest tier and to assist and direct economic development programs at local administrative levels. In principle the votes of the entire adult population of each province elected members of the first-tier assemblies. There were 80,000 members of such assemblies throughout the country—40,000 in each wing, east and west. The first-tier assemblies were known as union or town councils (union in the countryside, town in organized communities).

Basic Democracy assemblies were derived from traditional local institutions or administrative structures established by India's British rulers. The union councils under the new law were patterned on the ancient panchayat system of local government found in India. The second-tier councils were based on a British administrative invention designed to carry out local police operations. The third tier of Basic Democracy—the district—had originally been devised by the British to collect revenues and provide budgetary services. Above the districts were divisional councils, and above these, the provincial government and its provincial assembly, organized in accordance with British administrative practices.

The proponents of Basic Democracy, who presented it to the public as an affirmation of the importance of local government, implied that its hierarchy could substitute for provincial autonomy because it gave a voice to the people of each province. Most Bangalis saw it both as a propaganda device to lend the appearance of a popular representation organ to a highly centralized and controlled governmental structure and as an attempt to reinstate the structure of colonial rule.

AYUB'S SUCCESSES

Martial law controls over corrupt practices were gradually eased in 1959, but the vigor and extent of the Ayub regime's crackdown on its political enemies became more severe. The *Pakistan Times* of Lahore, which had long been a thorn in the side of the Muslim League because of its steady hostility to the domestic and foreign policies of that party, was closed down. Almost simultaneously the government lodged charges against members of the business community, largely headquartered in the then capital city of Karachi. Ayub announced that the capital would be moved to Islamabad, a new city in a suburb of the older Rawalpindi, a thousand miles to the north of Karachi and somewhat closer to Dacca, though still in West Pakistan. Islamabad was intended to symbolize the religious unity of Pakistan.

In December 1959 Ayub was elected "President Field Marshal Mohammad Ayub Khan" by the union and town councils in both wings. The council members had previously been elected by universal adult suffrage. To no one's surprise, the president garnered 96 percent of the vote. Basic Democracy had proved its worth to Ayub. The willingness of friendly conservative electors to give him a fair opportunity may have contributed as much to his success as did their dissatisfaction with the political turmoil that preceded martial law. But the council members in East Pakistan won their seats with a much smaller popular vote than in West Pakistan.

The president, formally sworn in on February 17, 1960, announced the selection of an 11-man commission to draft a Constitution to be submitted to him in early May 1961.

Pleased by his electoral success, the president moved to placate the Bangalis. He announced that Dacca would be the legislative capital of the country—that is, the national Parliament would meet in East Pakistan.[12] Because his Bangali opponents knew President Ayub favored a strong executive and had a low opinion of legislative bodies, they concluded he did not intend to make a major concession to them. However, his action pleased his followers in East Pakistan and gave them a modicum of increased political importance.

In April 1960 the president appointed Lieutenant General Azam Khan, a fellow Pathan who had also fought with the British Indian Army in Burma, to the governorship of East Pakistan. Azam initiated a vigorous campaign to rid the province of martial law opponents. But he soon came to sympathize with the Bangalis' case for a larger role in the country's economic development. Disillusioned with the reluctance of the Center to act on East Pakistani requests, he publicly vented his considerable wrath in the direction of the Karachi officialdom. His statements had little effect.

In 1961 President Ayub turned his attention to modernizing Muslim family traditions. In March of that year he promulgated the Muslim family law ordinance, which regulated inheritances, marriage registrations, polygamy, and divorce.[13] The most contested sections of the new law provided in substance that a man could not take a second wife without the consent of the first wife and that divorce must be dealt with by an arbitration council.

Conservative religious spokesmen criticized the law because it restricted the husband's freedom to take more than one wife. They argued that the Koran permits a man to have as many as four wives at a time, provided he treats them impartially. They ignored the serious abuses of the privilege that had occurred because they feared that even slight deviations from Islamic law would corrupt the religion.

THE CONSTITUTION OF 1962

In his autobiography, *Friends Not Masters*, President Ayub revealed that as early as 1954 he had planned a constitution in which strong executive authority would be vested in one man elected independently of the Parliament. He preferred the American presidency to the British parliamentary system because it strengthened the central government's ability to maintain law and order and permitted a freer range of action in foreign affairs.

The report of the president's commission on the constitution was submitted to him privately in May 1961.[14] Meanwhile, newspapers and politicians speculated about the kind of constitution he would propose and compared it with the kind of document they wanted. The announcement by the government that new "free elections" would be held drew skeptical comments from Awami Leaguers. When the president reaffirmed his support for Basic Democracy, his critics were even more doubtful of the kind of freedom that could be expected.

In East Pakistan antagonism to President Ayub soared. The students of Dacca University rioted. For some of them the death of the Congolese leader Patrice Lumumba and "American imperialism" served to justify their troublemaking. For others the rioting was a protest against President Ayub's jailing of Suhrawardy and other Awami League leaders, including Suhrawardy's lieutenant, Sheikh Mujibur Rahman. Suhrawardy had been arrested January 30, 1962, at his home in Karachi, accused of treasonable activities. The arrest was made because Ayub feared that the formidable Suhrawardy would oppose him in the upcoming debate on the Constitution. The riots at the university became more violent when the police hemmed the students into their residence halls. Governor Azam came to the defense of the students. President Ayub persuaded Azam to resign and, on the latter's return to Lahore, placed him under house arrest.

On March 1, 1962, the president declared the Constitution prepared by his commission adopted and set June 8 for its entry into effect. Martial law was to be terminated with the first meeting of the National Assembly elected under the provisions of the Constitution.

The Constitution, an exceedingly long document, established a strong presidential form of government. As chief executive the president was authorized to appoint ministers to assist him without approval by the legislature. The unicameral National Assembly and the provincial assemblies became talk shops. The president and the assemblies were given five-year terms, but because the first President and legislative bodies were to serve only three years, elections in 1965 were indicated.

The nation was named the Republic of Pakistan, without the adjective *Islamic,* which Jamaat-i-Islam and other conservative religious parties had wanted included. However, the president had to be a Muslim and no law could be enacted that was repugnant to Islam. The omission of *Islamic* may have indicated a decline in the political strength of the ulemas and a rise in modernistic thought, but the nation's commitment to Islam and to national unity stood unimpaired.

The federal structure of the nation was preserved by keeping the two provincial legislatures in existence and was presumably strengthened by naming Dacca the principal seat of the National Assembly, as promised by Ayub. The new capital at Islamabad was designated the seat of the government of Pakistan to maintain the authority of the Center and of Ayub. Bengali and Urdu were specified as national languages, and English was permitted to be used officially for ten years, at which time a commission would be appointed to consider its replacement.

The National Assembly did not give East Pakistan seats proportionate to its majority population. The total number of assembly seats was fixed at 156, and exactly half were assigned to each wing. A total of six seats were reserved for women to be selected by the president. Women were also eligible for elective seats. Each of the provincial assemblies had 150 elected members plus seats for 5 women, selected in effect by the president.

The president's powers under the Constitution were substantial. No bill could become law without his approval, although his veto could be overridden by a two-thirds majority of the National Assembly. The president could dissolve the assembly. If he did so, elections were to be held within 90 days, and he would have to stand for reelection in 120 days. The president's term of office was limited to two five-year terms, unless he was drafted for an additional period by joint action of the national and provincial assemblies. He had authority to appoint the governors of the two wings.

The powers of the central government were specific and extensive. All other powers were placed in the hands of the provincial governments, which the president controlled through the governor, the army, and the civil service. An independent judiciary and a list of fundamental rights and of individual civil rights were written into the Constitution.

The Constitution made no concessions to the Bangalis, nor was it meant to. The conservative document gave legal support to martial law, buttressed the centralizing features of Basic Democracy, and reduced parliamentary bodies to debating forums.

REBELLION IN EAST PAKISTAN

No sooner had the president promulgated the new Constitution in March 1962 than East Pakistanis of many political persuasions attacked the document and the regime.[15] Manzur Qadir, one of the architects of the Constitution, dared to defend the new law before a hostile crowd of Dacca University students and barely escaped serious injury at their hands. The students burned copies of the Constitution. The law minister in the president's cabinet, a mild-mannered Bangali named Mohammad Ibrahim, offered his resignation just after the promulgation of the Constitution. Although he refused to discuss his resignation publicly on his return to Dacca, it was widely believed that he left the government in a personal protest against the Ayub Constitution. The students of the university who esteemed Ibrahim, a former dean of the Law School, gave him an enthusiastic welcome when he spoke to them after his return to Dacca. In July leftist student groups called for strikes against the "fascist reactionary and antipeople forces" governing the country.

In September 1962 the students of Dacca went to the streets for the third time that year. Their protest was directed against the recommendations of an education committee set up by the president. A university ordinance proposed by the committee prohibited students from taking part in political activities and denied degrees to those found to have violated the law. In the course of the demonstration the police and students clashed, and two government vehicles were destroyed. A few days later the government gave in and accepted the students' demands sufficiently to halt further rioting. Students were now allowed to engage without penalty in nonviolent political activities.

Elections for the National Assembly under the Constitution went off smoothly enough in April 1963. More than 90 percent of the Basic Democrats cast ballots. A substantial majority of the legislators who were elected supported Ayub.

The favorable election results encouraged President Ayub to venture an appeasement program in East Pakistan. Tamizuddin Khan, a Bangali, former Muslim Leaguer, and moderate, was made Speaker of the National Assembly. The Bangali former prime minister, Mohammad Ali Bogra, was named foreign minister. Ayub replaced the technical expert Ghulam Faruque in the post of governor of East Pakistan with the Bangali Monem Khan, known contemptuously by leftist Bangalis as the "two-rupee lawyer" from Mymensingh (a city north of Dacca).

The National Assembly held its initial meeting in Dacca during May 1963; martial law came to an end. H. S. Suhrawardy and his associates were released from prison. Suhrawardy immediately announced the formation of a National Democratic Front, consisting of four anti-Ayub parties, to set to work on a new democratic constitution.

During the May assembly session the Bangali opponents of the Ayub regime lost no time in accusing the government of economic, political, and cultural discrimination against Bangalis. The anti-Ayub press, reporting on the proceedings of the provincial and national assemblies, retailed the sharp criticisms directed at the Center by the legislators. The provincial governor, closely allied with Ayub, clamped new curbs on the press in order to prevent what he called the "unauthorized" publication of legislative discussions. Newspapermen went on strike to protest the controls. Finally the president met with the editors and agreed to moderate the gag rules.

During the winter season of the assembly more arguments were heard on behalf of popular elections, the restoration of political parties, and the strengthening of civil rights. President Ayub promised to take favorable action on these proposals.

Suhrawardy died suddenly in Karachi on December 5, 1963, while the assembly was in session in Dacca. At a memorial service in Dacca enormous crowds demonstrated their affection for the Bangali leader and their hostility to President Ayub. The Democratic Front, however, was weakened by its leader's death.

Within a week of Suhrawardy's death President Ayub abandoned his antiparty stance and announced that he had accepted the presidency of a revived Pakistan Muslim League. He was pleased when the National Assembly passed a so-called bill of rights law, which assigned such extensive powers to the president as to virtually nullify the rights enumerated in the statute. Ayub announced triumphantly that recent by-elections won by the Muslim League endorsed his government and his party.

January 1964 was a time of dark deeds in East Pakistan. The year had hardly begun when a communal riot erupted in Dacca. For a week homes in and about the city were put to the torch and their inhabitants killed or maimed. By the end of the week as many as 5,000 persons were reported to have died. After the second day of rioting it became evident that the police could not put down the bloody affair and the army was called in.

The local opposition press, evading government controls, intimated that clashing Muslim elements—Biharis, West Pakistanis, and Bangalis—as well as Hindus and Muslims, had been at one another's throats. The local press sympathetically publicized the problems of beleaguered Hindus, large numbers of whom had found refuge in the compounds of Hindu-owned textile mills. Muslim families protected their Hindu servants and Muslim students at Dacca University gave safe haven to their Hindu colleagues.

One of the speculations concerning these events was that the riot had been fueled by anti-Indian and progovernment newspaper stories circulated in Pakistan and that the anti-Muslim press in India, especially in Calcutta, had contributed to the agitation.

The Dacca tragedy did not end with the conclusion of the disorders. A short time after the rioting had been ruthlessly put down, thousands of frightened Hindus left for Calcutta and West Bengal. There another, more deadly, series of Hindu-Muslim riots broke out. One account indicated that three times as many died in this horror as had been killed in Dacca. The riots were ended by Indian troops.

The result of the rioting in East Pakistan and West Bengal was a flood of two-way emigrations during the following several months. Estimates of the numbers of Hindus seeking refuge in India was placed in the neighborhood of 400,000. An equal number of Muslims left West Bengal, Assam, and Tripura to enter East Pakistan.

During the spring of 1964 the governments of Pakistan and India exchanged charges about alleged forced emigrations of populations.[16]

The complaints of the Pakistanis focused on the forced emigration of Muslims from Assam and Tripura. The Indian government justified its expulsion of Bangalis from these provinces of India on the grounds that the Muslims were squatters who had been encouraged by the Pakistani government to populate the mountain and hill regions north and east of East Pakistan. The Indian government may have been motivated by fear that the Pakistanis would revive a claim for Assam as part of the Partition. Not long after the massive migration began, the East Pakistani government, under the direction of the Bangali chief secretary, K. A. Haque, published a report on the Assamese and Tripura expulsions that concluded that the "real motive behind [the] action [of the Indian government] is not to deal with illegal migrants, but to free the border states of the Muslim population on the flimsy plea that they are Pakistani intruders, and to accommodate the Hindu refugees from East Pakistan in their homes and lands."[17]

Most of the Hindu refugees eventually returned to their homes in East Pakistan. However, the episode reaffirmed that anti-Hindu sentiments in the Pakistani government and among its supporters, as well as anti-Muslim antipathies to the Partition of India among fanatical and politically influential Hindus, were still alive and dangerous.

Another event took place in August 1964 that reminded the Pakistani government of the ill feelings between Bengali- and Urdu-speaking Muslims. East Pakistan's governor, Monem Khan, arrested labor leaders said to have been responsible for a strike at a jute mill that employed many Urdu-speaking Biharis. The governor ordered the strike leaders to sign a return-to-work agreement. They refused, the governor backed down, and the workers received the pay raise they had struck for. The government's decision was officially said to represent its desire to foster Bangali-Bihari cooperation.

THE ELECTIONS OF 1965

In preparation for the national elections, Bangali political opponents of President Ayub in January 1965 organized the Combined Opposition Party (COP), made up of such antagonistic groups as the Awami League (led by Sheikh Mujibur Rahman, Suhrawardy's successor), the Council Muslim League (a splinter group of the Muslim League headed by Kwaja Nazimuddin), and Jamaat-i-Islam and Nizam-i-Islam, both religiously oriented parties.[18] COP planned to name a single candidate to campaign against President Ayub. Its platform demanded a democratic constitution in which direct universal suffrage would replace Basic Democracy. Paramount power was to be lodged in a representative legislative body rather than the president. The judiciary would be independent and political parties legalized. Economic disparity between the two wings should be removed within ten years and the trend to the concentration of wealth in a handful of families reversed. Pakistan, the platform declared, should adopt an "independent foreign policy" and find a solution to the Kashmir problem with India. The Muslim family law issue was straddled out of deference to the religious parties in COP.

In April the Muslim League nominated Ayub as its presidential candidate. The 58-year-old Ayub's only serious rival, selected by COP, was Fatima Jinnah, the sister of Mohammad Ali Jinnah, who was then in her seventies. After 1958 she had become an advocate of democratic government and a critic of Ayub's rule. Her campaign was surprisingly vigorous. She traveled through West and East Pakistan, addressing large crowds. At the outset she had the help of Kwaja Nazimuddin in East Pakistan, but he died suddenly in the midst of the campaign. The former prime minister's brother, Kwaja Shahabuddin, then living in Dacca, supported Ayub Khan. General Azam Khan, former governor of East Pakistan, who until the onset of the campaign had been under house arrest, was permitted to return to East Pakistan to campaign for Miss Jinnah. This gesture of political generosity betokened President Ayub's confidence in his victory.

Leading members of the revived Muslim League, the governor, ministers, and other Ayub supporters in East Pakistan rallied to the president's cause. Ayub and Miss Jinnah made nearly half of their public appearances in East Pakistan.

During the long campaign Miss Jinnah pointedly referred to the president as Mr. Ayub Khan. In less complimentary terms, he referred to her as old, a recluse, weak-minded, and lacking in political experience, and he derided the idea of a woman president. In his speeches Ayub emphasized the achievement of political stability and the economic accomplishments of his regime. He frequently stressed the importance of Islamic ideology as a unifying force in the country. Miss Jinnah demanded the restoration of civil liberties and the installation of universal direct suffrage. She often evoked the memory of her brother. She repeated the frequently heard charge that Ayub's sons had amassed fortunes with their father's help, and she insisted that the government had created an undemocratic atmosphere by its ban on political parties, its constraints on the press, and its arrests of opposition leaders. In her speeches in East Pakistan she spoke at length and sympathetically about Bangalis' social and economic grievances.

President Ayub received 63 percent of the votes cast in the January 1965 election by the electoral college of 80,000 Basic Democrats. Miss Jinnah had to be content with 37 percent. Ayub's victory in East Pakistan by 53.1 percent of the vote was much narrower than in West Pakistan, where his margin of victory was 73.6 percent.

The president had prepared for the election with great care. Since 1962 Basic Democrats, especially in East Pakistan, had controlled a substantial share of agricultural development funds. The number of public works programs in the east prior to the election, double those of the west, may have tipped the scales of the Bangali vote in his favor.

After the election Sheikh Mujibur Rahman, his party workers, and 40 other oppositionists were singled out as unreliable political leaders and jailed. Ayub had not been opposed by Maulana Bhashani, presumably because the leftist leader supported the president's policy of friendship with Peking.

Ayub's victory created smoldering discontent among many groups in East Pakistan. The president's university ordinance, which limited the students' freedom of action, frustrated the political passions of the activists, although somehow their tempers were kept in check for many months after the elections and there was no rioting. The fundamentalist Muslims were displeased that the elections sanctioned the president's Muslim family law ordinance. His Bangali critics appeared to abandon hope of ending social and economic discrimination by the Center as long as President Ayub remained in office.

Khalid B. Sayeed, a professor at Queen's University, Ontario, Canada, claimed that the president had received material electoral support in the western Rajshahi and Khulna divisions of East Pakistan because these parts of the province were economically and politically less developed than the eastern division of the province. The politicians in the neglected areas, he said, held Dacca responsible for their plight. He also properly noted that the concentration of refugees in these areas tended to support the president. He did not, however, point out that many of the refugees to whom he referred were Urdu-speaking Muslims unsympathetic with Bangali causes.

Elections for the National Assembly were held throughout the country in March 1965. The Muslim League, with President Ayub as its champion, won handily, taking 115 seats of the 156 up for election. All but one of the opposition winners were Bangalis. In the East Pakistani provincial assembly, the league had a bare majority.

That Ayub should, despite his critics, win a majority in East Pakistan in his bid for the presidency and control of the nation's legislative bodies seemed to prove that his national integration policy and programs had paid dividends on the investments he put into them.

CHAPTER 6

The Struggle for Bangali Autonomy, 1965–71

From the election of 1965 until February 1968, when President Ayub became seriously ill, his tenure was an uneasy one. The first tremor of the political earthquake that eventually toppled Ayub from power was felt during the Indo-Pakistan war of August-September 1965. Ayub, elated by his electoral success but frustrated by his inability to induce the Indian government to carry out a United Nations mandate to submit India's claim to Kashmir to a plebiscite, plunged his country into a war with India. After two months the war ended in a stalemate. The Tashkent treaty of 1966, arranged by the Union of Soviet Socialist Republics, brought a legal end to the conflict but left a legacy of domestic troubles for Ayub.

The East Pakistanis found themselves in an exposed military posture during the short-lived war, although India, for its own reasons, made no significant hostile encroachment on their territory. However, the Bangalis had a weighty complaint to make about the war's impact on them. Scheduled economic development programs were cut 5 percent because of increased military costs. In the first year of the third five-year plan for 1965–69, which was to mark the beginning of provincial economic parity, funds from the central government were reduced by more than 20 percent, while military expenditures for 1965 and 1966 doubled. To make matters worse, agricultural production in East Pakistan fell off.

On the Bangali political scene a new man was ready to challenge the authority of the president. The Awami League, in disarray after the death of Suhrawardy, regrouped following the election of 1965. Sheikh Mujibur Rahman emerged as its new leader.

ECONOMIC DISPARITIES

Sheikh Mujib and the Awami League shaped increasingly vocal Bangali opposition to the inequitable economic policies and programs of the Center into a campaign against the Ayub government and a plea for provincial autonomy.[1] The cry of discrimination rallied members of the growing middle class and the peasantry to Mujib's party and gave his supporters a popular platform from which to criticize the regime.

Awami Leaguers diligently accumulated evidence of inequities. They noted that the economy of East Pakistan had been organized to accommodate the interests of West Pakistan. Although their combined economic growth rate—better than 5 percent during the sixties—was hailed as a model for a developing country, the figure obscured the persistent poverty of the Bangalis. The well-advertised level of Pakistan's prosperity was made possible to a large degree by the diversion of real resources from the east to the west.

Disparities were created by the allocation of private and public investments to West Pakistan or West Pakistanis rather than to East Pakistan and Bangalis. The west was also favored in the allocation of central government expenditures, including foreign aid.

In 1963 Mahbub Ul Haq, the chief planner of the central government, had revealed in his *Strategy of Economic Planning* that the government had transferred real resources from the east to the west. His economic evidence may be summarized as follows. The net balance-of-payments position of each wing revealed that the Bangalis had received a comparatively smaller share of foreign aid loans and foreign exchange reserves than did West Pakistan. Even if the distribution of these economic resources had been divided equally between east and west, the implied transfer of real resources would still have diverted 4 to 5 percent of East Pakistan income to the west annually.

Haq observed that the transfer of resources to West Pakistan made a major difference in provincial investment levels. West Pakistan's investments were substantially larger than its domestic savings because of the sizable flow of resources from East Pakistan and abroad. Total investment, according to Haq, was at least 12 percent of all goods and services produced in West Pakistan, while in the east total investments fell short of savings because of the compulsory transfer of savings from east to west. Haq predicted that, without a different pattern of planning, disparities between the two wings would grow.

Disparities in per capita income between east and west also angered Bangali politicians. No significant increase in per capita income in East Pakistan had occurred between 1947 and 1965, while income in West Pakistan increased substantially during the same period. Moreover, the standard of living of the vast majority of Bangalis, those in the lower income brackets (below $60 a year), had declined.

Disparities in distribution of foreign aid, likewise the consequence of central government policies, favored West Pakistani interests above those of East Pakistan. The sparse industries of the east were chiefly owned by West Pakistanis who were beneficiaries of financial aid from the central government and other forms of assistance. Traditional Bangali small-scale and cottage industries wasted away. The internal allocations of foreign economic and military aid by and large went to the Center and to the West Pakistani provincial government. East Pakistan received only 25 percent of the economic portion of the aid and hardly any of the military monies.

Although both wings produced about the same quantities of food grains, comparative nutritional levels of the Bangalis were lower. East Pakistan, during its quarter century of Pakistani rule, had millions more mouths to feed than did the west. Expenditures for food by Bangalis left them little to spend on other consumer goods.

Bangali agitation over economic disparity stirred President Ayub to a semblance of action. The third five-year plan of 1960–65 projected the attainment of parity between the east and west in 25 years, that is, by 1985. But the Bangalis, angered by what they regarded as an empty promise, made it clear they would not wait more than two decades to see their needs satisfied. Bangali riots and protests and Mahbub Ul Haq's advocacy persuaded Ayub in the late sixties to announce a fourth five-year plan, 1970–75, which for the first time allocated more than 50 percent of projected public funds to East Pakistan. The pledge came too grudgingly and too late.

OTHER BANGALI GRIEVANCES

Discrimination against the Bangalis in the civil and military services began with Partition.[2] The Muslims in the British Indian civil service had opted to go to West Pakistan, the promised center of political power, where they quickly acquired ample authority, because the politicians were a quarrelsome lot and the country needed experienced administrators. The civil service of Pakistan, an elite body made up mostly of West Pakistanis, became along with the military the decision makers at the Center and in the provincial governments. Under Ayub the civil servants, like the armed forces, were protected against provincial influences because they served at the pleasure of the president. Given their desire to gather power for themselves, they opposed decentralization and regional autonomy.

Of the 133 Muslim officers in the British India civil service, only one was a Bangali. Unwilling to be administered by other Pakistanis, some of whom looked down on their countrymen, the Bangalis demanded parity in the civil service. By 1955 there were only 55 Bangalis among 741 officers of the rank of undersecretary and above in the central Secretariat, and at that time all of the secretaries in Pakistan were non-Bangalis. (Undersecretary is the lowest rank in the senior service, the latter including the highest ranks in the civil services.) In spite of repeated promises to recruit more of them, by 1967 the Bangalis numbered only 186 out of 512 in the national civil service and only 382 out of 1,061 in other senior services, including the foreign service. After a 1967 change in the rules, there were more Bangalis in all the senior services.

Generally speaking, the Bangalis came from lower income groups than the West Pakistanis, and when posted in West Pakistan many of them felt out of place. They had little influence among the non-Bangali civil servants, businessmen, and senior military officers.

The ultimate goal of senior civil service officers was a post at the Center, but in the early sixties some were assigned to the province of their origin. In East Pakistan this "Bengalization" of the administrative services meant that fewer West Pakistanis and more Bangalis were assigned to the higher posts in that province. At the same time it resulted in greater central government control of Bangali politics—for example, the appointment of Bangali governors willing to serve as political agents of the Center.

In 1965 the Pakistani army had only one major general from East Pakistan among 17 officers of that rank. General Kwaja Wasiuddin, a member of the nawab of Dacca's family, served as martial law administrator at Dacca in 1961 and 1962. Of all army officers only 5 percent came from East Pakistan. In the navy and air force the Bangali contingent of officers ranged between 9 and 11 percent. The inferior standing of the Bangalis in the Pakistani army limited their opportunities to influence the policies of the government at a time when the army's officer corps was becoming the single most important group in the country.

Throughout the debate over disparities, Bangali politicians well disposed to the military service called for the speeding up of Bangali recruitment. They claimed that its officers did not think the Bangalis made good soldiers and that the physical standards for recruitment were designed to keep Bangalis out of the army.

THE AWAMI LEAGUE'S AUTONOMY PROGRAM

Sheikh Mujib led a delegation of the Bangali wing of the Awami League to a joint Awami League conference at Lahore in the spring of

1966. The six-point political and economic program for Bangali provincial autonomy that he presented to the meeting lighted the fuse of a national time bomb.[3] The program became the platform of Bangali politics and the rallying cry of the league's opposition to the government.

The first of the points declared that "the government should be federal and parliamentary, elected by universal, adult suffrage with legislative representation on the basis of population." Point two specified that the federal government be responsible only for foreign affairs and defense and have limited control over currency. Point three proposed the establishment of a federal reserve system to regulate dual currencies issued by individual federal units, e.g., East and West Pakistan. The fourth point centered on bestowing "fiscal responsibility on the federating units"; the federal government, however, was to be constitutionally guaranteed adequate funds to carry out its defense and foreign affairs functions. Point five lodged authority in federal units to control foreign exchange accounts. Finally, the manifesto demanded that the federal units be authorized to maintain a militia "which would contribute to the national security."

Critics of the program, more concerned with its political than its economic implications, said that Mujib's proposal for substantial control of the economy by the provinces would split West Pakistan into an undefined number of separate communities, leaving East Pakistan by far the most populous of the federating units. A central government almost wholly concerned with external affairs, it was argued, would have little influence on the overwhelming authority of the federal units.

The essentials of the plan were clearly unacceptable to West Pakistani politicians seeking to create greater national integration. The six points, they believed, proposed a loose confederation of disparate communities separated by distance, language, and culture, whereas the political wisdom of the West Pakistani elite would hold the country together. Many West Pakistanis feared that the six-point plan would lead to the dismemberment of Pakistan by encouraging dissident tribal and linguistic groups in the west. That view was more widely held than the idea that the Bangalis were incapable of managing their own affairs.

President Ayub responded angrily to the six-point program, charging that the document amounted to a demand for complete independence. From the viewpoint of those who believed in the necessity of centralized power, he was correct, but he did not see that the position of the Bangalis was negotiable.

THE DECLINE OF AYUB'S INFLUENCE

In the midst of a general strike in East Pakistan during June 1966, called to win adherents to Mujib's program, a riot occurred in which a dozen or more people were killed.[4] The government immediately arrested Sheikh Mujib and other Awami Leaguers, but rioting resumed at Dacca University. *Ittefaq*, the Awami League daily newspaper in Dacca, was closed by government order and its editor, Taffazal Hussain, jailed. The High Court of East Pakistan came to the rescue of the newspaper by declaring its closure unconstitutional. Hussain's detention, however, was upheld.

To mollify Bangali anger, the Ayub cabinet consented to a constitutional amendment that made it possible for the National Assembly to amend laws that had been promulgated by the president when the assembly was not in session. This concession to the assembly's desire for increased powers did not satisfy Fazlul Qader Choudhury, Speaker of the East Pakistani assembly; he joined a faction of the Muslim League opposing President Ayub. The government also released Taffazal Hussain in March 1967, presumably to placate the Bangali opposition, but it was an ineffectual gesture.

A few months later, the Pakistan Democratic Movement, a coalition of East and West Pakistani political parties, agreed on only one thing— dissent from President Ayub's policies.[5] Mujib's Awami League and Zulfikar Bhutto's People's party of West Pakistan joined forces in the movement with two religious parties, Nizam-i-Islam and Jamaat-i-Islam. (Bhutto, a graduate of the University of California at Berkeley, was a lawyer from the Sind. The strong man of this left-right coalition, he had resigned or was dismissed from the president's cabinet in the summer of 1966.) Three of the four parties in the Democratic Movement had only recently been allied in the Combined Opposition party.

A four-point program devised by the Democratic Movement proposed that the parties work for a Federation of Pakistan based on a parliamentary government directly elected by the people. The central government would control defense, foreign affairs, federal finances, and interprovince communications and trade. Residual powers would be vested in provincial governments "on the basis of full regional autonomy." The end of economic disparity and the attainment of parity in the civil service for Bangalis were to be achieved in ten years. Naval headquarters would move to East Pakistan. Bhutto, seeking ample countrywide authority for the Center, wrote a substantial list of federal powers into the program. This concession and others by the Bangalis showed they were not inflexible and, at least at this juncture, would have negotiated the demands of Mujib's six-point program.

For the time being the president and his advisors were not alarmed by the Democratic Movement. They concluded that the uneasy alliance among the parties, each of which harbored its own dissidents, posed no immediate threat to the president's rule. Not to be outdone in political maneuvering, however, President Ayub launched a minor "cultural revolution." In October 1967 East Pakistan's Governor Monem Khan, an Ayub appointee, distributed little green books entitled "Sayings of President Ayub Khan." The Islamic character of the nation was heavily emphasized in the sayings—a theme the dogmatic Monem Khan and President Ayub hoped would bring the people of East Pakistan together with their West Pakistani Muslim brothers. Such was the mood of the country that university students, instead of ignoring the book, were angered by it and denounced its publication. The appeal to religion as a national political unifier appears in retrospect to have been an ineffective propaganda ploy as far as the Bangalis were concerned. They regarded their Islamic faith to be as solid as that of the West Pakistanis.

The president tried to meet his critics partway by agreeing to broaden the base of the electoral system.[6] In December 1967, at his request, the National Assembly increased the number of members of the union and town councils from 80,000 to 120,000 for the next national elections. And, to make the National Assembly more representative, 50 legislators were added to its membership, and 50 apiece to each provincial law-making body. Tinkering of this kind confirmed Ayub's opponents in their view that, confident of his ability to control the assembly, the president was unwilling to abandon his hold on personal power. It is doubtful that he gained any friends among the Bangalis by such tactics, and he almost surely united his competiton.

The year 1968 was a baleful one for President Ayub. In October not only did he suffer a debilitating pulmonary embolism from which he recuperated slowly, but after his recovery he narrowly escaped assassination while attending a celebration of the tenth anniversary of his regime in West Pakistan. Bhutto was arrested in November as the leader of the rioting that followed the assassination attempt.

The president and his coworkers concluded at this point that the more time they spent on law-and-order problems, the less time was available for the exacting work of economic development. In consequence the president urged Muslim League party leaders to visit union and town council members, to discuss local problems with the people in the countryside, and to relay their complaints to the central government so that action might be taken. But the president's supporters in East Pakistan were more interested in holding onto their jobs than in going out to meet angry citizens to persuade them the government was listening to them. Moreover, the government needed no additional information about the peasants' grievances, which had been reiterated frequently for more than a decade.

One of the more spectacular events affecting the fortunes of President Ayub and Sheikh Mujib occurred in October 1968. A special tribunal meeting in Dacca tried 35 Bangalis, including Mujib, for plotting the secession of East Pakistan. Mujib, said to be the ringleader of the conspiracy, was alleged to have secretly visited Agartala (the capital of India's Tripura state, adjacent to East Pakistan) to discuss a secession scheme with Indian officials.[7] The Indian government denied the allegations. Defense attorneys for the Bangalis argued that the trial was a diversionary tactic by the government, intended to sabotage demands for political reforms by East Pakistanis, and that government witnesses had been coerced by the prosecution. The East Pakistani High Court ordered the government to show cause that the trial should not be declared illegal. President Ayub released Mujib and his fellow Bangalis a few months later; soon thereafter the High Court dismissed the charges.

Mujib was released on February 22, 1969, at a time when the Ayub government was faltering and the president was still in ill health from the embolism he had suffered. Commentators on Mujib's release suggested that the president, worried by the violent reaction of the Bangalis to the trial of Mujib, feared that the provincial government would collapse and the separatist movement gather popular support.

THE FALL OF AYUB

By autumn 1968 opposition to the ailing president had appeared throughout the west and east.[8] Maulana Bhashani, following a visit to Peking in 1963 that was supported by the Ayub government, had withheld his opposition because he favored a united Pakistan. At the end of 1968, however, he abandoned his love feast with the president to support a strike of Bangali ricksha workers. General Azam Khan, a stalwart of Miss Jinnah's in the 1965 electoral campaign, announced in December that he would oppose the president in the scheduled 1970 elections. Chief Justice Murshed of the East Pakistani High Court and several prominent West Pakistan figures joined the lists of candidates challenging the president. Asghar Khan, former commander in chief of the air force, came out actively against President Ayub. He made an extensive campaign tour of East Pakistan, advocating favorite Bangali causes—direct popular elections and provincial autonomy. His success was limited, however, because many Bangalis doubted they would be better off under another West Pakistani military man.

At the National Assembly meeting of December 1968, the opposition, chiefly Bangalis, staged a walkout and did not remain for the rest of the proceedings. In the East Pakistani assembly the opposition refused to agree to the government's tax measures and criticized its economic assistance programs for the province.

Two former chief ministers of East Pakistan, Nurul Amin and Ataur Rahman Khan, echoed the protesting chorus of the Awami League. They demanded direct popular elections, called for an end to inter-provincial economic disparity and to the concentration of wealth in a few industrialists' families, and decried the growing impoverishment of the Bangali peasantry.

President Ayub met this barrage from old and new political foes by announcing that he did not want to hold onto the presidency indefinitely and would name a successor. Despite this statement, the attacks on his regime persisted. During the closing weeks of 1968 he refused to talk to opposition leaders because, he said, he could not agree to arrangements that would disrupt the nation. The Bangalis interpreted his remarks to mean that he was unalterably opposed to regional autonomy in any form. In fact, Ayub was haunted by the fear that, with Indian complicity, the Bangali autonomy movement would lead to secession.

In both provinces political parties hostile to the president announced early in 1969 that they would boycott the 1970 elections unless direct voting was ordered, civil rights restored, and political prisoners released. On January 18 a newly formed Democratic Action Committee composed of eight party leaders staged a nationwide demonstration, in which the Student Action Committee of the University of Dacca—a coalition of student factions—joined with enthusiasm. The student committee had previously issued an 11-point anticapitalist, antiregime manifesto similar to the Awami League's six-point program. Party and student demonstrations drew large crowds in the west and the east.

The demonstrations in Dacca in January went on for three days. Students set fire to the offices of the government-supported newspapers *Morning News* and *Dainik Pakistan* (the latter owned by Governor Monem Khan). Several people were killed. The Student Action Committee called another strike to protest the killings. Vehicles were destroyed and there were more shootings as hundreds of students marched through the towns of East Pakistan.

On February 1 President Ayub said he would talk to the politicians of the Democratic Action Committee about constitutional issues, but he warned he would not accept any changes that might harm the national integrity. He also regretted the loss of innocent lives during the disturbances, blaming it on "enemies of the country." President Ayub's decision to talk to his political opponents was probably the result of pressures by army officers who believed that the extreme left would be the winner in further confrontations with the police. Left-leaning members of the Democratic Action Committee, however, refused to participate in the talks, saying that it was a maneuver to divide the opposition. Talks were held, however, with some members of the opposition. President Ayub, seemingly on his own, modified government control of student political activities.

During February violence was part of the daily life of East Pakistan. In Dacca the army was called out after mobs set fire to government buildings and the residences of President Ayub's political supporters. In the midst of the rioting the president belatedly announced the end of a state of emergency law that had been in force since the 1965 Indo-Pakistan war. The termination of the emergency law, which gave the government special authority to hold political prisoners without trial, was intended to clear the way for political talks. Ayub agreed to a demand for freeing political prisoners, and he released Sheikh Mujib, Bhutto, and others. He refused, however, to restore the civil liberties his opponents had demanded as a means of creating a proper atmosphere for the talks.

The Democratic Action Committee consented to meet with the president, but Bhutto, Asghar Khan, Sheikh Mujib, and Maulana Bhashani, the principal figures in the coalition, refused to attend the conference. Sheikh Mujib said he would not go to the talks until the government rescinded its indictment in the Agartala conspiracy against him and 33 others.

On February 21 the president announced he would arrange for free elections when his personally fixed term of office came to an end in March 1970. When the government also dropped its charges against those accused of the Agartala conspiracy, the opposition felt it had won. By the decision to hold elections in 1970, Ayub hoped to counter mounting dissatisfaction with his Basic Democracy system of indirect voting and defuse the opposition's demand for direct popular national and provincial elections. The law minister in the president's cabinet said that, after the election of President Ayub's successor, the next step would be the election of a National Assembly. His remarks were construed to signify that the regime would retain its presidential character.

Ayub announced that he had never intended to run for reelection and suggested that the presidency go to an East Pakistani. Bhutto, in a press conference, echoed the idea and remarked that only Sheikh Mujibur Rahman should be considered a likely candidate. But the tempting plum of the presidency was not acceptable to Mujib or the Bangalis. The prospect, in the absence of constitutional changes, was seen as an offer to join a regime that had sent Mujib to jail for long stretches. The Bangalis felt that however independent an East Pakistani president might try to be, he could be controlled by West Pakistani military and civil service advisors and that the Bangali campaign for regional autonomy would be brought to an end. At the end of January Bhutto, still a presidential candidate, had gone to Dacca to discuss the presidency issue with Mujib and Bhashani. The talks were without issue, for the Bangalis did not trust Bhutto any more than he trusted them.

In the last days of February President Ayub finally met with all the leaders of the Democratic Action Committee except Bhutto. Sheikh Mujib restated the demands of the six-point program. He objected to the equal representation provisions of the Constitution because of the greater population of East Pakistan, estimated by him at 70 million out of a total population of 125 million. He repeated that the powers of the central government must be limited and provincial autonomy guaranteed. Mujib's critics objected that the Bangalis simply wanted to take control of the country. Nevertheless, the president announced on March 14 that a broad agreement had been reached. The conferees, he said, were in accord on the establishment of a parliamentary system and direct popular suffrage. The problem of East Pakistan's autonomy would be settled separately. Sheikh Mujib, pleased with the results of the talks, said he would withdraw from the Democratic Action Committee. Bhutto, however, had an entirely different opinion. He dismissed the conference agreement as a halfway measure and demanded that President Ayub resign in order that a caretaker government be installed, evidently having himself in mind as its leader.

In East Pakistan the reforms forged by Mujib and the president were not enough to stem the tide of opposition to the government. For more than a week after March 24, 1969, mobs raged against Muslim Leaguers, regarded as henchmen of the Ayub government. More than 150 people were killed in a ten-day period during which the police lost control of the streets. Hundreds of people were made homeless and pillage was widespread. In areas of the worst disorders, medical services were unavailable to the injured and the dying. The jute industry came to a halt. The unpopular governor, Monem Khan, unable to exert effective authority, dared not venture out of his official residence for several weeks. Following a threat by students to invade his residence unless he promptly resigned, he and his family fled to the airport, whence they flew to West Pakistan. The economic life of Dacca came to a halt during the rioting when workers and professional people joined in a series of demonstrations and strikes, demanding better pay and working conditions.

The cabinet met, denounced mob rule, and invoked preventive measures. In West Pakistan, where riots like those in the east had begun in March, Bhutto was accused of leading the country into chaos with his insistence that President Ayub resign.

The president had appointed Dr. Mirza Nurul Huda, an U.S.-trained economist, as Monem Khan's replacement in Dacca on March 21. After a week in office, however, Dr. Huda resigned, on the grounds that groups (which he did not identify) were fomenting riots in order to bring on martial law. The government in Islamabad mingled appeals for unity and the promise of free elections with announcements that it was determined to maintain law and order.

A possible explanation of the March riot in East Pakistan was that students of the University of Dacca, demonstrating to force the resignation of Basic Democrats in the union and town councils, clashed with the police. The Basic Democrats were certainly hated in many quarters of East Pakistan, where they had been looked upon as agents of the president and of the Muslim League. But student demonstrations alone were hardly sufficient to have touched off the March horrors. Workers, encouraged by leftist agitators, joined the students, adding their muscle to the national revolt. Threats against Governor Monem Khan, intensely disliked as a sycophant of the government, had been made for some time. In many riot areas a struggle for jobs between Bengali- and Urdu-speaking Muslims contributed to the uprising.

In a broadcast to the nation on March 26, 1969, President Ayub resigned, admitting that his government had lost control of the country. He abrogated the 1962 Constitution and dissolved the national and provincial assemblies. If elections were held, he predicted, East Pakistan would get the autonomy it wanted. Maintaining that it was up to the army to prevent the country from collapsing into chaos, he named General Yahya Khan, commander in chief of the army, as martial law administrator.

Whether because of the people's exhaustion or their fear of martial law, the carnage in East Pakistan came to an abrupt end. Students and teachers went out of their way to assist the police in restoring order and in rounding up persons accused of assassination. Political leaders in Dacca demanded effective law enforcement.

Yahya Khan declared martial law on the day of Ayub's resignation. The death penalty, he said, would be imposed on persons caught rioting, looting, or burning. He had no other ambition, he added, than to create conditions conducive to the establishment of constitutional government. His speech bore a striking resemblance to the one Ayub made when he took over power in 1958.

YAHYA KHAN

General Yahya Khan appeared on the national political scene in 1969 without previous discernible political experience.[9] As a career officer in the British Indian army, he fought in North Africa and Europe during World War II, and after Partition in the Pakistani army against the Indians in the 1965 war. Earlier, from December 1962 to August 1964, he had been the general officer in command in East Pakistan, a post with little evident political significance but which in fact had served as a training ground for command of the country, since Ayub had previously held the job.

The liabilities Yahya inherited from President Ayub promised him an impossible political future, for nearly everything that could have gone wrong or could have been done wrong in the relationship between East and West Pakistan had been accomplished. Furthermore, General Yahya never understood how to combine effective military and political power. He made the mistake of assuming that political decisions would be obeyed if his government backed up those decisions with force. His heavy drinking further detracted from his judgment, and his political maneuvers were frustrated by the independent tactics of his wily civilian colleague, Bhutto.

General Yahya proclaimed himself president of Pakistan on April 1, 1969, predating his takeover from March 26, the day President Ayub relinquished his office. Yahya retained the post of martial law administrator. His assumption of the presidency was somehow interpreted as a promise to carry out constitutional reforms that would reconcile East Pakistan and the central government. It was also rumored that he was prepared to accord limited autonomy to the Bangalis and to make other amends, such as increasing economic benefits.

The first year of Yahya's incumbency under martial law was a relatively quiet one. President Ayub's military and civil servants stayed on to pursue the former president's mission—to maintain the central government's authority and the unity of Pakistan. Early on Yahya consolidated the power of the military by installing local military rule in each province in place of the discredited system of Basic Democracy. He authorized local military commanders to make on-the-spot decisions in putting down disturbances.

President Yahya moved cautiously in the direction of civilian rule. His first cabinet consisted entirely of military commanders. Echoing the 1958 announcement of Martial Law Administrator Ayub, Yahya said that elections could not be held until a sound basis of discipline had been achieved. To secure Bangali support for his regime, after a few months Yahya named four civilian Bangalis to his cabinet and selected another Bangali, Shafiul Azam, as chief secretary of East Pakistan, that is, its top professional administrator.[10] Yahya made other conciliatory gestures to the Bangalis, agreeing to double the recruitment of Bangalis into the army and announcing his budget would provide greater allocations for education and for lower income groups. He proposed the elimination of English as an official language within six years and the reorganization of the national educational system to encourage Urdu and Bengali; all government officials would be required to know both languages.

The Bangali reaction to these placatory proposals was generally negative. They saw the proffered budgetary assistance as tokenism, because the national economic plan provided larger development funds for West Pakistan. The language proposal read like a variant of one made by President Ayub that the Bangalis had rejected. President Yahya, like his predecessors, did not grasp the depth of feeling the Bangalis had for their language, nor the extent to which it figured in their cherished ambition for autonomy.

Now that Yahya had assumed the presidency, Sheikh Mujib returned to his attack on the Center.[11] The president, he complained, had not included the idea of a loose federation among his offers for change. Mujib repeated the charge that East Pakistan was being treated as a colony and a market for West Pakistani products, and he insisted that East Pakistan control its own economic and political development. Rejecting the Constitution of 1962 as the basic law, he called for a constitutional convention to be elected by direct suffrage. After the convention had completed its work, it should, he said, continue to serve as a legislative body. His proposals would have given the Bangalis a chance to exercise a decisive voice in the affairs of Pakistan. President Yahya and other West Pakistanis were not, however, willing to see the Bangalis acquire that much power.

Despite Mujib's criticisms, President Yahya pursued his own style of conciliation to weaken the influence of the Awami League. He altered martial law rules to permit political groups to hold meetings in preparation for the promised 1970 elections and maintained that the framework for a constitutional government should be settled before holding the elections—a position contrary to that of Mujib, which implied the acceptance of a parliamentary system prior to elections.

To increase Bangali support for his constitutional plans, Yahya selected Admiral S. M. Ashan as governor of East Pakistan and appointed G. W. Choudhury, formerly a professor of political science at Dacca University, to the fifth Bangali position in his cabinet, as minister of communications.

In November the election commissioners announced that ballots for the expected winter elections would be printed in Urdu only in West Pakistan and in Bengali only in East Pakistan. This action angered the Bihari Urdu speakers in the east, staunch allies of Islamabad, who threatened to boycott the elections. The threat could not have a serious effect on the elections, but it exacerbated animosities between Urdu and Bengali speakers.

On November 28, in a long speech intended to unify the country, the president proposed major constitutional changes within a Legal Framework Order and announced that direct elections for the National Assembly would be held October 5, 1970. Within 120 days after its first session the assembly would be charged with drafting a constitution. Yahya proposed the dissolution of the single provincial unit of West Pakistan and the creation of four provinces there: Sind, Punjab, North-West Frontier, and Baluchistan. He approved the one-man, one-vote principle, thus establishing a 56 percent majority for East Pakistan in future national assemblies. After January 1970 political parties could operate, but martial law would remain in effect to ensure the peaceful transfer of power to the newly elected government. He dodged the issue closest to Bangali hearts, provincial autonomy, leaving the matter to the proposed constitutional assembly. His plan also perpetuated a strong presidency. For his Bangali opponents, Yahya's concessions were insufficient and his promises ambiguous.

The year 1969 closed with the suspension of more than 300 administrative officials, who had been accused by military tribunals of corrupt practices and other forms of misconduct. The leaders of the principal political parties used the occasion to demand a full exposure of the millions of dollars said to have been illegally accumulated by former President Ayub and his family. They also insisted that Ayub be tried for crimes against the people. The government, however, took no action against the former president.

The return to party activity in January 1970 began intemperately in Dacca.[12] Several hundred people were injured during a chaotic meeting called by the fundamentalist party Jamaat-i-Islam. In the aftermath of the meeting another melee cost the lives of several persons and injury to others; several hundred demonstrators were arrested. According to Awami Leaguers, Jamaat-i-Islam members, opposed to Mujib's policies, had served as *agents provocateurs*. Throughout the early months of the year, security forces were augmented to control rumored student agitation.

In one of his innumerable public talks President Yahya discussed the forthcoming elections and his plans to end economic discrimination against the Bangalis. But he insisted that provincial elections be held 17 days after the national elections—a proposal intended to prevent a likely Awami League victory in East Pakistan from adversely affecting the outcome of the national parliamentary elections.

Yahya told foreign correspondents he would hold free elections, whatever happened to the Constitution. For their benefit, he pointed out that he had acted against business monopolies, had charged corrupt officials, and had arranged for more economic aid for East Pakistan.

By March Yahya had made more promises to the Bangalis. An oil refinery was scheduled to be built in East Pakistan with the help of Iran. Flood control measures were given top priority. Yahya's sanctioning of three cadet colleges and a better communication system between the provinces had military as well as economic significance, for these measures, if realized, would improve the posture of the military in East Pakistan.

THE LEGAL FRAMEWORK ORDER

President Yahya's concessions to the Bangalis and his promise to outline basic constitutional principles in a Legal Framework Order did not please the generals nor the West Pakistani politicians.[13] They insisted that a constitutional document be promulgated before the national elections, that the document define the limits of provincial autonomy, and that it be amendable by at least 60 percent of the total membership of the constitutional convention rather than the simple majority suggested by Yahya. In a word, they wanted a constitution that could not be readily changed by a Bangali majority.

G. W. Choudhury, a Dacca University professor serving as a civilian constitutional expert on the president's staff, reported that General Peerzada, the president's principal staff officer, General Hamid, chief of staff of the Pakistani armed forces, and other military officers in the inner cabinet of the president initially demanded that the changes mentioned above be included in the Legal Framework Order, which was then in preparation. Professor Choudhury further claimed that the military advisors were finally prevailed upon to substitute a statement in the order specifying the minimum conditions essential to the existence of the united Pakistan.

The order, published March 31, 1970, required that a future constitution respect four fundamental principles: first, that Pakistan adhere to an Islamic ideology and its president be Muslim; second, that a democratic constitution provide for direct, free national and provincial elections and guarantee fundamental rights and the independence of the nation; third, that the "maximum of autonomy" be granted to the provinces consistent with the authority of the government to discharge its federal responsibilities, including the maintenance of the country's territorial integrity; and fourth, that a pledge be made to eliminate disparities among the provinces.

The Bangalis did not object to the phraseology contained in the statement of principles in the order. But they did object to the sections of the order that gave the president final authority to authenticate a constitution and to amend the document within the framework of the four principles. They construed these provisions to mean that the president could interpret the principle of "maximum autonomy" to his own liking, and therefore that Yahya's promise to grant autonomous provincial rule was being withdrawn. They also believed that the order gave the Center excessive and arbitrary police authority.

The Awami League critics of the order responded to it by reissuing Mujib's six-point program of 1966 in a more elaborate and radical form. The new manifesto challenged President Yahya's claim to paramount power.[14] The people of Pakistan, it proclaimed, "have revolted against the perpetuation of injustice between man and man, between region and region." The new manifesto, it said, had been drawn up "to bring about a revolution through the democratic process and thereby to replace the present structure of injustice by a new constitutional, political, economic and social order" and "a comprehensive strategy for securing justice for each of the regions of Pakistan—for every citizen of the country." The document reiterated the ideals of parliamentary democracy, federation, and popular elections and reaffirmed the league's commitment to Islamic principles; it gave extended and detailed attention to finance and to agricultural reforms; finally, it proposed changes in social and cultural development programs. The document strongly asserted the need for Bangalis and Awami Leaguers to share in the country's government.

President Yahya interpreted the manifesto as a challenge to his authority. He seemed to react more vigorously to the manifesto than had President Ayub to the original program. A military court in May sentenced Mujib to seven years at hard labor, but the penalty was not carried out. Yahya believed he had sent a warning signal to the Bangalis and their leader. He wanted them to understand that he would not tolerate the kind of provincial autonomy demanded by Sheikh Mujib and the league. The Bangalis had no immediate reaction to the threatened jail sentence—perhaps they no longer took the president's threats seriously.

In August President Yahya took an action that further diminished his credibility in East Pakistan. He declared that, because of excessive floods in East Pakistan (which were not in fact disastrous), the planned October general election would be postponed until December 7. Bhutto, his political opponent in West Pakistan, asserted that the postponement was a ruse to keep Bhutto out of the National Assembly elections. In any case, the postponement was to cost Yahya dearly.

THE CYCLONE OF NOVEMBER 1970

On the night of November 12 a devastating cyclone, probably the region's worst disaster in centuries, struck a 3,000-square-mile area of the mid-coastal lowlands and islands of the Bay of Bengal.[15] A fair reckoning put the toll between 250,000 and 350,000 dead; thousands more were injured or left homeless. Winds of more than 100 miles an hour, whipping the shallow waters of the bay, created tidal waves as high as 15 and 20 feet. The raging waters met no obstacles for miles inland. The people, their villages, and their livestock were swept out to sea in the receding waters. Because their boats were lost in the storm, survivors were cut off from higher ground. Only swift relief could rescue them from the devastated areas. Prompt aid was not forthcoming from the government; it had not made sufficient preparations for such contingencies in spite of many discussions following a series of cyclones in the sixties. Some untroubled officials saw the cyclone as a technique of population control.

Two days after the cyclone hit, President Yahya, arriving from a brief visit to Peking, tarried in Dacca for a day—just long enough to order the governor, Vice-Admiral S. M. Ashan, to direct the relief work. Yahya then departed for Islamabad, leaving behind him a trail of animosities for his seeming indifference to the plight of the cyclone victims. Why had he not stayed on? One plausible explanation is that his advisors told him that Bhutto, his Punjabi army chief of staff, and other generals wanted to call off the postponed December election. They were convinced that Bangalis, angered by the government's inaction during the first hours after the cyclone, were prepared to vent years of unexpressed hostility at the ballot box and would win the election hands down, jeopardizing the future of his government.

Opposition Dacca newspapers asserted that West Pakistan had been in no hurry to provide relief. They noted that, although a Pakistani helicopter was on hand, most of its air force was idle. Although there were no landing strips for large aircraft in the disaster area, cargo planes might have dropped relief supplies. On November 20, a week after the cyclone, the International Red Cross in Geneva confirmed the correctness of news accounts that there was pile-up of relief supplies in Dacca and announced it would suspend relief operations there. Two small American helicopters stationed in Nepal and the first of a set of four larger British helicopters were flown from Hong Kong to assist the cyclone's survivors.

Dacca newspapers pointed out that there had not been sufficient warnings before the storm, although Calcutta radio stations had for hours repeated warnings about the impending cyclone, which could have hit that city. The government in Dacca, controlled by the central government, knew about the storm and its direction, for many officials and workers were sent home as a precautionary measure. An adequate warning system had not been set up in the cyclone belt south of Dacca.

On November 23, 11 East Pakistani politicians condemned the government's "gross neglect, callous inattention, and utter indifference" to aiding the cyclone victims. They telegraphed President Yahya that attempts had been made to play down or stifle news coverage of "the greatest single havoc in human history" and noted that "not one single [cabinet] minister is here; you yourself left the province after a cursory glance at the first flash of the news of the tragedy." The substance of the remarks was valid.

In order to save face, the government announced the release of $105 million in addition to the $11 million earlier granted for relief. The United States and other countries sent supplies, aircraft, and shallow-draft boats. U.S. public and private agencies gave generous amounts of aid. Twelve days after the disaster, President Yahya returned to Dacca to inspect relief operations. Government aid had belatedly begun, but it was foreign transportation facilities that broke the bottlenecks on land, river, and sea, and foreign missionaries who did much to assist the survivors. The president visited the cyclone area, where a foreign correspondent questioned him about the criticisms of the central government's relief work. He replied, "Criticism is beside the point. Let us get on with the work. My job is to see that people are saved." He went on to say, "Considering our resources and thanks to help from abroad, I think everything is going well. Things are better than expected. Most of the horrible news came from misinformation. I was absolutely horrified when I heard that cholera had broken out, but in the last 24 hours, I have been traveling around and I have not come across a single case." The president's statement about cholera was probably correct, but he failed to acknowledge that by the time he made his statement several hundred thousand people had died.

A few days after the Yahya visit Sheikh Mujib said in Dacca that the people of Bengal owed the press "an eternal debt of gratitude" for reporting the magnitude of the cyclone calamity and that he had visited areas where no relief had been received. He added:

> West Pakistan has a bumper wheat crop, but the first shipment of food
> grain to reach us is from abroad. While we have a substantial army

stationed in West Pakistan, it is left to British marines to bury our dead.
. . . While we have an army of helicopters in West Pakistan, we have
to wait on helicopters from across the earth. The feeling now pervades
. . . every village, home, and slum that we must rule ourselves. We must
make the decisions that matter. We will no longer suffer arbitrary rule
by bureaucrats, capitalists, and feudal interests of West Pakistan.

Belying Bangali conjectures that the government would use the
cyclone as a pretext for postponing the elections, President Yahya on
November 27 told a press conference in Dacca that general elections
would take place as scheduled on December 7. The president added,
"I want to make it clear martial law will continue in Pakistan if the
newly elected constituent assembly fails to frame the new constitution
as laid down in my earlier announcements. If, after the elections,
political parties do not participate in the constitution making, I will
continue martial law." Awami Leaguers construed these remarks to mean
that President Yahya was not prepared to accept the autonomy of East
Pakistan. With regard to criticisms of his government's relief efforts,
Yahya said defensively, "The effort was not ideal. Nothing is ideal. The
greatest possible was done with the maximum resources the country
could muster and with the help of friends abroad. My government does
not consist of angels. It consists of human beings."

Throughout November cyclone relief, at Yahya's urging and in response to worldwide sympathy for the victims, continued to come in
from the United States, Britain, and France; Communist China, too,
joined the dozen assisting nations. The Indian government agreed to
rush relief supplies. The U.N. Food and Agriculture Organization
announced the mobilization of $4 million in foodstuffs. On November
27 President Nixon appointed a citizens' Pakistan Relief Committee,
headed by former ambassador Robert Murphy, to channel aid to East
Pakistan.[16]

THE ELECTIONS OF 1970

Several days before the elections of December 7, thousands of people
swarmed into the streets of Dacca to demonstrate their support for
Mujib and his policy of autonomy.[17] President Yahya, worried by the
clamor of their demands, urged voters to elect candidates committed
to the ideology and integrity of Pakistan and threatened to veto any
constitution that jeopardized a united Pakistan. The failure of Yahya
to take action immediately after the disastrous cyclone was used
effectively by the Awami League to persuade the Bangalis that the
government did not really care about them.

The 1970 election, the first in the history of the country in which voters directly elected members of the National Assembly, was a national triumph for the Awami League. The league not only won all but two seats of 162 in the provincial assembly of East Pakistan, but also a majority 160 of the 300 seats in the National Assembly. The league's victory was a convincing demonstration of Bangali dissatisfaction with the West Pakistani regime. It was a vote for Sheikh Mujibur Rahman against Yahya Khan, but the general had the legions.

In West Pakistan Yahya fared no better. Bhutto's People's party took the largest number of West Pakistan's share of seats in the National Assembly—81 out of 138—but shared his voting strength with other West Pakistan parties. The election there was, nonetheless, a victory for Bhutto against the landlords, industrialists, and military officers standing behind Yahya.

An analysis of the election figures from East Pakistan shows that the 17.4 million registered voters who went to the polls cast 73 percent of their votes for the Awami League. The only other party to obtain more than 5 percent of the vote was Jamaat-i-Islam. Given the high rate of illiteracy, the fact that millions of women living in purdah encountered special difficulty in voting and that the standing of women in this male society made their voting less likely, the percentage of votes cast—58 percent of all those registered—should be considered a high one. The figure compares favorably with the 56 percent of registered voters who cast their ballots in the U.S. presidential election of 1972.

Two other Bangali parties contended in the elections along with the Awami League. The Council Muslim League, an antiregime branch of the Muslim League that had supported Miss Jinnah in the 1965 elections, was led in East Pakistan by Kwajha Kairuddin, a relative of former prime minister Nazimuddin. This faction drew its main strength from West Pakistan and its leader, Mian Daultana, a former chief minister of the Punjab. It supported the unity of Pakistan but thought it could work out satisfactory arrangments with Mujib and the Awami League with regard to autonomy for the Bangalis. The Council Muslim League won no seats in East Pakistan.

The second political party in the east to figure in the elections was the Pakistan Democratic party. Its leader, Nurul Amin, formerly East Bengal's chief minister, was later to become prime minister under President Yahya and vice-president under president Bhutto. The party represented a right-wing splinter group of the Awami League and opposed the six-point program of Sheikh Mujib as too radical. The Pakistan Democratic party, which included Nizam-i-Islam and the Justice party, had been invented for electoral purposes in 1965 to oppose

President Ayub. This alliance of middle-of-the-roaders, too feeble to challenge the Awami League and Sheikh Mujib, stood for autonomy, for an Islamic constitution, and for a modified brand of Islamic socialism. Its policies appeared to have little appeal to the Bangali voters in 1970. Nurul Amin, a gentle Bangali, could not brook the swift-moving and radical demands for an autonomy that ultimately spelled independence. His integrity, age (76), and desire for accommodation with Pakistan unity won his party few votes in the election. He, however, won the only seat the electors gave to his party.

In the East Pakistani provincial assembly, the Awami League gained 288 seats out of 300—better than a 90 percent majority. Members of Bhashani's National Awami party, reputedly better organized than the other small parties, did not vote in the election, on the advice of their maverick leader.

With the double Awami League sweep of the elections, the national and provincial legislatures were in the hands of the league's young leaders. The median age of the leaguers elected to the National Assembly was in the forties, and to the provincial assembly, in the thirties.

In their postelectoral elation, the leaguers did not take account of the fact that 27 percent of the ballots in the national elections were cast for anti-Awami Bangali candidates, most of whom bitterly opposed Awami League leadership. Compromise with its Bangali opponents was not attempted because the Awami League, which interpreted the vote as a mandate to put the six-point manifesto into effect, was more determined than ever to have full autonomy. Sheikh Mujib, two days after the league's capture of the East Pakistani provincial assembly, declared that there would be no new constitution except on the basis of the league's six-point program.

Although the Bangalis had won a majority in the National Assembly and, under normal circumstances, would have assumed control of the government, they never took office, and the assembly never met. Sheikh Mujib should have become prime minister, since he commanded a majority in the assembly that could have elected him to that office, but neither Yahya nor Bhutto would allow such an election. Besides, they unalterably opposed Mujib's idea of a confederated Pakistan.

SEPARATION

During the first two months of the year the voice of Sheikh Mujib and the sound of applause from his hundreds of thousands of supporters reverberated in the east. On January 3, at the ramshackle race track in Dacca, he reiterated his view that the constitution must be based on the six-point program. On the other side of the country Bhutto pleaded for the unity he hoped to bring about in all of Pakistan after his election victory. A preliminary meeting between Sheikh Mujib and Bhutto at the end of January produced a deadlock the day before the opening of a conference planned to settle their differences.

The cat-and-mouse game of politics continued. On February 13 President Yahya called the National Assembly to meet in Dacca on March 3, and a week later dismissed his cabinet with its five Bangalis, presumably because he wanted a free hand to deal with the east and with Sheikh Mujib.[18] On March 1 he indefinitely postponed the March 3 National Assembly meeting. The Bangalis believed that a threat by Bhutto to boycott the assembly unless Mujib gave up on full autonomy dictated the postponement.

Sheikh Mujib waited until March 3 to announce that he had turned down an offer from the president to discuss issues on which they disagreed.[19] He called instead for civil disobedience until the government was given over to the "people's representatives." He said that a general strike would be in effect in East Pakistan for four days to protest the postponement of the National Assembly meeting. The next day one death and a dozen injuries resulted from a clash between strikers and security forces; looting and arson were widespread. Crowds of youth ran through the streets shouting independence slogans. The government curbed the press.

As the troubles gathered momentum Mujib proposed the extension of the strike but immediately revoked the call because workers and others felt the economic pinch of payless days. His own supporters endeavored to maintain order while Pakistani troops put down rioting.

In the flurry of events Mujib suggested that Bhutto be made prime minister of West Pakistan and himself the prime minister of East Pakistan. The offer, obviously intended to advance the cause of provincial autonomy, was not accepted by Bhutto.

By March 1 Yahya had made up his mind to use force. He sent military reinforcements into Dacca. According to one correspondent, many arrived in civilian clothes. On March 2 the troops were observed flying into Dacca on Pakistan International Airlines unscheduled flights. In a clash with security forces on March 6, excited protestors were killed. Mujib put the number of deaths at 300.

Yahya and Bhutto conferred on March 7 and agreed that Pakistan was imperiled. Yahya proposed that the newly elected National Assembly meet on March 25. He then told the nation in a radio address that he would ensure the complete and absolute integrity of the nation and would not allow a handful of people to endanger the homeland of millions. He laid blame for the violence in East Pakistan at the door of its leaders.

The same day Mujib said the Awami League would not attend the March 25 meeting unless martial law was lifted, troops returned to their barracks, an inquiry ordered into the killing of civilians by the army in previous demonstrations, and power transferred to the people. He announced a tax strike for March 8. His speech barely stopped short of a call for independence.

On March 8 President Yahya appointed Lieutenant General Tikka Khan governor and martial law administrator in East Pakistan. The two jobs had traditionally been held by two men, one a civilian, the other a military officer. The chief justice of the East Pakistani High Court refused to swear the general in. The appointment of the general confirmed Yahya's decision to use force to put down what he viewed as an incipient rebellion.

Mujib called a partial strike and ordered schools and government offices closed, but he also announced he would participate in a March 25 meeting of the National Assembly if martial law was ended and the 1970 popular vote for his party in the assembly was accepted.

Talk of reconciliation was lost in the furor of events. Foreigners panicked and prepared to leave the province because they feared that students and other groups would use force to oppose martial law. Government officials refused to go to work. Mujib asserted control over the financial institutions of the province. By March 10 as many as 40,000 troops were stationed in cantonments near the larger cities of East Pakistan. The Awami League ordered that the black flag of anarchy be flown in defiance of the martial law administration. Maulana Bhashani, a longtime opponent of Sheikh Mujib, now came to his side. The military announced that civilian employees at military installations who failed to show up for work would be jailed. Mujib, taking the action to be a sign that an overt military crackdown was not far off, said the people would resist government force.

On March 15 Mujib issued a series of 35 decrees that announced that he was taking over the administration of East Pakistan in order to emancipate the homeland of the people of Bengal. For the first time he referred publicly to East Pakistan as Bangladesh. His decrees suspended the collection of income taxes for the central government and barred the remittance of other taxes normally transmitted to the central authorities. Arguing that he derived his authority from the election of the Awami League in December and his control of the provincial assembly, he still expressed willingness to meet with President Yahya.

On March 16 Yahya came to Dacca. His government issued directives that placed it in control of the administration of East Pakistan. Demonstrations against the regime persisted. Mujib and Yahya met on March

17 and 18 but reported no progress other than an agreement to investigate the killing of demonstrators by troops. Tensions mounted among civilians; Punjabis and other West Pakistanis left the east and Bangalis living in West Pakistan returned home. When the government proposed that a commission appointed by General Tikka Khan inquire into the deaths of the demonstrators, Mujib said it was merely a way to mislead the people. He asked citizens not to cooperate with the governmental inquiry and appointed his own three-man inquiry commission.

The build-up of troops increased to 60,000, according to local reports; only 25,000 troops had been present before the crisis. Just prior to the March crises in Dacca, India had cancelled air flights between the two wings after an Indian Airlines aircraft was hijacked by Pakistani guerrillas given asylum by Islamabad. Pakistan International Airlines was obliged thereafter to fly around India via Sri Lanka, three times the distance of flights over India. The move increased West Pakistani fears of Indian influence in East Pakistan.

The third and fourth conferences between Mujib and Yahya appeared to produce a compromise, notwithstanding new violence north of Dacca. But Bhutto's arrival on March 22 brought a mixed reception. Many Bangalis believed that he insisted on the unity of Pakistan under central control in order to succeed Yahya. After further conferences in which Bhutto participated, the National Assembly meeting, set for March 25, was again postponed to allow time to resolve differences. Reports from West Pakistan indicated that businessmen there favored a compromise with Mujib. The economic slowdown in the east had produced serious economic losses, because East Pakistan was the west's largest export market and supplier of foreign exchange.

Radio reports on March 24 of an agreement in principle turned out to be false. The failure of the conferences, the presence of sizable contingents of Pakistani troops, and Yahya's decision to use them to control the Bangalis by force produced a reign of terror beginning on March 25. Although Mujib clearly intended to make a unilateral declaration of independence, he had not organized a revolutionary force.

Mohammad Ali Jinnah's "moth-eaten" Pakistan was torn into two segments—Pakistan in the west and Bangladesh in the east. From the Awami point of view, General Yahya and his advisors had "lost" the Bangalis because they, like George III, "lacked the statesmanship to know the right time and manner of yielding what it is impossible to keep." Some observers believe that Sheikh Mujib was a tool of India who never intended to negotiate seriously, or that Bhutto's ambition to govern Pakistan sabotaged any possible reconciliation, or that, given time, the promise of greater economic benefits and a larger share in power would be attained in a united Pakistan. Others believe the evidence presented here that, after years of economic, political, and cultural frustrations, the national political visions of the Bangalis and the central government diverged so sharply that the events of the last days were inevitable.

CHAPTER 7

The Birth of
Bangladesh, 1971

On March 25 President Yahya declared the east-west talks finished. He returned to Islamabad and left East Pakistan's military governor, Tikka Khan, in command of occupied territory. Pakistan's authority over the Bangalis was being maintained at the end of a gun barrel.

The people of Bangladesh remember March 25, 1971, as a day of infamy and of liberation.[1] The Pakistani army, with a list of proscribed persons in hand, systematically killed several hundred Bangalis. The same day Sheikh Mujib was seized by the military and carried away to West Pakistan without his family. On March 26 his spokesman, Major Ziaur Rahman, declared East Pakistan independent of Pakistan and proclaimed himself president in Mujib's absence.

The occupying army, fearful of eyewitness reports of the killings, placed a strict censorship on newsmen, confiscated their films and notes, confined them to Dacca's International Hotel, and soon expelled them from the country. The Pakistani government complained that the BBC and the Voice of America reports had distorted the day's events.

The world waited only a few days to learn in detail what had happened on March 25. Simon Dring, a reporter for the conservative *Daily Telegraph* of London, and Michel Laurent, an Associated Press photographer, escaping the vigilance of the army, had scoured Dacca and roamed the countryside after other foreign journalists had been expelled. Dring described Dacca as a "crushed and frightened city" after ruthless shelling by the Pakistani army. He estimated that three battalions with ten tanks had attacked the virtually defenseless city. The first target of the army was the University of Dacca. Seventeen professors were killed in cold blood, and some 200 students in Iqbal

Hall, long a haven for militant antigovernment elements, were mowed down by firing squads. The offices of opposition newspapers were burned to the ground. Laurent reported on March 28 that the loss of life in the country had reached 15,000. Confirmatory eyewitness reports of violence during March subsequently came from many sources, including British and American officials, American missionaries, and other foreign residents.

By the end of March Pakistani troops controlled Dacca, but fighting went on in other East Pakistani cities. Hindus and Muslims fled to India, where the Indian military armed and trained Bangali contingents. Resistance radio broadcasts reported that the Pakistani army continued to kill Bangalis, burn their homes, and ruthlessly control the population. A total of 300,000 people were said to have lost their lives by the end of the summer. Bangali guerrillas were among the victims.

PAKISTAN'S PROPAGANDA CAMPAIGN

To counteract newspaper and radio accounts of wholesale atrocities, the government of Pakistan undertook a vigorous press and radio campaign justifying its actions.[2] Sheikh Mujib and his supporters, it was said, had been deceitful and unyielding in their March meetings with President Yahya. More than that, an armed rebellion, begun by Bangali students and other partisans of Mujib in collaboration with the Indian government to overthrow the Pakistani government in East Pakistan, had to be put down. Media support for Yahya in Dacca came chiefly from the quarters that had long been financed by the central government. As late as April 20 the *Morning News* editorialized: "The armed forces who were called upon to perform the duty of saving the country from disintegration and eventual enslavement (Hindu) of East Pakistan, were once again doing a magnificent job. All who have the interest of the country at heart are grateful to them and take pride in their performance. The voice of the vast majority, which was suppressed by the violent minority, has now been freed and can now assert itself." The government-aligned Dacca press played down reports of continued fighting by Bangalis, insisting that the situation was under control.

Early in May Islamabad invited a team of foreign correspondents to tour East Pakistan. British and American reporters reproduced the views of the officials who talked to them and added few comments of their own. Officials made a good deal out of stories that the Bangalis had killed hundreds of Biharis but said nothing about the number of Bangalis killed by the Biharis, who had been armed by the Pakistani army. Half-truths, whole lies, and a miasma of charges clouded the atmosphere. The one reality of Bangladesh in those days was that thousands lost their lives.

INDIA'S STANCE

One result of the slaughter was that Bangalis, Hindus, and substantial numbers of Muslims fled across the border into West Bengal, India.[3] General Yahya, who had commanded the East Pakistani army during the migrations of 1964, must have known what would happen. Whether he was indifferent to, or even welcomed, the migration is not possible to say. The immense flood of refugees did as much to align Indian and world public opinion against him as did journalists' accounts of the massacre.

After the tragic events of March 25 in Dacca, Indian officials and the general public did not hide their feelings for the Bangalis. Their sympathy soon turned to support. Many Indians, never reconciled to the existence of Pakistan, welcomed the Bangali revolt as evidence of the breakup of Pakistan and the return of "East Bengal" to the bosom of India.

Leftist members of the Indian Parliament interrupted legislative proceedings in New Delhi to demand that full moral support be extended to the "East Bangalis." On March 27 Prime Minister Indira Gandhi described the killings in East Pakistan "as not merely the suppression of a movement but a meeting of unarmed people with tanks."

In April an Indian parliamentary resolution accused Pakistan of slaughtering citizens of the eastern province and demanded that Mrs. Gandhi provide all possible aid to the rebel fighters in East Pakistan. She yielded partially by urging the people of India to lend their support to the independence movement, but she rejected a parliamentary request for diplomatic recognition of the independent government in East Pakistan, calling it premature. Pakistani charges of an Indian build-up on the East Pakistani border were denied by New Delhi.

It was the stability of the Indian regime that permitted it to pursue a policy of moderation with respect to events in East Pakistan, wrote U.S. journalist Selig Harrison. In an interview (*Washington Post,* April 14, 1971), Mrs. Gandhi averred that Pakistan was seeking to use India as a "scapegoat for its difficulties in East Pakistan." She defended her government's actions, adding that "any country, situated as we are, always has to be fully prepared for any contingency." In reply to a question from Harrison concerning the likelihood of a cooling off in East Pakistan, she remarked, "anything is possible," and then asked rhetorically whether there was any desire on the part of the central government of Pakistan to cool off. Demands for an independent East Pakistan, she said, "would not have arisen if Sheikh Mujibur Rahman and President Yahya had gone with their negotiations for a confederation agreement. It was only when Mujib was driven to the wall that there was a turn in the direction of independence." A message from Chou En-lai supporting Pakistan, she added, did not alter her announced solidarity with the rebels.

THE PROVISIONAL GOVERNMENT OF BANGLADESH

A clandestine radio broadcast on April 11, 1971, announced the formation somewhere in Bangladesh of a six-member cabinet of the "independent, sovereign republic of Bangladesh."[4] The government consisted of Sheikh Mujibur Rahman, president; Nazrul Islam, vice-president; Tajuddin Ahmed, prime minister; Khandikar Moshtaque Ahmed, foreign minister; and Captain Mansoor Ali and A. Kamaruzzaman as ministers. Colonel M.A.G. Osmani was appointed the general officer in command of the liberation army, originally called Mukti Fouj and later Mukti Bahini—that is, freedom fighters.

The cabinet, which included several lawyers, was a coalition of longtime middle-class Awami League members chosen to represent widely scattered parts of the country. The government's headquarters were discreetly located a short distance from the border of West Bengal. On April 12 the cabinet formally proclaimed the People's Republic of Bangladesh and then left for Calcutta. The following day the Pakistani army occupied—without bloodshed—the village from which they had departed.

The establishment of a presidential form of government, even though headed by the absent Mujib, was not in accord with the imprisoned leader's long fight for parliamentary democracy nor with the 1970 party manifesto that affirmed the party's demand for a parliamentary system in Pakistan. That Mujib's followers in Bangladesh would attempt to repudiate these positions was an early omen of discord in the ranks of the Awami League.

President Yahya, ignoring the existence of Bangladesh and its leaders, announced he would appoint a group of experts to prepare a constitution for Pakistan. The "secessionist" Awami League was excluded from the undertaking, which aimed at restoring civilian rule throughout Pakistan in four months. Yahya, counting on the support of Bangalis opposed to the Awami League and to the new government, won few Bangalis to his side. Under the circumstances such an assumption was so unrealistic as to convince even an outside observer that the president did not understand what had happened in the east.

With the formal announcement of Bangladesh's independence, assistance from the Indian government increased. Leaders of the Bangladeshi provisional government, self-exiled in West Bengal, were lodged at the government's guest houses in midtown Calcutta. When the Bangali personnel of the Pakistani deputy high commission (a diplomatic post) in Calcutta pledged their allegiance to the government of Bangladesh, the government of Pakistan demanded the ouster of the Bangalis and the acceptance of a new Pakistani deputy high commissioner in Calcutta. The Indian government moved the Bangali mission to new quarters. The Pakistanis thereupon shut down the Indian deputy high commission office in Dacca, one of India's largest diplomatic and consular posts. The closure of that office indicated to the millions of Hindus in Bangladesh that they would not be served by India as they had in the past; the flood of Hindu refugees became a torrent.

Animosities between the Indian and Pakistani governments went on. India, for example, accused the Pakistani government of preventing the repatriation of Indian diplomats and their families and retaliated in kind against Pakistani diplomats in India.

Soon after the Pakistani military occupation, the threat of famine in Bangladesh became serious. Although under heavy pressure to readmit United Nations relief agencies into the war zone, Islamabad did not reply to Secretary-General U Thant's offer of humanitarian assistance. However, private agencies of Western nations, including the United States, came to the rescue of the Bangalis.

Responding to a Pakistani charge in May that India had committed every act short of war to help the "secessionists" in East Pakistan, Mrs. Gandhi said that India was prepared to face war with Pakistan if forced into it.[5] Meanwhile both countries strengthened their armed forces in and around the borders of Bangali territory. Mrs. Gandhi, replying to Indian critics who accused her of not doing enough for the Bangalis, said recognition was under consideration. Later on in the month she said, "If the world does not take heed of the refugee influx, we shall be constrained to take all measures necessary to ensure our own security and to preserve the social and economic life of India." Thus was a military solution hinted at as an alternative to a political solution of the Bangali problem.

Early in June Mrs. Gandhi met for the first time with rebel leaders from Dacca and heard their request for her government's support of their cause. Soon thereafter the Mukti Bahini, the guerrilla forces of the provisional Bangali government, were armed and began training under Indian army officers. Regular Indian army units ignored the Indo-Pakistan treaty of 1947, under which both sides were to keep their forces five kilometers from the border. (The treaty had, in fact, not been strictly observed in the past.) With the help of Indian training, the guerrillas held their own against the Pakistani army.

BANGALI GUERRILLA FORCES

The Bangali guerrilla forces, led by the Mukti Bahini, consisted of civilian volunteers, soldiers from the Pakistani East Bengal regiment, and the East Bengal Rifles, border guards who were reported to have gone over en masse to the Bangali cause.[6] Other volunteers were later trained along the border for service in the Mukti Bahini by Bangalis with military experience. Independent guerrilla groups, organized by Bhashani's left-wing National Awami party and the Communist party of Bangladesh, also operated inside Bangali territory. The guerrilla forces, their total number estimated at between 30,000 and 100,000 (the lower figure is probably more accurate), operated out of the Sunderban forest in the southeast, the forested regions north of Dacca, the lowland around Barisal, and the Comilla region not far from the border of Tripura in India.

The guerrillas disrupted communications by destroying culverts and bridges connecting Dacca, Chittagong, and Comilla. They reduced rail and road deliveries to a trickle and sank a number of vessels in Chittagong Harbor. Because of their attacks on the port, foreign vessels stopped calling there. The guerrillas, too, took out after Bangali supporters and collaborators of the Pakistani army. The unpopular governor of East Pakistan, Monem Khan, was gunned down at his home in Dacca.

The horrors of the war were compounded by the disinterested savagery of West Pakistani troops, often fearful of their fate in hostile territory, and by Bihari guerrillas recruited as Razakars (civilian militia). The dirtiest jobs were allegedly undertaken by the Razakars. Both Pakistani forces looted and burned villages, raped women, and killed men, women, and children. Bangali guerrillas returned the atrocities. The destruction wrought by the opposing forces brought the economy close to a dead halt by the end of November; a majority of the working population of Dacca was without jobs as factory production shut down.

INTERNATIONAL SUPPORT FOR THE
PROVISIONAL GOVERNMENT

Prior to the intervention of India, the provisional Bangali government in Calcutta undertook an international campaign to advance its cause.[7] A consultative committee, consisting of four representatives of the Awami League and one representative each of the two factions of the

National Awami party—the Communist party of Bangladesh and the Bangladesh National Congress—was formed in Calcutta in September "to direct the freedom struggle." Maulana Bhashani represented the pro-Chinese faction and Professor Mussaffar Ahmed the pro-Soviet faction of the National Awami party.

The first overseas mission of the provisional government of Bangladesh, established in London in late August, directed the activities of Bangalis in Europe, the United States, and the United Nations. Justice Abu Sayeed Chowdhury, senior judge of the Dacca High Court and former vice-chancellor of the University of Dacca, headed the mission. A short while later an unofficial mission opened in Delhi, headed by a former senior Pakistani diplomat, H. R. Choudhury.

A number of Pakistani diplomats of Bangali origin gave up their posts to support Bangladesh, including the ambassador to Iraq, Abdul Fateh, and K. H. Panni, ambassador to the Philippines. Ranking diplomats in London and Washington also went over to Bangladesh, to be followed by others, such as M. Kaiser, the Pakistani ambassador to Peking. Unlike most new nations, Bangladesh was able to man its diplomatic and consular posts with experienced and capable personnel. The defections gave an international dimension to the depth of Bangali feelings.

TENSIONS BETWEEN INDIA AND PAKISTAN

The swelling flood of refugees during the summer of 1971 activated a stepped-up Indian campaign for international action.[8] Indian Foreign Minister Swaran Singh toured the principal capitals of the world to discuss the burden that the refugees placed on India and to voice his government's concern about continued foreign aid to Pakistan, which, he argued, only encouraged Pakistan's armed repression of the people of East Pakistan. During a visit to Washington the foreign minister admitted that a number of European governments were reluctant to say what measures they would take to end the fighting in East Pakistan or to deal with the refugee problem. Singh told the National Press Club in Washington that refugee aid was only a palliative and that international pressure to stop military action in East Pakistan was required. He proposed that all countries cut off economic and military aid to Pakistan. A State Department spokesman, referring to a conversation between Singh and Secretary of State William Rogers, made the innocuous comment that the flow of refugees into India "would be greatly facilitated by the restoration of peaceful conditions in East Pakistan" and the attainment of a political accommodation. He politely remarked that the department welcomed India's restraint in the situation.

That the administration had other views of the matter was revealed in the Anderson Papers, written by the American columnist Jack Anderson.

Meanwhile, the propaganda contest between Pakistan and India heated up. On July 19 President Yahya said he would declare war on India if that country "made any attempt to seize any part of East Pakistan. Let me warn them and the world it means total war. I am not looking for war and am trying to avoid it, but there is a limit to my patience." He also asserted Pakistan would not be alone. Was he counting on his American or his Chinese friends to rescue his army? In any case, the president was whistling in the dark. The Indian foreign minister in turn cautioned Yahya against using the "freedom struggle" in Bangladesh as a pretext for launching an attack on India. "We will defend ourselves," he added unnecessarily.

Pursuing its point-counterpoint tactics, the Pakistani government proposed that the United Nations Security Council defuse the situation along the border between India and Pakistan by sending a "good offices" team to visit the area. After letting it be known that Sheikh Mujib had been put on trial, Yahya replaced General Tikka Khan with General A.A.K. Niazi, who was to have the dubious honor of surrendering to the Indian army in December. At the same time the president appointed Abdul M. Malik, a Bangali of moderate views, as civilian governor of East Pakistan. He announced a general amnesty for all those who had committed "offenses" in East Pakistan after March 1. These last-ditch measures of appeasement, whether a sign of weakness or of generosity, did not pay off.

Pakistan and India moved closer to armed combat in August, when the Indian government signed a 20-year treaty of peace, friendship, and cooperation with the Soviet Union in Delhi.[9] The treaty, among other things, called for immediate consultation between the two countries in the event of an attack or threat of attack on either of them. The vague terms of the treaty made it possible to place a number of interpretations on it. Whatever its intended meaning, it signaled to Pakistan that it faced Soviet as well as Indian opposition and that the balance of the great powers on the subcontinent had at least for the time being shifted further toward the Soviets.

The treaty made it easier for India to obtain arms aid and "to accept" a Soviet naval presence in regions close to the Indian Ocean. Although the pact was described as "a treaty of peace against war" and claimed to reduce or eliminate the peril of war between India and Pakistan, it solidified Pakistani and Chinese opposition to India and Bangladesh.

At the end of the treaty sessions between the Soviet foreign minister and Indian officials, a joint declaration urged that steps be taken to achieve a political solution in the civil war in East Pakistan, because there could be no military solution to the crisis. The Indian-Soviet statement also contemplated the return of Bangali refugees to their homeland. Mrs. Gandhi used the occasion to appeal to heads of government to use their influence to save the life of Sheikh Mujib, on trial for treason.

The Pakistanis labeled the call for a political settlement "unnecessary and gratuitous advice. This is an internal matter of Pakistan and no one has the right to advise Pakistan how to deal with insurgents or handle law and order situations." A Pakistani spokesman, referring to Yahya's search for an anti-Awami Leaguer willing to assume the responsibilities of the eastern governorship, noted that the president was engaged in carrying out promised political reforms. This Pakistani political overture was described in the American press as another evidence of Yahya's political ineptitude.

REFUGEES

Refugees continued to stream into India throughout the summer months.[10] The Indian government alleged that almost eight million refugees had arrived by the end of August, and ten million by December 1. The Pakistanis claimed that only two million had departed for India. Outside sources thought the Indian figure to be more nearly correct.

The refugees' straits demonstrated the deadly character of the war in Bangladesh and created a world opinion hostile to Pakistan and favorable to India, whose propaganda machine solicited sympathy for itself as well as the refugees. Fears of cholera, famine, and wholesale death among the refugees were real but exaggerated. A cholera epidemic did kill several thousand refugees, but each year in Bangladesh the disease takes as many or more lives than died in the Indian outbreak. Conditions in the overcrowded refugee camps, filled with people of all ages suffering all kinds of diseases, were not too different from those in some of the villages the refugees had left behind.

By October an Indian official said that if the world did not help his country with its refugee problem, India would have to go to war against Pakistan to relieve the crisis there and stem the tide of refugees, which he estimated at about nine million. Although the refugees imposed a heavy burden on the economy of India, this argument alone hardly justified the war, because the United States, Western European countries, and the United Nations had already begun to give more aid to the refugees.

INDIAN INTERVENTION NEARS

By mid-October observers of South Asian affairs were nearly unanimous that both countries were in the grip of war fever.[11] Troops lined the border. Shouting matches resounded in the United Nations, propaganda filled the air, and the great powers aligned themselves—the United States and China with Pakistan, the Soviets with India and Bangladesh. More refugees tumbled into India.

Mrs. Gandhi, during a fall visit to the United States, talked to President Nixon but failed to improve the chances for peace. The Nixon administration, tilting toward Pakistan, wanted India to withdraw its border forces. The Indians refused to draw back until Pakistan pulled out its forces. The United States proposed that the Indian government negotiate with Pakistan, but the Indians insisted the Bangali problem lay between East and West Pakistan, although Mrs. Gandhi at this point must have known the Bangalis would not accept anything less than independence.

The Pakistanis, too, campaigned in the arena of world public opinion. Bhutto, as President Yahya's agent, visited Peking, where he was said to have obtained Chinese assurance of "resolute support should Pakistan be subjected to foreign aggression." A Chinese official in Peking, speaking more softly, urged Pakistan to seek a reasonable settlement with East Pakistan, but added that interference by any foreign country was inadmissible. Following his Peking visit, Bhutto warned Yahya there could be a repetition of the Bangali drama in West Pakistan if power was not restored to the people's representatives, meaning himself and his party.

Prompted by a U.S. proposal that Yahya confer with the Bangalis, Yahya said he would talk with Bangali politicians, although not with the imprisoned Sheikh Mujib. In the absence of Mujib, Awami Leaguers refused to meet Yahya. The Indian government, reacting to the U.S. proposal, saw it as an expression of U.S. determination to support Yahya and unwillingness to condemn his government for its use of force. On October 28 the working committee of the Awami League in Calcutta in effect rejected the U.S. proposal and announced it would accept nothing short of independence. The committee instructed Awami Leaguers elected in 1970 to the National Assembly not to make individual contact with foreigners.

The consolidation and strengthening of Indian and Pakistani forces on the borders began in earnest. Clashes between elements of each army increased on the East Pakistani borders. The Indians contended that the fielding of Pakistani armed forces in East and West Pakistan made India insecure. The Pakistanis' pride and their vaunted support by Communist China, as well as the successes of the Indian-aided Bangali guerrillas, reinforced Pakistanis' determination to keep control of East Pakistan as India and Pakistan drew closer to war.

November was the point of no return in the conflict.[12] Frantic efforts by the United States, both in and out of the United Nations, on behalf of Pakistan were frustrated by the unwillingness of either the Indian or the Pakistani government to compromise. The tilt toward Pakistan by the Nixon administration was encouraged by a Congress opposed to the Vietnam War and determined not to plunge the United States deeper into the affairs of Asia.

Four days before the Indian government openly admitted it was sending troops into East Pakistan, Indian and Pakistani troops fired on each other across borders in so-called defensive actions. The war had begun before the Indian army crossed the border.

THE INDO-PAKISTAN WAR OF 1971

An Indian army superior in numbers and aircraft to the 90,000 Pakistanis fighting the Bangalis took only 12 days, from December 4 to December 16, to execute an elaborate pincer movement on Dacca, moving from points in West Bengal, Assam, and Tripura to force the Pakistanis to lay down their arms.[13] The Pakistanis, held at bay along the Indian borders of East Pakistan by Bangali guerrillas since the end of March, were weakened by having to operate 3,000 miles away from their source of supplies. The government of Sri Lanka, unsympathetic to India, permitted the Pakistanis to use its port and air facilities to supply their forces in East Pakistan.

On December 6 India recognized Bangladesh, which it no longer regarded as an internal problem of Pakistan. The same day Islamabad severed diplomatic relations with India. On December 7 the United Nations General Assembly voted 104 to 11, with 10 abstentions, for a resolution calling for a cease-fire and the withdrawal of Indian and Pakistani forces to their own territories.[14] The Pakistanis accepted the resolution; the Indians ignored it. On December 13 the United States sponsored a Security Council resolution that called on India to accept the cease-fire and withdrawal of forces because India's intervention had defied world opinion. At that point U.S. action seems to have been dictated by a desire of the administration to fix the blame on India rather than to end the war. The U.S. resolution was vetoed by the Soviet Union, with Poland, the United Kingdom, and France abstaining: the vote was the same as that on a similar Security Council resolution sponsored by the United States a few days before. Although most commentators in the United States predicted its defeat, the administration persisted in showing its colors for Pakistan. In effect the administration echoed the Pakistani view that the war need never have taken place because a peaceful accommodation with the Bangalis was possible.

Three days after these charades the Pakistani army in Bangladesh surrendered, and India requested a cease-fire on the West Pakistani border, where fighting continued.[15] President Yahya, discredited by the war, was ousted from office and placed under arrest. Zulfikar Ali Bhutto replaced him on December 21, five days after the surrender of the Pakistani army in Dacca.

CHAPTER 8

The New Nation Sets
Its Course, 1972

A nation in an urgent plight at the end of a devastating war confronted Sheikh Mujib on his return from jail in West Pakistan. His most pressing task was to organize his government and, immediately thereafter, to prop up an economy so battered by natural disasters and the strife of war that it had to be rebuilt from the ground up.

Sheikh Mujibur Rahman was undeniably the leader of the Bangali nation and its 70 million or more inhabitants.[1] Born on March 17, 1920, in Tungipara, a small town south of Dacca, his parents were middle-class landowning peasants and pious Muslims. He was educated in Calcutta and later in Dacca and lived most of his political life in the latter city with his wife and children. For a time he sold insurance for a living.

With other leaders of new nations, Mujib could proudly assert he had spent years in jail for political offenses, and the longest time of any Bangali politician. He had opposed British rule prior to Partition and from the fifties onward had been an outspoken advocate of Bangali autonomy. His persistence in demanding home rule for East Pakistan made him the chief enemy of the central government and the hero of his people—at least for a time. He developed his political skills in the exacting school of party politics. As head of the Awami League since 1963, he had challenged the authority of Pakistan's rulers whenever their ill-advised maneuvers or intransigence had provided him the opportunity. At the beginning of his regime he had the considerable backing of the Dacca press and the adoration of his countrymen.

The original policies of Mujib were essentially those hammered out by the Awami League at its beginnings in the forties—autonomy for

Sheikh Mujibur Rahman, 1972 (courtesy of Ministry of Foreign Affairs, Bangladesh).

the Bangalis and neutralism in foreign affairs. From his earliest political years he had favored the withdrawal of Pakistan from the Southeast Asia Treaty Organization and later supported the North Vietnamese against U.S. military intervention. On coming to power he pragmatically accepted economic assistance from any country willing to give it.

He was regarded as a moderate radical except by his Pakistani adversaries. His political leanings, typical of a Suhrawardy lieutenant, placed him between the Maoist Bhashani and the pragmatic Bhutto. His political, economic, and social policies, initially based on the premises of a parliamentary socialist democracy, gradually changed during the four years of his leadership of the nation. By 1975 he had turned to authoritarian rule to subdue the anarchic frenzies that beset the country.

MUJIB TAKES CHARGE

Sheikh Mujibur Rahman came onto the political center stage on January 8, 1972, the day he was released from prison by President Bhutto.[2] Bhutto's reasons for releasing him were obscure. Perhaps he acted in the hope that Mujib would accept the post of prime minister of Pakistan; Bhutto made similar offers before the civil war and repeated the offer on January 18. Mujib firmly rejected every opportunity to play second fiddle to Bhutto.

Upon his release Mujib flew directly to London rather than to Dacca, in order, it is said, to allow his supporters in Dacca time to prepare a welcome and to give his return to power maximum international exposure. His stopover in London also afforded him an opportunity to catch up with happenings in Bangladesh and to make pressing political decisions before facing his people. It enabled him to meet with British leaders and begin an international campaign for recognition of his nation and for economic aid.

On January 10 he flew in a British Royal Air Force jet to New Delhi, where he met president V. V. Giri and Prime Minister Indira Gandhi. India and Bhutan at the time were the only countries to have recognized Bangladesh. During his 24-hour stay in the Indian capital Mujib conferred with a delegation of Bangali officials from Dacca and addressed a rally at a cantonment near New Delhi. His visit to that city disturbed right-wing Awami Leaguers, Maoist partisans, and others inimical to close Bangali ties with India.

A tumultuous welcome greeted Mujib on his arrival in Dacca on January 11. The crowds broke through cordons of guards to embrace their leader, proclaiming him *bangabandu* (friend of Bengal). All the pent-up enthusiasm and ebullience of the Bangalis was released as they surged forward to see, touch, and hail their liberator.

In his first public address, at the racecourse not far from the graves of "the Lion of Bengal," Fazlul Huq, and of H. S. Suhrawardy, Mujib boasted, "Noboby in the history of the world ever had one million people at a public meeting. I have got it." The numbers must have looked like a million to the exultant Mujib. He continued in the same vein: "I don't depend on anybody except God and my people. You know my people love me and nobody can suppress my people." This was the kind of talk the Bangalis loved to hear.

He told his followers, "Ours will be a secular, democratic socialist state." He would, he said, demand an international trial of those guilty of genocide in Bangladesh. Addressing the Biharis, he admonished: "No harm will come to you, but declare that you have become Bangalis."

Referring to President Bhutto and Pakistan, he said, "Mr. Bhutto wanted me to maintain some kind of links with Pakistan when he met with me in Rawalpindi. I told him I cannot say anything now, in fact I am not sure where I am. Let me tell Mr. Bhutto now that all links with Pakistan are snapped for good. I have no animus against the people of West Pakistan. Let them be free in their own country and let us be free in our country."

On the day of Mujib's return to Dacca, Bangladesh was recognized by East Germany and Bulgaria—thus did the Soviet Union make its standard sudden appearance in a newly independent country whose cause it espoused. Thereafter the global visibility of Bangladesh quickly enlarged. Mujib's appearance before the world in television and his numerous and widely reported speeches catapulted him and his country into the world arena. His choice of collaborators and the speed with which the government during its first year addressed itself to the huge problems of the country indicated that Mujib appreciated the seriousness of the situation, even though he and his people were not clear how to cope with the problems. The nation had discarded a worn-out regime and moved to a new, turbulent one.

THE PROVISIONAL CONSTITUTIONAL ORDER

The day Mujib returned to Dacca the government released the text of a Provisional Constitutional Order, which created the Constituent Assembly consisting of the representatives elected to the national and provisional assemblies in December 1970 and January 1971 and in the by-elections of March 1971.[3] Some elected members were later disqualified on legal grounds. For example, Nurul Amin, leader of the Democratic Front, was excluded because he had favored a united

Pakistan. No date was set for the first meeting of the Constituent Assembly.

The order replaced the presidential system by parliamentary government. The simple and literal justification for parliamentary rule, called for in the manifesto of 1970, was stated in the preamble of the order: "It is the manifest aspiration of the people of Bangladesh that parliamentary democracy shall function in Bangladesh." The political structure outlined in the order was modeled on the British parliamentary system, or, as some call it, the cabinet form of government. Mujib believed, at least then, that the new nation should reaffirm its political ties to the past.

A figurehead president was empowered to exercise "authority" on the advice of a prime minister who was supported by a majority of the members of the Constituent Assembly. Under the terms of the order President Sheikh Mujib swore in Justice A. M. Sayem as chief justice of the Supreme Court and thereupon resigned as president to take the post of prime minister.

Justice A. S. Chowdhury, ex–vice-chancellor of Dacca University, was named president. Mujib juggled the portfolios of the provisional government and gave himself four ministries: defense, home affairs, information and broadcasting, and cabinet affairs. He established 14 new ministries, which he filled with Awami League politicians previously elected to the National Assembly and their cronies. Three top permanent administrative officials were drawn from the ranks of former East Pakistani civil servants. Mujib gave no political plums to the Mukti Bahini, the guerrilla fighters, or to other established political parties. Nor did he include a military man in his cabinet. The Awami Leaguers who made up the cabinet represented a broad span of personal ambitions and of ideologies from right to left. President Choudhury stood close to the center.

THE CONSTITUTION OF 1972

The new government authorized a Constitutional Assembly to prepare a permanent fundamental law. The leadership of the Awami League, aware of the political difficulties that had arisen from the years of delay in adopting a constitution for Pakistan and confident that they commanded a considerable majority in the Constitutional Assembly, tried to speed the adoption of the document. To the surprise of league members, a draft document that they publicly circulated during the spring and summer of 1972 was criticized in the league's own ranks, by the press, and by left-wing politicians, each of them seeking to incorporate their conflicting ideological views into the Constitution.

The publication of the final document was delayed, ostensibly for consultations with legal authorities in India and Great Britain on technical matters and on account of the illness of Mujib. Finally adopted by the assembly at the end of October, the Constitution did not go into full force until December 16, 1972. It was not submitted to popular vote, perhaps in order to avoid a head-on collision with the left.

A long document of 83 pages, the Constitution created a parliamentary system comparable to the governments of India and Great Britain.[4] A president elected by a simple majority of an elective parliament was empowered to act in accordance with the advice of the prime minister, also an elected official (elected to Parliament by popular vote in a constituency and then named to the ministry by a majority in Parliament). The members of the 300-seat National Assembly (Jatyo Sangsad) were to be elected at least every five years by the universal suffrage of citizens more than 18 years of age. Fifteen additional seats were reserved for women to be elected by the sitting members of Parliament. An independent judiciary was also provided for.

The sections on fundamental principles and rights were written in language reminiscent of the Universal Declaration of Human Rights of the United Nations. However, these rights could be restricted by broad emergency powers, traditional in South Asian law. The emergency provisions gave the government authority to issue orders, notwithstanding the enumerated rights, "if the president is satisfied that circumstances exist which render immediate action necessary." The fundamental rights articles on freedom of the press, assembly, speech, association, and religion, too, were subject to restrictions "imposed by law in the interests of public order, decency or morality."

The day the National Assembly adopted the Constitution, the prime minister, his cabinet, and the chief justice of the Supreme Court were sworn into office. Two days later the 11-judge high court began functioning. The government was in full swing.

THE WAR'S LEGACY

Despite the exhilaration of independence, the vast problems plaguing the nation would take a long time to bring under control. The most immediate emergency, the need for relief supplies, was the most easily managed. According to preliminary estimates by Bangali economists, the country needed $3 billion to restore the war-devastated economy to the level of prewar standards.[5] The repair and reconstruction of transportation and communications, factories and power would be the most costly of these expenses. Another half-billion dollars, they esti-

Jute factory.

mated, was required to feed, shelter, and employ returning refugees and the war's homeless.

A United Nations report on conditions in Bangladesh at the beginning of 1972 concluded that the level of commercial, industrial, and other economic activities had probably fallen as much as 50 percent below the lowest figures for 1970 and that agricultural production had declined 25 percent. The Mujib government had virtually no foreign exchange, no overseas credit facilities, and wholly inadequate domestic financial resources.

The rapid return from India of the Bangali refugees, Hindu and Muslim, immediately after the war was insisted upon by the Indian government, which had spent millions of its own money in relief assistance in addition to sums given by other countries of the United Nations. The Hindu refugees, too, were unwilling to stay in India because that government required them to live in non-Bengali-speaking areas. By March 1972 nearly all of the refugees had returned, only to be greeted by lack of housing, scarcity of food, and unemployment.

The Bangalis living in the war zones were most numerous and their plight even more serious than that of the refugees. The survivors found their homes demolished, their property stolen, and their women raped. It had been nearly impossible to work amid military operations. The people of Dacca, Chittagong, and other cities and towns were badly off because most of the war was fought in and around those areas.

Power plants and factories were out of operation, although the factories, on the whole, fared better than other installations because

Pakistani troops had protected them and the guerrillas had concentrated their attacks on port and rail facilities.

EMERGENCY RELIEF

The new government arranged for relief. The war's disruption of the transportation and communications network for a time threatened to cause famine in many parts of the country, but the United Nations began monthly shipments of 200,000 tons of rice and wheat and airlifted food into areas that were otherwise inaccessible. Mujib asked aid-giving countries for building materials to replace the more than one million houses destroyed during the war; two and one-half million people, he said, were left without shelter.[6] He also requested that cash be given to refugees returning without possessions and to the millions of other Bangalis set adrift throughout the country.

His top priority after food and shelter was the restoration of the devastated transportation[7] and communications system. Relief operations, initially frustrated by mines and sunken hulks in Chittagong and Chalna harbors, before the war handled about six million tons of cargo, more than three million tons of which were food grains. During the first several months of 1972 relief carriers could not bring in supplies, nor could the ports be used for the limited available quantities of export jute and tea that earned precious foreign exchange. The ports were gradually cleared by a Russian salvage team of technical experts using specialized equipment.

To meet the internal transportation problems, the government in April took over the motor vehicles left behind by the Pakistani army and arranged to auction them off to replace the many vehicles damaged by the war. The strong rickshaw union got the government to sell the vehicles to private purchasers.

The railroads, which normally carried some 60 percent of the traffic to and from the ports, during the first several months of 1972 transported only 10 percent of the waiting loads because of war damage to tracks and railroad cars. With each passing month the percentage increased, and by the end of 1973 near-normal operations were resumed. The early restoration of the Indian rail link with the western border of Bangladesh made it possible to use Calcutta as a transshipping port.

The United Nations, many countries, and numerous foreign private relief agencies, both religious and secular, poured in relief assistance during 1972 and 1973.[8] As many as 72 foreign relief groups, including U.N. agencies, contributed to what observers considered the largest single and most successful emergency relief endeavor of our times. They assisted Bangali agencies in reconstructing homes, digging irrigation canals, rebuilding roads, sinking tube wells, and supplying medical delivery. The emergency was far from over by the end of the first summer, but the most crucial problem, that of saving lives and restoring confidence in the ability of the Bangalis to survive, had been accomplished.

The United States initially gave $35 million to the United Nations Relief Organization in Dacca to help break transportation bottlenecks, buy cargo-handling equipment and trucks, and charter inland waterway vessels. After the United States recognized the new government it established a relief and rehabilitation office of the Agency for International Development in Dacca. Its program included supplying of food, cash, and funds to build schools and other public facilities. By August 1972 the United States had contributed $267.5 million to the Bangalis' humanitarian needs.

When the United Nations relief program was terminated at the end of 1973, the world organization had given Bangladesh $1.3 billion in aid since 1971, of which $451 million had come from the United States. The official reason for the conclusion of the relief program was that severe droughts in Africa had to be dealt with. The expectation of better crops in Bangladesh may also have influenced its decision to withdraw. Francis Lacoste, chief of the U.N. relief body, said on his departure from Dacca that 40 percent of the aid funds on hand had yet to be expended. Other United Nations agencies continued the work begun.

GUNMEN AND SMUGGLERS

Within a week of his return to Dacca Mujib undertook to disarm the thousands of Bangali guerrillas. He flattered the Mukti Bahini, referring publicly to their fighting prowess, and promised them posts in a militia to be organized to assist in relief and rehabilitation. In a dramatic ceremony in the hometown of Kader "Tiger" Siddiqui, head of the Mukti Bahini, he persuaded the Tiger to give up his army's weapons. He pledged to award Siddiqui's followers certificates of national service and jobs in the national security forces. Siddiqui himself was given an army post.

Guerrilla activity and the Mukti Bahini organization officially terminated on January 30, 1972, but dissident students of both right and left and some members of the Mukti Bahini, having acquired a taste for violence or having found that they could make a living with guns, managed to keep their arms. Arms that had been surrendered at public ceremonies or seized by police were picked up again. Illegal armed bands continued to operate during Mujib's rule and later. During Mujib's administration government and party officials were prime targets of the gunmen. Critics of the government told the foreign press that the murders were committed by private armed gangs with Awami League connections. Groups of revolutionaries, criminals, individuals bent on personal vengeance, and party factions were all implicated in the terror.[9]

Its separation from Pakistan made Bangladesh almost wholly dependent on India's good will and trade. Since India's rupee exchange rate was more favorable than that of the Bangalis' taka, established in January 1972, substantial amounts of Indian goods were exported to Bangladesh. The large quantities of cheap and inferior-quality products that were smuggled into Bangladesh profited only the merchants. High-quality Bangali jute, much preferred by Calcutta's mills over the home-grown fibers, was once more smuggled into India after years of decline in this illicit trade. Rice and other essentials, too, fell into the hands of smugglers.

The Mujib government launched a jawboning campaign against smuggling. Threats of prosecution and the imposition of severe penalties were ineffective. Indian border police tried to limit the traffic, but their critics in Dacca maintained that New Delhi did not act vigorously enough. A June 28, 1972, agreement with India restricted border trade to foodstuffs and building materials in order to assure larger supplies of these products in Bangladesh and to stop the smuggling of shoddy goods. Contingents of the Bangali army, assigned to border duty to enforce the agreement, had little immediate effect on illegal transactions.

HOARDING AND BLACK MARKETING

In the immediate postwar period scarce food supplies, slack administration, and corrupt practices created serious social and economic problems for the government.[10] In one of his earliest messages to the nation Sheikh Mujib had issued a solemn warning against hoarding and black marketing in Indian rupees. The chaotic economic conditions of the first half of 1972 continued. On June 7, in a speech commemorating the sixth anniversary of the six-point manifesto, the prime minister warned hoarders that strong action would be taken against them if they failed to change their ways by June 22. Searches would be undertaken to unearth hoards of essential commodities and illegal arms. He also announced that force would be used to evict unauthorized occupants of abandoned houses and that the government would create 4,200 fair-price shops in an effort to reduce prevailing high prices for necessities. Mujib made good on his promise and on his threat. On June 22 about 40,000 policemen and Rakkhi Bahini (Mujib's national guard) began a mass drive against the possession of illegal goods, arms, and their purchasers and sellers. Cars were stopped at intersections and their contents, as well as the papers of their occupants, thoroughly examined. By the fall of 1972 more normal living conditions were apparent to foreigners arriving in Dacca. However, inflation, shortages of consumer goods, hoarding, and black marketing lasted throughout Mujib's regime.

Beyond emergency relief and the disruptions of the market, engineered by selfish interests and compounded by the fears of consumers, the formidable problems of planning and reconstructing the entire economic base of the nation had to be dealt with. To this challenge Mujib's government had ready-made answers—as it turned out, too many, too ready answers.

CHAPTER 9

Economic Policies and Programs, 1972

In the midst of its relief and rehabilitation endeavors, Mujib's government initiated programs for the upgrading of industry and agriculture that it hoped would bring a better life to the people. Aside from party politics, economic planning became the chief domestic preoccupation of the regime. Influenced by Mujib's economic policies, enunciated in the manifesto of 1970, and by the promptings of young intellectuals seeking an early break with the traditional economy of the country, the government nationalized the industry and commerce of the nation. They also initiated land, tax, and other agricultural reforms to which they had long been committed.

Mujib, moving swiftly to follow up on nationalization, appointed a central planning council composed of eager, experienced, trained economists to formulate plans aimed at balancing the national economic accounts. But the public ownership of key industries did not yield the economic benefits anticipated by the planners. Political interference in industrial and trade operations and a lack of competent managers, among other obstacles, foiled the planners. Sheikh Mujib, without giving up the goal of socialism, gradually enlarged the scope of private industry. Socialist planning, which began with enthusiasm, was modified when it became evident that plans did not match political and economic realities and the planners realized their programs were not being taken seriously. Sizable loans from United Nations organizations and from western nations kept the economy afloat. The insistence of the creditors on better economic performance and Bangali dissatisfaction with the operations of public enterprises convinced Mujib that he should take personal control of the economy. His political troubles finally led him to authoritarian rule.

116

SOCIALISM

The adoption of socialism, urged by doctrinaire socialists among Awami Leaguers and by partisan sympathizers of India and the Soviet Union, was also hastened by the dearth of private Bangali capital and industrial expertise as well as by the nation's inability to borrow in international private money markets.[1]

More importantly, economic relations between East and West Pakistan had made it impossible to attract and train any substantial number of Bangali industrialists. Among the 22 richest families of Pakistan only one was a Bangali. Industrial ownership in East Pakistan had been either in the hands of the wealthy West Pakistanis or of Bangali proprietors of small industries. Only about 11 percent of the total industrial assets of Pakistan were located in the east. The Bangali business community consisted of a small contingent of middle-class townsmen, a segment of the educated middle class that did not go into government service.

The socialist policy decisions of 1972 were foreshadowed in Part II of the Awami League manifesto of 1970, entitled "Fundamentals of the Economic Programme," which opened with the statement, "The basic aim of this economic programme is the creation of a just and egalitarian society free from exploitation. The vision is that of a socialist economic order." To meet the objectives of the new order, the manifesto stated, it is necessary "to nationalize the key sectors of the economy and to ensure the future development in the key areas in the public sectors." The document's list of priorities for nationalization included banking, insurance, heavy industries, foreign trade, and transportation.

The manifesto also demanded the alteration of tax structures to ensure a higher proportion of tax revenues from direct taxes rather than indirect ones, which burden the ordinary man. It called for a study of the feasibility of worker participation in ownership and management; insisted on the right of workers to bargain collectively and to strike; favored multipurpose cooperatives and demanded flood control measures. It proposed public support for education at all levels, technical training, and an attack on illiteracy.

The manifesto of 1970 became the cultural and economic Magna Carta of the new government. By the time Mujib had finished six months in office, hardly a sentence in the document had been acted upon legislatively. Experienced and talented personnel prepared the legislation, but in the absence of experienced business leaders and skilled workmen, party leaders and their followers interpreted and administered the laws to suit their private interests.

Awami Bangalis generally agreed with the observation of Professor Papanek, a member of the Harvard advisory group to Pakistan in the fifties, that the first Pakistani industrial entrepreneurs were "robber barons," but they rejected his claim that the operations of the barons were necessary to the development of the country or that the later generation of feisty trader-industrialists improved the well-being of the nation.[2] They looked on themselves as victims not only of the robber barons but also of the more genteel, sophisticated, and ingenious West Pakistani industrialists. It was an article of their faith that the private enterprise economy of presidents Ayub and Yahya, supported by U.S. aid, did not contribute to the fair distribution of the nation's wealth.

University students dedicated to radicalism, members of communist organizations, and individuals affiliated with the Awami League insisted on socialism as an ideological must. To their dismay the nation's foreign economic policy allowed the acceptance of assistance from any source, suggesting that domestic economic politics would follow a middle track. Moderate Bangalis, opposed on religious or ideological grounds to socialist politics of the Soviet Union type, awaited a more propitious time to express their misgivings.

NATIONALIZATION

The socialist enterprise took legal shape in March 1972 with the announcement of a series of nationalization orders.[3] The banks were the first to feel the winds of socialization. Existing banks (all Pakistani owned), which were promised compensation in the amount of the total paid-up value of shares held by the stockholders, were acquired by the newly established Bank of Bangladesh. Another order nationalized insurance companies. A third vested all properties of the former East Pakistani government in the Bangladesh government. The privately owned East Pakistan Shipping Corporation and the Pakistan River and Steamers Company were assimilated into a Bangali Inland Waterways Transport Corporation, a government agency itself, taken over from the government of Pakistan. Other firms operating in inland waters, owned by West Pakistani companies and by the Pakistani government and registered earlier under an Abandoned Property Order, were transferred to the government as abandoned and absentee owners' property of substantial value.

Two days later the Industrial Enterprises Nationalization Order gave the government the right to acquire certain industrial enterprises and to establish public corporations similar to those in Great Britain, which would coordinate and supervise the nationalized enterprises rather than manage them; compensation was to be made for the takeovers. A detailed schedule attached to the order nationalized jute and cotton textile plants and sugar mills. At the end of 1972 the government announced that 85 percent of the nation's industries had been nationalized.

Once the decrees were issued, Mujib asked the former Pakistani proprietors and executives of the nationalized enterprises to manage the property on behalf of the new owners. His appeal was indignantly ignored, and the jobs were taken by Mujib's followers.

Controversies within the government with respect to the place of private industry and foreign investment delayed the announcement of an official policy until January 1973.[4] Private investment in medium-size and small industries with a maximum capital of two and a half million takas ($350,000) was to be permitted for ten years, but the government had the authority to acquire a private industry if it was mismanaged. Foreign private enterprises were subject to 51 percent government participation; foreign holders of licenses and patents were given the right to remit their earnings and were guaranteed that their capital would not be subject to double taxation. An investment board, headed by the minister of industries, was authorized to control foreign investments.

The new industrial policy encouraged limited private small-scale and cottage industries by providing government funds and technical assistance. Other domestic private industries regarded as critically important, such as certain food-processing plants, agriculturally related plants, and pharmaceutical producers, were left intact.

The inability of nationalized enterprises to reach even modest production goals and the realization that the 1973 regulations did not allow for sufficient private capital investments induced Mujib in July 1974 to increase the domestic private investment ceiling from $350,000 to $4 million and to grant private enterprise greater tax benefits. The minister of industries said increases in the ceiling were made because of the high costs of land, building, and machinery suitable for setting up any sizable industrial plant. A new schedule of private industrial priorities was issued. Partnerships between private foreign and domestic enterprises were permitted for the first time.

The U.S. government's Overseas Private Investment Corporation (OPIC) reached an agreement with the Mujib government in January 1975 that enabled U.S. investors to receive U.S. government insurance coverage and other services of the corporation in order to encourage their investments. The Bangalis expressed their interest in U.S. financing of agribusiness and export-oriented light industries. OPIC operations began during the regime of Mujib's successor, Zia.

PLANNING

A closer look at Mujib's planning exercises throws light on the nature and range of the economic problems imperiling the nation.[5] His planning commission prepared a plan for 1972–73 that earmarked funds for the completion of projects included in Pakistan's unrealized fourth five-year plan for 1970–75. The latter plan had designated its largest expenditures in East Pakistan for agriculture, transportation, and communications. Mujib's planning commission in its 1972–73 plan over-optimistically projected the elimination of the nation's food deficit by 1975. Although the commission's members could not have foreseen the devastating floods of 1974, they erred in counting too heavily on the export potential of jute, tea, fish, and paper products. Substantial declines in the export of these commodities dashed their hopes for the development of the country's industrial base and worsened employment problems in agriculture and industry.

At a press conference in November 1973, members of the planning commission attributed declines in the economy to high levels of inflation in 1973, transportation bottlenecks, the underuse of import licenses, and international rises in prices on imported goods, as well as the weakness of the export earnings. They admitted, too, that the nationalized sector of the economy had performed poorly and suggested that decision making in the nationalized industries be decentralized. They advocated management training and guarantees of management incentives to improve industrial performance. They also noted that the statistical and other data available to them had been insufficient to meet their planning needs.

Nonetheless, the planning commission produced both a general first five-year plan for 1973–78 and a plan for the initial fiscal year, 1973–74. The plans conservatively emphasized economic revival rather than development. For the planners the scarcity of mass consumption goods, food, shelter, and clothing accentuated the need to increase their domestic production. Because improvements in waterways, transportation and communication, and industrial plants were essential to increased production, the planners allocated substantial funds to these projects.

A six-month delay in announcing the first five-year plan was indicative of the political controversies it stirred. The plan aimed at achieving an annual growth rate of 5.5 percent, to be accomplished by investing $7.5 billion during the five-year period, most of which was to go to the public sector. The intentions of the plan were laudable: to lower the prices of essential commodities, to concentrate on small-capital industrial programs in order that employment might be speedily increased, to reduce dependence on imports, to increase exports, and to continue reconstruction and the promotion of social goals in education, public health, and related fields.

The five-year plan's investment program was revised downward four months after its announcement because of price increases in oil and other imported products. A 50 percent reduction in the estimates of the 1974–75 plan caused its proposed expenditures to be cut back to the level of the previous year's plan. At the end of the 1973–74 period the commission made its second depressing report on the economy. It announced that available revenues were down about 25 percent and expenditures had been exceeded by 12 percent. The excess spending was attributed to the cost of moving Biharis to Pakistan and to pay raises for public officials. Consumer prices had increased 40 percent during the previous 12 months. A large deficit in the balance of payments was ascribed to the high price of imports.

In addition to inflation (which rose 120 percent from January 1972 to the end of 1973), a basic economic problem that plagued the economy was the low level of savings and investment. But inflation could not be controlled without savings and investment to step up farm and industrial production. The nationalized industries did not contribute to total production, nor did they yield surplus savings, because of poor management and corrupt practices by managers and staff. According to the critics of Sheikh Mujib, investable funds were draining out of the country into the banks of smugglers and other profiteers.

Mujib's planning advisors finally decided to abandon the five-year plan because increasing inflation had made it unrealistic. One by one, members of the planning commission quit their posts, disenchanted with the politicians, oppositionists, and bureaucrats and disappointed by their own lack of success. By the end of 1975 all of them had left the commission for university or research jobs in Bangladesh or elsewhere.

Mujib's acquisition of sole governmental authority early in 1975 made it possible for him personally to control industry. Meanwhile, he planned local administrative reforms to carry out his agricultural policies at ground level. He seemed to believe that this "revolution" would accomplish what the rational planning of his young economists failed to do.

LABOR POLICY

The labor movement in East Pakistan had been weak, corrupt, divided, and without significant influence on West Pakistani employers in the area.[6] However, during the period immediately preceding independence the workers joined in political agitation. On the heels of independence labor unrest became a way of life, especially when the workers were led by communist partisans. Union leaders, split by factionalism, were unable to control their membership. The government, although favorably disposed to labor, had no better luck.

In the fall of 1972 the minister for labor announced a policy he hoped would restore calm and increase productivity. A national wage board was set up to review wages and benefits in nationalized industries, and a productivity council was established to study and encourage the use of improved technologies. Industrial unions were encouraged, but contrary to the promises of the 1970 manifesto were not given collective bargaining powers in the nationalized industries. The top management board of each nationalized industry included two representatives each from labor and management, along with one member from a government financial institution. Worker participation did not please labor's leftist critics, nor did it improve the operations of industry. A separate joint management and workers' management council was established to settle labor disputes, subject to final decision by a labor court.

The labor policy of 1972 proscribed more than one union per industry and industry-wide collective bargaining. The unions, tied to divergent political parties, favored the British pattern of multiple unions and plant-by-plant collective bargaining. Union members in government industries refused to serve on management boards as long as single-union representation was required. Meanwhile, in the private sector, which was not bound by the labor policy, a variety of unions bargained individually with employers. In December 1973 an unhappy Mujib said he blamed the labor force in government enterprises for the current low level of production. The workers, he warned, needed discipline and training.

When Mujib attempted to take control of the economy in 1975, he addressed himself to the problems of unemployment and underemployment, estimated at a total of 30 percent of the work force. Moreover, 800,000 new workers were said to be entering the labor market each year. Mujib proposed to give work to the largest portion of those numbers by developing compulsory agricultural cooperatives, as well as investing further in the public and private sectors of industry. His 1975 "revolution" did not last long enough to test these ideas.

FOREIGN TRADE AND AID

Foreign trade, indispensable to an export economy such as that of Bangladesh, was placed under government control by Mujib. A federal trading corporation was assigned the responsibility of establishing minimum required quantities for essential imports and the licensing of importers of these goods. At first import licenses were issued only to private traders because the corporation was not organized to engage in trade. Favored businessmen and politicians were granted licenses in lucrative enterprises. The nation's trade deficits increased markedly through 1975, even though exports rose.[7] Foodstuffs and development capital required sizable external financing, as they had under Pakistan's rule.

On August 18, 1972, Bangladesh became a member of the International Monetary Fund (IMF) and the World Bank.[8] At the same time it joined the International Development Association (IDA), which enabled the country to obtain loans at low interest rates. Since its foreign reserves were depleted, the quotas for Bangladesh's deposits in the IMF and subscriptions to the lending agency were met in part out of its borrowings from other sources. In 1973 the IDA made 12 loans to Bangladesh— a total of about $221 million in long-term, easy credit arrangements. The funds were used to improve the water supplies of Dacca and Chittagong and to underwrite engineering studies for flood control and highway construction projects. Each year since then the IDA has financed other projects for Bangladesh.

Improvements in the economic prospects of the nation came from other quarters, too. Sheikh Mujib initiated political and economic connections with the Arab states. After the 1973 oil embargo the Arabs began to make loans to the Bangalis. Also, in spite of nationalistic misgivings about conferring with a consortium of western aid-giving countries, Mujib consented to a meeting with the European and U.S. group under the chairmanship of the World Bank to evaluate the nation's economic performance and to assess its need for aid. Between the fiscal years 1972/73 and 1975/76 Bangladesh received $2.86 billion from the Arabs, most of it in the latter years.

The financial aid Bangladesh received from the other countries and from international agencies rescued the new nation from sinking of its own weight. Most of the assistance had to be used for relief and rehabilitation rather than for investment. By mid-1975 the economy was slowly disentangling itself from a web of political and economic misfortunes and mistakes.

AGRICULTURE

The struggle of peasants to increase farm production made little progress during the Mujib regime. Actions taken by the government to revise landholding laws, obtain tax relief for landholders, and solve the gnawing problem of the landless were inconclusive. Reforms in the cooperative programs undertaken in the fifties failed, except in Comilla. Dissatisfied with his campaign to spur voluntary cooperatives, Mujib resolved to make them compulsory, but he failed to reckon with the character of the peasant, who was willing to accept advice and help but was hostile to political control. The rural works program for road construction and waterway improvements, inaugurated with the help of the Americans in the sixties, was reinstituted by Mujib with funds obtained from the United Nations and from bilateral national aid programs.

Landownership

Few economic problems in agricultural societies are more intractable than that of landownership.[9] Bangali attempts to wrestle with it were only partially successful. A look at the history of landholding and of legislation aimed at equalizing holdings reveals the bafflements of the problem.

Cultivable land covers two-thirds of the area of Bangladesh, that is, about 23 million acres. According to the latest available data, 80 percent of the population are engaged in agriculture and nearly 90 percent live in rural areas. The people have relocated to the cities more slowly than in most countries, partly because of poverty, the sluggish pace of industrialization, and the attachment of the Bangalis to the soil.

The disorders of 1964 and 1970 and the war of 1971 did not change the basic pattern of rural life. In 1969 agriculture accounted for 61 percent of East Pakistan's National Domestic Product—the highest percentage of any Asian nation, and almost 12 percent higher than mainland China's. Today more than 50 percent of Bangladesh's cultivated acreage is on farms of 2.5 acres or less, and the largest farms are seldom more than 40 acres. The wide dispersal of farms owned by a single landholder poses an additional problem for an agriculture dependent on benign monsoon rains.

The East Bengal State Acquisition and Tenancy Act of 1951 had limited landholdings to 33 acres per family and 3.3 acres in a homestead area. Outstanding rents owed by the cultivator to the government and intermediary rent collectors were rescinded by the act. Provision was made for the consolidation of small landholdings and restrictions were placed on the further fragmentation of the land. Landlords were to be compensated for land taken over by the government. Rents paid to the government by tenants were fixed at varying levels for different types of land.

The fulfillment of the law moved so slowly that it was not until March 1956 that the government announced the provisions of the act would be "immediately" applied and details of compensation arranged later. A revenue commission appointed in 1958 and a land administration enquiry commission established in 1962 investigated the legal and administrative problems of land acquisition. The enquiry commission recommended, and the government legislated, the maximum farm size at 125 acres; land and buildings in rural marketplaces were to be restored to their former owners. The absence of adequate records seriously delayed the carrying out of the law. Each of the districts had to be surveyed in order to determine ownership—a process slowed down by innumerable conflicts of interest.

The Awami League and its supporters planned to equalize farm holdings and to subsidize farm laborers. The ceiling on family holdings, fixed by the Acquisition and Tenancy Act of 1951, was modified in 1972 to limit individual as well as family holdings to 33 acres. Promises were also made to reduce the number of rich peasants. In the fall of 1972 the government began to distribute 400,000 acres of public land to landless peasants. Each landless family was to be given one and one-half acres; additional acres were alloted to cooperative farmers. But these measures hardly made a dent in the landholding problem.

Mujib met the peasants' complaint of excessive tax burdens by exempting landlords having less than 8.3 acres from payment of land taxes and accumulated arrears and by abolishing payments on peasant loans of 100 takas or less along with excise taxes on salt. Improved irrigation, the provision of seed, fertilizer, and insecticides, and credit arrangements were promised. But the elimination of land taxes produced a steep decline in government revenues not readily replaceable by taxes on other sources of revenue. Mujib's critics suggested it was time to tax profitable farms in the range of 3 to 8.3 acres.

Mujib's land reforms were criticized by socialist and nonsocialist economists and politicians. The 33-acre ceiling was attacked on the grounds that from 7 to 15 percent of rural families were completely landless and that the average 2.5 acres per farm was too high. It was pointed out that 80 percent of the land was held by peasants with farms larger than the average. For this reason and because employment and output inversely related to farm size, maximum landownership should be reduced to 8 acres, critics said. Mujib's challengers also claimed that bureaucrats, politicians, and professional people had become absentee owners of profitable farms.

Land reformers fall into two broad groups: those favoring small family farms and those preferring cooperatives. There is also a division among the advocates of cooperatives: some wish to strengthen voluntary cooperatives and others advocate compulsory cooperatives. Critics of Mujib's compulsory plan argued that it would perpetuate the basic inequalities of existing landownership by allowing Mujib's political friends to retain their large holdings.

Akter Hameed Khan, director of the Comilla Academy, in 1969 inaugurated a voluntary program to transform the peasant community of Comilla.[10] He established a multipurpose village cooperative to assist the peasant's use of mechanical farm equipment for power pump irrigation, to promote personal savings, literacy, and domestic hygiene, and to train village leaders in the management of these programs. In addition, American experts employed by the U.S. aid mission gave peasants instruction in U.S.-style farm extension work. U.S. Peace Corps volunteers, working with Akter Hameed, made striking contributions to the Comilla community as they did elsewhere in the countryside.

But the government of East Pakistan made slow progress in extending this type of cooperative to other parts of the country. New farm cooperatives found it difficult to recruit competent and dedicated persons to work in isolated communities. The breakdown of farm credit supervision and an exhausting debate on the scope of cooperatives' activities also stalemated their operations.

Rural Public Works

The government of Sheikh Mujib welcomed the idea of a rural works program, which had been initiated in 1962 in East Pakistan with U.S. aid. President Kennedy's Food for Peace program had authorized proceeds from the sale of U.S. export grains to be used in foreign countries for public works.[11] The government of Pakistan used the funds to pay landless workers to build or improve roads and irrigation ditches. The East Pakistan program employed thousands of workers and made significant improvements. Harvard University economic advisors to the Pakistani government had proposed the program and assisted in its administration.

Mujib gave the program a new title—Food for Work. In 1972 not only the United States but also United Nations agencies supplied foodstuffs to support projects. During the Zia years construction workers on canals and embankments in distressed areas were paid in food and cash. Foreign volunteer agencies also undertook Food for Work projects with the proceeds from grain purchases made by donors of the agencies. The program has been continued with an emphasis on the construction of culverts to aid in flood control. The immediate benefits of the program are widely acknowledged, but critics allege that in the long run it discourages self-reliant agricultural development.

WATER RESOURCES

The rivers, the living arteries of Bangladesh, provide water for drinking (if properly boiled), for transportation, and for crops.[12] The people depend for their food on the fickle ways of the monsoon. During the monsoon season the heavy rains swelling the Ganges, Brahmaputra, and Meghna rivers and their tributaries produce floods estimated to be comparable in volume to those of the Amazon. The *aus*, or early rice crop, is in serious trouble if the monsoon is late, that is, after June; the *aman*, or later crop, is hurt if the monsoon finishes early.

The irrigation of either crop can increase production as much as 100 percent. The *boro*, or spring crop, planted during the winter dry season, requires irrigation. Even though the rainfall in any area is 100 inches a year, during intermittent dry periods farmers must resort to irrigation for all food and cash crops.

By the middle of the sixties several large irrigation projects—the Ganges-Kobadak, Testa, and Dacca-Demrya—in the east-central part of the country were in partial operation. At the same time many other irrigation schemes using low-lift pumps were connected with the canals that pierce the countryside. In the past decade pumps, owned by farmers or rented from the original and reorganized Agricultural Development Corporation, have been increasingly employed. Tube wells, too, have been put into operation.

An India-Bangladesh Joint Rivers Commission was established by Sheikh Mujib and Mrs. Gandhi at their March 1972 summit meeting in Dacca. At the end of June the commission held its first meeting to consider development programs for the Ganges-Brahmaputra, whose headwaters are controlled by India. The commission also considered possible short- and long-term measures to reduce flood dangers to the region, and its members arranged to meet every few months. Both India and Bangladesh agreed for different reasons that the Farraka Barrage, being built on the Indian side of the Ganges close to the border of Bangladesh, merited special attention. Construction of the barrage, originally planned decades before, was started in 1955 to increase the flow of Ganges water into the Hooghly River, the westernmost channel of the Ganges delta that empties into the Bay of Bengal. Increased flow in the Hooghly would reduce or eliminate the silting of that river, which had gradually curtailed shipping into Calcutta. The Bangalis, however, believed that the barrage would diminish the flow of Ganges water into their country during the dry season. Following a compromise that lessened the amount of Ganges water to be diverted to the Hooghly, the barrage was dedicated in June 1975.

A comprehensive plan for regional water control, envisaged in a United Nations survey of November 1972, proposed the linkage of the major rivers of India in order to irrigate most of the regions of the subcontinent, including Bangladesh. The plan was estimated to cost $4 billion and take 25 years to complete, but it was never funded because of disagreements over its merit. After the issuance of the report the Bangalis turned their attention to a more comprehensive regional plan, which requires Nepal to build dams in its territory and China to consent to the use of the Brahmaputra, whose waters originate there.

CHAPTER 10

Foreign Relations Within the Subcontinent, 1971–75

South Asia includes seven nations. From east to west, they are Bangladesh, Bhutan, Nepal, India, Sri Lanka, Pakistan, and Afghanistan. Bangladesh, India, and Pakistan, occupying the preponderant part of the subcontinent, are contiguous and together are known as the South Asian Triangle. The size of the triangle's population is second only to that of China.[1] Each nation of the triangle is obliged by geopolitical realities to somehow get along with the others in order to preserve its national identity. The independence of Bangladesh, severed from Pakistan and virtually surrounded by India, made its foreign relations with these countries a matter of profound concern to the Dacca government.

As long as East Pakistan was ruled from West Pakistan, the public in Bengal had been little concerned with foreign affairs or foreign policy. However, by one of the paradoxes of the history of Pakistan, two Bangali politicians, Mohammad Ali Bogra and H. S. Suhrawardy, influenced the earliest initiatives of Pakistan in foreign affairs and steered its foreign policy in directions favorable to the interests of the United States and the West. Both briefly prime ministers of Pakistan, Ali Bogra and Suhrawardy shared a world view substantially different from the provincial outlook of Bangali peasants and the majority of the home-oriented leaders of the Muslim and Awami leagues.

Insofar as foreign policy found a voice in East Pakistan, the utterances were neutralist.[2] The Bangalis were not wrought up over Kashmir, an area remote to them. Their antimilitary sentiments, strengthened by opposition to the military posture of West Pakistanis, inclined them toward a nonalignment policy. The principal exceptions to neutralist

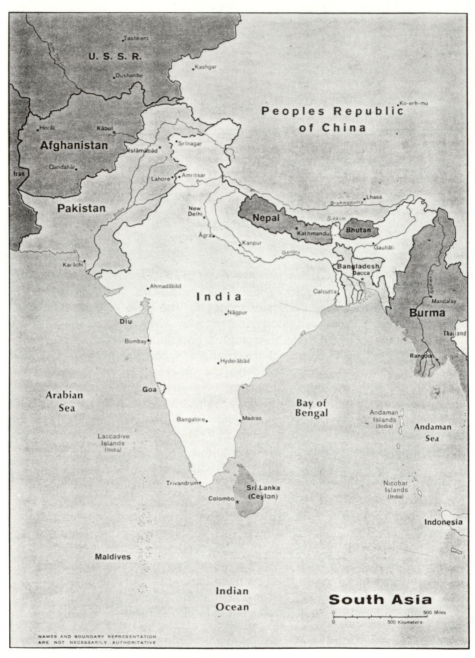

Map 4. The South Asian subcontinent

thinking were expressed by leftist students belonging to pro-Peking and pro-Moscow factions and by the followers of the maverick Maulana Bhashani.

The regional repercussions provoked by the separation of Bangladesh from Pakistan affected Bangali foreign policies as well as domestic affairs. The immediate postwar problems of the two countries, which revolved around the intervention of India, made India a partner in Bangladesh's postwar activities and deeply affected the course of relations in the South Asian Triangle. Extended tripartite negotiations over the repatriation of 90,000 Pakistani POWs held in India and the resolution of war crimes charges against Pakistani officers, although marred by heated propaganda exchanges, eventually produced accommodations acceptable to the three countries. Bangali differences with Pakistan over Biharis remaining in Bangladesh and Bangalis held in Pakistan, as well as the division of Bangali-Pakistani prewar financial assets and obligations, were partially patched up. The travail of these negotiations came to an end with the grudging recognition of Bangladesh by Pakistan and the initiation of economic relations.

INDIA AND PAKISTAN

In the weeks following the surrender of the Pakistani army in Dacca, relations between Pakistan and India were openly unfriendly. However, by March 1972 President Bhutto, in a spirit of conciliation, declared that he wanted a rapprochement with India on matters of deep concern to Pakistan, especially about the prisoners of war.[3] He insisted, however, that the Kashmir issue—the perennial Pakistani hang-up—not be discussed until overall relations with India improved. He said he favored an end to the fighting in Kashmir, a resumption of diplomatic ties, and cooperation in economic and communication matters, such as air freight flights and the installation of radio, television, and telephone lines. The first summit meeting between Bhutto and Mrs. Gandhi took place at Simla, an Indian hill town, on June 28, 1972.[4] The two governments had ordered an end to the fighting in the Kashmir region to permit the planned talks to go on.

The meeting opened with mutual expressions of hope for "a new beginning" but quickly turned to old grievances. The Indians demanded that Pakistan not rearm with foreign aid because India had no aggressive intentions against Pakistan. The Pakistanis defended their need for foreign military aid on the grounds that India made its own weapons and bought arms from the Soviet Union and that they had to be able to defend themselves against the threat of Indian aggression. Fortunately, the discussions did not go on in this ill-tempered manner.

On July 3 a limited agreement was reached calling for mutual troop withdrawals from the Kashmir area, the eventual resumption of diplomatic relations, and the renunciation of the use of force in the settlement of disputes. Talks on the repatriation of POWs and on land-sea commerce were promised for a later date.

The Indian press hailed the Simla Declaration as a momentous transformation of relationships in the subcontinent but warned that a long, hard road to peace lay ahead.[5] Many Indians felt that the agreement crowned the triumph of the war of 1971.

Prior to the meetings there had been some apprehension in Bangladesh that India might make untoward concessions to President Bhutto. Mujib had said that he must be consulted on the POW issue and on his government's right to try war criminals. Later, however, several Bangali papers hailed the Simla agreement as a triumph of reason. The U.S. press saw the agreement as evidence of good sense on the part of Bhutto and Mrs. Gandhi. Much of the comment was favorable to India. Mrs. Gandhi, it was noted, did not try to dictate a one-sided settlement in spite of the fact that she negotiated from strength.

BANGLADESH AND PAKISTAN

Mutual recriminations about the treatment of Biharis living in Bangladesh and of Bangalis detained in Pakistan was one factor that embittered the relations between the two countries. The war had worsened relations between Bengali-speaking and Urdu-speaking Muslims. Urdu-speaking Bihari guerrillas were blamed for the massacre of 125 Bangali professionals and intellectuals on December 14, 1971.[6] Immediately after the war, vengeful Bangali agitators, supported by a group of young Mukti Bahini, publicly tortured and killed four Biharis suspected of supporting the Pakistani army. The atrocious executions at the Dacca racecourse were photographed and spread across the front pages of the world press. In March 1972, Bangalis attacked Biharis living in Khulna, leaving hundreds of them dead or injured, according to foreign news reports. Mujib, upset by the incident, sent a telegram to the secretary-general of the Islamic secretariat (the executive staff of the Organization of the Islamic Conference, based in Jidda, Saudi Arabia), stating that the life and property of non-Bangalis were secure in spite of the Biharis' provocations. In May Mujib repeated his assurances regarding the safety of the Biharis, adding that many of them had returned to their former jobs. More than 2,000 Biharis were reemployed to operate the railroads when untrained Bangalis failed to run the trains properly. The following month the prime minister labeled as a brazen lie the Pakistani government's complaint that Biharis were being attacked and killed and noted that he had tried unsuccessfully to exchange Biharis who wanted to go to Pakistan for the several hundred thousand Bangalis stranded there.

The Red Cross posted teams at the principal points where Biharis lived to halt sporadic violence. The organization informed the governments of India, Pakistan, and Bangladesh that it would facilitate the exchange of Bangalis in Pakistan for Biharis. The Dacca government accepted the offer, but Pakistan linked the exchange to other issues, such as the release of the POWs in India and the cancellation of the war trials of army officers.

A matter of anguish to the Bangalis and an impediment to recognition by Pakistan was the presence, after independence, of an estimated 400,000 Bangalis in West Pakistan. Most of them were working people, domestic servants, and farmers with their families; about 10,000 were members of the Pakistani armed forces or civil servants.[7]

The *New York Times* of April 17, 1972, reported that the government of Pakistan refused to issue exit permits to the Bangalis or to permit communications between Pakistan and Bangladesh and that thousands of Bangali families were without financial support. Sheikh Mujib, in a June meeting in Dacca on the occasion of the sixth anniversary of the six-point program, accused President Bhutto of trying to bargain over innocent people. A few months later Mujib stopped in Geneva on his return to Dacca from surgery and convalescence in London to discuss the plight of the Bangalis in Pakistan with the United Nations high commissioner for refugees and asked for help in assuring the safety of his separated countrymen.

In October the prime minister renewed his expressions of solicitude about "a rapidly deteriorating condition of the Bangalis" in Pakistan. In a letter to United Nations Secretary-General Kurt Waldheim, he sought the secretary's good offices to secure their rapid return. The letter reasserted that non-Bangalis were being treated equitably in his own country.

A Columbia Broadcasting System reporter, speaking from Karachi in November, said that Bangali civil servants had been forced into subsistence living. Although the government of Pakistan denied charges made to the United Nations that the Bangalis were facing hardships or persecution, the reporter cited cases in which, to his knowledge, Bangalis dismissed from their government jobs were left to fend for themselves.

In mid-November President Bhutto told a *Washington Post* reporter that in secret talks with representatives of Bangladesh at the United Nations in New York, Pakistan had offered to repatriate the Bangalis. He alleged that the representatives of Bangladesh did not respond to his overtures. The Bangladesh mission at the United Nations denied there had been direct talks but admitted exchanges of views had taken place through a third party with regard to membership in the United Nations. Bhutto did not refer to the fact that the government of Bangladesh had previously requested the repatriation of Bangalis. Mujib held that the exchange of Bangalis for Biharis was a humanitarian rather than a political issue.

The Problem of Recognition

Close to the top of the foreign policy priorities of the Mujib government was recognition by Pakistan, for the Bangalis are a fellow Muslim nation. Generally speaking, the recognition of newly independent countries in the postwar world was a routine matter. It was very easy for countries that supported the Bangali cause; a problem for countries such as the United States, which played an ambiguous role; difficult for Muslim countries that supported Pakistan; and extremely difficult for Pakistan, still recovering from national surgery, offended pride, and a will to wreak vengeance on the Bangalis and their Indian collaborators. China was content to follow the lead of Pakistan as long as the course of action was unfriendly to Indian and Soviet interests. The two principal obstacles to recognition were Pakistani determination to obtain the immediate return of the 90,000 POWs held in India and the Bangali ultimatum that a number of the Pakistani military be put on trial for war crimes.[8] (Ultimately, the trials were not held.)

Mujib had rejected Bhutto's March 1972 offer of unconditional negotiation by insisting that Pakistan first recognize his country. Mujib's position produced a propaganda war between the two countries throughout 1972 and most of 1973, although Bhutto from time to time supported recognition in the face of opposition in the National Assembly and among anti-Hindu groups in his country. However, in July 1973 the National Assembly authorized him to recognize Bangladesh at a time of his choice. At an August 28, 1973, meeting with India, Bhutto agreed on a timetable for recognition. Bangladesh, although not a party to the August agreement, concurred in its decisions. Bhutto's recognition of Bangladesh represented a calculated hope that the Bangalis would distance themselves from India.

Recognition and Rapprochement

The year 1974 brought further improvements in Bangladesh's relations with Pakistan. Delegates from the Arab nations, on their arrival in Lahore to attend an Islamic summit, pressured Bhutto to recognize Bangladesh. At the same time, other delegates went to Dacca to persuade Mujib to attend the summit. The following day, February 22, 1974,

Mujib arrived at the conference and Bhutto announced Pakistan's recognition of Bangladesh.[9] Soon afterward the Bangalis agreed to an Indo-Pakistan accord of July 1973 that accepted the repatriation of nearly 140,000 Biharis already in Pakistan.

The relationship between the Muslim nations was further smoothed by Prime Minister Bhutto's visit to Dacca at the end of June.[10] Although the Pakistani president received a warm welcome at the airport by Mujib and thousands of Awami Leaguers, the mood was marred by the hostile shouts of Bangalis at an ensuing memorial ceremony in honor of the victims of Pakistani repression, which Bhutto attended.

At an official reception on the second day of the visit, Bhutto emotionally apologized for what he called "the shameful repression and unspeakable crimes committed in Bangladesh by the Pakistani army in 1971." He asked the Bangalis "not to equate those who ruled over us and over you." He said his trip was not intended to create a rift between Bangladesh and India, as Indian newspapers had asserted. Mujib intimated during the visit that efforts to reach bilateral agreements with Pakistan would not exclude India, because the peace of the subcontinent involved all three countries.

Bangali officials had hoped Bhutto would agree to take another 100,000 or more Biharis. The April tripartite agreement, as they read it, committed Pakistan to receive more Biharis than it had until then accepted. During the Dacca visit, however, Bhutto offered only to establish a joint commission to study the problem of emigration. In a letter to *Newsweek* in the spring of 1975, S. A. Karim, Bangladesh's permanent representative to the United Nations, said that about 350,000 Biharis who had applied for repatriation to Pakistan remained in Bangladesh. He also said 13,000 others who had received official approval for repatriation had not been able to move. The Bihari issue continued to trouble relations between the two nations.

A second serious difference also bedeviled them—the division of the financial obligations arising out of the war and independence. Mujib claimed the right to a share of the estimated $4 billion of Pakistan's preindependence exchange, bank credit, and certain movable assets. Pakistan insisted that the Bangalis accept their share of Pakistan's external debt accrued prior to 1971, a debt said to amount to some $6 billion. Foreign Minister K. Hussain said Bangladesh could legitimately claim 56 percent (the percent of the Bangali population in former Pakistan) of the total assets held by Pakistan at the time of liberation, which, he said, had been "usurped by Pakistan during its last two and one-half years of rule."[11]

At the June 1974 Dacca meeting Bhutto had suggested that a joint commission be set up to discuss conflicting claims. The Bangali foreign minister rejected the proposal and asked Pakistan to agree in principle that some money and property held by Pakistan belonged to Bangladesh. Bhutto turned down the Bangali request.

Nine months later Bangladesh, with the financial support of the World Bank and International Development Association, accepted its share of Pakistan's external liabilities. The Bangalis hoped by this move to be able to bargain with the Pakistanis, who steadfastly refused to grant the Bangalis a portion of its assets. Discussions about the assets were eventually opened and are still continuing.

BANGLADESH AND INDIA

The relations of Bangladesh with India were crucial to the young nation. Its geographical encirclement by India, the 14 million Hindus in its population, the military support given to it by India in 1971, economic arrangements with India, and other common concerns made relations with India an essential component of Bangali foreign policy. The intimacy of the initial relationship redressed some of the antagonisms that had developed since Partition. It also revived divisive political tensions among Bangalis, as well as conflicts of interest between the two countries.

At the end of a two-day meeting in March 1972, Mujib and Mrs. Gandhi signed a 25-year pact of friendship and cooperation.[12] The treaty, whose general content was similar to the pact India and the Soviet Union signed in August 1971, provided that if either country were attacked or threatened with attack, both would immediately enter into mutual consultation "in order to take appropriate effective measures to eliminate the threat." The treaty could hardly be construed to be a mutual assistance agreement, however. Bangladesh cannot readily be attacked from the outside except by nuclear weapons, to which it cannot respond, or by Indian forces moving across its borders. India's well-equipped armed forces, 800,000 strong, far outweigh the small military forces of the Bangalis.

The treaty also declared that neither party would enter into a military alliance against the other—a provision aimed at SEATO, CENTO (the Central Treaty Organization), and similar Western alliances. (Doctrinally speaking, the Indians have no military alliances.) A commitment in the agreement to refrain from giving assistance to any third party in armed conflict with one of the signatories prevented Bangladesh from allowing its territory to be used as a staging area—as it previously had been by the rebellious Mizos and Nagas in the Indian states to the east and north of Bangladesh.

The broad-gauged accord stipulated that policies of nonalignment and peaceful coexistence were to be carried out through mutual consultations. Cooperation in economic, scientific, and cultural fields was proposed to deal with such issues as flood and river control and trade and balance-of-payments problems. The treaty proclaimed the Indian Ocean a free zone—an area free of great-powers conflicts and nuclear weaponry and open to international trade.

Before the end of the year a five-year protocol was signed that opened transit and trade facilities in Bangladesh's inland waterways. These waterways, which had been closed to India since the Indo-Pakistan war of 1965, gave India convenient access to her states north and east of Bangladesh. In 1973 a cultural pact providing for scientific, technical, and cultural exchanges was concluded. At about the same time a three-year balanced trade and payments agreement transformed India into the Bangalis' most important export market.

In May 1974 one of the last in the series of comprehensive agreements reached by Mujib and Mrs. Gandhi fixed the land boundaries between the two countries and laid out a plan for economic integration.[13] The boundary agreement was intended to settle border disputes that had been going on since 1947. Bangladesh got four small enclaves on its eastern border and India obtained the important Berubari enclave on the northwestern edge of Bangladesh. In Dacca the opposition charged that the nation's representatives had yielded an enclave that legally belonged to Bangladesh. The compact on economic integration created four joint industrial enterprises, three in Bangladesh and one in India. Dacca received 300 million takas in credits for these projects. To forestall the criticism that the proposed integration would lead to economic domination by India, the prime ministers concurred "on the desirability of ensuring the sovereignty of countries over their natural resources and an equitable return on the products of raw materials and primary products."

During the several years of Mujib's regime, extensive negotiations between Dacca and New Delhi produced agreements on almost every matter of mutual interest. Mujib's consultations with Mrs. Gandhi on foreign policy were even closer than the traditional regional collaboration of the Scandinavian countries. He established a workable relationship with the Bangalis' most important neighbor.

BANGLADESH, PAKISTAN, AND INDIA

The future of Bangladesh is related both to its own ongoing relations with India and Pakistan and to Pakistan's arrangements with India. After the heated propaganda exchanges and bargaining of 1972–74,

Pakistan and India reduced the level of their hostility and began a cautious cooperation.[14] A meeting scheduled for June 1975 to deal with communications was postponed after India exploded a nuclear device close to the Pakistan border. India later announced that the experiment was for the peaceful use of atomic energy and that the nation did not contemplate the development of atomic weapons; Mrs. Gandhi expressed her willingness to exchange information on nuclear science if Pakistan wished it. The statements appeared to appease Bhutto. In September the two governments signed an agreement restoring postal, telecommunications, and travel services between them.

That same year the two countries agreed to end a nine-year-old trade embargo. The protocol outlined a timetable for the resumption of trade and included the activation of shipping services and rail links. Trade was to begin with an exchange of cotton and rice from Pakistan for Indian manufactures, iron ore, and tea.

The trauma of Bangali independence had scarred the relationships between the nations of the South Asian Triangle, but only for a relatively short time. The spirit of compromise that characterized events there during 1973 arose in part because the interests of the great powers were diverted to the affairs of the Middle East and the OPEC oil crisis. However, the involvement of the great powers in the 1971 drama of Bangladesh was not forgotten, nor did regional problems altogether disappear.

CHAPTER 11

Relations with the Great Powers, 1971–74

Barbara Ward, in her imaginative *Spaceship Earth*, identified certain regions of the world as "mush areas" where, because no unified authority or effective communications systems exist, outside interventions are likely. Her observation fits the situation of the South Asian Triangle. During the events of 1971 and the subsequent years of Bangali nationhood, great and lesser powers took advantage of turmoil in the triangle to advance their special interests.

The United States opposed the Bangalis but after a time gave them economic aid. The Soviets managed to keep Mujib more or less on their side. The Chinese stood behind the Pakistanis during their most insufferable moments. Great Britain and other European nations favored the Bangalis in their plight. The Arab nations tardily proffered economic assistance, while nations neighboring the subcontinent stood on the sidelines during the Bangalis' struggles. The United Nations, an arena of political debate over the recognition of Bangladesh, came to its aid through its social and economic agencies.

THE UNITED STATES

The Nixon administration, feeling its way toward a new China policy and wary of the war in Bengal, decided to tilt in favor of Pakistan— a CENTO and SEATO ally. In consequence, it refused to condemn Pakistani atrocities or to put pressure on Yahya to withdraw his troops. Instead, it dillydallied while it encouraged chimerical political solutions to Bangali-Pakistani differences.

U.S. representatives in New Delhi and Dacca attempted unsuccessfully to make the administration see the implication of the tilt to Pakistan.[1]

Public and congressional sympathy for the Bangalis, the revelations of the Anderson papers, and the media's indignation with the administration's policy eventually led to a new and more understanding policy toward the Bangalis.

The U.S. embassy in New Delhi advised Washington, following the Pakistanis' ruthless killings in Bengal and repeatedly thereafter, that Bangladesh was probably emerging as an independent country. Ambassador Kenneth Keating recommended that the United States encourage the Pakistani government to change its policy of military repression, make clear its displeasure over the use of U.S. arms in East Pakistan, and voice its concern over the imprisonment of Sheikh Mujib.

Time magazine, reporting on August 23, 1971 concerning the March 25 killings, said:

> After the shooting started last March, the U.S. Consul General in Dacca, Archer K. Blood, asked Washington for a quick, forthright condemnation of the Central Government's brutal crackdown. But Joseph S. Farland, the U.S. Ambassador to Pakistan and a Nixon political appointee, argued that the U.S. should do nothing to displease Yahya and thereby drive him into Peking's arms. In Washington, Farland's pleas for "quiet diplomacy" won out. The official policy was deliberately ambiguous. There was no condemnation, no reproach, only a promise to stop military sales and hold economic aid in abeyance for fiscal year 1972 (the House rejected the administration's $132 million Pakistan aid request outright and the Senate is expected to follow suit). In New Delhi again Ambassador Kenneth Keating, 71, protested that the quiet diplomacy was having no appreciable effect on Yahya and was confusing to the Indians. Keating, who is said to be in deep despair, was ignored, and Blood was transferred to the State Department's personnel office in Washington. Soon, word went out that the policy of not being beastly to Yahya had been personally endorsed by President Nixon. In India's view, U.S. diplomacy was not quiet but downright deceitful.

Secretary of State William Rogers, under pressure from Congress, warned Pakistan in August, five months after the Pakistani army's pillage, not to take any action in the trial of Sheikh Mujib because such action would increase the chances of a resumption of warfare in Pakistan. The secretary's statement, made to the Pakistani ambassador to the United States, Agha Hilaly, appeared to imply that Pakistan could lose the support of the United States if Sheikh Mujib was executed or received a heavy prison sentence. The secretary gave the ambassador copies of a telegram signed by 11 senators and letters signed by 50 members of the House urging compassion for the Bangali leader, as if to say that the administration felt obliged to give official recognition to the strong sympathy of many Americans for the Bangali cause. The Pakistanis remained confident they had the full support of President Nixon.

Senator Edward Kennedy suggested on August 25 that the United States consider breaking relations with Pakistan if its government did not give assurance that a peaceful solution to the problem of East Pakistan would be reached.[2] The Pakistani ambassador called the suggestion "bizarre" and said that the policies of Pakistan and the Nixon administration were in accord.

The *Wall Street Journal*, in an editorial on December 22, 1971, said in defense of the Nixon administration's South Asian policy, "We suspect that as events work themselves out, the diplomatic losses will prove to be less important than they now seem, while the principle that dictated the American attitude will be far more important than the pundits have grasped." "Even more important," the *Journal* editorialized, "we find it difficult to assume that any steps the Americans could have taken could have altered the chain of events in any significant way." Actually, the United States did influence events; its tilt toward Pakistan prolonged the stay of the Pakistani army in the east and enabled it to kill Bangalis during nine bloody months. "The war," the *Journal* said, "could have been averted only if Pakistan abruptly reversed its national policies and granted independence to East Pakistan. The critics imply that it is somehow an American responsibility that this did not happen." Many well-informed people believe that if Pakistan had accorded equitable treatment to the Bangalis over the years and, above all, had not launched its murderous attack in March and kept 90,000 trained soldiers at the throats of the infuriated Bangalis, a different outcome would have been possible. Successive U.S. administrations, however, had committed Pakistan to SEATO and CENTO and had befriended Pakistan, giving $4 billion in economic and military aid. The Pakistani army used U.S. weapons against its own citizens. U.S. military aid kept Pakistan on the U.S. side and attached the United States to its special interests.

President Nixon's ambition to make peace with China diverted attention away from the issue of South Asia and Bangladesh and gave Nixon every reason to support Yahya after the Pakistani leader's outrageous use of force. In a posthumous work, Edgar Snow relates that it was Yahya who delivered Nixon's first letter to Mao Tse-tung.[3] The game of power politics had immediate and devastating effects on the people of Bangladesh. The Soviets, not to be outdone, played their own game on the side of the Indian government.

The Anderson Papers

The most noteworthy criticism of Nixon administration policy with respect to Bangladesh was Jack Anderson's revelation on December 30, 1972, of a set of secret documents said to have come from three early-September 1971 meetings of the Special Action Group of the National Security Council.[4] The meetings, which dealt with U.S. policies toward India, Pakistan, and Bangladesh, were held about three months before the day (December 4) the Indian army crossed into Bengal. Anderson concluded, on reading the papers, that President Nixon tipped the scales of American policy against India and Bangladesh because he was a partisan of Yahya Khan and disliked Indira Gandhi.

The president, according to Anderson, overrode the advice of State Department professionals who recommended that he try to persuade Yahya to put an end to the use of troops in Bangladesh and grant the Bangalis a measure of autonomy. When the Indian army entered Bangladesh, the State Department proposed that the United States stay neutral because the Pakistani army was sure to lose.

Anderson suggested that the president's decision to order a naval task force to the Bay of Bengal increased Indian dependence on the Soviets. Relying on intelligence reports that Bangladesh had offered a naval base at Chittagong to the Soviets in exchange for economic aid, the president, it was said, concluded the Soviets would obtain the base. Anderson claimed that the official reason for sending the aircraft carrier *Enterprise* into the Bay of Bengal—to evacuate U.S. citizens—was not the real reason for the move. The United States planned to compel India to weaken its blockade of the Bay of Bengal, to divert the Indian aircraft carrier *Vikrant* from its military mission, and to force India to put its aircraft on the defensive, thus reducing its operations against Pakistan.

President Nixon was not the only culprit in the manufacture of a foreign policy that failed to recognize Pakistan's inhumanity. Marvin and Bernard Kalb, in their biography of Henry Kissinger, said that the secretary of state admitted he "did not devote much attention to the bloodshed in East Pakistan until October," seven months after the slaughter began. The Kalbs also wrote, "From his friends, right or left, there was deep disappointment that he had 'tilted' in favor of Pakistan against India in 1971 while the soldiers from Islamabad were conducting what is described as mass murder of the Bangalis in East Pakistan."[5]

Kissinger was quoted in the Anderson papers as inquiring, during the 12-day war in Bangladesh, whether assistance might be given to Pakistan by U.S. military equipment, particularly jet aircraft then in a Middle East country, such as Jordan.[6] State and Defense Department officials would have liked to have seen the transfer take place quietly. But one State Department official noted that the United States could not legally permit a third country to transfer arms to a nation for which direct arms sales had not been authorized. The position finally agreed on by U.S. officials was to keep the issue under study, in view of doubts that the transfer of arms would help the Pakistanis win. In Delhi Ambassador Keating, upset about the proposed transfer, warned against the plan. The war's sudden end made the transfer a moot point.

According to the Anderson papers, Kissinger said that the United Nations had been hurt by the Indo-Pakistan war because the wrangle in the U.N. Security Council over the issue of Bangladesh had been a farce and because the United Nations had failed to keep the peace. Kissinger made it plain that the president wanted the United States to be tough on India for its military intervention in Pakistan and to continue to support the Pakistanis. Tilting in their favor, Kissinger said, meant promising them help and making a statement in the United Nations protesting the Indian use of armed force, no matter what other countries did. Kissinger commented that Mrs. Gandhi was very tough and would not in any case give in to Russia, but that the United States "should not ease her mind over the employment of troops in an adjoining country." Anderson's account indicates that the United States contributed to the U.N. failure to keep the peace in South Asia.

Henry Kissinger devoted 76 pages of his 1979 *White House Years* to a detailed explanation of the "India-Pakistan Crisis of 1971."[7] He interlarded the text with replies to his critics and with reproofs of President Nixon, the secretary of state, and department of state personnel. The opening and closing sentences of Chapter 21 furnished clues to the preoccupations of the author. The first sentence tells us that "in every administration some event occurs that dramatizes the limits of human foresight" (p. 843). Kissinger then proceeds in the vein of former president Nixon to remark that "the United States could not condone a brutal military repression in which thousands of civilians were killed and from which millions fled to India for safety" (p. 854). But he justifies the tilt to Pakistan, as had Nixon, on the ground that India had set about "implacably to dismember Pakistan in 1971" (p. 916). He concludes that Pakistan offered the United States "the only channel to China" (p. 913).

His penultimate paragraph ends with the sentence: "I did not take kindly—or even maturely—to my first experience of sustained public criticism and Presidential pressures." The concluding sentences of the chapter heave a sigh of relief not shared by the people of Bangladesh: "And then suddenly it was all over. The crisis on the subcontinent did not linger and so there was no focal point for festering criticism.

. . . There was other business to turn to. . . . We had survived the storm with the rudder intact. We could resume our course" (p. 918). These expressions of self-satisfaction are a classic example of diplomatic aplomb and insouciance.

Kissinger's defense of his 1971 Bangladesh policies drew a searching critique by Christopher Von Hollen, senior associate of the Carnegie Foundation for International Peace and former deputy assistant secretary for Near East and South Asia affairs from 1968 to 1972. Von Hollen described Kissinger's "assumptions and conclusions" as "inaccurate and of ill service to U.S. interests." Unlike Kissinger, Von Hollen contended that the United States did not have to remain silent about Pakistan's military repression of the Bangalis in order to create a channel to China for President Nixon. Washington, he held, had failed to press Yahya hard enough to make concessions to the Bangalis. India did not aim to dismember Pakistan, nor did the Soviets encourage India in such a purpose. Kissinger's contention that Nixon's willingness to risk war with the Soviets had "saved West Pakistan and preserved the structure of peace" was simply "wrong," Von Hollen said. The secretary of state must have felt a twinge of conscience, for he visited Dacca in the fall of 1974 and arranged to have aid sent to the flood-stricken nation along with advice on the management of its economy.

U.S. Policy After the Indo-Pakistan War

Official antipathy toward India and support for Pakistan continued after the war. Secretary of State Rogers, in a televised interview on January 5, 1972, implied that the United States was taking a hard look at the continuance of foreign aid to India. The United States does not give aid in order to make other countries toe the mark, he said, but the United States had contributed $10 billion to India since 1947. "We have to consider in the future how much we want to contribute to other nations compared to needs at home," he remarked.

After Mujib's return the administration's support of Pakistan lingered on. When ambassadors Kenneth Keating (New Delhi) and Joseph McFarland (Islamabad) returned to Washington for consultation, it was agreed that a one-time exception would be made to a congressional arms export embargo enacted late in 1970.[8] As a result of the exception Pakistan eventually received personnel carriers, jets, maritime patrol craft, and replacements for other equipment. President Nixon, during his trip to Peking in February, talked about the recognition of Bangladesh with Chou En-lai after China had consulted Bhutto on this point. It is fair to surmise that the Chinese did not then favor recognition.

Early in 1972 congressional leaders, especially senators Adlai Stevenson and Edward Kennedy, demanded recognition of Bangladesh by the United States.[9] In a speech on February 3, following an unofficial visit to India and Bangladesh in January, Senator Stevenson attacked the administration's policy of nonrecognition and asked if the United States had urged restraint on Pakistan. On his visit to Dacca on January 29, Stevenson had said that President Nixon's policies toward India and Bangladesh were "despicable." Calling for U.S. recognition of Bangladesh, he had described the Pakistani army's actions as "butchery."

Senator Kennedy's subcommittee on refugees and migrants held extensive hearings in December on the plight of the Bangali refugees in India and the destruction the war had caused.[10] In February Senator Kennedy went to Dacca; in a speech there he said, "The people of the world recognize you, even if the United States government does not." He drew a parallel between U.S. and Bangali independence. Kennedy called on Sheikh Mujib and visited the devastated area of Khustia and the Adamjee jute mill, where thousands of Bihari refugees were living. Local reporters indicated that the Russians did not like the Kennedy speech.

The delay in the U.S. government's recognition of Bangladesh had been variously attributed to its continued support for Pakistan, to its SEATO commitment, to Pakistan's assistance in facilitating U.S. contacts with Peking, to the president's antipathy to Mrs. Gandhi, and to the Indians' intervention. It is likely that all of these considerations served to postpone action. The delay did not mean that the American public was indifferent to the fate of Bangladesh. U.S. public opinion, according to a Harris survey taken in January 1972, while unsympathetic to India because of its use of force in Bengal, also gave poor marks to President Nixon by a margin of two to one for his handling of the Bangali crisis. An overwhelming majority (ten to one) of the respondents polled felt that the people of Bengal were entitled "to rule their own country." Public opinion, a press favorable to the cause of Bangladesh, and sympathy for the Bangalis within the administration contributed to the decision to give substantial relief aid to the new nation.

However, on January 10, the day after Sheikh Mujib's release by Bhutto, a White House spokesman said that the United States was in no hurry to recognize Bangladesh and, indeed, the question of recognition was not under active consideration. President Nixon, prior to his February visit to China, remarked, "We are doing everything we can to develop a new relationship with other countries that will not be pro-Indian, pro-Bangali, or pro-Pakistan, but mostly pro-peace," but gave no reason for the delay in recognizing Bangladesh.[11]

By March 6 a spokesman for the State Department said recognition was under active consideration. In ambiguous official language, he explained that the delay was due to the "impact of our decisions on other countries, both within and without the region." One interpretation of this statement leads to the conclusion that the United States turned a deaf ear to Bangladesh in order to strengthen Pakistan internally and to bolster its bargaining position with India and Bangladesh. The *Washington Post* of March 9 noted that the last of the Indian troops were to leave Bangladesh on March 12 and asserted that the delay in recognition was due to the desire of the administration to give Bhutto a chance to control his disaffected army officers and political enemies. The columnist Flora Lewis visited Bangladesh in March and overdramatically reported that the delay in recognition "drains that much from the dying reservoir of friendliness to the United States and a chance for the United States to play a contributory role in Asia."[12]

Pressures for recognition were building up. The Senate Foreign Relations Committee held hearings on resolutions urging the United States to recognize Bangladesh immediately. Four senators, Stevenson, Kennedy, Hollings (Democrats), and Saxbe (Republican), urged immediate formal recognition on humanitarian grounds, saying that the failure to recognize Bangladesh prevented a free flow of necessary aid. (Most foreign aid sent to Dacca during the first several months after independence was channeled through the United Nations or through private groups.)

On March 8 the second annual report of the secretary of state to the Congress, discussing the U.S. position on Bangladesh, said, "however deeply the people of East Bengal" have suffered and however one views the legal situation, "clearly it is now separately governed." The statement used the word *Bangladesh* to describe the "nation" to which the United States was actively considering granting recognition. The secretary's statement, an obvious indication that the administration had made up its mind to recognize Bangladesh, referred to the staggering problem of recovery following the "tragic events of 1971" and promised that "a major purpose of U.S. policy in the area would be to alleviate the suffering of the people of Bangladesh." The secretary noted that $25 million had already been contributed and Congress had appropriated $200 million for relief and construction.

The Congress persisted in pressing its views and on March 22 the Senate passed a resolution calling for recognition; a similar resolution was adopted by the House. After a delay of 90 days from the date of the return of Sheikh Mujibur Rahman to Dacca, the United States on April 4, 1972, became the fifty-fifth nation to recognize Bangladesh.[13] According to a United Press story, President Nixon personally decided to recognize the new nation after he had surveyed the entire South Asian scene and concluded it would be best to "recognize the newly independent country now in order to maintain an American relationship with the new government."

On April 4, when Secretary of State Rogers formally announced the recognition of Bangladesh and the desire of the United States to establish diplomatic relations at the embassy level, he noted that the United States had had an official mission in Dacca since 1949 and that many U.S. officials and private individuals were associated with the development efforts of the people of the country. The United States expressed "its good wishes for the future" and reaffirmed the intention to develop friendly bilateral relations and to help in the immense tasks of relief and rehabilitation. The United States did not send an ambassador to Dacca until January 1974, 22 months after recognition.

The recognition of Bangladesh made it eligible for U.S. economic development aid. Up until 1975 the United States loaned or granted $500 million to Dacca and supported its borrowings from the World Bank and International Development Association. Secretary of State Kissinger on a visit to Dacca in October 1974 promised food and flood control assistance. As the United States continued to assist Mujib, anti-Americanism in that country subsided, but the American press, disenchanted by the crises in Dacca, soured on the authoritarian role of Sheikh Mujib.

GREAT BRITAIN

As the former rulers of India, the British tended to be nostalgic about the subcontinent where their predecessors had lived for more than 200 years.[14] British civilians and public officials remaining in India and Pakistan after Partition maintained a lively interest in the affairs of the two countries and exercised a moderating influence on the troubled foreign relations of the region. British universities, law schools, and other institutions for more than a quarter of a century helped to train a solid core of teachers, civil servants, and jurists in the Asian nations. During the Bangladesh crisis public opinion in Britain, as presented in its press, was sympathetic to the Bangalis. Many Bangalis had migrated to London and other parts of Britain during the years of Pakistani rule. Employees in the service industries and students of Muslim Bangali origin made up a passionately vocal constituency for Bangladesh.

During the Pakistani occupation the British government gave a hearing to representatives of the provisional government of Bangladesh. Britain was one of the earliest countries to recognize the Bangali nation. British missionary groups and technicians, along with experts from Canada, Australia, and New Zealand contributed to the development of East Pakistan prior to 1971 and continued to do so after independence. The first place visited by Mujib on his release from the Pakistani jail was London, where he was well received. The Bangali constitution makers used British models and consulted British constitutional experts in framing their fundamental law. British commercial ties with the new nation were substantial. Bangladesh was received as a member of the Commonwealth in April 1972.

The authoritarian turn of the Mujib team disappointed the British press less than American newspapers. There was no outward sign that the London government had devalued its sympathy for the Bangalis.

EUROPE[15]

Before independence, Bangali contacts with Western Europe were rare. The nation of Bangladesh has maintained diplomatic relations with Western European countries, from which it receives large amounts of financial assistance and friendly support.

During the Bangalis' conflict with the Pakistanis, French journalists in particular poured out articles and books sympathetic to the Bangalis. The French press followed developments in Bangladesh with the same interest as that of leading U.S. and British newspapers. Several French writers, especially André Malraux, wrote enthusiastically about the Bangalis' struggle for independence. Mujib made Malraux an honorary citizen of Bangladesh.

The Bangali foreign minister, Kamal Hussain, on a visit to Paris in September 1974, said he wished to establish firmer economic relations with the European Economic Community, noting that the community received 30 percent of the exports of Bangladesh and furnished 25 percent of its imports. Hussain sought investment assistance from the EEC for the construction of a new international airport at Dacca among other projects. In December of that year the EEC parceled out $120 million in aid to 15 of the Third World countries hardest hit by higher oil prices. Bangladesh received $22 million—the second largest share of the total.

THE SOVIET UNION

During the war of 1971 the Soviet Union "allied" with India and bestowed its friendship on the Bangalis.[16] A week after the Dacca massacre President Podgorny, in a letter to President Yahya urging him to halt the "bloodshed and repression," noted that the Awami League had won an overwhelming majority of seats in the December 1970 elections. Yahya, in reply, defended the action of his army and assured Moscow that he would hold discussions with "rational representatives in East Pakistan as soon as possible." The Soviets stopped arms shipments to Pakistan and, after the signature of the Soviet-Indian treaty of August, increased its arms exports to India. However, during the summer and fall of 1971 public Soviet statements about the war in Bangladesh were moderated, possibly out of fear that the Chinese would get involved if an Indian-Pakistani war took place.

When the Bangalis achieved independence, the Russians announced that they would meet with Mujib before they met Bhutto, but after Pakistan's recognition of the new country. The offer was regarded as an attempt to mediate between Pakistan and Bangladesh similar to Russia's mediation between India and Pakistan after their 1965 war. Diplomatic sources in Islamabad alleged that the Indian government prevented the Russians from acting as intermediaries. The truth of the story is not easily verified, but it can be read to imply that Bhutto wanted the Bangalis back in the Pakistani fold on his terms.

On January 25 the Soviets recognized the new nation and simultaneously sent a planeload of relief supplies. Soon after his arrival the Soviet consul general, V. F. Popov, drove Mujib to Tangail, a small town northeast of Dacca, where the Bangali leader prevailed on the Mukti Bahini of his hometown to surrender their arms. The Soviets quickly signed a barter agreement with the new government; similar agreements were soon concluded with Poland, Bulgaria, and Hungary.[17]

On February 28, 1972, Sheikh Mujib flew to Moscow with a sizable contingent of experts on the Soviet Union for a five-day stay. Met at the airport by Premier Aleksei Kosygin, Mujib expressed "the good will of the people of Bangladesh to the people of the Soviet Union" for their support in the Bangalis' fight for independence. News reports from South Asia indicated that Mujib hoped to get the Soviets to take over a major share of his $3 billion reconstruction program. The Soviet offer of aid was much less.

On March 5 the two countries signed a financial and technical aid agreement. Under it, arrangements previously made by the Soviets with Pakistan would be fulfilled in Bangladesh. The projects included an electrical equipment plant, radio stations, and offshore oil prospecting. The Russians also agreed to help in the reconstruction and development of Bangali merchant and fishing fleets and railroads, to provide helicopter service for the military and civilians, to train "national cadres for various branches of industry and agriculture," and to establish consultative services for the rehabilitation of the industry of the country. Russian technical assistance did not live up to expectations.

Although no formal treaty of friendship and cooperation was signed, the Soviets promised to undertake steps to broaden contacts with the Bangalis in science, art, education, and public health.[18] The Bangali delegation concurred in the Soviet position in the Middle East and supported the cause of the Viet Cong. Both sides favored the European Security Conference and disarmament and agreed to cooperate on the establishment of a 12-mile limit for territorial waters. The joint declaration at the end of the meetings contained muted anti-American and anti-Chinese statements and promised support for the Soviet-Bangali friendship societies in their countries.

The implications of the joint statements on foreign policy were offset by Mujib's insistence that he had accepted Soviet aid with no strings attached. The Russians obligingly agreed to honor his policy of nonalignment. If this exchange indicated that Mujib was wary of the Soviets, they too may have been unsure of his allegiance. The Russian press, which had for some time before independence described the Bangali leader as coming from a family of middle-class landlords, omitted this description at the time of his visit.

A trade agreement initiated by a Soviet delegation at the previous meeting in Dacca, calling for a modest $13.3 million in trade during 1972, was approved at the March Moscow meeting. The agreement projected Soviet purchases of raw jute, jute products, tea, goatskins, textiles, and spices, and Bangali imports of pig iron, kerosene, cotton, railroad cars, and machinery.

The trade, aid, and technical assistance agreements gave the Soviets an additional toehold in the Bay of Bengal and made it possible to influence the new nation in its socialist venture. The Soviets believed for a time they had championed another national liberation movement. The ink was not dry on the Moscow accords when the Russians raised their consulate general in Bangladesh to embassy status and rapidly doubled its size. By the middle of March several hundred Russians were active in all parts of the country. Almost all of them were alleged to be Bengali speakers trained at Moscow's Institute of Oriental Language Studies.[19]

The Soviet-oriented Bangladesh Communist party, legalized with other communist and noncommunist factions in 1972, collaborated with Mujib's Awami League in the new government. Soviet-Bangali friendship centers were installed throughout the country. Trade union leaders were cultivated by the Russians and newspapers were supplied with pro-Soviet and anti-American articles.[20] However, by 1974 Soviet-influenced news stories were less in evidence, and foreign news was given more even-handed treatment by the government-controlled press.

CHINA

Chou En-lai visited East Pakistan twice before the Bangalis became independent.[21] In both 1956 and 1963 the Chinese foreign minister was accorded the most enthusiastic welcome ever given to a foreign visitor to Dacca. In the latter year Chinese rivalry with India gave the Pakistani government every reason to encourage warm receptions for the Chinese. Maulana Bhashani's supporters swelled the crowds, as did Muslims happy to cheer a challenger of India.

The Chinese-Indian war in the fall of 1962 carried the Chinese military presence within 150 miles of the East Pakistani border. Government officials in Dacca, pleased with the ignominy of the Indian defeat, exhibited no fear that the Chinese intended any more than a sharp foray into Indian territory. In contrast to the frenzied war preparations going on in Calcutta and other parts of India, Dacca was calm throughout the month-long war. Pakistani military men may have taken too much comfort from the Indian military debacle in the North-West Frontier.

Chinese friendship with Pakistan was strengthened when the two countries agreed, in 1963, on a common border; India claimed the Pakistanis made excessive concessions to the Chinese. In diplomatic circles it was believed that members of the Pakistani embassy in Peking enjoyed greater prestige with the Chinese than most representatives of other countries. Yahya was delighted to make use of that prestige to help President Nixon achieve his vaunted diplomatic coup and to thank the president for his loyal support of Pakistan's Bangali policy.

The Chinese agreed with the Yahya program in Bengal on the grounds that the Pakistani government had a right to maintain the integrity and independence of the whole country. In the U.N. Security Council in 1971 the Chinese denounced the Americans, as well as the Indians and Russians, for interfering with Pakistan's internal affairs as part of a traditional antiforeign propaganda line.

At the insistence of President Bhutto, the Chinese in November 1972 blocked the entry of Bangladesh into the United Nations, although Peking itself had suffered the same fate for years. Conjectures about the opposition of the Chinese to the admission of the Bangalis ranged from the suspicion that they wanted to keep the Asian subcontinent unsettled to the notion that they were simply intent on supporting their ally, Pakistan, as long as nonrecognition served Bhutto's purposes.

During Mujib's regime relations with China were not unfriendly. A limited trade between the two nations developed. After Peking refrained from vetoing the entry of Bangladesh into the United Nations, the recognition of the Bangalis followed, as did the exchange of diplomatic missions early in 1976.

OTHER ASIAN NATIONS[22]

The two small nations neighboring Bangladesh, Nepal and Burma, quickly recognized the new nation and exchanged ambassadors with it. Arrangements for increasing trade between Bangladesh and Nepal were made and talks were held about establishing a land route between the two countries divided by an Indian corridor of some 18 miles. Cultural ties were also projected in 1972.

Burma borders Bangladesh at the latter's southeasternmost corner. Burma had very little to do with Bangladesh during Mujib's administration.

In June 1972 the Bangali foreign minister, Abdus Samad, made a week's tour of Malaya and Singapore to enlist the support of the governments there. Those countries agreed to extend diplomatic recognition to Bangladesh and expressed an interest in economic and political cooperation.

Sheikh Mujib traveled to Tokyo in the fall of 1973 to conclude arrangements for a substantial loan for Bangladesh and to discuss trade with the Japanese.

THE UNITED NATIONS

The provisional government of Bangladesh, in the midst of its war with Pakistan, dispatched a former jurist and future president of Bangladesh, A. S. Chowdhury, to the United Nations in the fall of 1971 to seek a hearing for the cause of his people, to enlist help for its refugees, and to lay the groundwork for recognition. The United Nations immediately began its efforts to assist the refugees and help the homeless and desolate of the civil war. In January a U.N. official, Sir Robert Jackson, was named to head a coordinated relief effort in Bangladesh called the United Nations Relief Organization Dacca (UNROD).[23]

By the fall of 1972 Bangladesh had received almost $1 billion in aid from international and national agencies, public and private. The UNROD effort coordinated the relief activities of 50 voluntary groups, including CARE, HELP, Oxfam, and CORR. Sir Robert Jackson proudly reported that UNROD was the largest relief effort ever undertaken by the United Nations itself. UNROB (United Nations Relief Organization Bangladesh), which replaced UNROD, went out of business at the end of 1973.

The Bangalis' campaign for admission to membership in the United Nations was supported by India and the Soviet Union. Later on, the Indonesian representative in Dacca said that his government would support Bangladesh's membership in the United Nations. On a brief visit to Dacca in early July John Connally, the U.S. secretary of the treasury, assured the prime minister that the United States would support his government in securing U.N. membership. The July meetings between India and Pakistan at Simla were thought by Bangalis to hold the possibility of Pakistani support for Bangali membership in the United Nations.

Bangladesh's application for a U.N. seat was scheduled for August 10, 1972. On August 9 President Bhutto announced that China would veto Bangladesh's admission. Bhutto claimed that if Sheikh Mujib could veto the repatriation of Pakistani prisoners of war in India, "we can also use the Chinese vote to block entry of Bangladesh into the United Nations."[24] At the United Nations the Chinese ambassador said Bangladesh was not qualified for membership, charging that the government in Dacca had collaborated with India in violation of the Security Council resolution of December that demanded a cease-fire. On a procedural resolution to send the matter to the Committee on Admission, the Security Council voted 11 in favor of admission and 1 (China) opposed, with Guinea, Somalia, and Sudan abstaining.[25] The arguments used by China to keep Bangladesh out were identical to those of Pakistan.

Indian news reports admitted that the Chinese veto was no surprise, because the settlement of the issue of Pakistani POWs was essential to Pakistan. On August 22 Pakistan asked the United Nations not to admit Dacca until India and Bangladesh had acted on a December 1971 resolution of the Security Council holding the detention of Pakistani POWs a violation of the Geneva Convention and requiring their repatriation. Pakistan also alleged that Biharis in Bangladesh were being mistreated. Islamabad cited the refusal of Bangladesh to enter unconditional dialogue with Pakistan as evidence of the unwillingness of the government of Dacca to carry out obligations essential to admission into the United Nations.

On August 25, 1972, China cast its first vote blocking the entry of Bangladesh into the United Nations. The vote was identical to that taken on the earlier procedural resolution. The abstaining states sponsored a compromise resolution that would have admitted Bangladesh immediately upon the implementation of the U.N. resolution on the POWs. This resolution, too, failed. China tried in vain to get an "indefinite" postponement of debate on the admission of Bangladesh.

China's veto statement included an attack on the USSR that accused the Russians of acting "with honey in their mouths and a dagger in their hearts." China said Soviet socialist imperialism played an insidious role in South Asia and that India, in concluding a military pact with the USSR, had stripped off its "cloak of nonalliance." Not to be outdone in the propaganda war, the Soviets likened the Chinese veto to previous action by the Security Council against China's admission. The foreign minister of Bangladesh ascribed the Chinese veto to a desire by China to promote tensions in the subcontinent.

On September 21 the United Nations Steering Committee approved a renewed discussion of the admission of Bangladesh by the General Assembly, but when the Chinese said they would use their veto in the Security Council again, the matter was dropped. On October 18 the secretary general awarded official observer status to Bangladesh, which gave Dacca representation on commissions and access to most U.N. documents but did not permit the country to vote. Six other nations, including South and North Vietnam, had such status.

By the end of 1973 Bangladesh was voted into membership of the most important U.N. specialized agencies and received substantial loans from the International Development Association. President Bhutto told the United Nations in September that Pakistan would recognize Bangladesh after all POWs had been repatriated.

The Bangali-Indian-Pakistani agreement of the spring of 1974, disposing of the POW issue, effected Pakistani and Chinese support for the admission of Bangladesh. The Security Council recommended admission in June. On September 17, 1974, the General Assembly voted Bangladesh the 136th member of the United Nations.[26]

CHAPTER 12

Internal Strife, 1972–74

Mujib's fortunes in domestic affairs did not match his foreign policy victories. The political objectives of nationalism, socialism, secularism, and democracy, which he intended to represent the nation's goals, confused the people by their ambiguity and divided the activists; interpreting the ideology became a part of the great game of politics.

Mujib's political adversaries, some of them more friendly to Pakistan than to him, decried the government's socialist and secularist policies, which they believed had been insisted upon by India. Every Bangali deemed himself a nationalist and democrat, but the religious-minded among his political opponents wanted the government to intensify the nation's commitment to Islam. Amid these complications, dedicated moderates held the nation together.

Mujib's early political troubles, however, were as much a consequence of Awami League factionalism as of his opponents' personal ambitions and ideologies. The first national elections of 1973, in consequence, represented a personal triumph for Mujib rather than a consolidation of his authority within the league.

Ideological debates among the factions gradually affected the workings of the civilian and military bureaucracies. An inadequately trained civil service was given major responsibilities for carrying out the social and economic programs devised by planners committed to a socialist industrial economy. The most disturbing, although barely visible, element in Mujib's problems was the burgeoning political consciousness of the newly organized Bangali armed forces. Personal and ideological differences among its officers and Mujib's distaste for things military limited the government's ability to control violence. During his first two troubled years in office, however, Mujib somehow managed to cope with the disarray of personalities, ideas, and institutions.

The current bon mot about politics in Bangladesh has it that one Bangali makes a poet, two make a political party, and three make two political parties. The University of Chicago professor Leonard Binder once described Pakistani political parties as "personal rivalries and motivations" that "remain for the most part cliques." Bangali political parties, similarly, may be described as factions fashioned by the fusion of personal political passions and ideological inclinations.

The Awami League, since its founding in the fifties, was the most readily identifiable and cohesive political movement among the Bangalis.[1] It retained its solidarity as long as it played the role of the opposition party. As socialist partisans joined it, the league, weighed down by the responsibilities of power, broke into power-seeking factions united only by the charisma of Sheikh Mujib. Among its opposition, an extremist minority known as the revolutionary faction of the National Socialist party resorted to violence and far-fetched propaganda to discredit the league. This group succeeded in raising the level of violence. Meanwhile the splintered league hindered the attempts of Mujib's government to fulfill its promises. Under constant pressure, internal and external, to modify its relations with India, purge itself of corrupt members, and move the economy forward, the government vacillated, satisfying neither itself nor its critics.

After independence the political parties aligned with Moscow, the National Awami party (Soviet faction) and the Bangladesh Communist party, acquired formal status alongside the Awami League. Mujib's arrangement with the "Moscovites" may have been an acknowledgment of Soviet and Indian solicitude for Mujib, an anti-Peking gesture, or an attempt to mollify a section of the left wing of his party.

Under Mujib's leadership three separate party committees were set up at local and national levels to administer law and order and to assist in the distribution of relief. With this stroke Mujib undermined parliamentary democracy in favor of party government. In response to demands from the left he outlawed the middle-of-the-road and fundamentalist religious parties of East Pakistan—Jamaat-i-Islam, for example—and sent their leaders to jail.

Mujib's alliance with the Soviet-aligned parties was hardly a response to popular demand. A U.S. intelligence report prepared in 1973 estimated the membership of all Bangali Communist parties at 2,500.[2] The Moscow-leaning Communist parties, for their own good reasons, did little to help Mujib. On the day in 1972 that the Soviets recognized Bangladesh, Moni Singh, the leader of the Bangladesh Communist party, told *Pravda* that his party supported the Mujib government in its striving for national independence but hinted that Mujib's dedication to Moscow's type of democracy might not last too long. *Pravda* noted that the Communist party of India, which supported the government of Mrs. Gandhi, regarded the Bangali Moscovites as a fraternal party.

EARLY OPPOSITION TO MUJIB

Mujib's political honeymoon lasted barely six months. The noisiest criticisms came from pro-Peking partisans, and especially Maulana Bhashani. They were later joined by student critics and by young, dedicated revolutionaries. Anthony Mascarenhas, reporting from Dacca for the *London Times* in June of Mujib's first year, described the coming months as a "summer of tigers."[3]

The first well-publicized signs of discontent with Mujib's regime came early in April 1972, when Bhashani, leader of the pro-Peking faction of the National Awami party, addressed a crowd in Dacca estimated at 25,000.[4] He warned the prime minister that not all of the millions of citizens were behind him. He denounced Awami League corruption and called for freedom of speech and a genuinely free press. In spite of the deference Mujib had paid to Bhashani when he returned to Dacca, the ailing 90-year-old politician seldom missed an opportunity to castigate Mujib's government until his death in 1976.

Political agitation among university students erupted with the re-opening of their institutions. The Bangladesh Students' Union was backed by Bhashani's Peking faction of the National Awami party; the Moscow faction of the party allied itself with Awami League supporters in the Bangladesh Students' League. In July 1972 a group of Mujib's student allies were attacked by dissident student organizers. Hundreds of students were injured in the fray. In separate incidents later in the year, anti-Mujib students attacked the U.S. Information Office near Rajshahi University, a similar group firebombed the Information Library in Dacca, and two students were killed in a clash with police, touching off rioting. To combat these antigovernment activists, Mujib organized the Jubo (youth) League, an adjunct of the Awami League whose political tactics were designed to attract younger voters.

Mujib dealt more harshly with avowed revolutionaries. He jailed the leaders of the Naxalists for their part in terrorist acts. Revolutionaries originally organized in West Bengal, India, the Naxalists counted Bangalis among their numbers. When their reign of terror in Calcutta was throttled in 1972, they decided they could employ their violent tactics more profitably in Bangladesh. They verbally attacked Moscow-oriented supporters of Mujib along with U.S. imperialism and "reactionary feudal" elements in Bangladesh. The government found them guilty of complicity in several riots.

In July Musaffar Ahmed, head of the Moscow-oriented wing of the National Awami party joined the chorus of criticism.[5] He attacked "American imperialists" and warned the people against "the nefarious consequences likely to crop up because of accepting American aid." He demanded immediate elections because many of the members of Parliament elected in 1970 had lost the confidence of the electorate. Maulana Bhashani, at a September demonstration held by his followers in Dacca, shouted: "We want food. We want clothing. We want a life worth living." Mujib responded to this protest against skyrocketing prices and corruption by discharging a number of party members and government officials.

The leftist, anti-Indian National Socialist party held its first meeting in Dacca in November 1972.[6] The party was correctly regarded as a greater danger to the Mujib government than the smaller left factions. Its members, young revolutionaries, a breakaway group of Awami League students, former followers of Mujib, and guerrilla leaders, dared to challenge the government and Mujib personally as corrupt and inefficient failures. They also organized a "people's revolutionary army," committed to abolish "bourgeois governments" and to prevent Indian intervention in Bangali affairs.

THE ELECTIONS OF MARCH 1973

The first national elections for the Parliament, scheduled for March 7, 1973, galvanized the opposition parties, which included some formerly banned parties, and the Awami League into a flurry of pre-election action.[7]

The Communist party of Bangladesh, putative partner of the Awami League, held a mammoth rally in Dacca in December after attempting in vain to arrange a separate alliance with Muzaffar Ahmed and with Bhashani. The rally attacked the Awami League for its failure to guarantee freedom and to establish socialism. It, too, assailed American imperialism and demanded the purging of the "feudal and capitalist elements" in the Awami League that frustrated the work of Sheikh Mujib.

Not to be outdone, Maulana Bhashani, acting on his own, called for the resignation of the government by the end of the year. If his request was not granted, he said, he would form his own interim government. He also called for a strike to be held in February, about a month before elections, to protest all pacts with India and the Soviet Union. As usual, nothing came of this kind of talk, save to add fuel to the fires of the opposition on the left and right flanks.

The campaign for Parliament was contested by more than 1,000 candidates and 14 political parties. Some of the parties released their election manifestos in Bengali, others in English. Of the 300 seats up for election, 11 of them, including Mujib's, were uncontested. The Awami League's electoral manifesto outlined a five-year program to accomplish socialist social and economic policies. Its announced foreign policy of neutrality, which vaguely urged the people and the government to be wary of foreign conspiracies aimed at undoing the freedom of the country, was probably intended to refer to Pakistan; the anti-Hindu opposition, citing this policy, accused Mujib of knuckling under to India.

On March 7 Sheikh Mujib and the Awami League won a hands-down victory at the polls. On March 11 the election commission announced that the league had taken 292 of the 300 seats. Five independents, one National Socialist party candidate, and one candidate of the newly formed Bangladesh Jatyo League won. Another seat remained vacant until a later by-election.

The number of votes cast in the election represented slightly more than 50 percent of the electorate—a lower level of participation than in the 1970 election. Voting was relatively quiet, although several fights broke out among students in Dacca. The government had prepared carefully against the threat of serious violence.

Concerning the Awami League victory, the *Bangladesh Observer*, an English-language newspaper sympathetic to the government, wrote blandly: "Today we stand on the threshold of a great happening in our national life and in the history of our nation. It is going to be an occasion for pledges redeemed and aspirations fulfilled for the Bangali nation."

A press roundup by the *Times of India* of March 13 quoted the London *Times* as commenting that "the election gives legal and constitutional status to Bangladesh's claim to recognition," and Peter Gill of the *Daily Telegraph* as observing that "the real issue is what, if anything, the Awami League can now do to implement an election manifesto which is almost endearingly optimistic." *Le Monde* was quoted as saying that "despite his triumph, the Bangali prime minister's prestige will not suffice to face the innumerable problems posed for his country."

On March 12 Sheikh Mujibur Rahman was reelected leader of the Awami League government. He promptly swore in a new cabinet of 21 ministers, most of whom were retained from the previous administration. Dr. Kamal Hussain was made foreign minister—a shift from his post as law and parliamentary affairs minister. The former foreign minister, Abdus Samad, was given the agricultural portfolio. Sheikh Mujibur kept four posts for himself: defense, cabinet affairs, establishment, and planning. Abu Sayed Chowdhury was reelected president on April 8.

The elections told a story to which neither Mujib nor the Awami Leaguers listened—the public had lost its enthusiasm of 1970. An *Economist* commentary of March 10 put the best possible face on the political apathy of 1973 when it suggested that more than half of the voters had stayed at home because they anticipated a landslide for the Awami League.

In the aftermath of the Awami League's electoral victory, more divisions, more criticism of the league, and more violence became the order of the day.[8] The vigor and range of press attacks on the government intensified. The Parliament, not without opposition, passed a printing presses and publication act that required licensing the operation of presses and the publication of newspapers. The home minister tried to meet objections to the measure in Parliament with the contention that the law was needed to protect the fundamental principles of the Constitution of 1972. The Bangladesh Federal Union of Journalists responded that any paper that attacked the independence and sovereignty of the state would be rejected by the people and that there was no need for the law.

Political differences widened among the league's factions and reputedly surfaced between key cabinet ministers Tajuddin Ahmed and Sayed Nazrul Islam. Some Awami Leaguers were encouraged by the elections to continue to enrich themselves by selling political favors. The party's absorption with its internecine quarrels while it ignored local party organizations hastened the erosion of its popular base.

The pessimistic economic reports of the planning commission, which objectively detailed serious declines in economic production and increases in inflation, gave the opposition sticks with which to beat the drums of criticism. Disparagement of Mujib and his colleagues became a daily political event.

THE BUREAUCRACY

The daily operations of the bureaucracy were disturbed not only by political turmoil but also by Mujib's reservations about the bureaucratic apparatus his government inherited from Pakistan, by the bureaucrats' added responsibilities for the administration of socialist economic programs, and by their distaste for political meddling in administrative affairs.[9] All of these anxieties made it difficult and sometimes impossible for civil servants to operate effectively. Too few of them had the kind of experience and competence required by the new nation.

In 1973 the Bangladesh civil service created by Mujib numbered 610,615 employees, of whom 80 percent were in the lowest categories and less than 1 percent in the top three. The two-year exile of many middle- and high-level civil servants had deprived the nation of badly needed talents at the worst possible time.

Mujib, speaking on the problems of the administration in March 1972, said: "We inherited a provincial administration unsuitable and inadequate for a free nation. . . . The old bureaucratic mentality exists in some quarters. . . . We hope their backward-looking outlook will change. My government will recast the entire administrative machinery to suit the new state and the new social order . . . and to bring the people and government officials closer to the people."

A thorough overhaul of the civil service did not take place. Disaffection with the government soon cropped up among the civil servants as it had in the political parties and the press. The return of civil servants from Pakistan created frictions with those competing for their jobs. To assuage bureaucratic irritations, to encourage civil servants to work more closely with the government, and to resolve inequities in pay scales, a pay commission in July 1973 recommended the reduction of pay differentials in the salary scales of civilian and defense personnel. Some salaries were increased, and a ceiling was placed on higher salaries. In-service training programs were also encouraged. But Mujib's earlier decision to give party members a whip hand in local administration deprived the civil servants of invaluable executive experience.

THE MILITARY

A Bangali armed force was a new and unique national institution, since the Pakistani army had completely controlled its Bangali contingents.[10] Bangali independence fighters, now integrated into the nation's military service, turned more and more to politics as civil unrest gave no signs of waning.

Given the protective power of India and the absence of threats from other neighbors, it might have been assumed that the Bangali military forces would devote their energies to controlling the violence that erupted during Mujib's rule. Instead, the military officers became deeply involved in the strenuous personal politics so dear to the Bangalis. Bangali officers who had been forced to remain in Pakistan during the war and after vied for positions with competing independence fighters.

Diplomats in Dacca estimated that by the end of 1973 the country had an army of 45,000 men. The air force was reported to number 6,000, its several squadrons equipped with Soviet MiG fighters, Soviet transport planes, and Soviet helicopters. The 2,000-man navy had three gunboats and other vessels. The forces were drawn from the Bangali troops in the Pakistani army stationed in the east who fought for independence, some guerrillas, and an estimated 8,000 to 10,000 Bangali officers and men released from compounds in Pakistan. The separate internal security forces comprised the police, the Bangladesh Rifles (border guards), and the Rakkhi Bahini, a home guard of 20,000. Training and equipment for the security and regular forces were supplied by other countries, including India.

Mujib gave a relatively low priority to his defense establishment. Expenditures for defense in the 1972/73 budget amounted to 11 percent of the total planned expenditures for the year, or one-twentieth of the normal defense expenditures of Pakistan. In the next fiscal year defense expenditures were increased to almost 19 percent of the total budget. At that rate the Bangalis were to spend less than 1 percent of their gross national product on defense. The nation had been saved large infrastructure expenditures because cantonments, other military facilities, and equipment, left behind by the Pakistani army when it surrendered, became part of the Bangali defense establishment.

Sheikh Mujib misjudged the military. Committed to civilian rule and to populist policies, he authorized the paramilitary Rakkhi Bahini, whom he personally controlled, to maintain order. Because many of the army's officers and troops were Pakistani trained, he feared that they might prefer accommodation to Pakistan rather than India. Furthermore, he did not take sufficient account, nor did other Awami Leaguers, of the factional discontents among the military, which were to spill over into domestic politics.

Mujib's attitude toward the military dimmed his perception of their revolutionary capabilities. Colonel Abu Taher, a brigade commander in Comilla who had been a wartime guerrilla fighter, and Colonel M. Ziauddin, commander of the Dacca Brigade, argued early in the first year of Mujib's rule that, because traditional military forces would be unable to defend the country against an attack by India, a peasant army should be created and trained to stop Indian interventions. Their anti-Indian bias and revolutionary ideas angered Mujib. But it was not until Colonel Ziauddin criticized Mujib in the opposition weekly *Holiday* that he and other like-minded officers were dismissed from the army. The cashiered officers joined underground revolutionary political groups. Colonel Taher, a cofounder of the National Socialist party, became the leader of the People's Revolutionary Army. Personal rivalries kept the flames of ideological factionalism lit among the military, engaging soldiers as well as officers.

NEW GOVERNMENT TACTICS AND A FEW SUCCESSES

In September 1973 the Awami Leaguers persuaded representatives of the National Awami party (Moscow faction) and the Bangladesh

Communist party to ally in a new coalition called the People's Solidarity Front.[11] It termed itself a patriotic party that would promote national unity. Perhaps Mujib and his followers hoped the front would eliminate the criticisms leveled at him by his leftist partners. Mujib's farther left opponents saw it as an attempt to sharpen divisions among them.

A few months later Mujib adopted a soft line toward the Bangali right, releasing 36,000 prisoners, mostly members of rightist pro-Pakistan prewar parties, who had been in jail since early 1972 under the Bangladesh Collaborators Order. It was at this juncture that Dr. A. M. Malik, the wartime governor of East Pakistan who had been sentenced to life imprisonment, was allowed to go to Pakistan.

By the end of 1973, however, nonparty professionals in the government's service began to leave the country because they were dissatisfied with the league's ascendency and doubtful of the government's ability to cope with the nation's economic and political crises. President Chowdhury resigned to give way to an Awami Leaguer, Mohammadullah, Speaker of the National Assembly. Chowdhury went to Geneva where he served as a representative to the international agencies of Europe.

Not all the news from Dacca was bad and some of it was good.[12] The recognition of Bangladesh in 1974 by Pakistan and a number of Arab countries, all of whom had previously been reluctant to accept the division of Pakistan, confirmed the standing of Bangladesh as a Muslim nation and expanded its opportunities for trade and aid.

In his National Day speech in Dacca on December 16, 1974, Mujib, employing the language of the United States' President Johnson, declared a "war on poverty." He called on everyone to help in the reconstruction of the nation. Among the achievements of the previous two years he cited the enactment of the Constitution, the return of Bangalis from Pakistan, substantial expenditures for economic development, the growing prestige of Bangladesh in the international community, the accord on the POWs, and his role at the Commonwealth meeting of prime ministers at Ottawa and at the Algerian nonaligned summit.

The domestic achievements did not bewitch many of the foreign correspondents who came to Dacca to write about current events, although a Chicago *Tribune* headline read: "Bangladesh—only despair is found in short supply." Some journalists warned that a revolution was at hand. Yet neither the dire predictions of the press, some of them garnered from local dissidents, nor the roster of achievements yielded an accurate picture of the country, which was indeed in the deepest trouble.

CHAPTER 13

The End of the Mujib Regime, 1974–75

The third year of the Mujib government, 1974, saw the country on the threshold of tragedy. The tenacity of Sheikh Mujib and financial assistance from Western nations helped the nation that year to avoid political and economic bankruptcy, even though summer floods occurring amid civil disorders and a shaky economy brought on fresh crises. Driven by floods and food shortages, thousands fled into the cities, worsening an already critical urban situation. Terror escalated, as did political propaganda.

Party politics and changes in political personnel marked the first quarter of Mujib's third year of rule. In the middle of January 1974, the Awami League held its last biennial council meeting, at which Sheikh Mujib warned the party that it had to go after the black marketeers, the hoarders, and the corrupt. He denounced the party's adversaries as those "wanting to set at naught the principles of democracy." His added admonition to party members not to engage in corruption was not taken seriously by the press or the party opposition. The complacency of the league itself is revealed in the general secretary's report of the session, which devoted more space to the glories of the party than to its responsibilities or to the serious problems facing the nation.[1]

Soon after the Awami League council meeting Sheikh Mujib quit the presidency of the council. By divesting himself of his party post, he believed he could devote more time to affairs of state and bring about political and constitutional changes that even then were in the making. His selection of Awami Leaguer Mohammadullah to replace A. S. Chowdhury as president of the nation was a nonevent.

On March 19 Sheikh Mujib was flown to Moscow for the treatment of a bronchial ailment; he remained there almost a month.[2] Speculation about his reasons for going to the Soviet capital rather than to London, where he had earlier been operated upon, wavered between the view that he preferred Moscow because there he might avoid the importuning pressures of the numerous Bangalis in London and the notion that he wished to reaffirm the friendship of his regime with the Soviet Union and to enlist its continued support. He could have had both motivations.

EMERGENCY POWERS

In response to the growing virulence of his opposition, Mujib and the Awami League majority in Parliament in September 1973 had obtained a second amendment to the Constitution that authorized the president during an emergency—that is, a civil war or a threat to national security—to set aside guaranteed political and civil rights. However, religious freedom, guaranteed under Article 41, was exempted from emergency authority. This exemption protected the Hindu and Christian communities that remained outside the political fray.[3]

In April, upon his return from Moscow, Sheikh Mujib invoked the emergency powers of the second amendment to control the nation's mounting political and economic disorders.[4] He authorized the use of his militia, the Rakkhi Bahini, and the army to arrest any person or search any house without showing cause. Those arrested or searched did not have the right to appeal to the courts against the actions of the military officers. Mujib's orders also provided for preventive detention and for the banning of political parties "if their activities were prejudicial to the national interests." These orders, like decrees of the Ayub regime, created special tribunals to try persons engaged in hoarding, black-marketing, sabotage, and printing, processing, or distributing "prejudicial reports." No appeal was allowed from the decisions of the special tribunals.

By the first of June several thousand persons had been arrested and substantial quantities of arms recovered. Harsher action was taken in July, when the government amended the Special Powers Act to allow firing squads to execute persons found guilty by the special tribunals. Although Mujib had installed a police state, his decrees did not stop opposition, agitation, or terrorism.

SUMMER FLOODS

The deteriorating economy was gravely battered in July and August by "the worst flood in the history of the country."[5] A swift and overflowing

Brahmaputra drowned several thousand persons and caused extensive damage to rice and jute crops. The Bangladesh Planning Commission gauged the damage at more than one million tons of food grains and from $10 to $15 million worth of jute exports. The country's food shortage was estimated at three million tons—in monetary terms, $320 million. By September the floods had propelled commodity prices to new heights.

The fear of a prolonged famine caused hundreds of starving Bangalis to flee toward India, but the Delhi government barred their entry. Dacca, badly overcrowded since independence, became the repository of thousands of refugees from flooded areas. The new arrivals lived in unbelievable squalor. Mobs fought for the free food distributed by the government at thousands of soup kitchens.[6]

When the damage done by the flood was assessed, Mujib and his government moved quickly to seek aid from abroad. Addressing the United Nations General Assembly, which had just admitted Bangladesh, Mujib presented his country's case for economic aid. He also visited President Ford in Washington and journeyed to the Middle East to plead for assistance.[7]

At the end of October Secretary of State Henry Kissinger visited Dacca to discuss relief measures.[8] Press accounts of the stay hint that he told the Bangalis they would have to do more for and by themselves. Nevertheless, during the last half of 1974 Bangladesh received as much as $400 million in cash and kind for emergency relief, chiefly from Western and Arab countries. This kind of help is indicative of the effectiveness of the Bangalis' pleas and the sympathy the Western powers retained for Bangladesh.

In November the minister for food and relief told Parliament that about 22,500 persons had died of starvation and disease during the previous several months. Government critics, while admitting that the floods had contributed to the famine, said that the huge amounts of foodstuffs being smuggled into India for better prices or being hoarded for the black market made large-scale starvation inevitable. The unhealthy internal political situation in the country at the time of the floods encouraged criticism by competing politicians and left the victims of the famine unaided.

A FAILING ECONOMY

The year-end news reviews of 1974 reported famine, death, and near despair in the aftermath of the summer floods and their consequent economic disasters, notwithstanding the aid the country had received.[9] Nonofficial sources said that as many as 100,000 persons died of starvation and disease during the latter half of 1974. An Islamic welfare organization collected nearly 2,500 unclaimed bodies in the same period, more than half of them from the streets. One critical foreign observer asserted that the Bangalis lacked the social structure and perhaps even the will to feed themselves.

The economic indicators portrayed a gravely afflicted economy. Jute mills, responsible for a major portion of the country's foreign earnings, were functioning at one-third of their capacity. The tea gardens were badly in debt. The Bangali taka, pegged at par to the Indian rupee, was purposely and frequently revalued for obscure political reasons. In January 1975 foreign currencies, including the Indian rupee, yielded a premium of 150 to 200 percent on the black market.

By mid-1974 the sad state of the economy and political turmoil provoked Mujib to further action. In July the armed forces were ordered to stop smuggling at the borders and seaports. Strikes by government and private employees were banned for three months. In August the imposition of newsprint quotas reduced allotments to opposition papers; many weeklies were forced to close down. The press control measures were similar to those the Awami League had protested during the Ayub years.[10]

At this point the courts intervened to halt the government's restrictive measures. The High Court struck down the government's legislation dealing with corruption and violence, holding that it imposed illegal penalties prejudicial to the fundamental rights provisions of the Constitution. Many of the persons arrested by the government had been Awami Leaguers and their supporters. Complying with the court decisions, the government ended its operations and released the prisoners.

Encouraged by the court decision, student adherents of the National Socialist party (JSD) demonstrated against the government. In October the party called for the resignation of the "inefficient and corrupt government" and the establishment of a national government by "progressive, anti-imperialist forces," including the underground parties. When the government did not respond, JSD declared a general strike for November to demand the dismissal of the government. The government rounded up and jailed party members, but the students and their sympathizers went on strike while underground groups renewed their guerrilla activities.

POLITICAL CHAOS

In October, following his trip to the United States and to a European meeting of a 22-nation Aid to Bangladesh Group, Mujib fired his finance minister, Tajuddin Ahmed.[11] According to the *Economist*, Ahmed was sacked to prove to Secretary of State Kissinger that Bangladesh would turn away from India and the Soviet Union toward the United States. A Bangali diplomat said that Ahmed had strongly opposed Mujib's trip to the United States and suggested that this may have been a cause of his dismissal. Ahmed, who headed the provisional government of Bangladesh in 1971, was reputed to favor closer Awami League ties with the Soviet Union while approving the idea of negotiating with local Maoists to form a government of national unity.

Another explanation of Ahmed's departure from the cabinet is that he had publicly urged the convening of a party congress to end the famine for which he held the party responsible. He cited official corruption and inefficiency as major causes of the decline of the nation's economy and lamented that the country had squandered the tremendous good will and generous aid it had received for three years. From the viewpoint of Mujib's Awami Leaguers, these remarks put Tajuddin Ahmed in the opposition. Prior to his exit from the cabinet, three state ministers and others believed to belong to the Ahmed faction of the league had submitted their resignations.

Youth organizations renewed their quarrels. Sheikh Fazlul Huq Moni, chairman of the Awami Jubo (youth) League and a nephew of Mujib's, was accused by other youth and student groups of backing "corrupt elements." Moni denied that his organization was connected with the Awami League but admitted it owed its loyalty to Mujib.[12]

The parliamentary system as well as the Awami League was under siege. The pro-Moscow associates of the league advocated the abolition of Parliament because it bred corruption. They urged the formation of a new government by Mujib supported by "honest" political parties, presumably those friendly to Moscow. It is likely they made their criticisms at this juncture because they knew that Mujib was planning an authoritarian government and hoped to have a role in it.

Led by the irrepressible Maulana Bhashani, the United Front, a group of opposition parties favoring China and hostile to India, had earlier in the year demanded the release of political prisoners, the rationing of food grains throughout the country, the eradication of corruption, smuggling, and profiteering, and the cancellation of "unequal" pacts, especially those with India.[13] A mass meeting was called for June 30, but on the preceding day the police arrested the United Front's leaders and placed Bhashani under house arrest. This action took the steam out of the group for the time being.

An added threat to law and order and to the progress of the economy came from revolutionary Chinese Communist partisans. A segment of this group, under the leadership of the National Socialist party (JSD), serving as a front organization for the underground pro-Chinese Bangladesh Communist party, launched a massive verbal offensive against the government. Besides accusing Dacca of such palpable shortcomings as inflation, smuggling, and corruption, the group labeled it an "Indian landlord bourgeois government" and denounced its collaboration with "Russian social imperialists."

Although the underground parties differed in their definitions of the real enemy—Americans, Indians, or Russians—they agreed the Awami League government had to be overthrown by violence to make way for a truly communist regime. They boasted that they had trained armed guerrilla cadres to overturn the government. They were responsible, along with roaming bandits, for killing Awami Leaguers, looting large farms, sabotaging industrial plants, and attacking police stations and the training camps of the Rakkhi Bahini, the paramilitary Home Guard. The underground professed to have seized food for distribution among the landless.[14]

Bangladesh celebrated its third birthday on December 16 amid a wave of bombings and armed raids and train derailment. In a national broadcast, Mujib reported that since independence 3,000 persons had been murdered, including four members of Parliament. They died, he said, "at the hands of miscreants who were creating terror under the darkness of night."[15] Diplomatic sources in Dacca said that many of the deaths were also attributable to infighting among local party leaders and to public outrage against corrupt public figures. Reports from other sources made it plain that armed terrorism had created an atmosphere of fear and hatred.

MORE EMERGENCY DECREES

On December 28, 1974, President Mohammadullah proclaimed a state of emergency that indefinitely suspended all fundamental rights in order "to protect the economy and restore law and order."[16] He also issued a decree "to contain internal subversion, lawlessness and secret killings." Troops and the Rakkhi Bahini moved into strategic positions in the cities and towns of Bangladesh. The government's press note accompanying the proclamation attributed the country's troubles to "collaborators of the Pakistan army, extremists and enemy agents in the pay of foreign powers." Government officials described the terrorists as Maoist guerrillas and gangs of criminals. They estimated the number of hard-core Maoists at about 1,000.

A January 3, 1975, emergency decree ordered the death penalty for persons hoarding food or other essential goods and for saboteurs, smugglers, and profiteers.[17] Lockouts and strikes were prohibited. Dacca authorities arrested a member of Parliament, prominent member of the

Awami League, and chairman of the Dacca Cotton Mill, a government enterprise, accusing him of "misappropriations and mismanagement at the mill." A well-known lawyer and head of a civil rights group was also arrested. Other emergency orders approved by Parliament gave the government broad powers to censure the press, intercept mail, deport foreigners, and eliminate political parties. This time the courts were not permitted to intervene. Ataur Rahman Khan, a moderate critic of the regime, declared democracy dead.

Addressing itself to the melancholy situation in Dacca, the government ordered the evacuation of thousands of destitute persons living wretchedly in the capital city.[18] The slum dwellers were transported to open areas near Tongi, about 12 miles away. Their belongings accompanied them to their new living sites where stores, schools, and water supplies were provided. Building materials were made available to the new arrivals, who were expected to build their own homes. Authorities in Dacca said the removal of the destitute would allow the government to recover land in Dacca. During the removal of the slum dwellers, abandoned vehicles of all kinds, including 60,000 rickshas, were cleared away.

The Western foreign press was sharply critical of the emergency decrees—the *New York Times* more than the British press.[19] Some of the unhappiness of the members of the media with the revolutionary government can be attributed to their steadfast antipathy to the press controls instituted by Mujib and to their disappointment with the failure of his Western-style democracy, the political system which had originally made them empathetic to Bangladesh.

The proclamation made Bangladesh the fourth country on the sub-continent to be brought under emergency rule with the suspension of basic rights, along with India, Pakistan, and Sri Lanka.

The *Bangladesh Times*, edited by Mujib's nephew, Sheikh Fazlul Huq Moni, commented on the decree: "The obvious intention of the government is to flush out centers of reaction and agencies of exploitation during the state of emergency." The *Bangladesh Observer*, in a front-page editorial on December 29, held the emergency law to be "in the greater national interest." The decree "was not unexpected considering the situation prevailing in the country for a pretty long time and the people welcome it for the sense of relief it has generated. Nothing short of it could cope with the threat to national survival." Acknowledging that Mujib did not find it easy to take such actions, the editorial added, "he waited too long before he reluctantly resorted to this measure, but incorrigible criminals and unpatriotic elements mistook his large heartedness and human gestures for weakness."

The British press saw the emergency law in a different light. The London *Times* lead story of December 30 regarded the decree as inevitable but warned that

> the government must now not only put an end to the violence it attributes to its opponents and to hooligans, but it must also restrain the brutality and indiscipline of its own paramilitary forces. No political factions can escape blame. Millions of pounds are needed to keep people alive and will not be forthcoming because aid givers lost heart. Governmental administrative corruption goes from top to bottom.

The editorial suggested that a government of a more authoritarian character, determined to impose discipline on the country, might well be the harsh answer needed; and it concluded that "somehow Bangladesh, not other powers, is going to have to find its own answer to its political problems." The *Economist* of January 4, 1975, raised the question of whether the decree "is an alternative or an addition to the long round of constitutional changes. Sheikh Mujib has never been short of authority. For some months he is believed to have been considering a move either to an authoritative presidential system or to a formalized one party system." The editorial concluded that if such a move were made, a change for the better might happen.

News reports from Dacca and New Delhi at the end of 1974 and the beginning of 1975 painted a picture of a nation in agony.[20] In a letter to the *New York Times* published January 30, 1975, C. Stephen Baldwin, an author and Baptist minister familiar with Bangladesh, repeated what other correspondents had been reporting during previous months when he labeled Bangladesh "totally bankrupt."

A desperate Mujib, moving toward authoritarian rule, launched a "second revolution" that swept away parliamentary institutions and installed one-man rule and control of the economy by the central government in the field of agriculture as well as industry.[21] Mujib told his cabinet on January 18 that he planned to change the form of the government, to which end he would submit a constitutional amendment to the Parliament. A few of the cabinet members expressed their resistance to such a drastic measure. But on January 21 the Awami League parliamentary party "unanimously authorized Sheikh Mujibur Rahman to take such steps as are necessary to resolve all the outstanding problems of the country." Favorable comments on the proposed changes came from Bangali leaders loyal to Mujib. A staff member of a major Bangali daily told an American reporter: "There has been a total lack of discipline in the country. As long as it's Mujib holding the reins of power and no one else, this could be the best thing that happened to Bangladesh."

AUTHORITARIAN RULE

By a vote of 293 to 22, the Parliament on January 25 approved a constitutional amendment making Sheikh Mujibur Rahman president of his country with almost unlimited powers. He was given authority to select his own prime minister, vice-president, and cabinet. The Parliament stripped itself of effective legislative power by awarding the president full authority to veto any legislation and to dissolve the chamber. It salvaged one of its controls over the president by reserving the right to remove him by a three-fourths vote "for violating the Constitution, grave misconduct or on the ground of physical or mental incapacity." The Parliament also removed the constitutional provision that gave "effective participation of the people through their elected representatives in administration at all levels." Total executive authority was bestowed on the president, "either directly or to the officers subordinate to him." The Parliament allowed itself to serve out the remaining three years of its five-year term.

Two independents and one opposition member walked out of the proceedings, and some Awami Leaguers absented themselves. The Awami party members who did not show up knew that the proposed legislation approved by the Parliament dissolved the league and empowered President Mujibur Rahman to rename it, formulate its program, and choose its membership.

Sheikh Mujib, automatically replacing President Mohammadullah, was sworn in as president immediately after the parliamentary vote on the Constitution. The following day Mujib's appointees took the oath of office—former minister Sayed Nazrul Islam as vice-president and former minister Mansoor Ali as prime minister. The cabinet included six new members.

In his address to the Parliament on January 25, Mujib said that "free-style democracy" had encouraged corruption, smuggling, and black-marketing. During his talk he promised that the new system would "bring smiles to the faces of the common man." He acknowledged the breakdown of law and order and called for a total effort to make the country self-sufficient in food. How long, he asked, would friendly countries continue to give food, aid, and other assistance? Answering his own question, he said: "We must have population control. This free-style cannot continue. We must discipline ourselves. I do not want my people to be a nation of beggars." He blamed Pakistan and its local supporters, floods, and foreign newsmen for the difficult state of affairs of the nation. Foreign newsmen misrepresented the situation, he said, because local people gave them a false picture of the country. At the end of his speech he boasted that he had acquired full powers "to do away with colonial injustices, to stop colonial exploitation of the people and to guarantee their security and prosperity. We have established democracy for the downtrodden and not for the 5 percent rich." Mujib's justification of the second revolution bore a family resemblance to Mrs. Gandhi's speech of July 22, 1975, in which she was to explain her shift to authoritarian government.

Media Reactions

The *Economist* commented that Bangladesh "cannot afford to waste any more time. If Mujib fails now, as he has failed so many times in the past, to produce immediately measurable results—like a fall in the price of rice, a decrease in civil violence, or the revival of the jute industry—the blame will be wholly his." Although the weekly saw that "a logical justification for dropping the parliamentary system might have been to facilitate a whopping big cabinet purge to eliminate the obviously corrupt and incompetent . . . yet the Sheikh's first act after his swearing in was to reappoint every last minister; of six new ministers, only two came from outside his Awami League." But *Time* pointed out, "most observers believe that Mujib retained his Cabinet more or less intact primarily for the sake of continuity and that major changes will come later."

The London *Times* commented: "It is an irony that Sheikh Mujib seems to be moving inexorably towards the kind of absolute rule from which he and his countrymen sought to escape in a bloody civil war. But many people in Bangladesh will happily accept that if he can halt the drift towards total economic collapse."

A *New York Times* editorial on January 30, 1975, sought to write Mujib off:

The abolition of parliamentary government and the assumption of full dictatorial power by Sheikh Mujibur Rahman are . . . the desperate and futile. . . acts of a bankrupt regime. They cannot retard or even hasten the infant Bengal nation's descent toward chaos. Sheikh Mujib enjoyed absolute authority since independence. The corruption, incompetence and indifference he assails and which have driven foreign relief officials to despair are centered in his own party to which he assigned the exclusive role in a one-party state. His party's dismal performance must be assigned to the Sheikh himself. . . . It may be that the problems are of such magnitude to overwhelm any potential leadership. That is all the more reason why Dacca should not lock itself into one-man rule,

closing off all opportunities for legitimate challenge and for the orderly
emergence of new leaders and new ideas.

The One-Party State

A month after the establishment of presidential rule, Mujib proclaimed
Bangladesh a one-party state. A series of decrees wiped out 13 political
parties, ranging from conservative Islamic groups to communist factions
on the left. The Awami League was renamed the Bangladesh Krishak
Sramik Awami League (peasants', workers', and people's league), BAKSAL
for short.[22] All members of Parliament were required to join BAKSAL.

The inception of the one-party state brought an immediate dividend.
The wily nonagenarian, Maulana Bhashani, in early March acceded to
the second revolution. Never at a loss for words, Bhashani told the
press that he supported the revolution "as he did the six-point movement
led by Mujib," adding, "I will support any policy of Mujib's government
which will aim at attaining a self-reliant economy for the government."

The former Bangladesh National Awami party faction of which
Bhashani had been the leader joined with representatives of the defunct
Awami League and the Soviet-oriented Communist party of Bangladesh
in a public demonstration with BAKSAL on March 26, the date Mujib
chose to celebrate the Pakistani siege of Dacca. President Mujib used
the occasion to reply to his critics, defend his regime, and put forward
substantive proposals for politico-economic reform.[23] Admitting that
corruption was the responsibility of the 5 percent rich to whom he
belonged, he accepted the burden of ending it. In response to taunts
of foreign critics, he announced a four-point program: (1) to rid the
nation of corruption; (2) to increase farm and industrial production;
(3) to institute family planning to control population increases; and
(4) to use BAKSAL to create national unity.

The success of his anticorruption program, he said, awaited the
roundup of the culprits by his security forces. Dissatisfied with the
sluggish progress of voluntary cooperatives, he proposed the establishment of compulsory cooperatives in every village. Repeating an
earlier unfulfilled promise, he said workers' councils would be organized
in industry. Western officials had criticized his previous reluctance to
insist on population control, and Mujib's emphasis on family planning
sounded as though he meant business. He said BAKSAL would include
all elements of the population in a diversified party structure that would
give representation to groups and localities. His pledge to reorganize
local government to include party politicians, youth, and peasants
sounded like a revised version of Ayub's Basic Democracy with an
added emphasis on party control. Fearing that the nation's courts might

interfere with his revolution, he excoriated the colonial style of the court system and proposed to establish lower courts closer to the people. He wound up his speech with a denunciation of the trade practices of the developed nations and a plea to his fellow countrymen to increase industrial and agricultural production.

The programs Mujib outlined in his speech, although only a part of the revolutionary campaign, were among the first things he planned to accomplish domestically. The heavy emphasis in the speech on the need for total governmental control of the social, political, and economic life of the Bangalis underlined his determination to be rid of what he considered outworn traditional democratic institutions and policies.

The government quickly eliminated a statutory minimum price on jute in the hope of aiding the growers. On April 8 all bank notes of 100 takas ($13.20 at the existing official rate) were recalled in order to halt the illegal hoarding of cash, to slow down inflation, and to penalize persons who kept their cash out of the bank to avoid paying taxes. Both measures helped the economy.

Mujib was as much disturbed by the criticisms of the press as was Mrs. Gandhi in India; he moved more quickly than she to shut down all opposition newspapers. A newspaper ordinance, adopted in the spring, gutted the free press.[24] Anwar Hussain, the editor of *Ittefaq* and son of Taffazal Hussain, an early associate of Mujib, was replaced by a government-selected editor. After the issue of the ordinance, readers of the well-regarded *Bangladesh Observer* were able to learn only the things the government wanted them to know. Stories on government programs such as family planning, antihoarding stories, and accounts of arrests in smuggling cases were prominently displayed in the news columns and documented upon in editorial pages. Photos and stories about Sheikh Mujib's activities were as numerous as always.

Within a few months of his inauguration as president, Mujib instituted programs to renovate local government, to install multipurpose compulsory cooperatives, and to arrange party structures.[25]

The revision of local government called for the creation of 60 new district governments headed by centrally appointed governors and representative district councils. The revision was planned to go into effect in September 1975. Party control was assured because the governors were to be chosen by the president from among party members in Parliament—civil servants, politician figures, and loyal men from other occupations. The councils were to be made up chiefly of workers and peasants representative of the national political party.

The economic counterpart to local government was to be a system of compulsory multipurpose agricultural cooperatives in each village.

From 50 to 75 of them would serve as experimental stations. Seven members of the BAKSAL Central Committee were to head seven of the cooperatives. Mujib described the co-ops as a form of socialism adapted to the history, culture, and traditions of the Bangali people. Details of this adaptation were not revealed, save that the government would not take ownership of the land; landholders, however, would have to share their output with the cooperative and the government.

BAKSAL, said Mujib, would involve the participation of people in all walks of life. Four or five candidates from the party would contest for elections in order to permit the people to select the best man. The short life of the party makes it impossible to judge whether such elections would have introduced a democratic element into the promised authoritarian system.

In foreign affairs, Mujib to all appearances followed the course he had successfully pursued prior to 1975—the resolution of wartime disputes on the subcontinent, membership in the United Nations, recognition by Pakistan and the Arab countries, easier relations with Communist China, and substantial economic aid from the West and the United Nations.

With the second revolution in place, Mujib moved to cement relations with New Delhi. He publicly accused the Pakistanis of intervening in Bangali domestic affairs and entered into agreements with India that settled two long-standing disputes with regard to land boundaries and Indian control of the Ganges by the Farraka Barrage. Neither of these arrangements were popular among the Bangalis, some of whom feared that they symbolized Indian hegemony and Bangali dependence. As much as any other of his actions, Mujib's pacts with India consolidated his opposition.

THE ASSASSINATION OF SHEIKH MUJIB

During the early hours of August 15, 1975, a group of angry young army officers in command of several hundred troops armed with machine guns and mortars attacked and killed Sheikh Mujibur Rahman, his family, and some of his followers in their Dacca home. His wife, children, two nephews, and several of his cabinet ministers, altogether about 20 people, were gunned down.[26]

Shortly after the killings a Major Dalin, one of the coup leaders, went on Radio Bangladesh to announce Mujib's death. He said that Khondikar Moshtaque Ahmed, a minister in Mujib's cabinet, would take over the presidency. Martial law was proclaimed and a 24-hour curfew imposed.

The coup had been engineered by a faction in the army led by young officers unhappy, among other things, with what they regarded as Mujib's denigration of the regular armed services and his reliance on the better-equipped paramilitary Rakkhi Bahini. Their public justification of the killings on the ground that Mujib was "a megalomaniac, corrupt and unpopular," failed to acknowledge their desire for personal vengeance. The officers, like some others, feared that Mujib had diluted Muslim culture by leaning too heavily on India and its good will.

The three and one-half years of Mujib's government revealed the strengths and weaknesses of the man, the Awami League, and Bangali democracy. Mujib's charisma, which won him the support of the people, arose largely from his ambition to prove that he knew how to govern. His excessive optimism, stemming from his political vision of a "mighty world nation . . . free of all injustice and sorrow," betrayed his ambitions, as did his reliance on the Bangali habit of believing public utterances. Unlike his mentor, H. S. Suhrawardy, an intellectual who had studied law, Mujib was a pragmatically oriented populist wedded to an ideology he did not fully understand. He tried to use his commanding position to master the nation's problems and to keep his opponents at bay. His lieutenants were not as supportive as they should have been and his opponents more ruthless than he knew. He depended too much during his first years in office on his party colleagues and their political performance. He had to learn that many of them placed their personal ambitions above the party and the nation. Perhaps, with independence, the Awamis and their supporters believed they had earned both the right to office and to its spoils. Other Bangalis, too, discovered how to use the system to make lucrative personal deals. Passionate opponents resorted to terrorist tactics, and Mujib could not control the violence of his partisans.

Mujib was not the first leader of a Third World nation to learn how difficult it is to curb the greedy and to help the desperately poor. The destruction of the 1971 war and the problems of organizing relief and rehabilitation, of building new governmental structures, and of establishing and maintaining critical foreign relations demanded his immediate and constant attention from the time he assumed office. The additional need to achieve national unity, move the economy forward, and heal the wounds of neglected social problems overloaded his agenda. He became disenchanted with Western-style parliamentary democracy and turned to authoritarian one-party rule to accomplish what he had previously failed to do. His forceful political and economic measures had only been proposed when he was assassinated.

The assassination of Mujib shocked his followers, deprived them of his dynamic leadership, and produced deep fissures in BAKSAL membership. It also had the effect of permitting the armed forces, downgraded by Mujib, to acquire a share in the government's operations.

The nation survived the trials of Mujib's years in office and the trauma of his assassination in part because the peasantry that had supported the Awami League in the election of 1970, although disillusioned with the Mujib government, remained willing to support other leaders who would look after their needs. The peasants' fatalistic attitude toward life, too, made it easy for them to accept changes they could not control.

CHAPTER 14

Unsteady Progress, 1975–81

THE AHMED REGIME

Moshtaque Ahmed, a former member of Mujib's cabinet who was named president by the leaders of the revolt that ended the life of Mujib, went on Radio Bangladesh several hours after the coup to urge his countrymen to cooperate with his government, adding, "Anybody trying to resist the new revolutionary government or violating any instruction given so far will be dealt with severely."[1]

Ahmed's announcement within hours of the assassination that he would accept the presidency suggested that the killers had made prior arrangements with him. Although Moshtaque Ahmed and other members of Mujib's cabinet had been dissatisfied with Mujib's leadership and discord was rampant among the military, it remains questionable whether Ahmed was directly involved in the actions of the young officers. However, he was eager enough to take advantage of the coup, and his government did not investigate the assassination.

The day after the assassination Ahmed was sworn into office at a ceremony attended by the chiefs of the armed services.[2] He appointed a cabinet to replace "the autocratic government of Sheikh Mujibur Rahman." Most of the members of the new cabinet had at one time or another been in Mujib's cabinets. The president selected former president A. S. Chowdhury as foreign minister.

Although early official radio reports insisted "all is quiet in the land; people are back at work, at school and on the farm," bewilderment typified the new government's first several days in power. Sheikh Mujib's body lay in his residence a full day because no one could decide what to do about it. The day the government was installed, Mujib was buried in his home village, but no one was there to praise him.[3] The next day, however, Radio Bangladesh interspersed its broadcasts with tes-

179

timonials to the dead president prepared by his former colleagues, who also avowed their allegiance to Moshtaque Ahmed.

President Ahmed declared himself martial law administrator on August 19, empowering himself to set up special tribunals to punish violators of his orders, which he placed beyond the jurisdiction of the constitutional courts.[4] Security police were organized. More than 30 former Mujib associates were arrested on charges of corruption. Among the detainees were Tajuddin Ahmed, finance minister until 1973, several members of Mujib's 1975 cabinet, and other top officials of Mujib's administration.

Fearful that Mujib's supporters would riot in Dacca, the government posted tanks there for many weeks. Occasional gun battles between government and Mujib sympathizers were reported. President Ahmed abolished Mujib's one-party system, BAKSAL. Two of the influential Bangali dailies in Dacca, both of which had been critical of Mujib, were restored to their original owners. To divorce his regime from that of Mujib, possibly at the insistence of the military, Ahmed ordered the Rakkhi Bahini absorbed into the army and thereby abolished. The army acquired the equipment of the paramilitary outfit.[5]

The president and his advisors, greatly troubled by the threat of social disorders and by the hostility of the political opposition, experimented unsuccessfully with a variety of hard and soft measures in order to keep their hold on the reins of government. Progressively harsher policies played into the hands of the military, who contested among themselves for a larger share of political authority.

A general amnesty declared in September for those depositing illegal arms by the following week did not work.[6] The seizure of arms and arrests of the culprits continued throughout the three months of the government's stay in power.

President Ahmed announced on October 3 that parliamentary democracy would be restored, beginning with the withdrawal of restrictions on political activities on August 15, 1976, and culminating with the calling of a general election on February 28, 1977.[7] He praised the achievements of the armed forces, in pointed acceptance of their political influence and his reliance upon them. He proposed that an independent judiciary be given a place of honor in the new government.

To accent the greater freedom to come, the president released 1,000 of Mujib's political prisoners. The cases of other detainees were reviewed. Death penalties were commuted to 14 years of hard labor. More newspapers, released from governmental control, were given back to their owners; but when press leaders requested the repeal of Mujib's press control acts, the government refused.

The political reforms promised by the president won the support of Maulana Bhashani but not of many parliamentarians. Prior to his announcement of a return to parliamentary government, the president had called a meeting of the parliamentarians, but less than half the membership showed up. Two weeks after the October 3 address, another meeting attracted 260 parliamentarians, better than two-thirds of the assembly, but many openly attacked the "murderers of Sheikh Mujibur Rahman."

Although he owed his office to a military coup, the president could not settle the personal and ideological differences that plagued the armed forces. Michael T. Kaufman's valid but incomplete analysis of these differences, which appeared in the March 11, 1982, *New York Times*, identified two principal alignments among the military factions. One of them was described as a nationalistic group made up mostly of men who fought for independence in East Pakistan and supported the basic lines of Mujib's domestic and foreign policies; the other, so-called Islamic, faction, controlled by Bangali officers returned from prisons in West Pakistan, demanded closer ties with the Islamic world and a sharp curtailment of relations with India. This distinction is basically sound but too simplistic; for one thing, most independence fighters favored closer ties with Islamic nations. Moreover, there were among the military many pro-Maoists, revolutionary officers, and men agitating for a complete reorientation of the nation's political and economic life.

President Ahmed endeavored to achieve a balance between the nationalists and pro-Islamic factions. He appointed General Khalilur Rahman, repatriated from Pakistan, to a new post as chief of defense staff and another repatriate as head of the Bangladesh Rifles, the border security forces. He promoted General Ziaur Rahman, Mujib's deputy chief of the army staff, to its chief, because, it is said, he believed the general had foreknowledge of the Mujib coup.[8]

At first the pro-Maoist JSD (national socialist party) and its military adherents welcomed the government of Moshtaque Ahmed because the government opposed Mujib's Indian tilt and rejoiced over the Chinese recognition of the government, but the JSD quickly turned against the regime, condemning the rightist complexion of the cabinet and demanding its dismissal.[9] Pro-Mujib forces, said to be responsible for labor unrest in the Adamjee jute mill, blamed the Ahmed government for the death of Mujib.

THE NOVEMBER COUPS

President Ahmed had not learned that political assassinations often beget other revolutions. Just as the death of Mujib in August brought him to power, a series of military coups ended his regime. The first outbreak of violence occurred on November 3 with the murder of four former members of Mujib's cabinet and other officials jailed in Dacca by President Ahmed. Ahmed had also imprisoned the "August majors," who were well known as Mujib's assassins, on the grounds of the presidential palace. Somehow they escaped the palace, went to the Dacca jail, and killed the officials of Mujib's government.[10]

The day after the killings, senior officers led by Brigadier Khalid Musharaf, next in command to General Ziaur Rahman, staged the second coup of the year, with the backing of India, according to one source.[11] The brigadier made himself a major general and chief of the army staff and placed General Zia under house arrest. The two had been bitter personal enemies since serving as brigade commanders of the Bangali forces in the 1971 war. General Musharaf, known as a Mujib sympathizer, resented the favor shown by President Ahmed to the assassins of Mujib.

After the coup the August majors immediately fled to Bangkok.[12] On their arrival in the Thai capital their leader, Lieutenant Colonel Sayad Farook Rahman, told the Dacca press that the jailed prisoners had been killed by senior military officers he refused to name. He alleged that he, his fellow officers, and their families had been allowed to leave the country "in order to avoid bloodshed" and that senior officers were holding President Moshtaque Ahmed "virtually a prisoner." The four ministers killed in jail, he explained, had been eliminated by the unnamed killers because they were the only possible civilian challengers of the new military rulers—a reference to General Musharaf. All but one of the August majors subsequently flew to Libya for asylum.

President Ahmed, seeking to absolve himself from suspicion in the Dacca jail murders, immediately ordered a judicial inquiry committee to probe the situation in which criminals were given safe passage out of the country and into the "circumstances in which four prominent persons were murdered in the Dacca jail." Four of his ministers of state resigned, two of them accused of corruption. Both moves appeared to have been taken to keep the president in power.

On November 5, the day the inquiry was announced, Mujib sympathizers staged a half-day strike and held a procession to Mujib's former residence, where wreaths were laid at the gate. Students and other followers of Mujib rioted to protest the escape of the August majors.[13] At this juncture President Ahmed, believing he could not prevail, issued a proclamation enabling him to nominate a successor to whom he could transfer the authority of the presidency. At midnight on November 5 he resigned and turned over his office to Chief Justice Abusadat Mohammad Sayem. The new president, reputed to have been an associate of Sheikh Mujib, had been appointed by Mujib to the Supreme Court position.[14]

On November 6 President Sayem said, somewhat mysteriously, that the armed forces had triggered welcome changes in the country and smoothed the transfer of power. Describing his government as "unified, nonpartisan, and interim," he affirmed his intention to establish a rule of law and an impartial administration, to uproot corruption, to dispel domestic disorders, to establish a self-reliant economy, and to expand the nation's export markets.

The Sayem statement on the role of the military was partially explained in subsequent reports of violent contests for power in the armed forces. Prior to General Musharaf's coup of November 3, the highly volatile JSD (national socialist party) had created an underground Association of Revolutionary Soldiers to persuade the rank and file of the Dacca cantonment to revolt against the self-appointed general. On November 6 the revolutionaries killed the general, whom they accused of being an Indian agent collaborating with New Delhi to reestablish control over Bangladesh. General Ziaur Rahman, who had been placed under house arrest by President Ahmed, was released by the revolutionaries because they believed him to be friendly to their cause. The day after the release of General Zia, President Sayem named him chief of the army staff and deputy martial law administrator. Sayem also freed JSD leaders who had been imprisoned by Sheikh Mujib, presumably out of gratitude for their party's role in the release of General Zia.

A third coup appeared to be in the making when Radio Bangladesh on November 7 reported that General Zia had made a "heroic come-back."[15] A broadcast by Zia himself announced that he had been requested "by the people of Bangladesh, the armed services, and others" to take over for the time being as chief martial law administrator of the Bangladesh army. He held the post of martial law administrator for eight hours, at which time President Sayem reasserted his constitutional authority. One plausible explanation for this rapid switch is that the president persuaded the young and ambitious general his actions had no legal basis and might not bring him the popular support he needed. General Zia was renamed chief of the army staff. The president, as the chief martial law administrator, appointed the general, along with the chiefs of the navy and air force, as deputy martial law administrators and divided the former ministries among them. General Zia got the important portfolios of finance, home affairs, industry, and information.

In his proclamation establishing the martial law administration, the president dissolved the Parliament but advanced the date for parliamentary elections to an unspecified time prior to February 28, 1977. The president also gave himself authority to appoint zonal martial law administrators.[16]

In his first public address under President Sayem, General Zia, although declaring himself "a soldier, not a politician," plainly spoke with authority when he promised that martial law would not be extended beyond the time it was needed.[17] He later espoused the president's programs to restore democracy and to maintain a nonaligned foreign policy.

The military came to dominate the government with the establishment November 11 of a National Economic Council, consisting of the president and three deputy martial law administrators, each with voting rights.[18] A nonvoting civilian was named deputy chairman of the council. Because the deputy martial law administrators were also in command of civilian ministerial offices, they were for the moment in effective control of domestic affairs, save for the superior constitutional authority of the president.

Shortly after the appointment of General Zia as army chief, the JSD's Association of Revolutionary Soldiers circulated pamphlets among army personnel demanding the elimination of preferential treatment for officers. Noncommissioned officers cooperating with ranking officers were labeled antirevolutionaries. The rank and file were urged to form revolutionary councils with industrial workers, peasants, and intellectuals to launch a revolutionary government. General Zia was accused of antirevolutionary sympathies. The association incited mutinies among troops in and around Dacca.

The government promptly arrested JSD leaders, including the chief of the association, Lieutenant Colonel Abu Taher (a wartime guerrilla fighter), the association's district leaders, and others, charging them with disruption of national unity. In June 1976 a special secret military tribunal tried 33 members of JSD for attempting to overthrow the government and to subvert the armed forces.[19] A month later 17 of the accused were found guilty and the remainder acquitted. Sixteen of the accused were given jail sentences ranging from 1 to 12 years. Lieutenant Colonel Taher was sentenced to death and hanged on July 21. The sentence meted out to Taher, who was a member of the November 7 group that brought Zia into the government, was approved by President Sayem and General Zia.

The penalties did not discourage the rebels in the army, for JSD had won the backing of many officers and soldiers. To counter their influence, General Zia removed a Dacca tank regiment thought to be friendly to JSD to a location 100 miles from the capital and disbanded the Bengal Lancers, a unit known to be under the thumb of revolutionaries. By making concessions to the demands of other army units, he kept a lid on agitation among the military for the time being. General Zia had earlier consolidated official control over the armed forces when, in April 1976, he engineered the resignation and the exile to Europe of his fellow martial law administrator, Air Marshal M. G. Tawab. Tawab, who had contested Zia's authority, represented extremist Islamic and pro-Pakistani groups in the country.

General Zia was not without a political base, and he gained power over President Sayem as he broadened that base. He had the enthusiastic support of the left-leaning *Holiday*, the cooperation of most of the Dacca press, and the confidence of nonrevolutionary pro-Chinese and anti-Indian factions, including Maulana Bhashani. They held that Zia represented most of the patriotic elements among "the national bourgeoisie," who were willing to stand up for national independence and to consider Indian interference in Bangali affairs the greatest danger to the country.

To broaden his political base, the general had embarked on a program that propitiated the uncommitted and conciliated his political opponents, except members of JSD. At the end of 1975 wartime collaborators with Pakistan had been pardoned. Islamic leaders were permitted to make political speeches at religious assemblies. In the spring of 1976 pro-Mujib military men involved in the first of the November coups were released from jail. The officers who assassinated Mujib were invited to Dacca from Libya to discuss their reinstatement in the army. However, they were implicated with the exiled Air Marshal Tawab in a coup plot and were expelled.

PUBLIC ORDER REESTABLISHED

The civilian population, whose lives had been disrupted by revolutionaries and criminals during the Mujib years, had a respite from disorders in the months immediately following his death. The government organized special armed police forces to reduce armed robberies, thefts, and other crimes of violence. It also stepped up efforts to repress the circulation of illegal arms. In November and December 1975, hundreds of guerrillas and professional bandits were brought to trial in special district martial law courts.[20]

To control smuggling, estimated to have involved $4 billion worth of goods during Mujib's rule, the government increased its surveillance of ports and borders. By May 1976, 8,500 cases were on the docket of the Bureau of Anti-Corruption. General Zia and President Sayem, like their predecessors, made innumerable speeches exhorting the citizenry to help reduce smuggling, which, they reminded their listeners, did great harm to economic development.

From time to time in 1976 the government employed drastic means to keep order. Martial law decrees divided the country into zones under the command of a military administrator. Laws were promulgated imposing the death penalty for numerous offenses, including smuggling, arson, and the subversion of the armed forces and the police. In June 1976, Mujib's press orders of 1975, which placed the press under overall governmental control, were rescinded, but new regulations forbade the publication of materials critical of martial law.

General Zia's promise to improve amenities in the universities, in the hope students would give up or moderate their penchant for political violence and antigovernment agitation, was ineffective. Violence between rival political factions continued, and students died in the clashes.

POLITICAL ACTIVITY AND THE PROMISE OF ELECTIONS

From a Western point of view the most conciliatory step General Zia could take was to restore popular elections, as promised by presidents Ahmed and Sayem. The general soon concurred; in late November 1975 he said the government should revive democracy with free and fair elections.[21]

At a July 1976 meeting of 39 political leaders, President Sayem said the government intended to permit political parties to resume political activities by August 15 and to hold general elections by the end of February. The leaders, who did not include former president Moshtaque Ahmed or Sabur Khan, a Muslim Leaguer and former supporter of President Ayub, agreed to holding elections on the condition that no "undesirable or unsubstantial" political parties be allowed to contest.

Extensive publicity about plans for February elections temporarily smothered rumors circulating in political circles that the elections might be postponed. Prior to the July meeting General Zia had held talks with leading politicians to ascertain their attitudes toward the holding of elections. The rightist parties favored immediate elections, but leftists and militant opponents of Mujib did not. M. Toaha, leader of the Maoist Communist party of East Bengal, proposed the convening of a national assembly to form a national party before the elections.

An election commission prepared electoral registers throughout the country. Regulations issued after the July meeting required political parties to submit for government approval a constitution, manifesto, program, and list of their affiliated organizations. No parties were permitted to advocate opinions inimical to national independence and security, accept foreign aid, or form paramilitary cadres. Parties claiming to represent the political views of Mujib were also outlawed.

Although 57 parties (or more accurately factions) applied to the government for approval, by the end of November only 21 had been sanctioned. Their manifestos emphasized nationalism and democracy;

secularism was muted. The government in October had announced it would recognize religiously oriented parties.

The spectacle of innumerable political factions bidding for popular favor bewildered or disgusted many citizens. In a roundabout fashion the government revealed its doubts about the merits of a February election. The November 9 and 14 issues of the *Bangladesh Observer*, friendly to the government, published long statements by Maulana Bhashani urging the postponement of the elections until the issues of the Farraka Barrage and "Indian border incursions" had been settled, as 90 percent of the people did not want elections anyway.

Discussions about the election date came to an end on November 21. The president announced its postponement because, he asserted, the public feared that an early election "would jeopardize national unity and solidarity." Personal and party interests, he said, had in too many such cases prevailed over national unity. He also cited a gradual deterioration in law and order, contributed to by "antistate elements" and by border troubles. Noting that other political leaders favored postponement, he promised to hold earlier local elections in January and February 1977.

The week following the postponement of the general election, General Zia assumed the full powers of government as the chief martial law administrator, the post previously held by President Sayem.[22] He forthwith arrested former president Moshtaque Ahmed along with Awami Leaguers and pro-Moscow National Awami party members; in all, more than 100 persons were jailed for actions "prejudicial to the state" because they had opposed the postponement of the elections. A pro-Peking party and other left-wing groups praised the arrests. The indicted political leaders were later sentenced to serve from one to five years for "political corruption and the abuse of power."

The resolute actions of General Zia as martial law administrator suggested he was ready to take on the presidency. The results of so-called nonpartisan local elections in January and February 1977 for union council members (a union council area includes several villages having approximately 10,000 eligible voters) indicated Zia would not be a shoo-in.[23] Awami Leaguers, the general's opponents, won a larger share of the votes than did Muslim Leaguers, his political allies. In fact, however, the results did no more than momentarily delay the general's drive toward the highest office. He had only to wait until April 21 to be named president. On that date President Sayem announced his resignation for reasons of health.[24] Temperamentally inclined toward the courtroom rather than the rough-and-tumble of politics, Sayem had earlier accepted the ceremonial and advisory role of president in Mujib's parliamentary government. He probably exercised a moderating influence on the ambitious general.

PRESIDENT ZIAUR RAHMAN

The 43-year-old Ziaur Rahman, born January 19, 1936, in Bogra, a small town 90 miles northwest of Dacca, belonged to a family of lower-level bureaucrats.[25] He joined the Pakistani army at the age of 17, and most of his military training was in Pakistan. He rose to the rank of major, fought against India in the 1965 war, and served briefly in the British Army of the Rhine. In the late sixties he was known to be sympathetic to the cause of Bangali autonomy. In 1971, as a regimental commander in Chittagong, he became one of the heroes of Bangali liberation and the first Bangali officer in the Pakistani army to revolt against Pakistan. On March 27, immediately following the Dacca killings, his troops captured the Chittagong radio station; he declared himself for national independence. During the resistance he commanded the so-called Z (for Zia) guerrilla forces. In August 1975 he was appointed deputy chief of the army by Sheikh Mujib and in November was promoted to chief by Ahmed.

He was described by foreign correspondents as "dapper" and "immaculately turned out" in the style of a British Guards officer. One observer said, "He marches rather than walks." An interviewer wrote that he gave the impression of a "serene hesitancy" and assured authority. A hardworking politician, he knew every inch of the country and spent more than half his time out of Dacca. He was regarded as a ruthless man, yet moderates "mostly [acclaimed] him as the best thing since independence." During most of the years of Zia's regime from 1975 to 1981, he lived a simple life with his family in the military cantonment on the outskirts of Dacca.

On assuming the presidency, Zia immediately barnstormed the country to muster public support for his government and his policies. He announced a popular referendum would be held on May 30, 1977, referring to it as an exercise of the democratic franchise.[26]

The election commission reported that more than 70 percent of the registered voters went to the polls on May 30 to mark a Yes or No ballot in response to a single question: "Do you have confidence in President Major General Ziaur Rahman and the policies and programs enunciated by him?" The commission declared that a fraction over 98 percent of the electorate voted Yes and noted that about 10 percent more people had voted in the referendum than in the immensely popular election of 1970 that preceeded the advent of Bangladesh.

Ziaur Rahman.

Critics of the referendum complained prior to the vote that no one was permitted to campaign against the general and that many of his opponents were still in jail. The leader of the National Awami party said the announced results of the vote were absurd. He claimed that at selected polling places more votes were reported than had been indicated by his party's estimates of voter turnout.

President Zia said he was surprised by the percentage of the voters voting and in the size of the favorable vote. He thereupon promised to hold general elections in December 1978, but he refused to say whether he would form a political party or bring politicians into his government prior to the 1978 elections. He did say he would turn the country toward democracy little by little. Elections would first be held in municipalities and in districts, the largest local unit of government in rural areas. Until the national elections were held the martial law administration, established by Mujib in 1975, would remain in effect, but political parties would be permitted to hold private meetings.

Apart from his desire to win domestic support, Zia wanted the May referendum to demonstrate to other countries his nation's stability. More immediately, the referendum was intended to give him a firm voice in the June Commonwealth meeting in London and at a later conference in Paris with aid-giving countries.

In one of the most far-reaching acts of his presidency, Zia moved quickly to redirect the course of the nation by modifying its ideology. He revised the Constitution's statement of fundamental principles—a nonjusticiable and political part of the document—altering the language of the principles to bring them in line with a Muslim rather than a secular state. In their rewritten form, the fundamental principles dedicate the nation to "a complete trust and faith in Almighty Allah."[27] The socialist aim of the principles was modified to make that objective consistent with Islamic ideas of social justice and economic equality. The restatement of principles required the government to maintain close relations with all Muslim countries. In making these changes, Zia believed, correctly, that he had responded to popular wishes. The new language did not differ substantially from Mujibist interpretations of the principles, but for Zia the changes symbolized a nationalistic assertion of independence from India. His rejection of a secular ideology invigorated his nationalistic coalition of pro-Islamic and anti-Indian blocs and those favorably disposed to cooperation with Pakistan and Peking.

Ideological nuances did not seem to count when the Awami League won a slight majority of the August election of municipal council chairmen, a repetition of their earlier local election victory.[28] The returns cast doubt on Zia's 98 percent victory in the May referendum. But the president's confidence in his ability to hold onto his office remained unshaken.

MILITARY MUTINIES, 1977

The rise of General Zia to the presidency revived the struggle for power among the armed forces. On September 30, apparently to the surprise of the Zia government, an army tank regiment in Bogra tried to seize the local air force base in order to negotiate the freedom of Colonel Farook Rahman from prison in Dacca. The colonel, leader of the Mujib assassins, had returned to Dacca earlier in the year and had immediately been jailed. President Zia's soldiers surrounded the base, and the president himself is said to have persuaded the rebels to surrender.[29]

Two days later the mutiny spread to the Dacca cantonment a short distance from the airport, where Zia's officers were negotiating with Japanese Red Army hijackers who had forced a Japan Airlines plane to land. One group of rebel soldiers seized and killed several Bangali senior officers at the airport. Another contingent occupied a nearby radio station and announced that an armed rebellion was in progress, "led by armed forces, students, peasants, and workers." A few hours later all the rebels were captured. President Zia said the same day that the attempted coups at Dacca and Bogra were undertaken by "some misled soldiers trying to disrupt the peace at the instigation of interested elements." Officially, 11 air force officers and 10 soldiers on the loyalist side were reported to have been killed and 40 to have been wounded during the mutinies. Unofficial estimates reported that as many as 230, mostly soldiers, had died.

The revolts, which attracted worldwide press attention, were ascribed in Dacca to a conflict between air force enlisted men and officers over pay and service conditions. *Le Monde,* however, suggested they had been planned by the military wing of the JSD organizers of the November 1975 uprising. The Paris paper reported that the air force was decimated—that 18 officers had died in the shoot-out and that half the remaining officers had resigned when Air Marshal Gaffar Mohammad was superseded on October 9 by a group captain. Only 11 officers, said *Le Monde,* were left at that time in the air force.

Trials of rebel officers and men began October 7 before military tribunals. Nearly 100 were executed, about 50 given life imprisonment, and 77 acquitted for involvement in the two rebellions. A justice of the Supreme Court who conducted a probe of the mutinies warned against "antistate elements" who might still try to cripple the economy. The justice accused "illegally armed" elements of endangering the economy; he was understood to refer to the JSD revolutionary army. On October 14 President Zia banned three political parties that he accused of attempting to infiltrate the armed forces and incite violence: the Democratic League headed by Moshtaque Ahmed, the Nationalist Socialist party, and the pro-Soviet Bangladesh Communist party. Their leaders were jailed.

THE PRESIDENTIAL ELECTION OF 1978

Having tried the mutineers and imprisoned his most-feared political opponents, President Zia prepared for a popularly contested election during the following summer, which he hoped would testify to his popularity and constitutional legitimacy. In November he relaxed martial law orders and turned over some of their local administration to the judiciary. At the close of 1977 he said he would form a political front "with the people as the source of all power," because at present "a political vacuum exists which can only be filled by a democratic process."

The vigor of party campaigns in the earlier local elections must have reminded the president that Bangali fondness for parties could not be denied. General dissatisfaction with Zia's uncontested referendum and its misleading ballot count revealed that he had to face opposition at the polls.[30] He moved cautiously toward the creation of a party coalition, after an unsuccessful attempt to establish a broad consensus among all parties similar to the Indian Congress party. The core of his coalition was a revived Muslim League. The Awami League led another coalition to oppose Zia's presidential ambitions.

Zia waited until April 21, 1978, to announce a presidential election to be held six weeks later on June 3.[31] The election, he said, would assure a stable government and "pave the way" to democracy, adding that the Constitution would be amended to provide for an independent judiciary and a general election to establish a "sovereign Parliament," with the president as chief executive and a cabinet headed by a prime minister, like the French presidential system. At the same time he announced that, after the gradual lifting of restrictions on party activities, parliamentary elections would take place in December 1978.

After May 1, 1978, political parties were permitted to campaign publicly in anticipation of the June election, the first presidential vote in the new nation.[32] The Awami League immediately attacked the government for the suddenness of the election call and questioned Zia's authority to perpetuate the presidential form of government, ignoring the fact that it was Mujib who switched to the presidential system.

The temporary coalition supporting President Zia's candidacy, calling itself the Nationalist Front, comprised six parties: a National Democratic party; a Bangladesh Muslim party; the pro-Peking wing of the National Awami party; a United People's party, also pro-Peking; an Islamic Socialist Labor party; and a Hindu minority organization. The opposition coalition, the Democratic United Alliance, consisted in the main of former BAKSAL members of the Awami League, along with the pro-

Moscow branch of the National Awami party and the Janata party of General M.A.G. Osmani. The alliance selected the general as its presidential candidate.

General Osmani, a 65-year-old retired senior general of the Bangali army and the only well-known candidate to oppose President Zia, was in Mujib's first cabinet but soon left it and had remained outside of politics. He was not a strong candidate. At one point he told the press he would not challenge the president if Zia agreed to resign the posts of army chief and martial law administrator and to postpone the elections for 90 days.

Zia's campaign was effective. The economic situation had improved and food crops were more plentiful, even though urban and rural poverty had not mended. Zia toured the countryside, where the Awami League was strong; he told the peasants he would launch more rural development programs. Osmani had little to offer except a discredited parliamentary system.

The electorate went to the polls June 3 without great enthusiasm; only 54 percent of the eligible voters cast their ballots. President Zia won 77 percent of the votes, a better than three-to-one margin.[33] Osmani and his coalition lodged official complaints alleging serious electoral frauds, but they did not pursue their charges. The foreign press reported the election was reasonably fair. The *Statesman* (Calcutta) said there was "little evidence of the rampant lawlessness as under Mujib."

At the end of June the president announced the formation of a cabinet, including a large number of bureaucrats, to assist him in the "economic emancipation of the people."[34] He named Masihur Rahman, leader of the pro-Peking National Awami party and "architect of the Nationalist Front," as senior minister. Members of a revived Muslim League and of the United People's party, consisting of young socialists, were also appointed to the executive body. One-third of the cabinet was made up of party stalwarts as diverse in their political ideologies as the coalition that elected President Zia.

Restless Bangali politicians did not keep their electoral combines together for long. The first to break up, the defeated Awami League, split into two factions. Members of Zia's coalition reestablished their original party independence or dispersed into sectarian fragments. Masihur Rahman's pro-Peking party splintered right and left because of differences over the division of cabinet offices and patronage.

In the wake of party disintegration President Zia found out how to benefit from opposition party turmoil. During the November national holidays he appeased his political rivals by releasing several thousand political prisoners and disconcerted them by organizing the Bangladesh

Nationalist party to assist his followers in the upcoming parliamentary elections.[35]

The next month he held a series of talks with opposition leaders who were threatening to boycott the January 27 elections. His political foes claimed that the date did not give them enough time to organize their campaigns. Zia agreed to postpone the date until February 12, and then to February 18. The elections, he said, would be fair; he appealed to his opponents to participate in order to produce a government elected by the people. He met other opposition demands halfway by suspending martial law and press censorship and by promising to release all political prisoners.

The Awami League, Zia's most formidable opponent, saw his concessions as a victory for its cause and agreed, on January 10, to put up candidates, as did Moscovites. Ataur Rahman Khan, leader of liberal democrats, organized an alliance of splinter groups with his Jatyia League to participate in the elections.

THE PARLIAMENTARY ELECTIONS OF 1979

President Zia opened the campaign of the Bangladesh Nationalist party on January 2 at a mammoth meeting in Dacca.[36] He repeated his previous promise that the majority leader in the Parliament would be prime minister and that the cabinet would be responsible to the Parliament. He also announced the release of 10,000 political prisoners, most of whom, he said, had been jailed before November 1975; presumably they were not friends of Mujib and the Awami League.

Observers in Dacca surmised that as many as 50 parties and more than 2,000 candidates would contest for 300 elective parliamentary seats. They reported that the formidable Bangladesh Nationalist party coalition President Zia had pulled together assured him of majority control. Moderate religiously oriented parties entered the campaign, along with the fundamentalist Jamaat-i-Islam.

In spite of the rhetoric of many parties and candidates, the campaign failed to arouse the expected public enthusiasm, perhaps because the people had already placed their confidence in President Zia. The public also believed Zia had outmaneuvered the more practiced politicians, especially those in the quarrelsome Awami League.

Only 40 percent of the voters turned out for the February 18 elections. Twenty-nine parties and a large number of factions and independents participated. Members of President Zia's party and cabinet won 205 seats; the Malik wing of the Awami League captured 40, although its leader was defeated by a Zia minister. (The Malik wing favored a return to parliamentary government as it was established in the Constitution of 1972.) The right-wing faction of the Muslim League—the Islamic Democratic League, formed by former Ayub minister A. Sabur Khan—gained 19 seats. A few pro-Moscow and pro-Peking factions were elected. Sixteen seats went to independents and the remainder to the leaders of smaller opposition parties. With the 30 seats reserved for women to be selected by the president's party, President Zia had the backing of at least two-thirds of the legislators.

The day after the election the president told foreign correspondents he contemplated no changes in domestic or foreign policy. He said he attached great importance to agricultural development, family planning, and the reduction of illiteracy. He remarked that the government had already decentralized segments of commerce and industry and would continue to encourage private investment, including foreign private investment. He hoped the country would be able to double food production in three to five years, noting that, although the population had increased by five million in 1977/78, grain imports had been halved because of good weather and production increases.

Zia promised to lift martial law within a week after the Parliament met in April 1979, but he refused to resign his military posts until he saw how the Parliament worked. Only a few thousand political prisoners jailed by Mujib, he said, remained to be released. The fate of these prisoners, who also included former president Moshtaque Ahmed, was under "constant review."

The coverage of the election by the world press was much sparser than for previous contests, perhaps because it generally believed President Zia was a certain winner and Bangladesh had begun to settle down. A *New York Times* editorial voiced guarded optimism that the elections held the promise of future stability.

Zia, the first popularly elected president of the nation, had been voted in for a five-year term. His commanding majority in Parliament made it unlikely that the impeachment procedures of the Constitution could be effectively invoked. But the nearly 100 highly vocal opposition members of Parliament were sure to attack the government, the execution of its policies, and its personnel. The promised restoration of fundamental constitutional rights, especially freedom of speech, assembly, and press, offered the politicians and the newspapers opportunities to air their grievances and to test the president's political skills.

ORGANIZING THE NEW GOVERNMENT

With the successful conclusion of the presidential election, which Zia described as a "passage to democracy," he turned to the tasks of establishing relations with Parliament, selecting a cabinet, and addressing the problems presented by divisions within his party and by opposition criticism.

Before the first session of the legislative body, the parliamentary members of the president's Bangladesh Nationalist party selected Shah Azizur Rahman as prime minister, replacing Masihur Rahman, senior minister of the preparliamentary cabinet, who had died March 13.[37] Azizur Rahman, a moderate man of the right and a long-standing member of the Muslim League of East Pakistan, had been a member of President Zia's cabinet since 1978. He was ostensibly chosen for his reputation as a speaker and parliamentarian.

The Parliament convened on April 2, 1979, and in its first five-day session adopted the Fifth Constitutional Amendment Bill of 1979, which confirmed all laws and decisions previously made under martial law.[38] The prime minister said that martial law, the source of recent law-making, had provided continuity between the parliaments of Mujib and Zia and that the enactment of the bill would "make it possible to lift martial law in the shortest possible time." The opposition, led by the Awami League's parliamentary spokesman, unavailingly objected to the amendment on the grounds that it confirmed martial law court punishments against which no appeal was allowed. At the end of the Parliament's session President Zia announced the end of martial law rule, which had been in effect since August 15, 1975.[39] He appealed to the political parties to help the government maintain law and order.

On April 15 the president appointed a cabinet of 29 ministers, with Shah Azizur Rahman prime minister. Four members of the previous cabinet, chiefly former civil servants, were dropped.[40] Zia kept the secretariat, defense, cabinet affairs, and science and technology ministries under his wing. Dr. Mirza N. Huda, the planning minister, also won the finance post. The foreign minister, Professor Shamsul Huq, a nonparliamentarian like Huda, was reappointed. Dr. Amina Rahman was named minister of women's affairs. Five of the cabinet ministers were retired military officers.

From the time General Zia had become martial law administrator he had expanded his political power with the help of a civilian bureaucracy that included a sprinkling of retired military officers in key positions.[41] The martial law regime, which lasted three and one-half years, enlarged the responsibilities of the bureaucracy and heightened its prestige within the government's structures. In 1979 the government modernized the bureaucracy. It instituted a Senior Service Pool, similar to Britain's Administrative Service and the more recently established top categories of the U.S. civil service. The government later approved in principle the organization of 14 cadres (categories of service) in all of which able and efficient civil servants could reach the highest posts in the bureaucracy. Although in theory the plan placed all civil servants on an equal footing, critics feared it would bring more army officers into the Senior Service Pool. Press complaints of the arrogance and excessive numbers of military men in the government echoed the views of civilian Bangalis.

President Zia, well aware that his regime could not get along without political parties, also knew he would have difficulties getting along with them. His Bangladesh Nationalist party, a confederation of left- and right-wingers, was held together by his personality and drive and the adroit use of political favors.[42] In order to consolidate the electoral gains of the party, in the early fall he organized a power base within it. A 12-man standing committee made up of government officials and party representatives, including four members of Parliament, became the party's top policy-making body.[43] At the same time a 120-member national committee was appointed to represent the interests of the districts. In an attempt to ward off a struggle over these organizational changes, Zia talked with party members prior to the selection of the committees. He yoked the party to the cabinet and the Parliament by naming the senior deputy prime minister, A. Badruddoza Choudhury, the party's secretary-general. Choudhury resigned his second cabinet post of health minister to devote more time to party work and to the party's parliamentary group.

Local newspaper critics labeled the standing committee a politburo that would leave the 450 members of the party's general council out of the decision-making process. The opposition regarded the move as evidence of another corrupt political deal designed to hold the Zia party together.

OPPOSITION PARTIES

Opposition parties stalked the government throughout 1979. The Muslim League and the Islamic Democratic League called for an Islamic republic, although the Awami League and leftist parties generally disapproved of the demand.[44] Prime Minister Azizur Rahman told an Indian news agency that the government "had no plans to make the country into an Islamic republic nor a plan to change the national anthem [Tagore's 'Golden Bengal'] or the flag." The Awami League tried to blame the government for a threatened food shortage brought about by winter and spring droughts.[45] When President Zia and his party colleagues toured the countryside, assuring the people the problems would be resolved, Awami League spokesmen following the government entourage alleged the president had questioned the patriotism of the Awamis and had accused them of being foreign agents. By the end of

1979 the food issue lost its relevance as large imports of food grains brought supplies to normal levels.

On the fourth anniversary of the death of Sheikh Mujib, August 15, 1979, the Awamis and the pro-Moscow Bangladesh Communist party for the first time observed a "day of mourning," while rightist groups celebrated a "day of deliverance." Heavy rains spoiled both events.

During 1979 student political organizations renewed their quarrels.[46] Anti-Zia student unions at Dacca and Rajshahi universities fought pitched battles with government-affiliated students in which several students were killed. In the springtime student union elections, both of the unions supported by the Awami League and by the president's Bangladesh Nationalist party lost to the National Socialist party students. The new leaders asked the universities to establish a "gun-free zone." The student conflicts of the seventies were at once more violent and more confusing than those of the sixties. In the earlier decade students were unarmed and factionalism among them less fragmented.

PARLIAMENTARY AND PARTY MANEUVERS

The "sovereign" Parliament opened its 1980 session in February. Perhaps it was the political rebound of Mrs. Gandhi that inspired the Awami-led coalition of 80 opposition parliamentarians to back a legislative boycott and a 24-point charter, which they proclaimed was the first step toward the reestablishment of parliamentary democracy.[47] The government accepted two of their demands. It agreed to hold more frequent and longer parliamentary sessions and to make available to the Parliament all international agreements signed by the government. Zia also promised at a later date to meet other demands, such as the release of political prisoners. The concessions did not satisfy a majority of the opposition—the Awami League, the National Socialist party, and a scattering of smaller parties. They boycotted the Parliament until the end of the session. However, members of rightist parties and many independents who initially joined the boycott ended their action in response to the president's concessions and promises; some said they were swayed by more practical considerations, like preserving the powers of the presidency. The president had let it be known that parliamentary sovereignty meant rule by the majority party; the best the minority could expect was for the majority to listen and respond to its demands. The opposition sought more than that; its members wanted to attract the support of politicians in the president's coalition-ridden party.

President Zia matched his opponents' moves and simultaneously carried out a promise on March 24, two days before the ninth anniversary of independence, releasing 1,600 political prisoners jailed under Mujib's emergency law of 1974.[48] Among those released, the most important included former president Moshtaque Ahmed and two National Socialist party leaders, both of whom had been sentenced in 1976 for plotting to overthrow the government of President Sayem. All those released were anti-Awami politicians. An earlier brief strike by prisoners convicted by military tribunals may also have influenced Zia's decision. Soon afterward he jailed the leaders of the Communist party's pro-Soviet branch and of the Awami League for encouraging industrial strikes in the spring. In June he jailed Awami Leaguers who had called a six-hour strike to denounce the execution of four of the league's members.[49] Later in the year Zia turned the other cheek and declared a general amnesty for most categories of prisoners, except those sentenced for violent crimes or by martial law courts. Zia's policy of divide and rule undermined the strength of his rivals.

Government action against party enemies did not stop dissension among the military. In June the government revealed a threatened military coup and arrested four senior army officers, along with other military personnel, for "spreading disaffection among the armed forces" by promoting a rebellion in the army and for holding secret meetings in Dacca and Bogra.[50] The rebels did not go on trial until March 1981.

Private vendettas reported by the local press may have prompted Vice-President Abdus Sattar on July 25, 1980, to tell the members of a conference on crime that it was "no longer safe to live in Dacca."[51] Although the home minister tried to play down the extent of personal violence, the police told the press that crime had increased among young people and better families and increased disciplinary action had had to be taken in the police force itself. *Holiday* claimed most cases of violence were traceable to personal quarrels among the government's youth leaders. Trial delays and shortages of judges increased law enforcement problems. The situation was similar to that in the cities of many Western countries, save that much of the Bangali violence was politically inspired.

A different order of problems confronted the government in March, when 700,000 low-paid civil servants held a five-day nonviolent strike to demand improvements in allowances, pensions, and the system of appointments to the service as well as the right to unionize.[52] Government officials contended that civil servants had recently benefited from increased emoluments. The officials opposed unionization out of fear of future civil service strikes. The strikers had the support of opposition parties and trade unions.

The establishment minister, Major General Majedul Huq, on September 1 put into effect a modified version of the 14-cadre reorganization plan for the bureaucracy approved the previous November. He said that new administrative structure would abolish "the colonial concept of 'rank and status'" because all civil servants would have equal opportunities for promotion and all hiring decisions would be made on the basis of competitive examinations. However, advancement to the top posts was limited by length-of-service requirements. In the view of the high-level bureaucrats the new service became a "lottery" rather than a "personnel system." Those who had gone on strike in March, however, accepted the reforms.

Zia's reduction in the size of his cabinet to improve the quality of its work and to eliminate corruption appears to have been a juggling act,[53] for the numbers of ministers of state and deputy ministers increased. The changes may have strengthened party loyalties to the president.

The year 1980 ended peaceably enough, but political controversies resumed during the first five months of 1981. President Zia celebrated both National Day (December 16), and the tenth anniversary of national independence, March 26, 1981, on the same spring day.[54] A three-hour parade by 50,000 troops was witnessed by such guests as Sekou Touré of Guinea and the Palestine Liberation Organization's Yasir Arafat. Zia's critics remarked that by merging the two days the president sought to placate Islamic parties that had opposed the war of independence.

The Awami League in March adopted a new tack to challenge President Zia. Members of the league traveled to New Delhi to elect Mrs. Hasina Wajed, the daughter of Sheikh Mujib, as their president in absentia.[55] Since the death of other members of her family in 1975 she had lived with her husband in New Delhi. In mid-May they returned to Dacca. The Dacca press remarked that her selection followed the South Asian pattern of crisis politics, in which relatives of former leaders are chosen to lead. More important, her election indicated that the Awami League had been unable to agree on one of its members as president. The Indian press, which frequently criticized the Zia government, supported the Awami League's choice of Mrs. Wajed.

The selection of Hasina, as she was popularly known, set off an exchange of political fireworks. She charged that President Zia had rewarded her father's killers with choice diplomatic posts; she vowed to see them tried for murder. President Zia, said to be unperturbed by the Awami League's election of Hasina, ascribed it to the influence of Mrs. Gandhi. According to the London *Times,* President Zia, addressing members of his Bangladesh Nationalist party, predicted that "Awami

League followers were out to create a law and order situation with the objective of restoring the one party system."[56] However, it was neither the Awami League nor Hasina, but Zia's fellow army officers that would haunt the nation with the spectre of authoritarian rule. On May 30, 1981, three years after his election to the presidency, Ziaur Rahman was assassinated by his officers.

CHAPTER 15

Economic Policies and Progress, 1975–81

The political, social, and economic strategies that make up a policy of interdependence must include national self-development programs and mutually advantageous international trade and aid arrangements. Once the Dacca government understood the need for a policy of interdependence with other nations, it devised and carried out domestic social, agricultural, and industrial programs and pragmatically pursued better relations with its neighbors and with more distant nations. The social and economic policy of self-reliance inaugurated by Mujib and transformed by Zia into numerous other practical programs has yet to get up a full head of steam, not because international agencies and other governments failed to advise on and assist in its accomplishment, nor for want of trying by Dacca, but because political turmoil slowed its progress. In the depressed economic conditions of the world since 1981, however, it has become clearer that progress in national self-reliance depends not only on a manageable level of political debate in Bangladesh, but even more on the willingness of rich nations to maintain a high level of aid and trade with the Bangalis.

During most of President Zia's administration the economy improved, with the help of good weather.[1] The improvements owed much to the government's enthusiasm for development programs. Per capita income increased, notwithstanding population growth, and export earnings grew. Consumer price indices, after climbing as much as 80 percent in some earlier years, steadied around 15 percent. The production of food and cash crops, the improvement of rural roads, and the establishment of irrigation and flood control measures took the highest priority in development budgets. Food crop damage caused by a 1979 drought and a 1980 flood was offset by food imports. Local private capital entered the domestic market and an improved climate for foreign investment attracted companies from abroad—trends that upset dedicated socialists and others fearful of the consequences of foreign participation in the nation's industries. Factories and mills, underutilized since independence, began to produce. Through 1980 aid-giving countries and international agencies increased their commitments. However, in 1981 the assassination of President Zia, the worsening world economy, and cutbacks in foreign assistance presented a new government with major economic dilemmas.

BUDGETS AND PLANS

Yearly budgets prepared by post-Mujib governments from 1975/76 to 1980/81 organized fiscal programs intended to advance self-reliance in agriculture, industry, commerce, and social welfare.[2] Government expenditures for these purposes in 1980/81 more than doubled those of 1976/77, and the development budget for 1980/81 increased nearly twofold over 1978/79. Although inflation accounts for much of the increases, major economic and social programs greatly benefited from increased allocations.

The political victories of the president and his party in 1978 and 1979 made it possible, with assistance from abroad, to combat the food shortages threatened by drought and floods, to limit increases in the cost of living, and to reinforce hopes for more vigorous development of the economy. Budget increases reflected the confidence of the government in its ability to manage the economy and to bring in generous amounts of foreign aid (more than half of it from grants by the United States, Japan, and European and Arab countries) for its development programs. President Zia's optimism and enthusiasm were never in short supply.

Fiscal planning inaugurated by the young economists of the Mujib government fell out of favor upon his death because of its socialist slant. The Zia government in 1977 substituted a two-year economic strategy and later launched a second five-year plan for 1980–85 to justify its private and public development budgets to foreign donors and to guide rather than control their expenditures.[3]

Zia's finance minister said that the five-year plan aspired to a radical transformation of the nation's socioeconomic structures and to a new emphasis on developmental over current expenditures. By allocating one-third of development spending to rural development and by encouraging private industry, the minister declared, the plan would ensure a broader distribution of the nation's wealth and increase job opportunities. Outlays of rural development funds, it was believed, would staunch the flow of unemployed peasants to the cities. He held out high expectations for greater economic growth levels derived from indigenous industry and from rural and urban construction work. Admitting the foreign aid component of the plan for fiscal year 1981/82 would be about 13 percent less than under previous economic plans, the minister stated that new taxes and the self-financing of the public sector would make up for the decline in foreign aid. He also underlined the vital importance of sustained foreign aid. From an outsider's point of view, the second five-year plan looked overoptimistic, which in fact it turned out to be.

In an interview with a *Far Eastern Economic Review* correspondent not long before his death, President Zia admitted that the plan was in trouble because of world economic conditions. A revised plan, he said, would trim less essential projects. New sources of aid would be sought and domestic taxes increased. The cost of projects like road and building construction would also be reduced. Zia asked for more bilateral aid in view of the decision of the multilateral aid group to cut back its previous year's assistance.

PRIVATE AND PUBLIC INDUSTRIES

On the advice of World Bank officials, General Zia in 1975 had begun to denationalize the shipping and jute industries. In April 1979 the minister of industries repeated the government's commitment to encourage private domestic and foreign enterprises.[4] He offered liberal tax exemptions or reductions for specified periods, invited foreign firms to bring in management teams, and promised an efficient investment coordinating office to accelerate the repatriation of profits. An interim two-year plan for 1978–80, devised by the finance minister, projected larger public and private investments in agricultural production, housing, and industry. Independent of government action, the moribund Dacca Stock Exchange planned reforms in its operations to encourage private investment.

The finance minister later said the private sector was expected to increase its investments during the lifetime of the second five-year plan. He asserted that the private sector, accorded tax incentives, would cooperate with the public sector in order "to play a role within the framework of social justice." The remark, it was hoped, would reassure doubters that the government would hold the private sector publicly accountable.

Nationalized industries were also assured of a future in the economy.[5] A 1979 government report stated these enterprises had recovered from the losses they suffered in previous years. Government corporations, it said, had been streamlined and their performance improved by more effective handling of labor-management relations, updated management and technical skills, and closer supervision of operations. The report cited production figures showing that recent improvements had been made in the output and exports of the corporations.

The government acknowledged that industrial progress depended to a great extent on cooperation with trade unions.[6] Large-scale industries, principally in the hands of public corporations, were completely unionized. The right to bargain collectively, abridged by 1975 laws, was restored in 1978. Although strikes in these industries were illegal, they were normally tolerated. However, in 1979, during a government jute mill strike in Chittagong, union leaders were jailed and their union supporters dismissed from their jobs. The government then promised to adopt a labor policy consistent with that of the International Labor Organization, permitting strikes except in essential industries such as power, water supplies, and communications, and assuring higher levels of workmen's compensation and minimum wages.

RURAL DEVELOPMENT

Before 1977 rural development programs had scarcely gone beyond the Food for Work projects that Mujib had reinstituted in the sixties. His government and its economic experts had been too preoccupied with the promotion of public industrial development to devote sufficient attention to agriculture. Mujib's critics thought that, for the most part, he took the peasants for granted. In 1977 General Zia heeded the advice of international lending agencies that rural development should be given first priority.[7] He acted for political as well as economic reasons, since he was at that time searching for a constituency. Before the referendum of public confidence of May 1977, Zia issued a manifesto announcing his intention to accentuate rural development.[8] He proposed to increase food and textile production, eradicate illiteracy, improve health services, and encourage private investment. He asserted his plan would mean the "emancipation of the people."

Increased production of cash crops and foodstuffs, including wheat and vegetables, was mandated in 1978 for a five-year period in the neglected northwest region of the country. The plan called for the irrigation of more than a million nonirrigated acres, the application of fertilizer, and the building of facilities to process farm products. Integrated development projects were undertaken in other rural areas with funds provided by the World Bank, foreign government, and domestic sources. The projects included cooperative programs, training for cooperative management, drainage improvements, and special educational programs to help women participate more fully in rural development and in family planning.

The economic agenda of rural development was increasingly merged with programs to slow down population growth.[9] Family planning facilities and personnel were expanded through generous budgetary allocations to rural organizations. The press and the government's radio and television stations conducted campaigns to popularize the idea that population control is an integral part of the war on poverty.

The government's estimate of the population in 1980—just short of 90 million—indicated a growth rate of 3.6 percent since independence. Population increases had hardly been slowed. Zia, supported by some Muslim religious leaders, encouraged the use of contraception and sterilization. In March 1981 the president asked people to adopt a program of one child to a family, an idea fostered by the Chinese. It seemed unlikely, however, that families would be willing to follow his suggestion. A proposal by members of Parliament in 1981 to raise the legal marriage age from 16 to 18 for women and from 18 to 21 for men was more practical. The introduction of the proposal was symptomatic of a change in public attitudes toward population control. It did not become law, however, because of conservative Islamic opposition.

A rural industries program to increase the processing of agricultural products and give jobs to the unemployed and underemployed in villages and towns was funded in development budgets of the seventies.[10] Roughly 20 percent of nonurban workers were reported to be employed in more than 57,000 existing small industrial units, most of which were privately owned. However, the shortage of energy and intermittent shortages of raw materials hindered their progress. The government proposed to finance the correction of these deficiencies and to introduce vocational training to protect the "infant" industries.

A more spectacular and controversial program—a large-scale canal-digging project—formally began on December 1, 1979.[11] The drought that earlier in the year had forced the government to import several million tons of food grains precipitated the execution of President Zia's pet scheme. He planned to create a network of 103 canals stretching over 500 miles of the countryside, which would irrigate 550,000 acres of land and produce an additional 350,000 tons of food by 1981. Part of the cost of the digging was borne by the Food for Work program. Popular enthusiasm for the undertaking, spurred by the president's well-publicized visit to the countryside to work alongside the diggers, attracted many volunteer workers.

Engineers and bureaucrats criticized the digging as reckless because it neglected structural engineering considerations such as drainage and the nature of the soil. Opposition politicians argued that landlords alone would profit from the newly irrigated areas and sharecroppers would become mere hired hands. According to a correspondent of the *Far Eastern Economic Review,* President Zia favored land redistribution but was unable to persuade his landowning cabinet members to commit themselves to that policy. The strict enforcement of Mujib's eight-acre limit on individual and family holdings would go a long way toward more distribution of presently available land and of the maximum possible acreage within the boundaries of the nation. On the basis of present evidence, five-acre Bangali farms have proved to be the most efficient. An eight-acre limit could, therefore, be counted on to increase rather than diminish farm productivity. Since such a reform leaves sizable numbers of sharecroppers and hired hands, additional improvements are required—the further development of cooperatives, for one. Sharecroppers everywhere in the country, not, as at present, only in isolated areas, should be able to have a larger share of the crops they harvest. Farm workers' unions would give a forum to the hired hands.

The Food and Agriculture Organization, the United States, and private foreign agencies, such as CARE and the Catholic Relief Services, which help to distribute food grains, had made it possible for the Zia government to continue the Food for Work program.[12] American AID officials claimed that in 1975/76 the program employed 600,000 rural workers, and the next year 790,000; they estimated that more than one million would be employed in 1977/78 for an average of 35 days a year. The workers engaged in road building, railroad maintenance, and the clearing of irrigation channels, according to AID, as well as contributing to better transportation and the availability of farmland water.

Critics of Food for Work like to cite a Food and Agriculture Organization (FAO) evaluation that praised the program's employment objectives but contended that it is not a long-run answer to rural unemployment. FAO noted that the program, because it lent itself to the misappropriation of grain, the misuse of funds, and false reporting, could create a new class of profiteers and might encourage poor-quality construction work. The organization seemed to be surprised that workers in the program received less than urban workers performing similar tasks. The report concluded that Food for Work brought greater benefits to surplus farmers than to the rest of the country, but it did not comment on the productivity of those benefited or propose a better alternative.

For all its limitations, the program is likely to continue as long as U.S. food grains are available, but it could be reduced or eliminated if the government's higher food production plan nears its self-sufficiency goal. Besides, as Bangali economists point out, a decline in food imports automatically reduces project assistance because local funds generated by the government's sale of the imports help it to pay for the projects. Fewer productive structures limit the ability of the economy to increase export earnings. These arguments were accepted when the Mujib government carried on its earlier food program. Longer-run solutions have been built into other development programs.

FOREIGN TRADE

Export earnings, with which the Bangalis buy the goods they need to increase production and to meet their external obligations, increased slowly.[13] Better food crops in 1977 and 1978 temporarily reduced food imports and made it possible to import other necessities. Improvements in trade will result in the future from the renewal of trade agreements with the Soviet Union, India, Pakistan, and other nations and from new agreements with China and Indonesia.

Increased industrial production made it possible for 1980/81 exports to surpass those of the previous fiscal year. An increase in the exports of nonjute products resulted from an agreement with the European Economic Community providing for duty-free entry of certain Bangali textiles produced in garment factories and financed by private foreign capital. Trade promotion centers were opened in Europe in 1981, where Bangali officials and private traders sought to attract technical and financial assistance as well as direct investment. They have been quite successful. The Dacca government also granted trade concessions to domestic producers to encourage their export business. These actions, however limited, registered a new aggressiveness and self-confidence.

The large excess of imports over exports in recent years goaded the government to take further trade action. Import procedures were revised in 1980 and public aid allocated to export-oriented industries. Increases in garment and textile exports made a dent in the nearly total dependence on the jute trade. The substitution of domestic natural gas for expensive diesel oil imported from the Soviet Union helped to improve the balance of trade. To attract foreign investment and expand employment, three processing zones (where imported raw materials or semifinished goods are turned into more finished products) were authorized in 1981.

INTERNATIONAL ECONOMIC AID

It was not until the Bangladesh Aid Group, established in 1974 by 22 governments and international agencies, met in Paris around the end of May 1976 to consider aid for the next fiscal year that a balanced industrial and agricultural self-reliance program was spelled out.[14] The group agreed that conditions for development had improved. It exacted pledges from Bangali officials to modernize their administrative procedures, decentralize government decision making, set up task forces to report on critical problems, encourage private investment, emphasize population control, increase agricultural production, and improve grain storage management. With Bangali assent to these changes, the group recommended the investment of $1.1 billion for development assistance to begin July 1, 1976.

Robert McNamara, president of the World Bank, visited Dacca in early November 1976.[15] The Bangalis gave him a pessimistic report on the economic state of the nation, including alarming deficiencies in nutrition. They told him that a policy of income redistribution, advocated by many critics of the government, was utterly impracticable because of the narrow range of national per capita incomes; at the end of 1976 the per capita income was $90. They noted that all Bangali per capita incomes were at low levels and 80 percent of them were below the poverty level. The Bangali statement concluded that to avoid absolute poverty, an annual growth rate of 5 percent was an economic imperative and impossible without outside help.

The dramatization of Bangladesh's problems rather than its successes was part of Zia's campaign to persuade the World Bank and other donors that the nation's economy could not improve without significant foreign assistance. As long as McNamara was the head of the bank he strongly supported the proposition that aid should first go to the poorest countries, a category for which Bangladesh easily qualified. On his 1976 visit McNamara told the local press the World Bank was interested in promoting projects that would reduce rural unemployment, increase agricultural production, and raise the level of industrial production. He said he was satisfied that the Dacca authorities were giving high priorities to agricultural development and family planning.

During the month of McNamara's visit Zia responded to the recommendations of the Bangladesh Aid Group to decentralize decision making in economic administration.[16] He ordered the direct election of the chairmen of the basic unit of government, the union council. An elected chairman, Zia said, would be able to persuade the government in Dacca to pay attention to local needs. He also directed the nation's banks to expand their activities in rural areas.

Later, when President Zia organized his Bangladesh Nationalist party and development programs were well under way, he gave important responsibilities for local development to his rural party members. His critics charged him with imitating Ayub's Basic Democracy—Awami

Leaguers did not mention Mujib's suggested administrative reforms of 1975, which hinted at a similar type of local party control.

Domestic controversies over the administration of aid did not hamper the government's drive to obtain outside help.[17] From 1977 to 1981 moderate levels of grants and loans from the International Development Association, the Asian Development Bank, and from other nations nearly doubled. Large portions of the monies from the West took the form of grants. For example, in 1979, in addition to the several million tons of foodstuffs loaned or granted to the Bangalis to cover the losses from that year's drought, European, Asian, and Arab countries (alone or in conjunction with international agencies) helped to finance agricultural and export programs, industrial plants, and vocational training and educational programs.

The deteriorating world economy of 1980/81 and changing international assistance policies brought a decline in the aid the Dacca government had hoped for. The suspension of a previous grant by the IMF after the assassination of President Zia presented Dacca with a new set of problems (see chapter 17).

Notwithstanding the nation's prolonged economic struggle, Bangali diplomacy since independence improved regional relations and established its credentials in global matters. In the long run the nation's economy will profit from the nation's diplomatic stature.

CHAPTER 16

Foreign Relations, 1975–81

Bangali quiet diplomacy during the last half of the seventies contrasted pointedly with the brouhaha of its internal politics. The hundreds of millions of dollars in aid obtained from international organizations and rich nations testified to its successes. Faithful to a homegrown, non-aligned policy, Bangali diplomacy commanded respect among the world of nations, a respect demonstrated by the nation's election to the United Nations Security Council and its selection as a representative of the Third World at the North-South Conference at Cancun. The continuity of its policies with respect to Asian, Muslim, and Western nations reinforced that esteem. Its persevering dialogue with neighboring countries, especially with India, despite the region's recurring problems, represented a realistic use of diplomatic skills and helped maintain peace on the subcontinent. In response to a variety of international and domestic influences the government improved its human rights record and supported regionalism and a better international economic order.

SOUTH ASIA

Three days after Mujib's assassination Mrs. Gandhi hailed him as a man "dedicated to peace and friendship on the subcontinent."[1] To counter the suspicion that the government in Dacca would loosen its ties with India, the high commissioner of Bangladesh to New Delhi called on the Indian foreign secretary to appeal for friendship and cooperation. Plane flights between the two countries were resumed. Radio Bangladesh on August 20 reported that President Ahmed had conveyed his profound regrets to Mrs. Gandhi over Mujib's death. India kept its diplomatic mission in Dacca. Indian officials, however, must have resented the anti-Indian and pro-Chinese editorials of Enayetullah

Khan, editor of the *Bangladesh Times,* a government organ. One editorial denounced India and the Soviet Union for threatening hegemony and imposing unequal treaties on the Bangalis. President Ahmed prevailed on the editor, however, to commend India for its support of Bangali independence.

The day after the death of Mujib, President Bhutto announced that his government would immediately recognize the new regime and urged Islamic and Third World countries to do the same.[2] He promised the Bangalis a gift of 50,000 tons of rice and a large donation of clothing. Bhutto was obviously pleased by the removal of Mujib.

Several weeks later President Ahmed announced the imminent exchange of ambassadors with Pakistan and China. The government of Mrs. Gandhi reacted coldly to the news, although China had had a diplomatic mission in New Delhi since 1947 and her government had greatly improved its relations with Pakistan.

Sayem and the Zia governments nurtured the international good will the Bangalis had attained among the Western and Eastern powers during and after the fight for independence. It reached out to other Muslim nations, solidified its ties with the Arab states, and made new contacts with Southeast Asian nations. Perforce, Zia's regime gave its closest attention to the problems of the subcontinent, and especially to those with India.

Many of the problems, exacerbated by Indian support of Mujib dissidents and by Muslim Bangali suspicions of India, focused on new and old grievances. With the emergence of Zia border frays between Bangali troops and Mujibist guerrillas sheltered in India whipped up anti-Indian reactions among Bangalis.[3] Dissatisfaction with Mujib's agreement on control of the Ganges waters eventually led the Zia government to reopen the Farraka Barrage issue with Mrs. Gandhi's successors.

Stories from Dacca in November 1975 alleged that Bangali border troops and pro-Mujib insurgents had engaged in pitched battles. In December the two governments tried but failed to end the clashes. Mrs. Gandhi, wary of the Zia government and troubled by mounting anti-Indian sentiment in Dacca, attributed the border problem to the interference of "foreign powers in the affairs of Bangladesh," presumably referring to Pakistan. Mrs. Gandhi's statement, offensive to the Bangalis, did not improve the situation. Throughout 1976 the Mujibists, several hundred strong, made sporadic border raids. Foreign observers in Dacca agreed that India was training and arming the guerrillas. The Zia government in response increased its military expenditures.

The unhappy relations of Dacca with Mrs. Gandhi obscured the fact that the two countries continued to cooperate in matters of mutual advantage. A meeting of Indian and Bangali experts in the fall of 1976 completed the demarcation of their common boundaries in accordance with an agreement negotiated by the Mujib government. The two governments also extended earlier trade agreements for another three years.[4]

Where national economic interests conflicted, however, settlements were hard to come by. During 1976 the media of both countries engaged in a ferocious battle of words over an Indian decision to limit the flow of Ganges waters into Bangladesh through the Farraka Barrage. General Zia brought the issue to the U.N. General Assembly at the beginning of its 1976/77 sessions in the hope that that body would intervene on his side. Because most U.N. members saw no way to settle the dispute, the Political Committee of the assembly politely returned the problem to the contending parties with the suggestion they resume bilateral discussions.

The rout of Mrs. Gandhi's government early in 1977 improved the atmosphere for bilateral talks. In mid-April 1977, after an acrimonious discussion in Dacca, the two delegations announced they had reached "an understanding" on sharing the Ganges waters. Details were to be worked out by officials meeting in New Delhi. But the first talks, held in May, reached no conclusions.

Indian Prime Minister Morarji Desai and General Zia, meeting in London in June, arrived at a second understanding calculated to make future detailed discussions more fruitful. After many months of bargaining, on November 3 the two nations came to a settlement.[5] The pact, which was to run until 1982, or later if mutually agreeable, set out the quantities each country would take from the Ganges during the dry period of January 1 to May 31 each year. Because the governments realized that the Ganges cannot adequately supply both countries during the dry season, they reactivated the Joint Rivers Commission to explore other measures to improve the regional distribution of the delta river systems.

The agreement did not satisfy the West Bengal government, which argued that it sacrificed the interests of the port of Calcutta. The Bangalis rejected the complaint on the grounds that the new agreement gave India more water. Many Bangalis, on the other hand, saw the agreement as a sellout to India.

By the spring of 1978 the Joint Rivers Commission had come up with two different long-run solutions to the water shortage problem.[6] New Delhi, viewing the Ganges and Brahmaputra as one river system, proposed the excavation of a 100-mile-long canal in Bangladesh, connecting the Brahmaputra with the Ganges to regulate its larger flow of water. The Bangalis maintained that such a canal would result in the loss of significant quantities of cultivable land and would uproot thousands of people. They also argued that dams along the Brahmaputra are not technically feasible and, because the Brahmaputra flows through Tibet and China (which claims control over the river's headwaters) as well as India and Bangladesh, the government of China must be involved in the project. The Bangali alternate plan envisaged the building of reservoirs in Nepal and India that could store monsoon waters in the Himalayan country and augment the Ganges during the dry season. The Bangalis claimed that studies of Nepalese water resources indicated dams built in that country could also be used for irrigation and hydropower.

U.S. President Jimmy Carter, speaking to the Indian Parliament at the end of December 1977, and British Prime Minister Callaghan, addressing news conferences in New Delhi and Dacca in early January 1978, both promised that their governments would assist in developing regional water uses. Continuing disputes between Bangladesh and India on such uses postponed action.

An Indian journalist watching the February 1979 parliamentary elections in Bangladesh noted that the anti-Indian voices heard during the presidential campaign of 1978 were muted. During that campaign President Zia had remarked that relations with India had improved with the victory of the Janata government.[7]

The meetings of President Zia and Prime Minister Desai in Dacca during April 1979 gave a fillip to the hopes of Bangalis looking for improved relations with their giant neighbor.[8] At the conclusion of the sessions the two leaders agreed to negotiate "the optimum use" of their water resources, to hasten "a mutually acceptable long run increase" in the flow of the Ganges waters, and to deal with "problems relating to some of the border rivers." They instructed the Joint Rivers Commission to begin action on these issues. Separate negotiations were to resume on the problem of the maritime boundaries of Bangladesh and India in the Bay of Bengal. The leaders also promised to act promptly on cooperative arrangements in the fields of agriculture, shipping, technology, education, and culture. India agreed to buy cement, fertilizer, and other Bangali products in order to reduce existing trade imbalances with Bangladesh.

The Joint Rivers Commission quickly decided to establish a committee to discuss approaching Nepal about the Bangali proposal to increase the flow of the Ganges from its headwaters—a proposition Mrs. Gandhi had been unwilling to consider.[9] Discussion of other river problems was scheduled for a later date.

The joint communiqué issued by the president and prime minister did not mention arrangements they had entered into to dispose of the sticky issues between the two nations.[10] Prime Minister Desai, however, told his Parliament that illegal migrations between the two countries would be halted. The prime minister agreed informally to turn over to the Bangalis the Mujibist guerrillas operating in areas north of Dacca and to repatriate some 21,000 Indian Muslims who had fled a short time earlier into Bangladesh following communal riots in West Bengal. In its own interest the Indian government sealed off its borders to prevent 50,000 Biharis from marching across India to Pakistan.

The return of Mrs. Gandhi to power on January 8, 1980, amid turmoil in the Muslim world, moved President Zia to meet with her at a working luncheon while he was in New Delhi addressing a late January meeting of the United Nations Industrial Development Organization.[11] The meeting stimulated speculation that friendly relations with India would be the order of the day. But the Dacca government worried that Mrs. Gandhi would resume her hard-line policy with regard to the Ganges water problem. The concern seemed justified.

Press reports coming from India in 1980 predicted the 1977 agreement regarding the flow of the Ganges into Bangladesh would be allowed to end in 1982, the terminal year of the accord.[12] The Indian government maintained that its share of Ganges water permitted by the agreement was not enough to clear out the accumulated silt at the port of Calcutta. The Indians also alleged the Joint Rivers Commission had not investigated the river's flow into the Hooghly. Meanwhile, the Bangali proposal of a Nepalese storage reservoir and India's scheme to connect the Brahmaputra with the Ganges by a canal through Bangladesh were in limbo. The Dacca government, according to *Holiday*, rejected the Indian proposal as "legally unjustifiable, technically impractical, economically and ecologically disastrous."

"It is comic but symptomatic of relations between India and Bangladesh that the two countries are arguing about competing claims to an island that may not exist," said the *Economist.*[13] Its wry comment referred to the government of West Bengal's claim for India of a "new island" which, it said, had appeared in the Bay of Bengal. After that government sent an expedition to the island, called New Moore, to plant an Indian flag, Dacca protested. New Delhi officials, however, intervened to say the island had been there since 1971, was claimed by both countries and lies closer to India than to Bangladesh. However, a bigger second "island" formed by the silt from the Ganges remaining under the waters of the Bay lies closer to Bangladesh. By the end of the year, the Bangali and Indian foreign offices agreed to a study of both islands to help settle their claims. Anti-Zia forces in Dacca denounced the study as a concession to India's "big power chauvinism." India later sent a naval ship to New Moore (also known as South Talpatty) but subsequently withdrew it.

An old Indian-Bangali dispute with serious social and political implications cropped up again. During the Ayub years thousands of Bangalis living in neighboring Assam had been forced to return to East Pakistan.[14] In the seventies Indians and Bangalis migrated to Assam in search of employment. The migrants became caught in the middle of a complex quarrel between New Delhi and the native Assamese, who demanded that the government deport all non-Assamese entering from Bangladesh and West Bengal. The Assamese claimed the immigrants competed with them for jobs and threatened their political future. Under the pressure of an oil blockade, boycotts, and violent outbreaks between the Assamese and migrants, Mrs. Gandhi reasserted control over law and order but also agreed to deport many of the migrants. The issue between Mrs. Gandhi and the Assamese remains unsettled and, because Bangali Muslims are among the deportees, adds to her differences with the Bangalis.

Population pressures on the Chittagong Hill Tracts and the tribal people who lived there, which had been building for several decades, led in 1976 to tribal guerrilla resistance and a round of recriminations between the Bangali and Indian press and governments over Dacca's military actions against the guerrillas.[15] The predominantly Buddhist tribal people, who numbered about 700,000 in the seventies, had lived an isolated life for centuries in the Hill Tracts, an area of some 5,000 square miles in southeastern Bangladesh, bordering India and Burma.

Prior to the Partition of India the British government had protected the tribes from outside influence and forbade nontribal people to settle in the area or buy land there. Tribal resentment flared in the sixties when the Pakistani government built a hydropower dam in the hill country that flooded thousands of acres of tribal land. Pakistani promises to resettle the displaced families went unfulfilled. The Pakistanis tried to encourage the tribes to abandon their practice of moving from place to place, turning over new land for cultivation, and to take up settled farming, but the effort was unsuccessful.

After Bangali independence the tribes, fearful that nontribal settlements begun by the Pakistani government would greatly increase, asked Mujib and Sayem to grant them local autonomy. When they received no response, a tribal leader organized a guerrilla group called Shanti Bahini (peace force). Its spokesmen charged that Dacca intended to force the tribes out of the Hill Tracts. Bangali officials replied that settlements had ceased and that homeless tribal families would be settled on cooperative farm estates. Bangali military garrisons in the tribal areas were strengthened to combat the guerrillas. A parliamentary commission from Dacca in April 1980 held talks with the leaders of the Shanti Bahini, but nothing came of them. Clashes between government troops and guerrillas and among villagers resumed. The armed conflicts led the Parliament of the Zia government in November 1980 to adopt a disturbed areas bill, which increased the security forces in the Hill Tracts. The battles there grew fiercer.

The desire of the tribes to live their own lives and the determination of the Zia government to dedicate the land resources of the country to increased food supplies was complicated further by the opposition of the Indian press, which vigorously supported the cause of the tribes in the name of religion. The *Statesman Weekly* in May 1980 described the situation in the Hill Tracts as a "Buddhist struggle for survival."

The disturbed areas act inflamed the anger of the guerrillas and divided the Bangalis. Increased Indian sympathy for the tribes exacerbated Bangali-Indian relations. Many Bangalis remembered that the Indian government had for years used troops to fight other tribal guerrillas in northeastern India.

Nearby Nepal opened a consular office in East Pakistan in the early sixties and exchanged ambassadors with Bangladesh.[16] President Zia in December 1977 visited Kathmandu to discuss the Bangali proposal to build reservoirs in Nepal. At the end of a subsequent visit of the Nepalese royal family to Dacca, a joint communiqué stated that water resources were a proper concern of all countries in the region and one in which Bangladesh and Nepal would cooperate. Meanwhile, economic relations between the countries have prospered.

In 1980 the Bangalis established diplomatic relations with Bhutan, whose foreign policy is technically guided by India. The exchange was read as a desire on the part of Bhutan to make diplomatic contacts beyond India. The Bhutan embassy in Dacca is only the country's third diplomatic mission, one of which is at the United Nations.

The exchange of ambassadors between Dacca and Islamabad in 1976 was followed by the conclusion of a three-year trade pact, the establishment of a joint committee to encourage private trade, a mutual commitment to establish branch banks in Dacca and Karachi, a telephonic linkage of Dacca and Islamabad by satellite, and the resumption of Pakistan Airlines flights to Dacca.[17] When the Bangalis offered to pay fair compensation to Pakistani industrialists whose factories had been nationalized in 1972, the Bhutto government in turn promised to help in the rehabilitation of plants idled by the lack of technical and managerial skills.

The Pakistani army coup of 1977, which removed President Bhutto and put General Zia-ul-Huq in command of the country, did not alter Bangali-Pakistani relations. Soon after the coup the Bangali General Zia visited his counterpart in Islamabad. He told the press that the two countries reaffirmed their intention to strengthen economic, technical, cultural, and educational relations, to establish joint industrial ventures, and to cooperate in agricultural matters. On his return to Dacca General Zia said he had also discussed the repatriation of the Biharis. In 1977 about 130,000 of them who refused Bangali citizenship lived in Bangali camps. After Zia's visit to Islamabad, Pakistan reportedly prepared to accept 25,000 more of them. Since then only a few Biharis have been repatriated. The remaining Biharis are, for the time being, people without a country.

REGIONALISM

Ever since Partition officials and others on the subcontinent and outside it have talked and written about the feasibility of regional economic arrangements. President Zia in the summer of 1980 proposed a six-nation subcontinental summit as a forum to discuss regional cooperation.[18] He later said informal talks were under way and agreement could be reached on telecommunications, commercial aviation, and scientific and cultural exchanges, and that a link could be established with ASEAN. Perhaps, he said, the forum could become a South Asian common market.

A loose network of bilateral economic, technical, and cultural agreements has been entered into among the South Asian nations. These agreements, established on the principle of live and let live, have so far protected the independence of the subcontinental nations.

The political ramifications of Zia's proposal may be as important as the economic issues. President Zia could have been implying that the military and political preeminence of India should be accepted as a fact and dealt with collectively. He was well aware of Pakistan's distrust of India and was concerned that his own country lies, geographically speaking, in the palm of India's hand. He hoped that the settlement of differences among Bangladesh, India, and Pakistan after the 1971 war would serve as a precedent for regional action and saw that his country would be in a better bargaining position with India if he could muster the support of other nations in the region for causes the Bangalis espoused. The Bangali initiative was rewarded when a South Asian Regional Cooperation (SARC) organization was formally established by the South Asian countries in August 1983. The secretariat has yet to be set up.

OTHER MUSLIM NATIONS

The Zia government expanded and strengthened its ties with other Muslim nations.[19] President Zia, on a visit to Cairo in September 1977, vowed with President Anwar Sadat to maintain solidarity with Muslim states and affirmed "the right of the Palestinian people to establish their own government." After condemning Israel and the apartheid policies of Rhodesia and South Africa, Sadat and Zia, seeking more favorable trade terms with the developed countries, carried their quest to North-South conferences, including the one held at Cancun.

The Bangalis benefited from the growth of fraternal relations among the Muslim nations in the seventies. Members of the Organization of Petroleum Exporting Countries (OPEC) gave them an interest-free loan payable in 25 years. The planned migration of hundreds of thousands of Bangalis to OPEC countries dramatically illustrated the character of Muslim brotherhood. In 1978 President Zia journeyed to the easternmost tip of the Islamic crescent to meet President Suharto of Indonesia; the two committed themselves to Third World objectives and to cooperation in the development and sale of gas and oil supplies. Bangladesh in 1979 enjoyed friendly diplomatic relations with nearly every Muslim nation.

In the spring of 1979 Saudi Arabia pledged the Bangalis special consideration in meeting their requirements for oil. President Zia visited Iraq in March to discuss the nonaligned movement. Zia and the Iraquis condemned "Zionist aggression" against the Arabs and supported the idea of a Palestinian homeland; the Iraqis agreed to recruit workers from Bangladesh. The following month President Zia journeyed to Kuwait, repeated the pro-Palestinian stance, and signed trade, economic, and cultural agreements. By August 1980 the OPEC nations had made $263 million available to the Bangalis. The following December the United Arab Emirates agreed to jointly finance a fertilizer plant and a limestone-mining project. Trade and cultural arrangements were also concluded.

ASIAN NATIONS

The normally cordial relations between the Bangalis and Burma were set back in the spring of 1978 when thousands of refugees, described by Dacca as "Burmese Muslim nationals," began to pour across the Burmese borders into the Chittagong Hill Tracts.[20] By June 150,000 or more refugees, the majority of them women, children, and the elderly, had encamped there. The Burmese government explained that they had been expelled because they were citizens of Bangladesh. A census of Burmese citizens begun in April, it said, had revealed that large numbers of illegal Bangali immigrants had entered the neighboring Burmese state of Arakan. When the "illegals" began to be prosecuted, nearly 20,000 "Bangalis" fled across the border.

The Dacca government replied that the refugees had been forcibly evicted from an area in which they had lived for centuries. Some outside observers supported the Bangali case, explaining that the Muslim refugees consisted of two groups: the largest of them, the Rahingyes, had settled in Arakan centuries ago, and the ancestors of a second group, consisting of Bangali farmers and fishermen, had traditionally entered Burma to plant paddy and to work as farm laborers.

Burmese hostility to the presence of Muslims appears to have stemmed from the Rangoon government's desire to wipe out a Muslim guerrilla group that began fighting in the fifties to create an independent state of Arakan. Bangali accusations of inhuman evictions were denied by the Burmese. In response to Bangali requests, the United Nations appealed to its members to aid the refugees. Food and other supplies came from United Nations agencies—WHO and UNICEF—and the International Red Cross. The United States, the United Kingdom, and other countries made substantial financial donations and gave other relief assistance.

A series of conferences between the Bangalis and Burmese produced an agreement in July 1978. The Burmese promised to repatriate "all refugees" and both sides decided to open negotiations about their respective boundaries. The good offices of the United Nations and of the Saudi Arabian ambassador in Dacca hastened the conclusion of the agreement. By the end of the year thousands of refugees remained in their camps, but in accordance with the agreement batches of 200 were being repatriated every three days.

By the end of May 1979 three-quarters of the estimated refugee population had been repatriated. President U Ne Win, on a visit to Dacca that month, agreed with President Zia to demarcate 123 miles of their land boundaries and to begin discussions on a maritime boundary.

The earlier interest of the Bangalis in Southeast Asia was again demonstrated when President Zia visited Thailand and Malaysia in March 1979 and vowed his government's support for the Association of South East Asian Nations (ASEAN).[21] Agreements on trade, technical cooperation, and civil aviation were reached in Malaysia. In June 1979 Bangladesh sponsored a United Nations Security Council resolution that called on "all foreign powers" to withdraw from Cambodia.

General Zia's visit to China in January 1977 was hailed in Dacca as a great success.[22] In the exchange of greetings with Communist Party Chairman Hua Huo-Fang, the chairman challenged the South Asian role of the Soviets and indirectly that of India. The Bangali and Chinese leaders signed a modest trade protocol and economic and technical agreements under which China would send experts to help the Bangalis control their water resources and establish a fertilizer plant and a textile mill. Following the visit the Chinese supplied the Bangalis with fighter planes and training teams. Through the early eighties hundreds of Chinese economic and military experts have been in and out of Bangladesh to carry out the economic and technical agreements.

Events inside China delayed the return visit of Vice-Premier Li Hsien-Nien to Dacca until March 1978. He signed an economic, scientific, and technological agreement with Zia during that visit. The Chinese also agreed to make a $60 million interest-free loan for a fertilizer project.

Japan had interested itself in the development of the Bangali economy since the sixties. In 1979 the Bangladesh Shipping Corporation ordered 19 dry-cargo tankers and 3 oil tankers to be built in Japan. In June 1980 a delegation of Japanese businessmen came to Dacca to discuss industrial development investments of $1 billion during the second five-year plan for 1980–85.

Japanese rice-growing experts, fertilizer plant engineers, and television technicians had come to East Pakistan.[23] Trade between Bangladesh and Japan has steadily increased, and Japanese businessmen plan to participate in agricultural and engineering industries. In recent years Japanese economic aid has been a close second to that of the United States.

THE SOVIET UNION

With the emergence of General Zia the decline of the Russians' and Europeans' influence in Dacca was publicly marked by less Bangali press coverage of their local activities and by diminished attention to Bangali affairs in the Soviet press.[24] Diplomatic bickerings between the Bangalis and India and the increase of Peking's influence with the Zia government contributed to the change. Russian support for a pro-Soviet National Awami faction suffered a momentary setback when General Zia jailed its chairman. However, he was later released and his group participated in the presidential and parliamentary elections, with meager results.

Although General Zia in September 1979 told the Russians to reduce their 100-man staff in Dacca, the Soviet diplomats stayed on, continuing to interest themselves in Bangali politics. Prior to Zia's 1979 admonition, the Soviet deputy minister Nicholai Fernin had come to Dacca on a visit officially described as "forging friendly relations with all." This visit was followed by open Soviet support for the pro-Moscow parties and factions contending in the 1978 elections.

Relations with the Soviet Union in 1979 could be described as quietly normal. Pro-Moscow critics of the Bangali government accused it of tilting toward China and the United States. The Soviets kept up their amicable relations with pro-Moscow Bangali parties and factions. They sponsored training programs and encouraged trade. During the 1980 session of the Parliament in Dacca, the president's party condemned the Soviet invasion of Afghanistan but did not break off diplomatic relations with Moscow, as earlier proposed by the Islamic Conference meeting in Islamabad.[25]

THE WEST AND THE UNITED NATIONS

The calm and cooperative relations of the Bangalis with the Western nations and the United Nations from 1975 to 1982, evidenced mainly by economic assistance programs, encouraged further sympathetic arrangements.[26] In August 1980 President Zia met with the Bangladesh Aid Group in Paris. Later that month he addressed the U.N. General Assembly on his nation's need for agricultural development. He also met with President Carter. His search for expanded aid was only partially successful. In October 1982 Bangladesh's ambassador to the United Nations was installed as chairman of the Group of 77, a U.N. group of 124 Third World nations dealing with trade and development.

Bangladesh, elected to the U.N. Security Council on November 10, 1978, for a two-year term beginning in January 1979, was drawn into decisions about Iran. In December 1979 the Bangali permanent representative to the council cosponsored a resolution condemning Iran for holding American diplomatic hostages. The Bangalis were also among the sponsors of a January 1980 council resolution deploring the Soviet Union's armed intervention in Afghanistan, demanding respect for that country's sovereignty, territorial integrity, and independence, and calling for the immediate withdrawal of all foreign troops. Bangladesh was one of the 104 members of the General Assembly that voted for a resolution reaffirming the Security Council's position. The refusal of the Bangalis to support a council resolution favoring sanctions against the Soviets seems to have been motivated by their commitment to a nonaligned policy and to doubts about the efficacy of sanctions.

A highly vocal member of the U.N. Conference and Trade and Development (UNCTAD), Bangladesh championed the establishment of an international economic order that would, among other things, give developing nations greater access to world markets and resources, encourage the adoption of commodity agreements to stabilize world prices, and yield a more universal system of technological information exchanges.[27] At the 1979 Manila meeting of UNCTAD the representatives of Bangladesh strongly supported the organization's program for collective self-reliance and a framework for future international economic negotiations.

In an address to the United Nations in August 1980, President Zia voiced the desire of the nonaligned countries in the Third World that OPEC, nations with "centrally planned economies," and the West should increase their economic aid. The U.S. press played up Zia's remark that OPEC countries have a special responsibility to contribute as much as 50 percent of the funds needed by poor countries for development and that they should invest a part of their assets in the least developed nations. Spokesmen for OPEC suggested that increases in economic aid to poor nations depended on the outcome of international discussions and the settlement of broad economic problems, presumably inflation. That response, in which other donor nations concurred for other economic reasons, offered slim prospects for early increased aid for the developing world from the oil states.

HUMAN RIGHTS

The introduction of human rights as a foreign policy issue by the Carter administration, promoted by Western governments and by private groups such as the London-based Amnesty International, resulted in public reports critical of half the world's nations, including Bangladesh.[28] Freedom House, a U.S. organization, categorized Bangladesh, India, and Pakistan as "partially free." The 1977 Department of State Human Rights Report described martial law in Dacca as a "temporary regime whose role is to restore stability, law and order, and equal justice." Although the regime did not appear to encourage or condone torture, the report said, rough treatment of prisoners is a South Asian tradition. The report singled out for criticism the largely segregated situation of the Biharis, but it admitted the resolution of the problem depended on negotiations with Pakistan. The report concluded, "With the exception of the Biharis, whose lot is somewhat improved, citizens of Bangladesh move about freely."

Following the execution of some of the officers implicated in the mutinies at Bogra and Dacca, Amnesty International (AI) cabled the Dacca government to stop the executions. In December 1977 AI officials visited Bangladesh to inquire into the situation. Their report stated that the Dacca government had executed hundreds of dissidents in the armed forces and had jailed 10,000 to 15,000 persons.[29] The secret martial law trials of the accused, they said, fell far short of internationally accepted standards. American newspapers had reported that as many as 217 military personnel were executed in the aftermath of the mutinies.

The Bangali home secretary responded that the estimate of 10,000 to 15,000 political prisoners was a "grave exaggeration," but he admitted that some had been "detained to prevent them from indulging in prejudicial activities." The special martial law courts, he said, were established "to deal with grievous offenses speedily," with a view to curbing the incidence of crimes. He pointed out that the death sentence must be confirmed by the president. On December 30, 1977, President Zia told an AI official the executions had stopped.

The 1978 and 1979 human rights reports of the U.S. Department of State to the Congress recorded progress toward freedom in Bangladesh. During 1979 political prisoners continued to be released. The Department of State estimated that "no more than 50" political prisoners were being held in 1979. In March 1980 two of the most important of them—former president Moshtaque Ahmed and the former leader of the National Socialist Party (JSD)—were freed. Restrictions on press freedom were relaxed and some banned newspapers resumed publication.

The 1979 report focused on the plight of the stateless Biharis. It also found that the treatment of political prisoners was harsh, prisons were overcrowded, and preventive detention was tolerated. As if to attenuate these shortcomings, however, the report outlined the problem of the nation's poverty. The 1980 report stated, "Following an earlier trend, 1980 was a year of continued gradual improvements in respect for and promotion afforded to human rights." To fortify its conclusion, the report added information about Bangali social and cultural programs.

Bangali ideological critics of the Zia government regarded the reported human rights record as unbalanced and too optimistic. Up to 1980 the reports certainly reflected the Carter administration's sympathy for the Bangalis and the conviction of its officials that the Bangalis needed the aid the Dacca government requested. The rights violations included in the reports were not categorized as "excessive," which would have caused a congressional ban on aid to Bangladesh. The report on Bangladesh did not differ from those of other countries believed to be moving in a democratic direction.

BANGLADESH'S NEUTRALIST STANCE

Bangladesh lives on the periphery of the world of power politics. As a Third World nation it is a nonpower. The limited defense capabilities of its armed forces and the low level of its economy means that its security is at the mercy of its neighbors and other nations.

Given their geopolitical and economic situation, the Bangalis' attachment to an open-ended neutralist posture is realistic and morally practical. Their diplomats, aware of the limited bargaining potential of their country, have shown that they know how to cope with great and near-great powers. Bangladesh's reliance on the United Nations, through which it receives economic assistance and a forum to discuss its grievances, is instinctively correct, even though the great powers have yet to make the United Nations into an economic and political peace-making body. Association with the nonaligned nations gives the Bangalis a voice in the world of have-nots, even though the diverging interests and politics of those nations make their conferences more useful for stirring up the great powers than for immediate economic betterment.

CHAPTER 17

Transition and Reorganization, 1981–83

President Zia reached the height of his political power in 1981, notwithstanding factional violence, differences within his party, and his stern treatment of armed forces rebels. The progress of his foreign policies imparted dignity to the nation. Domestically, the distribution of favors among politicians and military officers gave him the backing of middle-class conservatives; his rural development program won peasant support. But on May 30, 1981, he was gunned down by dissident military officers, for reasons that remain controversial but were perhaps related to political rivalry.

Certainly the violence among political activists and the Bangali military had over the years created a political atmosphere that emboldened the violent.[1] *Ittefaq* reported in July 1981 that 185 political murders had been committed during the first six months of that year. The majority of the murders were attributed to the military wing of the National Socialist party, an organization that killed landowners and distributed their crops among landless farmers, and to the Kadir Bahini, 1,000 deserters from the army led by the pro-Indian "Tiger" Siddiqui. Political factions within the armed forces had attempted more than 26 coups since 1975. Swift punishment of the rebels, including death sentences by the military-backed governments of presidents Sayem and Zia, did not stop the attempts.

President Zia's successor, Abdus Sattar, a 75-year-old leader of the Bangladesh Nationalist party, eased the tensions attending the assassination. He and his right-wing cabinet prevented a threatened food shortage, persuaded the International Monetary Fund to restore part of a cutback in promised foreign aid, increased private industrial enterprise, and held the Awami League at bay in a popular election for the presidency.

However, Sattar's inability to hold the Nationalist party together and, above all, the determination of General H. M. Ershad, army chief of staff, to install a government with a strong military presence resulted in .a bloodless coup led by the general. A martial law administration was promptly put in place. During the first months of the general's administration he inaugurated far-reaching political and administrative reforms. With party activity suspended and the press under control, the general decentralized the government's bureaucracy and judicial system, further expanded the scope of private industrial enterprise, established an austere budget in anticipation of declines in foreign aid, and planned a larger role for the military in development programs. Although Ershad promised on several occasions to return the country to democracy within two years, he let it be known that he strongly preferred an Asian type of government suited to the conditions of a poor nation rather than the unworkable colonial models of Western democracy.

ZIA'S ASSASSINATION AND ITS AFTERMATH

In a style reminiscent of Mujib's assassination in Dacca five years earlier, dissident army officers killed President Zia and several of his aides in Chittagong during the early hours of May 30, 1981.[2] The leader of the rebels, according to the government of Acting President Abdus Sattar, was General M. A. Manzur, commanding officer of the Chittagong district. Opposition leaders immediately questioned the allegation.

Zia had gone to Chittagong the previous day to inspect local development projects, to settle quarrels among his Nationalist party supporters there, and perhaps to talk to General Manzur. The same day General Manzur received transfer orders to Dacca as commandant of the Staff Training College—a step down for the ambitious general, a former freedom fighter and colleague of the president.

Immediately after the death of Zia a Chittagong radio broadcast announced that a revolutionary council headed by General Manzur had taken power, dismissed the government, suspended the Constitution, proclaimed martial law, abrogated the 1972 treaty of friendship with India, and affirmed the Bangali claim to New Moore Island.[3] The *Statesman* (Calcutta) characterized the broadcast as a "peculiar brand of pro-Islamic, pro-Freedom Fighter, anti-Indian and anti-capitalist attitudes." Perhaps the rebels were appealing to as many Bangali factions as possible.

The same day, Vice-President Sattar publicly revealed the assassination of President Zia and announced he had taken control of the government, in accordance with the Constitution, as acting president.[4] He invoked emergency powers, established a curfew in the larger cities, and called on the rebels to surrender immediately. His government, he said, would make no changes in foreign policy and would honor agreements with foreign countries—a conciliatory gesture to New Delhi. At a meeting of government officials and members of the opposition, the latter declared "their adherence to constitutional and democratic politics and their abhorrence of the politics of violence." The cabinet and the chiefs of the armed forces pledged their loyalty to Sattar. These actions contributed to a political calm.

According to Dacca press reports, General Manzur shortly after the Chittagong broadcast reduced his demands to a cabinet reshuffle and a guarantee of safe passage for himself. Sattar, rejecting the new demands, told him to surrender.[5] A deadline for the surrender was fixed and then postponed. During the 48-hour standoff, General Manzur and several of his associates left the Hill Tracts. The government reported "angry troops" had killed them. Others alleged the fleeing officers were hunted down and slain on government orders. Government troops quickly retook Chittagong and arrested 20 officers said to have been involved in the attempted coup.[6] A special military tribunal immediately convened to establish the identity of the officers responsible for killing President Zia.

The president's body was disinterred from a shallow grave near Chittagong and flown to Dacca. At a state funeral the following day he was buried in a military ceremony. Hundreds of thousands of mourners along the funeral route shouted, "Zia is blessed, Allah is great." He was buried in a plot close to the Parliament building, symbol of Bangali democracy.

In August 1981 the government issued a white paper saying the coup had been organized by General Manzur and six of his senior officers.[7] One of these officers is said to have persuaded the president's personal secretary, Lieutenant Colonel Mahfusur Rahman, to cooperate in the coup. The paper concluded that in the early hours of May 30, a group of officers with the assistance of the secretary shot Zia and two of his security guards.

The opposition refused to accept the government's claim that Manzur was responsible for the assassination and the reasons given for his action.[8] Its members asserted that a group of Manzur's officers killed the president without Manzur's knowledge but that the general, when he learned what they had done, accepted it. The government's first broadcast announcing the president's death, they noted, did not mention

Manzur by name. In his subsequent Chittagong broadcast Manzur referred to himself by his military rank and made no attempt to hold Chittagong. The opposition charged that Manzur had been killed by government troops in order to prevent him from disclosing the facts of the conspiracy.

Speculation about the reasons for Manzur's involvement in the plot variously portrayed him as a patriot, a traitor, or a politically confused general.[9] Some said he believed his action was necessary to redress the failure of the Zia government to put a stop to party rivalries and to widespread corruption. These observers refrained from implying that a government headed by General Manzur would have eliminated party rivalries and corruption, but they insisted he preferred a political to a military solution to the government's dispute with the Hill Tracts guerrillas.

The Indian government expressed relief that the rebellion had been quashed.[10] Earlier, Mrs. Gandhi and the Indian foreign minister signed the condolence book for the president at the Bangladesh embassy in New Delhi. The foreign ministry, responding to nonofficial Bangali charges of Indian involvement in the assassination, called attention to the demand of the Chittagong rebels for the abrogation of the India-Bangladesh Treaty of 1972 and to Acting President Sattar's declaration his government would honor all agreements with neighboring countries. Pakistan sent a message of condolence that hailed Zia as a statesman dedicated to the national unity of Bangladesh and the cause of Islam.

The world press gave generous and prominent coverage to President Zia's assassination.[11] Most papers wrote respectfully of Zia as a charismatic leader who improved the stability of the country and attracted the devotion of a sizable number of his people. They described him variously as energetic, a one-man show, ruthless, determined, and nationalistic. On the other hand, the initial press evaluation of the effects of Zia's death on the future of the nation was generally pessimistic. A *Times* (London) editorial of June 1 predicted the killing of President Zia was "likely to throw the country into despair at the unending military rivalry from which the country has suffered from its birth." The *Economist* of June 8 thought Zia's death "the last thing" Bangladesh needed and offered the opinion that his death had "set back the nation's hope of curing its ills, probably for years." A *New York Times* correspondent observed that the "dominant Bangladesh party, never better than a loose coalition, may fall apart without Zia."

When it later appeared the Sattar government had weathered the storm of the assassination, the *New York Times* editorialized on June 12: "Events since Zia's violent death imply some progress. . . . Internal power passed smoothly to a frail Acting President and plans have been announced for new elections in six months. President Zia's unheralded achievements contain a lesson of sorts. No third world country should be glibly written off. No society wants to be a basket case."

The *Nation*, hostile to Zia's regime, painted a dismal picture of the nation's future in a June 13 editorial:

> Bangladesh is now almost certainly entering a new period of political upheaval. Zia's successors are political nonentities and the army is thoroughly discredited. But after years of military repression, the left has been virtually shattered and the social-democratic followers of the assassinated Mujibur Rahman seem intent only on settling old scores with the military. . . . An impasse has been reached which probably can only be broken by violence. Such is Zia's legacy.

The violence and dissension of the Zia years resembled the turbulence of Mujib's regime, but Zia did what Mujib was unable to do—move the nation's economy. His shift of economic priorities from industry to agriculture and the zeal with which he pursued agricultural productivity displayed a sensitivity to the problems of the peasants that Mujib was not given time to exhibit. Zia's improvements on Mujib's foreign aid programs also nudged the nation ahead. Zia's manipulation of party members and the appointment of fellow officers to government posts to offset the severe treatment meted out to dissident officers gave his government the appearance of stability. However, from the beginning of his steep climb up the ladder of power he was the prisoner of his officers, as Mujib had been the prisoner of his political followers. Neither the charisma nor the accomplishments of either leader gave them sufficient power to prevail over disorder. The present period of unsettling quiet finds the nation at a crossroads where democratic and conservative forces, civilian and military, ready themselves to contest in the future.

SATTAR'S NEW GOVERNMENT

The transition began with the unexpected calm of the transfer of power to the Sattar government.[12] Its partisans ascribed its smoothness to Sattar's prompt decision to affirm his constitutional authority, to maintain civilian control of the military, and to allay the fears of the Indian government. He wisely announced that presidential elections would be held in six months "to foil any conspiracy to disturb the democratic process in the country."

The military, to avoid the implication that they sympathized with the rebels, immediately declared their support for constitutional government. The nation and the politicians, too, perceived the futility of resort to political violence. Suspicions of the political ambitions of the military lingered. Abdus Sattar in July retired a number of military officers from his official family. Others were dismissed for their failure to return to duty after the Chittagong coup or forced to retire without explanation.

By mid-June Sattar, turning to party affairs, announced the presidential election would be held on September 21.[13] The opposition justifiably complained that the September floods would make it very difficult for voters in rural areas to reach the polls. Moreover, the Awami League and other parties, struggling to agree on their presidential nominees, said they needed more time to prepare their campaigns.

Rumors in the press that Zia's widow and the 35-year-old daughter of Mujib would be candidates of the Bangladesh Nationalist party and the Awami League, respectively, soon dissipated.[14] Party leaders decided they needed older and more experienced male candidates. Although Sattar had declared on May 31 he was not a candidate because of his age and ill health, a joint committee of the government's party hierarchy of committees on June 22 made him its choice. Sattar's career suggested he might draw election support from the left as well as the right.[15] In his youth he had been an aide to the Awami League's H. S. Suhrawardy and later served as a justice on the Supreme Court of Pakistan. Since as acting president Sattar was not eligible under the Constitution to stand for the presidency, the Parliament amended the Constitution to qualify him. During the debate the Parliament rejected an opposition proposal to change the presidency to a British form of parliamentary government.

Sattar's nomination probably hastened the ejection of two young, ambitious retired army officers from the cabinet.[16] They nonetheless remained in the party, perhaps on the chance their political fortunes would change. The Calcutta *Statesman*, which had often criticized post-Mujib governments in Dacca, said the ministers had been singled out because as freedom fighters they had taken part "in the struggle for independence." The *Statesman* depicted the ousted ministers as more democratic and more sympathetic to India than Sattar. The ministers no doubt figured in the ultimate collapse of the Nationalist party.

To contest the election, opposition parties organized into three broad alliances.[17] Two of them represented mainstream parties—an anti-Indian, anti-Soviet front of 18 parties headed by former president Khandikar Moshtaque, and a 9-party coalition of pro-Indian, pro-Soviet parties and factions led by the Awami League and its president, Hasina Wajed. Both alliances agreed to fight for parliamentary democracy. A third opposition combine, which included an exhausted National Socialist party and splinter groups of the Awami, Muslim, and Democratic leagues, supported the candidacy of Kwaja Wasiuddin, a former lieutenant general in the Pakistani army and commanding officer in Dacca and Lahore who had returned to Bangladesh after independence and served as Bangali ambassador at several posts. He, too, favored parliamentary democracy and was influential in military circles.

The unity of the three fronts on the issue of parliamentary democracy put them in palpable opposition to the government, but their differences of outlook and history revealed them to be as much opposed to one another as to the government. Nor did the several factions among them see eye to eye. Their fragmentation made the government party the odds-on favorite to win the election.

THE TRIAL OF ZIA'S ASSASSINS

When the government on June 3 announced that 17 officers (later increased to 31) would be tried on charges of complicity in the Chittagong coup, the parliamentary opposition demanded an inquiry into the death of Mujib as well as Zia.[18] The Awami League urged a public trial for the indicted assassins of both presidents. Amnesty International advocated an open trial for Zia's killers.

The release of sections of a white paper on the Chittagong coup during the trial of the officers reheated the controversy. General Osmani, a presidential candidate in the 1978 election, and General Wasiuddin questioned the morality of trying officers who had surrendered in response to assurances of safe passage. The government replied that the officers had been forced by their troops to surrender and therefore could not be pardoned.

A secret court-martial opened in Chittagong on July 10. In early August the court found 29 of the 31 officers guilty and acquitted two. The court blamed General Manzur for the death of the president and for the coup. It concluded he was politically ambitious, had won over other officers in the Chittagong district to his critical views of the government, and had formed a revolutionary council to seize power on May 30. Twelve of the 29 accused were condemned to death, 12 others imprisoned, and the remaining 5 discharged from the armed forces. On September 22 the Supreme Court confirmed the death sentences; the 12 officers were executed the next day. Riots in Dacca set off by the executions were quelled by police.

PREELECTION MANEUVERING

Acting President Sattar, after his selection as his party's presidential candidate, set up a kitchen cabinet to advise him on the day-to-day operations of the government.[19] This group consisted of Shafiul Azam, a top civil servant, Dr. Mirza Nurul Huda, advisor on economic affairs, and Lieutenant General H. M. Ershad, chief of the army. The president and other cabinet members, particularly those standing in for the government party, remained responsible for making basic policy and program decisions. Sattar's advisory group, however, gave the impression that he had a tight rein on government operations; it improved his election posture as the nation's strong man.

During the summer the opposition resumed its activities.[20] The Awami League declared it would participate in the election only if the government complied with a four-point program: postpone the election until the third week in November, provide adequate media coverage for opposition candidates, lift the emergency laws, and prepare a new list of voters. A freedom fighters' association named General Osmani as its presidential candidate. The Muslim League nominated Sabur Khan, a staunch ally of former president Ayub. To force the government to alter the election date, a combine of opposition parties threatened strikes. The government headed off the strikes by postponing the election until November 15. The Awami Leaguers then asked that their other demands be met. The government replied that adequate media coverage "would be assured" and emergency laws lifted after nomination papers had been filed on September 21.[21] Voter lists, it claimed, were updated as the election commissioner registered new voters. The opposition accepted the concessions.

In the fall political agitation surfaced among the bureaucrats. Employees of government banks and other public corporations, including steel, chemicals, and food processing, demanded larger bonuses.[22] Several civil service associations, including the police, which opposed the September 1980 democratization of the administrative hierarchy, demanded the elimination of lateral discrimination among all of the services.

The government's bank employees went out on strike to emphasize long-standing demands. Their defiance of the government presented Sattar with one of his most serious challenges. The striking union had been affiliated with the Bangladesh Nationalist party until President Zia expelled it because the union's leaders, according to the *Far Eastern Economic Review* of September 18, 1981, "forced the bank to pay increased salaries and benefits retroactively to 1972 and the bank management to sanction loans and advances for questionable projects." Zia had instructed his finance minister to obtain the return of funds illegally granted to employees. Members of the cabinet had reportedly protected accused members of the union. When the union threatened a strike for September 24 and insisted the Sattar government sanction their earlier actions, Sattar ordered the arrest of the leaders. The union employees struck. Sattar promptly dismissed about 4,000 strikers and began legal proceedings against the union leaders. The government won hands down.

THE PRESIDENTIAL CAMPAIGN OF 1981

As the government party closed ranks behind him, political pundits in Dacca confidently forecast Sattar as the winner of the election.[23] The party leaders counted on popular abhorrence of political violence and Sattar's firmness in dealing with the assassins and the bank strikers to attract conservative voters. The party's campaign slogan, "an orderly transfer of power," and the manifesto of the party proclaimed its fidelity to the 1978 platform on which the charismatic Zia was elected.

In what was to prove to be a fateful line of decisions, Sattar prior to the election reduced the number of military officers in the civilian branches of the government. In addition to this reduction and to previous eliminations of officers from the cabinet and the armed forces, a week before the election a board that had inquired into the involvement of officers in the Chittagong coup retired 19 other ranking officers.

Sattar's determination to limit the political influence of the military produced an instant confrontation with General Ershad. The general, in a press interview during the campaign, said, "We considered Zia an army man who would look after our interests. . . . Zia knew our needs. Obviously Sattar won't have the same knowledge."[24] He added ambiguously, "I don't think the army has a role to play now. . . . The army might step in, if law and order completely breaks down or the government loses control of the situation." In a later interview with *Holiday* the general suggested that if Sattar was not elected the Awami League would benefit and violence would ensue. In a subsequent "clarification" of this remark, he asserted that the army would support the verdict of the people. The Awami League presidential candidate, Kamal Hussain, upset by Ershad's earlier remark, accepted the general's explanation.

A few days before the election a *New York Times* correspondent in Dacca wrote that General Ershad had considered and rejected an army intervention after Zia's death and had supported the democratic constitutional process. The general also was reported to have said that the process would be best protected by giving the military an opportunity to participate in the government and to have hinted that this could be accomplished by reserving cabinet posts for the military, as Zia had done.

The constant plea of General Ershad for a share in government and President Sattar's effort to restrain the military put the two men on a collision course. The general, like Zia before him, was patient enough to rein in his ambition for power until a more opportune moment presented itself.

The Awami League no longer insisted it would withdraw from the election.[25] Kamal Hussain, after entering his name on the presidential candidates list, said, "We believe in elections." Hussain, a lawyer, intellectual, and moderate, pledged himself to most of Mujib's policies, including the nationalization of key industries. He denied a government accusation that he would restore Mujib's single party, BAKSAL, although the notion was approved by many Awamis. The league, Hussain said, would seek a multiparty parliamentary government. In response to the criticism that his party was too partial to India, he recalled that as Mujib's foreign minister he had learned the meaning of hard bargaining with India. He might have added that his manner of dealing with India had been conscientiously pursued by the Zia government. In spite of Hussain's reasonableness, the chances of the league's success in the 1981 election, as in 1978, were low, in large part because the party was in disarray over policies and tactics. Although Hussain had the backing of Hasina, the president of the league, he was at loggerheads with the league's militant secretary-general, Abdur Rassak. Hussain's solid, respectable personality could not arouse the devotion accorded Mujib. Moreover, he had been living in Dacca only since 1980, after a self-exile in London following the death of Mujib.

Hussain's campaign meetings drew good crowds but fewer than he expected. He alleged that the government, during the few days left before the election, failed to provide him with the transportation he had been promised to reach more rural voters. Perhaps he could have avoided being the victim of this election trick if he had concentrated on the rural vote earlier on. Instead, he complained "the ruling party is preparing to rig the polls." After a big rally in Dacca he told a *New York Times* reporter, "If we are made to lose, then we reserve the right to protest in the streets," because he was certain the only way he could lose would be through vote frauds. Government supporters viewed Hussain's remarks as a "total admission" that he was "trailing."

Hussain appealed to the memory of Mujib and attacked the government's economic and political shortcomings. He held it responsible for a decline in rice production and a rise in consumer prices and criticized its willingness to permit luxury imports. He implied what Awami Leaguers had been saying for a long time, namely that the economic policies of post-Mujib governments favored the affluent over the poor. He compared Mujib's Awami League role in the struggle for independence and the construction of a grass-roots organization with Zia's creation of the Bangladesh Nationalist party from the "top down" and his seizure of power in the style of a military dictator.

A *Le Monde* reporter who attended rallies of the two leading parties contrasted the "disciplined" character of the crowds listening to Sattar with the "vibrant, tumultuous and militant atmosphere" of Hussain's meetings. A Bangali reporter described Hussain's speeches on the election circuit as "more like professional expositions than election-eering," but he concluded they commanded attention.

ELECTION RESULTS

The election returns came in slowly over several days. The earliest count foretold a "sweeping victory" for Sattar.[26] Hussain, plainly distressed, said the results were "fictional" and "laughable." When official election returns showed Sattar leading in all districts of the country, Hussain alleged "widespread intimidation of the voters by the government party." Election officials routinely denied the charge.

A *Christian Science Monitor* reporter, after a tour of rural and urban polling places, concluded there was "a large orderly turnout with no obvious signs of interference or rigging." Diplomatic observers at the polls more cautiously described the election as reasonable and peaceful. The Manchester *Guardian* representative reported that at the voting centers visited by journalists and diplomats there was little evidence the voters had been intimidated.

The day after the election began Sattar had referred to the voting as peaceful, free, and fair. With the results in, the opposition insisted the election was unfair. Awami League spokesmen said demonstrations would be held November 20 to protest the election results. Sattar called on Hussain to concede the election and to call off the demonstration. Hussain acquiesced.

Slightly more than 55 percent of the electorate voted in the election. Sattar received two-thirds of the ballots cast and Dr. Hussain somewhat less than one-third. On November 20 Abdus Sattar was sworn in as president in a brief ceremony attended by members of the cabinet, judges, chiefs of the armed services, and diplomats. Sattar's election, however, was less a personal victory for him than an expression of popular concern for political stability. The voters appeared to have cast their ballots to protect the gains of previous years and to reject a change in leadership because they feared a return to political violence.

GOVERNMENT REORGANIZATION

President Sattar faced the same kind of political, economic, and international problems that had troubled the nation for years.[27] The demand of General Ershad for a greater share in the conduct of government by the armed forces presented the disquieted democracy with its greatest dilemma. How could a Bangali democracy preserve stability if it had to rely on defense forces which since 1971 had caused more violent ruptures in democratic processes than the faction-ridden political parties? That a general such as Zia had been able to stick to democratic processes was largely due to his willingness to listen to the advice of moderate civilian colleagues among bureaucrats and politicians and to his appreciation of the democratic aspirations of the people.

Sattar began the reorganization of the government on November 24 with the appointment of Dr. Mirza Huda to the vice-presidency. Huda, a professional economist who had served Zia as finance minister and Sattar as an adviser, was chosen because of his experience with the nation's ongoing economic development problems. The appointment annoyed Sattar's ambitious party colleagues, who looked on Huda as an outsider. A 42-member cabinet selected on December 4 gave strong representation to the party's right wing and precipitated a struggle between the party's parliamentary members and party officials, each demanding a larger share of power.

On January 1, 1982, Sattar announced the establishment of a National Security Council to replace President Zia's National Defense Council. He proposed a council structure made up of himself, his vice-president, four ranking civilian ministers, and the three chiefs of the armed services. The council's responsibilities were to include exploring the ways in which the armed forces would be used in social and economic development. If Sattar hoped his proposal would assure civilian control of the government yet mollify General Ershad, he was mistaken. The general objected to the preponderance of civilians on the council and to the manner of its establishment. Sattar gave way and reconstituted the council to include only the three highest civilian officials along with the three armed services chiefs.

The new council met to discuss the possibility of emergency action to eradicate corruption and inefficiency in the government and of the declaration of a state of emergency. Sattar prevented the adoption of the latter course. The council, however, agreed to dissolve the 1981 cabinet, to reduce the cabinet's size, and to prepare a list of politicians eligible for appointment to an uncorrupted council of ministers. Sattar later told Bangali citizens through the media that he had dissolved the cabinet because of "doubts and dissatisfaction arising in the minds of the people about the honesty, sincerity, and integrity of many a member of the council of ministers." He further admitted the country faced a crisis because former officials had failed to do their jobs. Sattar's Security Council action and his admission of a crisis meant that General Ershad

had won his anticorruption campaign and increased his authority in the government.

Shortly thereafter the army arrested Awami League leaders, one of whom was said to have confessed to India's involvement in arming a pro-Awami League group and a Bangladesh Nationalist party youth organization that planned to assassinate government leaders. Kamal Hussain said the arrests were "a conspiracy to malign the league and its leadership by false, malicious, and motivated reports based on words put into the mouths of recently arrested criminals."

SATTAR'S PROBLEMS

The March 16, 1982, issue of the *Far Eastern Economic Review* predicted the military would soon take over the government. It cited General Ershad's remark that the Sattar government had not offered "a strong and decisive government." The general's elaborate political crusade for power, activated by the death of President Zia and encouraged by the problems of the Sattar government, had by mid-March come to a point at which he could say, with the tacit approval of Sattar, that the country needed a savior.

During the ten months of Sattar's government, economic adversities beset the nation and added to his political woes.[28] The worsening world economy, which slowed the streams of foreign aid to Bangladesh, curtailed the nation's development budgets. Foreign exchange was in short supply and financial reserves depleted. By the end of the fiscal year 1980/81 consumer prices had risen 19 percent. Because of these and other difficulties, the International Monetary Fund withheld already promised aid. Nearly a year elapsed before the agency restored a portion of the aid. Food shortages, the result of a reduced 1981 crop, were made up for by drawing on national reserves and taking advantage of donations that had previously been promised by other nations. The Sattar government's offer of new opportunities to foreign private investors, and its agreement with the Saudis for a joint investment corporation to establish a Bangali telecommunications equipment industry along with a Saudi promise of $180 million in aid, were regarded as evidence of the progress of private enterprise.[29]

Relations with India after Zia's death kept their usual uneven course.[30] During the November election campaign the press and the political parties of both countries traded charges. The Bangalis accused the Indians of interfering in the national election; the Indians said they had been the object of anti-Indian tirades during the campaign. At the same time talks between their foreign ministers about New Moore Island, which the Bangalis call South Talpatty Island, ended only in an agreement to meet again to discuss the issue further. It had not been resolved by the end of 1983.

A second, more serious dispute that began in the fall of 1981 was settled by the end of that year. When guerrillas of the Shanti Bahini in late September launched an attack on Bangali security forces in the Chittagong Hill Tracts, not far from the Indian border, the Bangali foreign ministry said the attack appeared to come from inside India, to which the guerrillas had returned. An Indian newspaper, citing official sources, asserted that about 25,000 tribals had been driven into India by Bangali forces. Bangali authorities denied the story and claimed India had established refugee camps to receive the tribals. The Indian government warned Dacca of its concern about the influx of refugees, called attention to reported brutal treatment of the tribals by Bangali forces, and requested that they be permitted to return to their homeland. The debate heated up when the Bangalis accused India of complicity in the tribal rebellion and of supplying arms to the rebels. The Indian government said what it wanted was a frontier zone of peace. In November Dacca and New Delhi signed an accord expected to ease the return of the tribals to the Hill Tracts. Dacca recognized the importance of creating "an agreeable, peaceful atmosphere" to encourage their return. On its face the agreement represented a turnabout in the domestic treatment of the Hill Tracts tribals and an improvement in Bangali-Indian relations.

The U.S. Department of State human rights report for 1981 was more critical than that of the previous year.[31] It complained about political prisoners remaining in jail, the overcrowding of jails, and press controls that limited freedom of expression. The concern of the department for social rights was evident in the tone of its comments on the problems of Hindu property rights, the plight of the Biharis, and restrictions on women's rights. The report stated that improvements were made under President Zia, but it also said, "The threat of natural disaster and economic breakdown must continue to be taken seriously." The report as a whole reflected a judgment that the Bangalis should continue to receive U.S. help.

In the world arena, U.N. respect for Bangladesh's representatives was in evidence during the contest for the presidency of the General Assembly.[32] After two ballots Kwaja Kaiser, head of the Bangali delegation, tied with Ismal Killai of Iraq, who won the post in a lottery ballot.

The day before the nation's celebration of its eleventh year of independence President Sattar, under pressure from his party, appointed Mohammadullah vice-president to replace a frustrated Dr. Mirza Huda. The military, battling for recognition of the armed forces' constitutional rights to have a share in the governing process, wanted General Ershad to be named vice-president. The general, who had not been consulted about the appointment of Mohammadullah, interpreted Sattar's action to mean the president had resolved to retain civilian and party control of the government. He decided the time had come to take power.[33]

ERSHAD'S BLOODLESS COUP

During the predawn hours of March 24, 1982, General Ershad told the nation by radio that he had deposed President Sattar and his government to end "corruption in public life" and "the fight for power within the ruling party," and to check the decline of the economy.[34] The general "suspended" the Constitution and declared martial law. He named himself martial law administrator and commander in chief of the armed forces, banned political activity, public assemblies, and strikes, and imposed a night curfew in Dacca.

Echoing President Zia in 1975, he said, "I am a soldier. I have no political ambitions. My whole and sole aim is to reestablish democracy in accordance with the hopes and aspirations of the people." The people, he insisted, "expected the army to step in and put matters right" because the Sattar government had completely failed to meet the threats of a grave economic crisis and of food shortages. On a positive note, he added that the country's foreign policy would remain unchanged and all treaties and agreements would be honored.

He spoke in general terms about his plans to reorganize the government. He would select a president to serve at his pleasure and a council of advisers to head the government's administrative services. He would head martial law administration along with the chiefs of the navy and air force, and the country would be divided into five zones, each headed by a military officer.

Abdus Sattar had gone on the air before the general to tell the people that "deteriorating law and order, economic and political problems make military rule necessary." He extended his "best wishes to the present rulers of Bangladesh. I fully support the loyal armed forces' effort to help the nation."

General Ershad, who first made himself heard and felt during the November 1981 election campaign demanding a constitutional allotment of political power for the military, had won his tilt with the politicians.[35] The new chief of state, described by a *Le Monde* reporter as "reserved" and even colorless, said when asked about the charisma of President Zia, "The élan Zia was here yesterday. Today it is the élan Ershad." His first months in office showed him to be a man of great ambition

H. M. Ershad.

and an organizer in the military mold, possessed by grand political ideas.

He was born in 1928 in Rangpur, a town in North Bengal, one of the poorest areas of the country. He graduated from the University of Dacca and rose to the rank of lieutenant colonel in the Pakistani army. After his training most of his service was spent in East Pakistan. During the war of independence he was imprisoned in Pakistan. After returning to Bangladesh he was appointed army chief by President Zia. He is interested in literature and sports, especially golf and tennis.

The populace accepted the coup quietly.[36] Signs of martial law began to disappear from the streets within a week. Satisfied that no blood had been shed and that the transfer of power had not stirred the political activists, the people had nothing to say. Some foreign observers suggested that they lacked enthusiasm for the new regime. However, hostility among university professors, students, and politicians persisted. Some believed that General Ershad had not intervened at the time of Zia's death because he was unsure of the support of the armed forces and not, as he claimed, because he was devoted to democracy. Critics of the general also believed that Sattar had ousted most of the corrupt politicians and reduced patronage.

But Sattar gave in to the coup, and he was not the only one. The Awami League, according to *Le Monde*, was "traumatized" because it had favored a takeover that aimed at eliminating corruption in the Nationalist party. Some Awamis were said to hope Ershad would invite them to join his government. Hasina Wajed accepted the coup "with no regrets" because "the self-imposed leaders [of the Zia government] brought the latest coup on themselves." Her remark reflected her penchant for complaining about the past.

Upon hearing the news of the coup, the U.S. Department of State sent a stiff message to Dacca: "We regret that constitutional processes in Bangladesh have been overturned. . . . We had repeatedly stressed to Bangladesh leaders the importance we attach to constitutional and democratic government and economic development. . . . We hope that there can be a return to constitutional government at the earliest possible opportunity." This message was quickly followed by a softer communication that said the United States had a long-standing humanitarian interest in Bangladesh. U.S. officials in Dacca promised the coup would not affect aid but said the situation would be kept under review. The U.S. ambassador was present at the swearing ceremony of President Choudhury a few days later.

Tass reported that Leonid Brezhnev had sent congratulations to General Ershad; Peking announced the news of the coup without comment. The ambassador of Saudi Arabia was the first foreign envoy to call on Ershad. Mrs. Gandhi greeted the news of General Ershad's new government with the remark that it was "a sort of coup d'état." She also expressed her concern that India now "faced so much instability on her borders—an instability that if drawn out would encourage intervention." She may have intended her remarks to warn Pakistan to keep out of Bangladesh. The Indian external affairs minister saw the coup in a different light. He told the Indian Parliament the situation in Bangladesh seemed to be under control and that developments there were an internal matter. The Indian president sent congratulations to General Ershad.

The only major newspapers to comment on the coup were *Le Monde* and the Manchester *Guardian*, both more sympathetic to the Awami League than to other Bangali leaders. *Le Monde* believed the coup, which it said had arrested the course of the nation's democratic process, took place because the military found it could not hold on to the power it enjoyed under Zia. "Ershad's ascendancy," the editorial said, "means that freedom fighters have been bested by the military trained in Pakistan, but changes in domestic affairs will not affect foreign policy."

The *Guardian* commented that it accepted the sincerity of General Ershad when he said he had not launched a coup to establish a military dictatorship, but "there is every reason to doubt the General will return to the barracks." The editorial noted that the military as civilians are not exempt from the temptations of corruption and wondered whether "they will be more efficient."

GENERAL ERSHAD AND MARTIAL LAW

Martial law, justified by General Ershad as representative of the will of the people, imposed draconian penalties on politicians guilty of "corrupt practices," that is, the use of political power for private benefits and the use of planned political violence, which often accompanied overheated factionalism.[37]

Martial law regulations allowed the confiscation of property, life imprisonment, or the death penalty for those found guilty of corruption or the possession of illegal arms. The penalties applied to former presidents (Ershad exempted Sattar), vice-presidents, ministers, and members of the armed forces, among others. Antigovernment activities carried 7-year prison sentences. Hoarders and black marketeers might serve 14 years at hard labor. Not only were political activities and strikes prohibited and their perpetrators subject to punishment, but student unions were dissolved and special regulations issued to prohibit student participation in politics.

The first martial law courts, headed by senior military officers, opened April 5, 1982, throughout the country. Although no appeals from their decisions were allowed, trials were to be public and the accused were allowed defense counsel.

By the end of the first month of martial law nearly 700 persons, including 6 former cabinet ministers, had been jailed.[38] One-third of that total were held on charges of corruption or endangering the state, and about half for breaking curfew; more than 100 wanted criminals were caught in the martial law net. Most of the first third of those jailed belonged to the Bangladesh Nationalist party. Four persons held in the death of a villager near Dacca were the only ones reported to have been given the death penalty.

The foreign press diligently reported criticisms and defenses of martial law.[39] Some businessmen and diplomats doubted the Ershad government's ability to deal with high-level corruption, because they believed that the government had erroneously charged some politicians and bureaucrats with such activity. In a *New York Times* interview the editor of *Ittefaq*, M. Hussain, remarked, "If martial law continues for long, there will be trouble. People do not like it. What I fear is that martial law cannot be as harsh as it is on paper; there will be excesses, and if Ershad is not inclined to be harsh, what about the next martial law ruler?" His pessimistic comments reflect the opinion of moderate Bangalis discouraged by protracted political violence. Defenders of Ershad said he was a moderate who had forestalled harsher action by middle-level officers; they also claimed that his press controls were no more stringent than those imposed by previous governments.

REORGANIZATION AND DECENTRALIZATION

Within four months General Ershad had completed a calculated program to reform the nation's political, social, and economic structures.[40] He first established a powerful council of advisers (in fact a trimmed-down cabinet) whose members filled the shoes of previous ministers as heads of national civilian services. Two weeks after its formation it included 7 retired and active military officers and 5 civilians; later it was expanded to 11 civilians and 8 officers and was called a cabinet once again.

Two of the highly regarded former civil servants attracted the attention of the foreign press. A.M.A. Muhith, minister for finance and planning, had served on Mujib's planning commission, as economic minister in the Washington embassy, and as executive director of the Asian Development Bank in Manila, and had returned to Dacca as secretary of the external resources division of the ministry of planning until his retirement in 1981. His experience in foreign aid agencies and his broad economic outlook was expected to contribute importantly to development programs. Shafiul Azam, head of the ministry of industries, commanded the respect of all political parties for his administrative competence. Other civilians headed the ministries of foreign affairs, law, local government, land reform, agriculture, rural development, irrigation, and information. Military officers were placed in ministries that related to national security, including transportation and energy.

Since the general regarded the bureaucracy as a prime source of corruption, he set about to ensure its purity. To this end he planned to place ombudsmen in each ministry and a committee of ombudsmen in the armed services. He also notified the private sector he would investigate racketeering.

For his second change in government organization, Ershad chose A.S.M. Choudhury, a former judge, to occupy the titular post of president. Serving at the pleasure of the general, President Choudhury was to perform ceremonial duties.

A third change reorganized the administration of economic development funds and a portion of the judicial system. One or another of these reforms had been proposed by Mujib, Zia, and Sattar, but none had acted on them. General Ershad's decision to decentralize came to this: it was an accepted idea, the World Bank and the IMF had strongly urged it, and, in addition, it would rid the nation of centralized colonial institutions or modernize them, bring the government closer to the people, disperse the bureaucracy now largely concentrated in Dacca, and stop the population flow to the cities. To ensure local health services, the government decreed that doctors would not be allowed to go abroad unless they had served five years in rural areas.

Decentralization of economic development divides decision-making authority between Dacca and local governments and requires Dacca bureaucrats to live in rural areas. Officers in the 19 districts have additional authority to establish local industries. Zi-ullas (formerly called thanas), administrative units that embrace a cluster of villages and number about 400, have additional responsibility to collect taxes for limited local development programs. Ershad's decentralization program began operation in the most powerful of the zi-ulla subdistricts. Ershad counts on the subdistrict economic development programs to further his political fortunes.

To curtail the costs of litigation and speed up the judicial process, General Ershad in May 1982 announced a plan to decentralize the judiciary. The High Court, a part of the Supreme Court, was independently organized into a hierarchy of courts, regional, district, and thana. Despite protests by the Supreme Court Bar Association, transfer orders were issued to judges on June 15.

The economy in 1982 sustained "zero economic growth," according to Finance Minister Muhith. The economic crisis was partially explained by the political and economic uncertainties that followed the death of Zia. Other important factors were the worldwide recession, poor crops, and declining foreign aid.

By means of large budget cuts and downward revisions in the second five-year plan for 1980–85, the economy weathered a fiscal debacle. To stave off trouble and compensate for the decline in the year's food production, the government began a huge program of rice and wheat distribution and pressed for more food from abroad.[41] By the spring of 1983 good rains and more irrigation facilities had increased food supplies well above the previous year's level. General Ershad stepped up the disinvestment of public enterprises and greatly extended the scope of private ownership. However, the economy's basic public and private managerial deficiencies, its structural limitations, and the global recession prevented the nation's industries from making more than slow progress.

A new industrial policy, announced on June 3, expanded opportunities for domestic and foreign private investment.[42] At the heart of the 15-point program was the decision to denationalize all but defense-related industries and a few others. The remaining public corporations were to be made more efficient and less corrupt by improving management and production, disinvesting abandoned units, and engaging private management contractors to operate the enterprises. The government agreed in principle to return several hundred public enterprises, such as jute, cement, paper, fertilizer, and sugar plants, to the private sector. Twenty-five of them were offered for disinvestment. The nation's banks and a specialized government agency were instructed to help new private companies planning to invest in new technologies and manufacturing for export. Investment decisions could also be made at the district level, unless more than 20 percent of a new company's raw materials had to be imported, in which case a central investment board would have to approve the proposal. New light industries, such as textiles, transportation equipment, and chemicals, would be open to both public and private companies.

A large number of nationalized jute and textile mills were designated in October to return to their former owners, a step that was interpreted as a move toward total disinvestment in these industries. Former owners were invited to take back their mills by returning the compensation they had received in 1976.

The Industrial Promotion and Development Company of Bangladesh, a joint public-private and domestic-foreign venture, began business in Dhaka* in January 1983. The government of Bangladesh held 30 percent of the initial capital; included among the investors were a World Bank affiliate, a West German development agency, and an industrial service organization owned by the Pakistani Aga Khan. The IPDC immediately took on several industrial projects.

---

*The spelling of the city's name was changed in October 1982 to more closely approximate the Bengali pronunciation.

To provide financial assistance to private enterprise, a joint Bangali-Arab bank, one of three private commercial banks (the other two are locally owned), opened its doors for business in Dhaka in the spring of 1983. Other nationalized banks may be turned over to private hands. The Bangali-Arab bank has become the most successful of private banks.

The government continues to exercise strong control over the economy through the national Bangladesh bank and the governmental administration of heavy industries. The minister of energy, for example, is actively planning for the installation of a modest 300-megawatt nuclear power plant to be built 90 miles north of Dhaka. Heavy foreign financing is required. The reasons given for the plant's construction are the lack of fossil fuels in Bangladesh and the desire to conserve gas resources. British and French firms are bidding for the construction work, which is expected to be completed in 1990.

The success of the ambitious and optimistic private enterprise program depends on a better trained and more skillfully managed private sector, less open to the temptations of corruption. Its future, too, is at the mercy of domestic political forces and almost equally depends on improvements in the emerging international world order, still in a state of confusion.

The government soon learned it had to do something about "black money" generated by illegal, untaxed transactions, which were estimated to amount to 40 percent of the total money supply.[43] The government decided to allow businessmen to invest this money after the payment of a 15 percent tax, provided they used it for productive purposes; otherwise the tax rate would be 30 percent. By September more than 1,000 individuals had declared $180 million in unpaid taxes.

Dedicated officials, too, had to administer Finance Minister Muhith's revised budget for 1982/83, which cut back spending for development and increased taxes.[44] A "rationalization committee" under the minister's direction reviewed development projects and reduced the original estimates 15 percent by dropping nearly one-third of the projects. A realistic appraisal of domestic growth also lowered its previous estimate. The revised budget, taking into account the state of the world economy, calculated foreign aid at the same level as in 1981/82. The pessimistic assumptions of the new budget were more realistic than the earlier one, which had boosted expenditures for defense, debt service, and food subsidies.

The finance minister's budget for 1983/84 proposed increased expenditures for agricultural subsidies and higher taxes. Greater expenditures for development programs were to be met by larger disbursements of foreign aid. The minister dared to predict a 6 percent growth

Bank of Bangladesh, Dhaka.

rate for the economy in 1984. However, he reduced the scope of the second five-year plan by concentrating its expenditure estimates in immediately productive projects and by reducing its balance-of-payments gap.

The most surprising and far-reaching proposals for structural changes in the economy came from a land reform commission appointed by General Ershad.[45] Its report recommended restrictions on absentee landowning, the seizure of unused land, reduction in the size of landholdings, and limits on urban landownership. The report also proposed the five-year extension of sharecroppers' tenancy rights and the distribution of sharecropper farm products on the basis of one-third share each for land, labor, and energy input. When rural landowners complained that the government was threatening to take their property away and further limit the size of their holdings, General Ershad assured them that the aim of the reforms was not to deny their entitlements but to increase the productiveness of the land and to protect the rights of sharecroppers. The U.S. AID administration had previously cast doubts on the economic merits of similar reforms advanced by the Zia government, which supporters of the landowners in the Nationalist party had smothered.

The commission's recommendations are essentially those supported for years by middle-of-the-road politicians and partially introduced in previous administrations. Such reforms, the commission believes, would benefit both the peasants and the economy. The carrying out of the commission's recommendations will be long delayed if large landowners have their way, but the Awami League and its allies will continue to demand land reforms.

In fiscal 1981/82, a record harvest was offset by the rising cost of imports and tight external payments.[46] The gross national product for that fiscal year amounted to 1 percent, a decline from the previous year. The government in 1982/83 met its domestic expenditures by actions, including soliciting increased foreign aid, that moderated balance-of-payments difficulties and budgetary pressures. Import increases were restrained and the taka depreciated. By the spring of 1982/83 the nation's gross national product had returned to its previous higher levels.

RELATIONS WITH INDIA

If India worried that Pakistan's Islamic regime would exert undue influence on General Ershad's martial law regime, it did not allow its fears to stand in the way of its ambition to become a dominant Asian power by negotiation with its neighbors.[47] In May 1982 the Indian external affairs minister came to Dacca, and an agreement was reached to resume talks on common problems and to engage in cooperative undertakings.

After several more months of negotiations, General Ershad and Mrs. Gandhi held a summit meeting in New Delhi October 6 through 8. They reached a settlement or authorized additional studies on several long-standing disagreements. Most significantly, they issued a memorandum of understanding with regard to the troublesome Ganges water issue. It contained an interim agreement extending for 18 months the validity of the existing 1977 pact on sharing Ganges water below the Farraka Barrage. Further, the memorandum initiated a study by the Bangladesh-India Joint Rivers Commission to decide on the level of the river's flow during future dry seasons. The commission's decision is to be final. The memorandum also dealt with highly controversial long-range water resource programs. It authorized a study by experts of the economic and technical feasibility of the Bangali plan to build storage reservoirs in Nepal and the Indian plan to dig a broad linking canal between the Brahmaputra and the Ganges within Bangladesh.

The two leaders agreed to try to close the trade gap between India and Bangladesh, which for years had been unfavorable to Dhaka, by increasing Bangali exports to India, including those produced by Indian technical and cooperative programs. Their Joint Economic Commission was requested to encourage private trade and economic cooperation.

Further talks were promised to deal with the issue of the Bay of Bengal islands and the maritime boundaries. India gave a perpetual lease to Bangladesh for a corridor connecting two Bangali areas separated by a West Bengal enclave. The lease establishes a free zone for the movement of Bangali and Indian citizens and tax exemptions on Bangali goods moving through the area. A protocol agreement was signed to facilitate Indian river services between Calcutta and Assam.

The cooperative measures undertaken by the two leaders in 1982 contrast pointedly with the death the following year of hundreds of Bangalis in Assam. The events of 1983 had their origins in the migration of Bengali-speaking Muslims and Hindus from East Pakistan, Bangladesh, and West Bengal into Assam, which created deep resentment among the Assamese majority. When in February 1983 the first state elections for local assembly and for national representation in New Delhi were to be held, Mrs. Gandhi—for constitutional reasons, she said—decided to use electoral rolls made up in 1978, which included the names of the immigrants. Assamese students began protesting their inclusion on the rolls and participation in the elections. Negotiations between the protestors and New Delhi reached an impasse.

In the hope of stifling protests, New Delhi imposed press censorship. Rioting by Assamese students began immediately. Throughout February, before, during, and after the elections, 3,000 or more Bangalis, Hindus, and Assamese were killed and hundreds of thousands left homeless by incendiaries.

Mrs. Gandhi denied any direct responsibility for the deaths and blamed "agitators." The elections gave an overwhelming victory to the Congress party. Because most Assamese refused to go to the polls, only 32 percent of the eligible voters participated in the elections. The Assamese nonvoters refused to accept the legitimacy of the newly elected bodies.

The government in Dhaka initially said little about the Assamese affair. When India added new troops to its border security forces during May, two units on the West Bengal border of Bangladesh and one on its Assam border, Bangali officials said the moves were an internal Indian affair, but the foreign minister instructed the Bangali high commissioner in New Delhi to make a report. The head of Indian border security said the forces were strengthened to prevent "infiltration" from Bangladesh.

OTHER FOREIGN RELATIONS

Among the many contacts of the Bangalis with other Muslim nations during General Ershad's administration, two are representative. King Khalid of Saudi Arabia visited Dhaka shortly after the general's takeover, and Finance Minister Muhith went to Riyadh in search of $300 million (half of which he obtained) needed to meet a development budget shortfall.[48] The Saudis during the previous six years had given the Bangalis $500 million in assistance, most of it in the form of grants. The commerce minister of Pakistan, meeting with his Bangali counterpart in Dhaka, agreed to increase the value of trade both ways to $120 million a year. The two ministers noted that trade between the two countries had been increasing and promised to maintain regular contact in order to remove existing trade barriers.

Pakistan's relations in the 80's followed a steady and largely un-documented course.[49] Trade agreements were renewed and banking arrangements reached. Pakistan's President Zia was sympathetic to the Bangali military regimes. Conservative Bangali politicians shared Pakistani distrust of India.

The common interest of Bangladesh and Nepal in a regional water resources program was reaffirmed in November 1982, when General Ershad visited his neighbor to the north. Landlocked Nepal expressed an interest in using the facilities of the Chittagong port and in constructing an 18-mile-long road to connect northern Bangladesh with Nepal.

In February 1983 Bangladesh concluded its thirteenth barter trade agreement with the Soviet Union. However, the economic advantages of the trade did not deter President Ershad, after his return from an official visit to the United States, from ousting all but 14 Soviet diplomats and closing down the Soviet Cultural Center. He justified his action on the ground that the diplomats had meddled in domestic politics. The diplomats had left the country by January 1984. China has gradually replaced the Soviet Union as the great power nation most favored by Bangladesh.

FOREIGN AID

Bangladesh obtains about 80 percent of its development aid from abroad, and the bulk of that from Western nations and United Nations agencies.[50] Prior to the Bangladesh Aid Group meeting in Paris toward the end of April 1982, Finance Minister Muhith prepared a basic development program to submit to the group. The consortium agreed to contribute $1.58 billion in aid during the fiscal year 1982/83, an increase of 3.5 percent but less than Dhaka's request for $2 billion. The group commended the Ershad government on its fiscal management.

The International Development Association approved $250 million in aid for 1982/83. Later the International Monetary Fund (IMF) agreed to grant $78 million in special drawing rights to compensate for trade deficits. Earlier the IMF had cancelled a much larger similar loan because of the Sattar government's failure to meet IMF criteria for reduced public expenditures.

The dependence of the nation on foreign aid was on the mind of General Ershad when he attended the United Nations General Assembly's special session on disarmament on June 17, 1982. In his address he said that the $600 billion spent worldwide on armaments should be "cut sharply" so that the savings could be directed "to the teeming masses of the global unemployed."

PROSPECTS FOR DEMOCRACY

General Ershad has insisted he plans to return the nation to democratic rule by 1984.[51] His statement that the political crisis required him to take over power and his political and economic maneuvers under martial law cloud the future of Bangali democracy, although for many other reasons it has a good chance to survive.

The general's public avowals of determination to restore democracy were sown with plausible and self-justifying conditions. He first stated he wanted to see democracy returned "as soon as possible," but later admitted it would take two years, that is, until 1984, when his term as army chief expires. At his news conference for foreign correspondents after the 1982 coup, when he asserted he was a military man, not a politician, and added he would return to the army on the resumption of civilian rule unless the people called him to power, he concluded, "I would surely like to come, but not in uniform." That statement made him the leading candidate for prime minister or president in 1984.

The success of martial law, too, became a condition for a return to democratic government. Corruption, the general repeated obsessively, must end, law and order must be restored, and a beginning must be made in political, social, and economic reforms. Moreover, he would lift the martial law ban on politics only if the situation enabled him to do so. And before democratic rule was established, he insisted, a popular referendum would be held to settle the issue of parliamentary versus presidential government. That referendum could turn out to be a popularity contest the general expects to win. Beyond all of those hurdles on the road to democracy, Ershad maintained a new constitution must be framed that gives the military a role in the democratic process. On this point he argued, "The army created the nation and should be heard," ignoring the fact that he was not in the fighting army and independence would have been barely possible without India's help.

In a national radio address on June 20, 1983, the general talked about his vision of the nation's future. He said plainly that democratic government requires the military to weigh in as the "balancing power." The armed forces would bolster the nation's administrative, technological, and engineering sectors and rebuild "an integrated, powerful, and unified nation." In point of fact, martial law gave the military the dominant position in making public policies and filling important posts in the council of ministers. Is democracy, then, a mere extension of martial law?

Ershad attacked the present Constitution as a failed imitation of Western democracies on the grounds that Bangali political parties would not voluntarily abandon power and did not understand that their power depended on the support of the people. He suggested that constitutional models better suited to the nation could be found in the political systems developed by Singapore, South Korea, and Japan. Since political parties operate freely only in Japan and are handcuffed in the other two countries, this suggestion cast doubt on the future role of Bangali political parties. In a December 1982 interview with correspondents of the *Far Eastern Economic Review*, Ershad said he had decided to reduce the number of political parties. The leaders of the Awami League and the Bangladesh Nationalist party each formed coalitions with like-minded smaller political parties.

Ershad's determination to use the military to move the nation toward a regime of purity and efficiency will be widely challenged. His economic programs have yet to prove their worth. If the politicians can act responsibly and propose a popular alternative to the general's balance of military and civilian power, there will be a critical showdown.

ELECTIONS PROMISED AND POSTPONED

During the first months of martial law, which General Ershad devoted to governmental and economic reforms, the ban on political action imposed by the law vexed the Bangali political spirit. The general's early promise to return to democracy in two years seemed hard to believe. Even the preliminaries to the local elections in 1983 did not end the waiting period soon enough.

General Ershad chose his own time to open the Pandora's box of politics and to begin his moves leading to a bid for the presidency. He made it plain that he would be responsible for the nation's return to democracy, and that a prerequisite was a state of law and order maintained by the military. His critics, on the other hand, pointed to the fact that military coups were responsible for the assassinations of Mujib and Zia and for martial law.

The general threw down the political gauntlet on August 17, 1982, when he proposed the drafting of a new constitution that would legitimize a political role for the military. He then said he would not become president while in the army. Although his term as chief of the armed forces was later extended to December 1984, he still had the option of resigning before presenting himself as a civilian presidential candidate. His August speech suggested, significantly, that the election of the president be decided either by popular vote or by an electoral college comprising members of Parliament, local administrators, and popularly elected union council members. The latter proposal, geared to the general's decentralization plans, read like an updated version of Ayub's Basic Democracy. Ershad went on to repeat an earlier proposal that the constitutions of other Asian nations be studied, but this time he mentioned Muslim nations.

As if to announce a preference for the electoral college idea, the government in September began to implement its plans for decentralization and local elections.[52] The chairmen of all municipalities (centers of opposition leadership) "ceased to hold office" and their authority was given over to the commissioners. The government, it was said, would subsequently appoint municipal chairmen and hold elections for municipal commissioners. Work was also to start on the designation of wards and the registration of voters for all local elections.

With an eye to his standing in the international community, General Ershad acquired the title of prime minister in anticipation of his attendance at a regional Commonwealth conference. A week later the council of ministers made him its president to enhance his status in world capitals. The new titles may also have been intended to add luster to his office at home.

Also during September the general said in a public address that a return to civilian rule would come only after a "healthy political situation" prevailed. He told the High Court judges the establishment of three provincial high courts outside Dhaka was imperative. Although hundreds of lawyers had boycotted the court to back up the resistance of the Dhaka High Court to Ershad's initial decision, the government position held.

The government also challenged several hundred University of Dhaka professors who had been living abroad for some years, contrary to established rules. Forty of them were terminated and more than 400 requested to return within a specified time. In February 1983 another 150 were dismissed because they refused to return.

On January 14, 1983, the general surprised politicians and, perhaps, the public, when he told a meeting of teachers from Muslim religious schools that "the ideals and principles of Islam will be reflected in every sphere of state and national life; the place of Islam as a religion will be maintained above all in the Constitution of the country. Our struggle," he added, "is to fight the enemies of Islam and turn Bangladesh into an Islamic state."[53] Whether the general meant that he wanted an Islamic state similar to that of Pakistan or of the conservative Arab countries is unclear. He had previously appeared to reject the fundamentalism of an Islamic state. Several weeks after the January 14 address, he told reporters he realized it was a mistake to have allowed his emotions to carry him away on that occasion.

Prior to the annual Martyrs' Day observance on February 21, commemorating the death of two students who opposed Pakistan's imposition of Urdu as a second language, General Ershad made another venture into the mine field of language, religion, and politics. On the occasion of Martyrs' Day, which also celebrated the survival of Bengali, he ordered the Koran to be read in order to stress the importance of an Islamic state. For the critics of the general, this remark paralleled the Urdu threat of 1952 which would have made Bengali "an endangered species."

Twenty-three opposition leaders, responding to the statement about the institution of an Islamic state, warned that it could lead to civil war—communal strife between Muslims and Hindus. The British Broadcasting Company aired a report (not heard on local radio stations) that students affiliated with the secularist opposition had declared the general's proposal to read the Koran at the Martyrs' Day celebration a negation of the achievements of the February movement by "changing basic state policy and promoting the interests of a group and a person in the name of religion."

The controversy ignited by Ershad's politico-religious remark did not end with words. Two student groups, the secular-minded Student Action Committee and the fundamentalist Student Front Organization, engaged in a bloody battle at Dhaka University. The front organization held a parade to mark its founder's day, February 6, while rumors were circulating on the campus alleging that a student of the action committee had been killed by the fundamentalists. Members of the action committee attacked the front organization marchers; more than 200 students were injured.

The Student Action Committee organized a procession on February 14 to confront a police barricade near the Dhaka University campus. The committee announced it would stage a sit-in to protest the government's educational and other policies. Students and police exchanged a variety of missiles, and when a sizable body of students breached the police ranks, the police opened fire; 100 students and 60 police were hurt.

The following day the government arrested 30 political leaders of an Awami League coalition, sponsors of the Student Action Committee, including Hasina Wajed and Kamal Hussain. Four hundred students were jailed; a night curfew was imposed on Dhaka and the university was closed.

In a broadcast on February 18 General Ershad adopted a conciliatory stance. Referring to the local elections to be held in 1983 and the general elections of 1984, he called for a "national dialogue" between himself, politicians, and intellectuals to begin on Independence Day, March 24.[54] On the eve of the broadcast he had released most of the prisoners taken in a few days earlier, but not the party leaders nor the students.

On February 21 a heavily guarded General Ershad quickly laid a wreath at the martyrs' shrine and departed. Students took over the shrine area; they chanted slogans such as "End martial law" and waved banners in memory of Mujib and Zia. The police stood quietly by.

As the time neared for the national dialogue the rest of the recently jailed political leaders were released. The government at the same time

Shahid Memorial to students killed in 1952 language riots.

warned the students not to make any more trouble and later freed all of them.

At a March 24 ceremony celebrating the twelfth anniversary of independence, the general repeated his promise to hold local and national elections. The ban on "indoor politics," he said, would be lifted on April 1 and the dialogue would then ensue. He restated his commitment to a constitutional role for the armed forces, saying that is was necessary to achieve a peaceful transfer of power, which had not happened for 12 years. He intimated he would take the issue of the armed forces' role to the country in the elections.

In the same speech he expressed his willingness to discuss foreign policy, defense, and the national economy with the opposition. He severely limited the scope of the dialogue, however, by observing that these subjects were above party politics. In a published article he had outlined the kind of opposition the country needed: one that would accept the verdict of elections without question and support the government on issues of national interest. The government, in return, would "consult" the opposition on major policy issues. Ershad here strongly implied that he would only agree to the establishment of a "sovereign" executive. The opposition demanded the recognition of their "full political rights," such as open campaigning and free elections. If Ershad's statements amounted to more than political rhetoric, there may be no escape from confrontation and a martial law crackdown in the future.

Political coalitions were formed and the promised dialogues began, notwithstanding the general's admonitions. A 15-party alliance, dominated by Hasina Wajed's faction of the Awami League and the radical JSD and also including right and left splinter groups, was put together in April. The coalition issued a manifesto of 11 demands that called for an end to military rule, restoration of human rights, a judicial inquiry into the February riots, the release of all political prisoners, and the holding of parliamentary elections. Another coalition of 11 right-wing parties, calling itself the United National Front and led by former president Khondakar Moshtaque Ahmed, announced its formation the same month.

The first of Ershad's talks began at the end of April with Ataur Rahman Khan, the respected moderate leader of the well-established moderate Jatiya League coalition. Khan emerged from the meeting with the comment that he was convinced the general supported democracy. In a subsequent meeting with other oppositionists on June 6, the general was reported to have rejected their demand for parliamentary rule. A few days later an alliance of leftist and centralist parties asked the military to hold general elections immediately and hand over power to a civilian government. Although most of the opposition parties rejected Ershad's plan to give the military a role in the constitution, they were as divided as ever on the issues.

POLITICS AND ELECTIONS

By the middle of 1983 General Ershad seemed confident that he could bring democracy to the country.[55] In August he hinted that he might retire from the military and enter politics. After his return from a visit with President Ronald Reagan in Washington, he announced on November 14 that presidential elections would be held six months earlier than previously planned, on May 24, 1984, to be followed by parliamentary elections November 25. On December 3, 1983, President Ahsanuddin Chowdhury launched the Jana Dal (people's party) to support the candidacy of General Ershad. The principal adherents of the party were military officers. Eight days later the general declared himself president, as Zia had done before him. He did so, he said, in order to pave the way for democracy; he invited the opposition to talk with him.

The following day Hasina Wajed, leader of the Awami League and the 15-party alliance, and Begum Khalida Ziaur Rahman, leader of the Bangladesh Nationalist party and a group of seven parties, were released from house arrest, where they had been confined for a month for alleged involvement in political protests.

On her release Hasina said talks with Ershad could not begin until restrictions on political activities and press censorship were lifted. She also demanded the immediate release of political prisoners and the holding of parliamentary elections prior to the presidential poll. President Ershad quickly lifted the ban on political activities. Local observers said he acted to attract the support of Begum Rahman and her allies.

The dialogue between President Ershad and the main opposition leaders, scheduled to start January 7, 1984, did not take place, for the opposition leaders refused to participate. At the end of the month the opposition parties debated among themselves whether to boycott the rural elections in February. The 15-party alliance, which included the Bangladesh Communist party, condemned Ershad's expulsion of the Soviet diplomats. The seven-party coalition led by the Bangladesh Nationalist party demanded firmer action by the government in its dealings with India on issues of Ganges water, New Moore Island, and India's plan to build a fence along its border with Bangladesh to keep Bangalis from entering Assam. The year 1983 ended in a standoff between President Ershad and his opposition.

On May 12 leaders of the opposition coalitions won the agreement of President Ershad to hold parliamentary elections prior to a presidential election. Earlier in the year, Ershad held off opposition demands for the scheduling of elections in late May. On July 13 he agreed to set the date for parliamentary elections for December 8, 1984. No date was fixed for an expected presidential election.

QUESTIONS FOR THE FUTURE

The period from the death of President Zia to the beginning of 1984 presented Bangali democracy with a set of new and old questions. The most important of them are the following:

1. Will a civilian or a military government formulate and execute the public policies of the nation? General Ershad made this a paramount issue with his demand for a constitutional role by the military.

2. Will General Ershad's decentralization plan be used to control the popular vote or will it allow the citizenry to contribute to social, economic, and political development? The decentralization plans of Mujib and Zia were never completed.

3. Will the spiritual values of Islam, now debated globally, inspire democratic institutions, democratic social reforms, and human rights such as religious freedom and freedom of expression?

4. Will party candidates successful in the 1984 elections form a center to hold the nation together peacefully and accelerate national development, or will political instability resume?

5. Will financial aid from abroad and terms of trade be sufficient to meet the nation's needs? Will the serious effects of the worldwide recession persist, or will the world of rich nations find ways of equitably assisting the poorer nations and of waging peace?

Epilogue

Madame de Staël once said the battle for independence precedes the battle for freedom. Twentieth-century political experience tells us more. The struggle to realize the democratic values of equality and justice as well as freedom do not readily follow the winning of national independence. As Polish Solidarity leader Lech Walesa has remarked, "Freedom must be gained step by step, slowly." So too must other democratic values.

As long as chance and errors in judgment exist in political life, political action falls short of political ideals. For these and other reasons the government of Bangladesh, like many new nations, has vacillated between democracy and authoritarian rule. The Bangali popular democratic spirit, however, staved off doctrinaire authoritarianism and sustained a battered but promising democracy. To progress in democratic ways the nation can no longer afford embittered personal and factional struggles for power. Its divided ruling middle class must refrain from political partisanship and enlist the participation of the people in its political, social, and economic endeavors, broaden opportunities for education and cultural development, and safeguard the national interest.

The factionalism that activated violence and corrupt practices took hold when presidents Ayub and Yahya pressed their national integration campaign and the Bangalis assailed them. A more adroit and sympathetic administration of Bangali affairs could have reduced the incidence of factionalism and assuaged Bangali sensibilities. With independence Bangali politicians indulged their fondness for political wrangles, which divided the major preindependence coalitions into less stable combinations. Charisma and popular support carried Mujib and Zia through their short presidential years. Awami League factionalism panicked Mujib into a frustrated authoritarian posture that ended in his death. Zia's frontal attacks on factional divisiveness—his popular economic

Street scene, Old Dacca (U.S. Information Service, Dhaka).

Street scene, modern-day Dhaka.

programs, severe punishment of military rebels, and favors to loyal conservative politicians—aroused a second coterie of dissident military officers who staged his assassination. The interim civilian government of Abdus Sattar gave way to a bloodless coup by a military junta that justified its action with a promise to end corruption. General Ershad, its leader, asserted the superior ability of the military to control violence. The general did not refer publicly to factionalism, but his announced programs indicated that he hoped to control its effects. The politicians for whom religion is a serious, private matter deeply resented his efforts to introduce religion into politics.

Commentators have popularized the idea that two antagonistic nationalistic outlooks, which divide the ruling middle class, explain factionalism and its erosion of the nation's governability. One of the nationalistic groups consists of Bangali civilian politicians who before independence supported a united Pakistan and opposed independence, but nevertheless remained in or returned to the new nation of Bangladesh. After 1975 they participated in the government of President Zia, espoused his domestic and foreign policies, and allied themselves with partisans of pro-Islamic causes. The second group, identified with Sheikh Mujib's Awami League, opposed Pakistani rule, supported independence, and, after holding power for three and one-half years, became the principal opposition party. Its government, representing popular causes, established a mixed economy with substantial governmental participation, friendly relations with India, and a pragmatic nonaligned foreign policy that brought billions of dollars in relief assistance.

Pro-Moscow factions, it should be added, clung like barnacles to the sides of the Awami League, while pro-Peking and anti-Indian groups aligned themselves with conservative nationalists. Officers of the armed services at first divided their allegiance among revolutionaries and the supporters of both nationalisms. As time passed increasing numbers of them rallied to the conservative front.

A close look at the record of the Mujib and Zia administrations discloses that their nationalisms were not as far apart as the commentators suggest. On coming to power Sheikh Mujib sprinkled his anticolonial nationalism with the salt of socialism, secularism, and democracy, which he gradually adapted to the nation's circumstances. As his industrial socialist program floundered, he encouraged domestic and foreign private investors to participate in the economy. In accordance with the national tradition, his "secularism" was Islamic in temper and tolerant in practice. His nonaligned foreign policy extended a hand to the Soviets, China, and India, and later to Pakistan, while he sought and obtained aid from the West. When factionalism in his party and growing opposition to his administration threatened, he resorted to one-party government in the hope of recovering his original popularity.

Zia's nationalism differed from Mujib's mainly in degree. Domestically, he retained public enterprises and expanded private industries, and he emphasized the Islamic character of the nation while preserving religious freedom. Although on the way to the presidency he was alleged to have employed a rigged plebiscite, his popularity was later confirmed in a fair and open election. The conservative coalition he put together with patronage directly engaged the government in the development of the economy, as Mujib during his last days planned to do. His foreign policies, built on foundations laid by Mujib, confirmed the nation's international standing. Bangali-Indian relations stabilized, even though Zia met with more resistance from India than had Mujib.

Mujib and Zia, each in his own way, largely succeeded in reconciling the two nationalisms. Their pragmatic bent and charisma appealed to Bangali political tastes and held the nation together. The trauma of their assassination wounded but did not break the national spirit they had evoked, nor did it stifle the nation's democratic inclinations.

The nationalism of the austere General Ershad is an open question. He must deal with demands for early elections by opposition politicians, a struggling economy, the continuing need for large amounts of foreign aid, and tensions with an India distrustful of military rulers. He has wisely promised to return the government to democratic ways.

That Mujib's and Zia's reconciliation of the conflicting nationalisms did not prevent outbreaks of political violence or control corrupt practices suggests that reasons other than factionalism threatened the governability of the nation. A combative political egalitarianism among the middle class is an alternative explanation for violence and corruption and suggests additional remedies for the ill effects of factionalism. The egalitarian spirit affected the peasants and the middle class in differing ways. The peasants' tradition-freighted life rounded the sharp edges of competition and preserved their strong sense of community.

After independence combative egalitarianism among the members of the middle class committed to politics—sparked by their struggle for power—sharpened party factionalism, created a hostile political atmosphere, and encouraged corrupt practices, although their leaders tried with varying degrees of success to maintain social order. When middle-class officers in the Bangali armed forces gained some political stature, they earned a place in the struggle for power. During Mujib's and Zia's regimes revolutionary egalitarianism among civilians and the military worsened the power struggle. Nevertheless, a traditional egalitarianism, favoring a nearly classless society, persists. The recent emergence of two women as heads of the principal parties demonstrates this sense of equality.

As long as politics remains a middle-class status symbol, competition for partisan power will remain a force in Bangali government, as it has been in the past. In the Calcutta of the 1930s Muslims bested Hindus only in the political arena. In Pakistan the Bangalis' long struggle for political influence against economic and political discrimination whetted their political steel. Independence inaugurated an open season for politicians. Sympathy and support from other countries gave some politicians additional reasons to pursue the game of politics.

Because military extremists were responsible for most of the anti-government violence, strict control of military factionalism has become an obligation of the present and of future governments. Popular revulsion to the assassinations of Mujib and Zia may help to stop the bloodletting, and the peasantry's preference for orderly change, expressed by its votes, could moderate partisan violence. Practical self-help programs that engage politicians and the people offer a peaceful alternative to political frenzy.

During the past dozen years corrupt practices have been used principally to create and maintain political coalitions and to guarantee middle-class interests. The system in all nations provides jobs, contracts, licenses, and other favors for party loyalists and the friends and families of those in power, and for those that party leaders hope to attract to their cause. More serious are the cases in which charges of corruption are used to justify political coups and the leaders of the coups then revert to those practices. The political cynicism and indifference which such actions generate tend to demoralize democracy.

Professor Carl Friedrich, in *The Pathology of Politics*, presented a realistic view of these practices and their reform.[1] He distinguished between "functional" and "disfunctional" corrupt practices. Preferential political treatment that did not significantly harm the political system, he held, could be tolerated, provided it is kept under control. In Western democracies the history of legislation establishing enforceable ethical standards of political conduct tells us that control of political corruption is very difficult and possible only to the extent that it is supported by public concern. "Disfunctional" corrupt practices, often sanctioned by legislation or public policies, are those capable of undermining the "values, interests and beliefs" of a nation. Two kinds of corruption that have done great harm in Bangladesh are the political favors that satisfied private interests but added to the numbers of unemployed, and those that deprived the poor of a fair share of food supplies. Bangali democracy has expected the government to accept responsibility for the reduction of social and economic discrimination.

Beneath the abundance of partisan rhetoric, another cause of factional disarray is a continuing debate among Bangali politicians over the political institutions best suited to its democratic ambitions. Four leading questions are at issue. How should the government, the governing party, and the people be related to one another? Should the government be parliamentary or presidential? How should the bureaucracy be reformed? What political role, if any, is proper for the military?

The endeavors of Mujib and Zia to encourage closer relations between their parties, the government, and the people passed through periods of neglect and faced political opposition. The grass-roots support given to the Awami League from its beginnings gradually declined after independence. But Mujib in the final months of his administration planned local party organizations to stimulate and assist in administering extensive rural programs. Zia, after he became president, plunged into similar programs in which he took a leading part. Their deaths ended their plans and experiments before they had proved their worth. General Ershad's decision to decentralize the administration of economic programs and of the courts testifies to the acceptance of the need for government contacts with the people.

Critics of Mujib's and Zia's actions, who accused them of attempting to reestablish a form of Ayub's Basic Democracy, failed to make their case. Neither Bangali leader could rely on the local party organizations to deliver what Ayub's pyramid of beneficiaries was able to do. Nor had the Basic Democrats, a political minority, ever been tested in a general public election, as were Mujib and Zia. The critics overlooked the fact that the success of local party democracy depends in the last analysis on the ability of the government to obtain the freely willed cooperation of the people with its programs. General Ershad's decentralization moves have yet to pass the inspection of popular judgment.

For a dozen years the Bangali people lived under parliamentary and presidential governments and interim martial law administrations. During Zia's 1978 presidential campaign the Awami League linked its demand for a return to parliamentary government with the populist cause of independence. The acceptance of the presidency by Mujib and the election of Zia, however, indicated a popular preference for the presidential system, perhaps because Bangali voters rally more readily to charismatic figures. The austere General Ershad's hint that a plebiscite would be held on the issue of parliamentary versus presidential government affirmed the importance of the matter.

In the poorer democracies of the Third World a large share of the government's responsibility for the direction of the economy devolves on its bureaucracy. Although Sheikh Mujib curtailed industrial nationalization, Zia made substantial cutbacks in public enterprises, and both of them encouraged private enterprises, their bureaucracies continued to manage major segments of the economy, including banking, transportation, energy, and communication. Public administrators, too, assigned public incentive programs to private enterprise and channeled foreign grants and loans into the economy.

Zia's democratization of the bureaucracy, in response to the egalitarian spirit of the lower ranks of its hierarchy, initially upset top bureaucrats. His reforms and General Ershad's administrative decentralization will for a time shake up the bureaucracy's organization and morale but in the long run should improve its competence and impartiality and, contrary to some Western orthodoxies, increase its ability to defend a system of democratic social justice.

Geopolitical limitations on the nation's military capabilities have restricted the traditional defense role of the military and contributed to military involvement in domestic affairs. General Ershad's insistence on a political role for the military and his assertion of political leadership required him to confront civilian opponents and to win the favor of the peasantry. However, his imposition of martial law will keep alive the memory of two presidential assassinations by military officers and the possibility of continued factionalism among them. If Ershad increases the constitutional role of the military, the politicians left out in the cold will become more restless and will agitate to restore civilian democracy.

Modernizing social and economic development, rather than instituting political reforms, is the everyday preoccupation of the government and its people. Short-run programs such as Food for Work and Zia's canal-digging project put the nation's goal of self-sufficiency by 1985 within reach, barring natural disasters. The longer-range problems of over-population, unemployment, inequitable distribution of landholdings, use of water resources, and industrial development, which resist easy and early improvement even with combined domestic and international action, touch the vital interests of the nation.

In this overpopulated nation of limited rich farmland and even more limited natural resources of other kinds, the equitable distribution of land and its better use are, as in many other Third World countries, the most far-reaching and urgent problems before the nation. Critics of the present landholding situation note that 16.7 percent of the rural population in 1980 controlled two-thirds of the land, while almost 60 percent of that population held less than one acre; in 1975 only 38 percent of the population held less than an acre. The accumulation of land by relatively few owners occurred during these years, it is said, because a majority of landowning members of Parliament had blocked remedial changes in the law and because Bangalis working in the Middle East used their large earnings to buy up farmland. The critics, however, do not acknowledge that Bangali inheritance laws, which distribute land among the children of a family, had over time increased the number of minuscule farms. Land reformers claim that farms of five acres or more, half of which are managed by tenants, are less productive than smaller farms worked by their owners and their families, even though half of the larger holdings profited most from new crop technologies.

Whether or not the present 33-acre limit on holdings is lowered, other measures are needed immediately to improve levels of rural employment and food production. The expansion of existing privately financed arrangements, which have increased the tenants' share of crop earnings from one-half to two-thirds, to include tenant farms over five acres would boost productivity and invigorate community action pro-grams. Cooperatives of the type pioneered at Comilla in the sixties by Aktar Hameed Khan would, with government encouragement, augment the knowledge, skills, and efficiency of small-acreage farms. The long-term future of Bangali agriculture hangs on the conclusion of inter-national agreements that would maximize the water resources available to the farmers of the region.

Advances in social well-being depend equally on progress in economic productivity and distribution and on social and political action. Increased budget allocations have modestly improved health services and population control. Further reforms related to overpopulation and the traditional larger intake of available food by males will come when the public learns the need for change. But the debilitating malnutrition that results from preferential allocations of food requires government action.

Existing cultures are the seedbeds of political and economic development in a nation, but governments, too, can create conditions in which national cultural talents can flourish or decay. With the assistance of the government, science and technology studies have progressed along with primary and secondary education. Thus the Bangali imagination, which soars beyond its love for poetry and drama, was eloquently expressed in the American career of the skyscraper engineer Fazlur Khan, a graduate of Dacca University and the University of Illinois. The visual arts, which miss the leadership of Zainul Abedin, and literature have stagnated under the pressures of political turmoil. University students' absorption with politics, excited by factional alliances, remains a problem that needs to be addressed by the government, faculties, and students. The press, with honorable exceptions, reflects the factionalism of the ruling class. Temporarily shut down during episodes of martial law, it has nevertheless remained reasonably free.

Significant progress in obtaining foreign aid and in other negotiations with its neighbors attended the foreign policies of Mujib's and Zia's governments. In view of the decline in the world economy, Bangali diplomacy has now turned its attention to trade and aid arrangements that will prevent a worsening of its economic condition. It has succeeded in restoring a portion of promised IMF aid. Other international and regional aid arrangements and a growing number of trade agreements buttress the economy. Bangali diplomacy, which keeps a sharp focus on the nation's wide-ranging interests on the subcontinent, has profited from recent signs of improving relations in the region.

The British economist Joan Robinson wrote in *Freedom and Necessity*, "Anyone who writes a book, however gloomy its message may be, is necessarily an optimist. If the pessimists really believed what they wrote, they would have no point in saying it." This book, written from the perspective of a realistic optimist, sees many reasons for a better outcome in the fortunes of the Bangali people.

In the Third World peasants and workers have much more modest ambitions and appetites than the people of rich nations. They want enough to eat, a roof over the heads of their families, gainful work in their community, and a peaceful existence. They seek a life in which they are free to follow their religious beliefs and to attain a level of income that makes it possible to educate their children and to exempt their families from the misery they know only too well.

The majority of Bangalis, because of population pressures and numerous other difficulties, have had to live in greater poverty in this century than in the last one, yet they have survived, partly because they shared their material goods with others as an obligation to their extended family and their village. Their fatalism, induced by experience and influenced by Sufi mysticism, helped them accept their lot. Although in recent years the modernization of political, economic, and social life troubled their traditions, the peasantry generally accepted moderate changes. Less divided than the middle class, they endured more. Future governments that fail to attend to their needs cannot count on prevailing.

The ill fortunes of the Bangalis made more dramatic news than their less instantly visible improvements. The nation's natural disasters, political upheavals, and low standard of living gave it the inaccurate reputation of a nation without hope. Prosperous countries cannot rightly accept the proposition that impoverished and politically insecure societies are condemned to extinction and penury, for many developed nations began their march into history from much the same conditions. In our times developing nations, like older, more prosperous ones, have progressed with the help of technology, economic assistance, trade, and investment and, above all, of a people determined to do as much as possible for themselves.

The Bangali people have never doubted that life has meaning. This certainty, although tinged by fatalism, generates hope. If they have from time to time betrayed their hopes or misplaced them, they have also been spurred to action by them, for hope has to do with things as they might be, not with things as they are. The good things accomplished during the past by the Bangalis attest to the underlying strengths of the nation. The hard problems that remain are a constant reminder that politics is every nation's unfinished business. However, the future of Bangladesh depends not only on the Bangalis, but also on a worldwide commitment to a better world order that includes a more equitable distribution of wealth and political influence in our global village.

Chronology

From 7th century B.C.: Recorded civilization in Bengal (the Ganges-Brahmaputra valley)

7th to 12th centuries A.D.: Hindus and Buddhists predominate in Bengal

9th to 11th centuries: Bengali vernacular develops

From the 12th century: Soldiers and missionaries convert Bengalis to Islam

12th to 16th centuries: Muslim rule

16th to 18th centuries: Mogul rule

Mid-18th century to 1947: British rule of India, including Bengal

1905–11: Separation of East from West Bengal

August 1947: Partition of British India and establishment of independent Pakistan, including East Bengal

1951–53: Kwaja Nazimuddin, a Bangali, serves as prime minister of Pakistan

1953–55: Mohammad Ali Bogra, a Bangali, serves as prime minister of Pakistan

March 1956: Pakistan adopts its first Constitution; East Bengal becomes East Pakistan

1956–57: H. S. Suhrawardy, a Bangali, serves as prime minister of Pakistan

1958–69: General Mohammad Ayub Khan rules Pakistan under martial law

Spring 1966: Awami League demands autonomy for East Pakistan under six-point program

1969–71: Yahya Khan's presidency

December 1970: National election victory of the Awami League

March 1971: Bangali independence

March–December 1971: Indo-Pakistan and Bangali guerrilla war

January 1972: Sheikh Mujibur Rahman returns to Dacca

April 1972: United States recognizes Bangladesh

October 1972: Bangali Constitution adopted; Sheikh Mujib sworn in as prime minister of the parliamentary government

February 1974: Pakistan recognizes Bangladesh

September 1974: United Nations recognizes Bangladesh and admits it as a member

January 1975: Sheikh Mujib sworn in as president

August 1975: Sheikh Mujib assassinated

August–November 1975: K. M. Ahmed serves as interim president

November 1975–April 1977: A. M. Sayem's presidency

December 1976: General Ziaur Rahman becomes martial law administrator

April 1977: General Zia becomes president

May 1981: General Zia assassinated

May 1981: Abdus Sattar becomes acting president

November 1981: Sattar elected to the presidency

March 1982: General H. M. Ershad deposes Sattar in a bloodless coup and names himself martial law administrator

October 1982: Spelling of Dacca changed to Dhaka

December 1983: General Ershad names himself president

Notes

CHAPTER 1: THE LAND AND ITS RESOURCES

General Sources: William S. Ellis, "Bangladesh: Hope Nourishes a New Nation," *National Geographic,* September 1972, pp. 295–333; contains beautiful photographs and an excellent small map of Bangladesh. Ian Stephens, *Pakistan: Old Country/New Nation* (London: Penguin Books, 1963), pp. 39–45; presents a fine description of East Pakistan (Bangladesh). U.S., Department of State, Bureau of Public Affairs, *Bangladesh: Background Notes* (Washington, D.C.: Government Printing Office, 1981); summarizes geographic, social, economic, and political data. Six of the best maps of Bangladesh were published in the seventies by the World Bank, 1818 H Street N.W., Washington, D.C. 20433.

1. Geography. Nafis Ahmed, *A New Economic Geography of Bangladesh* (New Delhi: Vikas Publishing House, 1976), which supersedes his earlier *Economic Geography of East Pakistan* (London: Oxford University Press, 1958). Articles in the *Oriental Geographer,* published in Dacca since 1953. Haroun Er Rashid, *Geography of Bangladesh* (Boulder, Colo.: Westview Press, 1978).

2. Boundaries. *Indian and Foreign Review* 11, no. 16 (June 1, 1974), pp. 7–8, contains the text of the boundary agreement with India. See also Talukder Maniruzzaman, "Bangladesh in 1974: Economic Crisis and Political Polarization," *Asian Survey* 15, no. 2 (February 1975), pp. 126–127. With respect to the maritime boundary see *Bangladesh,* February 15, 1975 (fortnightly; published in Washington, D.C., until 1977; now published in Dacca) and *New York Times,* April 6, 1975. In January 1973 the Dacca government claimed the 12-mile limit in the Bay of Bengal to be within the territorial jurisdiction of the country. New islands emerging in the bay could change the maritime boundaries of Bangladesh and India: *Economist,* August 9, 1980, pp. 33–34, and *Far Eastern Economic Review,* December 26, 1980, p. 6; *Keesing's Contemporary Archives,* November 5, 1982, p. 31796.

3. Cyclones. Dom P. Moraes, *The Tempest Within* (New Delhi: Vikas Publications, 1971). *New York Times,* November 15, 16, 24–26, and 30, 1970. *Far Eastern Economic Review,* September 29, 1978, pp. 20–21.

4. Water resources. George Ball, *Diplomacy in a Crowded World* (Boston: Little, Brown, 1976), pp. 241–243. Roger Revelle and V. Lakshiminarayana, "The Ganges Water Machine," *Science* 188 (May 9, 1975), pp. 611–616. Marcus F. Franda, "Politics and the Use of Water Resources in Bangladesh," *American Universities Field Services Staff Report,* South Asian Series 18, no. 3 (September 1973), pp. 1–11. See also note 12, chapter 16.

5. Transportation. U.S., Department of the Army Corps of Engineers, *Transport Survey of East Pakistan,* 3 vols. (Washington, D.C.: Army Corps of Engineers, 1961). Donald N. Wilber, *Pakistan: Its People, Its Society, Its Culture* (New Haven, Conn.: HRAF Press, 1964), pp. 28–41. The governments of Bangladesh and India agreed at a New Delhi summit meeting in May 1974 to carry out a joint survey for a new rail line west across Bangladesh to eastern Indian territory at Agartala; more recent progress by the railroads and Biman airlines is reported in *Far Eastern Economic Review,* January 20, 1978, p. 66, and in *Bangladesh,* February 1, 1979.

6. Oil. The awarding of contracts to foreign oil companies, including American operators, and the start of their explorations are recounted in *Bangladesh Today* (published in London by the Bangladesh High Commission), December 1, 1974. See also *Bangladesh,* November 15, 1975, and *Far Eastern Economic Review,* December 12, 1975, p. 38, and August 25, 1983, p. 72.

7. Nuclear reactor. *Asian Recorder,* September 24–30, 1977, p. 13945. *Far Eastern Economic Review,* October 1, 1982, pp. 57–58. Bangladesh was the one hundred and eleventh nation to sign the non-proliferation treaty; *Department of State Bulletin* 79, no. 2032 (November 1979), pp. 49–50.

8. Natural gas. *Far Eastern Economic Review,* July 25, 1980, p. 6. *Green Horizons* (Dacca: External Publicity Division, Ministry of Foreign Affairs, 1974), p. 19.

9. Industry. *Europa Year Book 1982: A World Survey* (London: Europa Publications, 1982), vol. 1, p. 1601. *World Bank Annual Report 1981* (Washington, D.C.: World Bank, 1981), p. 52. *World Development Report 1980* (Washington, D.C.: World Bank, 1980), pp. 112, 114, 120, and passim.

10. Agriculture. Richard F. Nyrop et al., eds., *Area Handbook for Bangladesh* (Washington, D.C.: Government Printing Office, 1975), pp. 227–248 and passim. *Europa Year Book 1982,* vol. 1, pp. 1599–1600. *World Bank Annual Report 1981,* pp. 51–52. *World Development Report 1980,* pp. 90, 112, and 114. See note 46, chapter 17, this volume.

CHAPTER 2: THE SOCIETY AND ITS PROBLEMS

1. Society. Peter J. Bertocci, *Bangladesh, History, Society and Culture,* South Asia Series, Occasional Paper no. 22 (East Lansing: Asian Studies Center, Michigan State University, 1973); bibliography of secondary materials. Richard F. Nyrop et al., eds., *Area Handbook for Bangladesh* (Washington, D.C.: Government Printing Office, 1975), pp. 134–145. Kamruddin Ahmad, *The Social History of East Pakistan* (Dacca: Pioneer Press, 1967); this historic survey

favored Bangali separation from Pakistan; it was banned by President Ayub in 1969.

2. Status of women. *Far Eastern Economic Review,* January 5, 1984, pp. 26–27. *Bangladesh,* May 18, June 2, and November 3, 1972. Rounaq Jahan speech, *Bangladesh Observer,* November 6, 1974. Betty Hartman and Jim Boyce, "Roshina," *Internationalist* (London), October 1977, pp. 122–123; an account of a Muslim woman's life in a Bangali village. Rounaq Jahan, "Women in Bangladesh," *Women for Women in Bangladesh* (Dacca: University Press Ltd., 1975).

3. Middle class. Abu Abdullah, "The Class Bases of Nationalism: Pakistan and Bangladesh," in Barbara Thomas and Spencer Lavan, eds., *West Bengal and Bangladesh: Perspectives from 1972,* South Asia Series, Occasional Paper no. 21 (East Lansing: Asian Studies Center, Michigan State University, 1973), pp. 245–264. Peter J. Bertocci, "Bangladesh in the Early 80's: Pretorian Politics in an Intermediate Regime," *Asian Survey* 22, no. 10 (October 1982), pp. 988–1008.

4. Population. The 1980 population estimate of 90 million is based on a probable annual increase of 2.4 percent over the 1970 census figure of 71,479,073 reported in the *United Nations Demographic Yearbook 1977* (New York: United Nations, 1977), p. 182. For 1980 census figures see *Europa Year Book 1983: A World Survey* (London: Europa Publications, 1983), vol. 1, p. 1594. D. S. Halavy, Jr., *The Geometry of Hunger* (New York: Harper and Row, 1971). *War on Hunger,* A Report from the Agency for International Development (Washington, D.C.: Government Printing Office, 1975). The youthfulness of the Bangali population is discussed by Rounaq Jahan in *Pakistan: Failure in National Integration* (New York: Columbia University Press, 1972), pp. 10–12. Nyrop et al., eds., *Area Handbook for Bangladesh,* pp. 78–89. Roger Revelle, "Possible Futures for Bangladesh," *Asia* (Spring 1973), pp. 34–53. *World Development Report 1980* (Washington, D.C.: World Bank, 1980), p. 110.

5. For President Ayub's Muslim Family Law of 1961 see Donald N. Wilber, *Pakistan: Its People, Its Society, Its Culture* (New Haven, Conn.: HRAF Press, 1964), pp. 134–136.

6. Population control. William Rich, *Smaller Families Through Social and Economic Progress* (Washington, D.C.: Overseas Development Council, 1973). John Stoeckel and Mobqual Chowdhury, *Fertility, Infant Mortality and Family Planning in Rural Bangladesh* (Dacca: Oxford University Press, 1973). *New York Times,* January 25 and September 30, 1976. C. Stephen Baldwin, "Catastrophe in Bangladesh: An Examination of Alternative Growth Possibilities, 1975–2000," *Asian Survey* 17, no. 4 (April 1977), pp. 345–357. *Bangladesh,* August 15, 1978, and September 1, 1978. Nurul Islam, *Development Strategy* (New York: Pergamon Press, 1978), pp. 63–72. Marcus Franda, "Moral Implications of Bangladesh," *Asia,* supplement, Fall 1974.

7. Emigration. Nazrul Karim, *Changing Society in India and Pakistan* (Dacca: Oxford University Press, 1956), pp. 93–96. *New York Times,* March 11, 1979, re the effects of emigration on the skilled labor supply in Bangladesh. See also chapters 16 and 17, this volume.

8. Health. Wilber, *Pakistan,* pp. 333–345. Lincoln C. Chen, ed., *Disaster in Bangladesh: Health Crises in a Developing Nation* (New York: Oxford University Press, 1973). Lincoln C. Chen and Jon E. Rhodes, "Famine and Civil War in East Pakistan," *Lancet,* September 11, 1972, pp. 557–560. *New York Times,* October 13, 1975, re cholera. *World Development Report 1980,* pp. 150 and 152.

9. Malnutrition. *Pakistan Nutrition Survey of East Pakistan, March, 1962–January, 1964,* A Report of the Ministry of Health, Government of Pakistan, in collaboration with the University of Dacca and the Nutrition Section, Office of International Research, Public Health Service, National Institutes of Health, U.S. Department of Health, Education, and Welfare, May 1, 1966, pp. 1–14. Chen, ed., *Disaster in Bangladesh. New York Times,* November 24, 1981, regarding the nutrition study at the University of Dacca.

10. Housing. *The Annual Plan, 1972–1973* (Dacca: Planning Commission, 1972), pp. 59–62. *Bangladesh,* September 22, 1972. Karim, *Changing Society in India and Pakistan,* pp. 96–97 and 123–137. *CORR Bangladesh* 2, no. 1 (1972), pp. 13–14; CORR, a group of U.S. and European Christian relief agencies, contributed significantly to relief and rehabilitation.

11. Urbanization. Hafik H. Hashani and Garth N. Jones, eds., *Problems of Urbanization of Pakistan* (Karachi: Institute of Public Administration, 1967), pp. 99–100. Alex Inkeles and David R. Smith, *Becoming Modern: Individual Changes in Six Developing Countries* (Cambridge: Harvard University Press, 1974); Inkeles summarized his findings, which included a study of East Pakistan during the early sixties, in "Making Men Modern: On the Causes and Consequences of Individual Changes in Six Developing Countries," *American Journal of Sociology* 75, no. 2 (September 1969), pp. 208–255. K. Maudud Elahi, "Urbanization in Bangladesh," *The Oriental Geographer* (January 1972), pp. 1–15.

12. Dacca. "Development of Dacca," *Round Table,* no. 275 (July 1979), pp. 259–260. *Statesman Weekly* (Calcutta), May 3, 1980. *World Development Report 1980,* p. 148.

CHAPTER 3: BANGALI CULTURE

General Sources: There is no comprehensive account of Bangali culture. Muhammad A. Rahim, *Social and Cultural History of Bengal* (Karachi: Pakistan Historical Society, 1963), and Peter J. Bertocci, *Bangladesh: History, Society and Culture,* pp. 1–17, contain bibliographic materials. See also the annual U.S. Library of Congress *Accession List, Bangladesh,* for Bangali publications. Trevor Ling, "Creating a New State: The Bengalis of Bangladesh," *South Asian Review* 5, no. 3 (April 1972), pp. 221–230, maintains that social and cultural forces differentiate the Bangalis from their Indian brethren.

1. Language. G. W. Choudhury, *Constitutional Development in Pakistan,* 2nd ed. (London: Harlow Longmans, 1969), pp. 81–83. Selig Harrison, *The Most Dangerous Decade* (Princeton, N.J.: Princeton University Press, 1962).

Keith Callard, *Pakistan: A Political Study* (New York: Macmillan, 1957), p. 183, passim.

2. Religion. Wilfred C. Smith, *Modern Islam in India and Pakistan,* 2nd ed. (Lahore: Ripon Printing House, 1947), pp. 262–270. Leonard Binder, *Religion and Politics in Pakistan* (Berkeley: University of California Press, 1963), pp. 123–124. Richard S. Wheeler, *Politics of Pakistan* (Ithaca, N.Y.: Cornell University Press, 1970), pp. 93–109; Donald E. Smith, ed., *South Asian Politics and Religion* (Princeton, N.J.: Princeton University Press, 1966); see especially the contribution of Khalid Bin Sayeed, pp. 408–443. Callard, *Pakistan: Political Study.* Jean Ellikson, "Believer Among Believers" (Ph.D. diss., Michigan State University, 1972); Ellikson was a member of the first (1961) U.S. Peace Corps group serving in East Pakistan. Louis Gardet, *L'Islam: Religion et Communauté* (Paris: Desclée de Brouwer, 1970), pp. 230–242 and 313–314. Ian Stephens, *Pakistan: Old Country/New Nation* (London: Penguin Books, 1963), pp. 22–37. Richard V. Weekes, *Muslim Peoples* (Westport, Conn.: Greenwood Press, 1978), pp. 89–99.

3. Other religions. Donald A. Wilber, *Pakistan: Its People, Its Society, Its Culture* (New Haven, Conn.: HRAF Press, 1964), pp. 106–114. Marta Nicholas and Philip Oldenburg, comps., *Bangladesh: The Birth of a Nation* (Madras: M. Sesrachalam, 1972), pp. 33–34, re Hindus in Bangladesh. David Pearl, "Bangladesh, Islamic Laws in a Secular State," *South Asian Review* 8, no. 1 (October 1974), pp. 33–41.

4. Education. John K. Galbraith, *Economic Development in Perspective* (Calcutta: USIS publication, n.d., 28 pp.). *Education in Pakistan,* a report prepared by the Ministry of Education, Government of Pakistan, reproduced by the Pakistan Embassy, Washington, D.C., 1965; Karl Von Vorys, *Political Development in Pakistan* (Princeton, N.J.: Princeton University Press, 1965), pp. 19–24. Recent enrollments of eight million in primary and secondary schools and of two million in secondary schools are reported in *Europa Year Book 1982,* vol. 1, p. 1597.

5. Universities. *Commonwealth Universities Yearbook 1977–78* (London: The Association of Commonwealth Universities, 1977), pp. 150–176, contains a history and description of the administration and subjects of study of the six Bangali universities and their colleges. See also *The World of Learning 1982–83* (London: Europa Publications, 1983), vol. 1, pp. 146–149, and *World Guide to Higher Education* (Paris: UNESCO Press, 1977), which reports on the system of degrees and qualifications for admission to the universities of Bangladesh on pp. 11–20.

6. Bangali letters and arts. *Bangladesh,* June 30, 1972. *Crescent and Green* (London: Cassell and Company, 1955), pp. 106–111. See *Accession List, Bangladesh,* for entries of the work of Bangali poets and dramatists.

7. (a) Mass media: Information about the press was obtained from the United States Information Agency and Bangali editors. The formation of a nonaligned news agency was reported in the *International Herald Tribune,* April 16, 1975. Later statistical information about the Bangali press will be found in the *International Yearbook* (New York: Editor and Publisher) and

issues of the *Newspaper Press Directory* (London: Benn Brothers). *Europa Year Book 1982,* vol. 1, pp. 1610–1611, lists the daily newspapers and periodicals published in English and Bengali. (b) Wire services: See *Bangladesh Observer,* July 18 and August 26, 1976.

8. Press controls. *New York Times,* December 6, 1968. Donald Wilber, *Pakistan: Its People,* pp. 282–287. Press controls since independence are discussed in chapters 13, 14, and 17, this volume.

9. Radio and television. *Bangladesh Observer,* September 20 and 24, 1973, and March 6, 1975. *World Radio and TV Handbook 1979* (Havidovre, Denmark: Billboard Publications, 1979), pp. 201, 346. *Europa Year Book 1983,* vol. 1, p. 1609.

10. Science and technology. *The World of Learning 1982–83,* vol. 1, pp. 145–46, lists the Bangali learned societies, research institutes, libraries, and museums. Ward Morehouse, *Science and the Human Condition in India and Pakistan* (New York: Rockefeller University Press, 1968). *Bangladesh Observer,* June 14, 1975.

CHAPTER 4: THE ROOTS OF THE BANGALI NATION AND THE PARTITION OF 1947

General Sources: Vincent A. Smith, *The Oxford History of India,* 3rd ed. (New York: Oxford University Press, 1956). Richard V. Weekes, *Pakistan, Birth and Growth of a Nation* (Princeton, N.J.: Princeton University Press, 1965). Jadunath Majundar and Ranesh Chadu, *The History of Bengal* (Pre-Mogul), 2 vols. (Dacca: University of Dacca, 1943 and 1948); written when East Bengal was part of India. P. M. Holt, Ann K. Lambton, and Bernard Lewis, eds., *The Cambridge History of Islam,* vol. 2 (Cambridge: The University Press, 1970), pre-Mogul period, pp. 3–34, Mogul period, pp. 35–63. Another interpretation of events in Pakistan prior to Bangali independence will be found in Y. V. Gankovsky and L. R. Gordon Polonskays, *A History of Pakistan* (Moscow: Nauka Publishing House, 1964); the Russians present a picture of British and American imperialism supporting feudal landlords and the "big bourgeoisie" in the development of Pakistan.

1. Colonial period. (a) Mogul rule: Richard Symonds, *The Making of Pakistan* (London: Faber and Faber, 1950), pp. 24 ff. Kamruddin Ahmad, *The Social History of East Pakistan* (Dacca: Pioneer Press, 1967), pp. 1–47. Hafeez Malik, *Moslem Nationalism in India and Pakistan* (Washington, D.C.: Public Affairs Press, 1963), pp. 108–111. Barrington Moore, Jr., *Social Origins of Dictatorship and Democracy* (Boston: Beacon Press, 1966), pp. 315 and 317–340. (b) British rule: Malik, *Moslem Nationalism,* pp. 146–153; Malik claims that during the first 75 years of British rule in Bengal the Muslim upper and middle classes either disappeared or were overshadowed by new Hindu upper classes as a result of the Permanent Settlement, the land tenure system established by Lord Cornwallis. See also Moore, Jr., *Social Origins,* pp. 343–347.

2. Mutiny of 1857. Wilfred C. Smith, *Modern Islam in India and Pakistan,* 2nd ed. (Lahore: Ripon Printing House, 1947), pp. 193–194, 199–212. Christopher Hibbert, *The Great Mutiny* (New York: Viking Press, 1978).

3. Rural Bengal. Akter Hameed Khan, "Rural Development in East Pakistan," South Asia Series (East Lansing: Asian Studies Center, Michigan State University, 1965). Peter J. Bertocci, "Patterns of Social Organization in Rural East Bengal," in Alexander Lipski, ed., *Bengal, East and West,* South Asia Series, Occasional Paper 13 (East Lansing: Asian Studies Center, Michigan State University, 1969), pp. 105–137. Feroz Ahmed, "The Struggle for Bangladesh," *Bulletin of Concerned Asian Scholars* 4, no. 1 (Winter 1972), pp. 2–3; a critical analysis of land-ownership in East Pakistan.

4. "Partition" of Bengal. Khalid B. Sayeed, *Pakistan: Formative Phase 1957–1958* (London: Oxford University Press, 1968), pp. 24–28. Percival Spear, *A History of India,* vol. 2 (London: Oxford University Press, 1968), pp. 176–180. Richard Symonds, *Making of Pakistan,* pp. 24–40 and 49–50. John R. McLane, "The 1905 Partition of Bengal and the new Communalism," in Lipski, ed., *Bengal, East and West,* pp. 39–77. Mohammad Ali Chaudhri, *The Emergence of Pakistan* (New York: Columbia University Press, 1967), pp. 55–202. K. K. Aziz, *The Making of Pakistan: A Study in Nationalism* (London: Chatto and Windus, 1967), pp. 17–143. Holt et al., eds., *Cambridge History of Islam,* vol. 2, pp. 91, 94, and 97.

5. Muslim League. Sayeed, *Pakistan: Formative Phase,* pp. 30–33 and 213–216. Symonds, *Making of Pakistan,* pp. 40–42.

6. Calcutta. Geoffrey Moorhouse, *Calcutta* (New York: Harcourt Brace, 1971); a journalist's fascinating account of the city. The social and political life of Calcutta's Hindus and Muslims is treated in H. H. Broomfield, *Elite Conflict in a Plural Society: Twentieth Century Bengal* (Berkeley: University of California, 1968). For a different view see Leonard A. Gordon, *Bengal: The Nationalist Movement, 1876–1940* (New York: Columbia University Press, 1975), especially pp. 265–293; see also Gordon's "Divided Bengal: Problems of Nationalism and Identity in the 1947 Partition," *Journal of Commonwealth and Comparative Politics* 16, no. 2 (July 1978), pp. 136–168, and K. McPherson, "The Muslims of Madras and Calcutta: Agitational Politics in the early 20's," *South Asian Review* 8, no. 5 (December 1975), pp. 32–48 passim.

7. Lahore Resolution. Sayeed, *Pakistan: Formative Phase,* pp. 118–125. Isthiaq H. Quershi, *The Struggle for Pakistan* (Karachi: Karachi University Press, 1963), pp. 116–140. Smith, *Modern Islam,* pp. 300–326.

8. United Bengal and Partition. Henry V. Hodson, *The Great Divide: Britain, India and Pakistan* (New York: Atheneum, 1971); contains a detailed analysis of the events surrounding the Partition of 1947. Leonard Moseley, *The Last Days of the British Raj* (London: Weidenfield and Nicholson, 1961).

9. British plans. Spear, *A History of India,* vol. 2, pp. 233–237.

CHAPTER 5: BANGALIS IN PAKISTAN, 1947–65

General Sources: Keith Callard, *Pakistan: A Political Study* (New York: Macmillan, 1957). From a socialist point of view, Tariq Ali, *Pakistan: Military Rule or People's Power* (New York: Morrow, 1970).

1. National Assembly. G. W. Choudhury, *Constitutional Development in Pakistan,* 2nd ed. (Lahore: Ripon Printing House, 1947); discusses the National Assembly and events leading to the Constitution of 1956, pp. 6–132.

2. Hindus and the provinces. Leonard Binder, *Religion and Politics in Pakistan* (Berkeley: University of California Press, 1963), pp. 123–124. Wayne Wilcox, *Pakistan: The Consolidation of a Nation* (New York: Columbia University Press, 1963), pp. 123–124 and 165–172. Lawrence Ziring, "The Failure of Democracy in Pakistan: East Pakistan and the Central Government, 1947–1958" (Ph.D. diss., Columbia University, 1962).

3. Jinnah's successors. Leonard Binder, *Religion and Politics,* pp. 130–131. Re Nazimuddin see Mustaq Ahmed, *Government and Politics in Pakistan* (Karachi: Pakistan Publishing House, n.d.), pp. 37–41.

4. Provincial elections. Wilcox, *Pakistan: Consolidation,* pp. 20 and 31–33. Callard, *Pakistan: Political Study,* pp. 29–30, 56–59, and 72–73. Donald N. Wilber, *Pakistan: Its People, Its Society, Its Culture* (New Haven, Conn.: HRAF Press, 1964), pp. 219–223. Jyoti Sen Gupta, *Eclipse of East Pakistan* (Calcutta: Renco, 1963), pp. 85–89, 189–197, and 241–244.

5. Fazlul Huq. *New York Times,* May 7 and 23, 1954.

6. Pakistan's first Constitution. Choudhury, *Constitutional Development,* pp. 1–132, re electorates, p. 125. Ian Stephens, *Pakistan: Old Country/New Nation* (London: Penguin Books, 1963), pp. 279–297.

7. Suhrawardy. Gupta, *Eclipse,* pp. 272–278, passim. The *Dacca Times,* May 1964, published a 49-page supplement in honor of Suhrawardy shortly after his death. Sheikh Mujibur Rahman wrote one of the articles in the issue, entitled "My Leader—A Messenger of Peace, a Fighter for Hindu-Muslim Unity." The supplement contains the text of Suhrawardy's speech as leader of the opposition in the Constituent Assembly of Pakistan, January 31, 1956, at which he warned a storm was brewing in East Bengal and stated Islam is not the link between the two provinces. "We are," he said, "a different state, altogether." He then demanded regional autonomy. Suhrawardy and the Awami League: See Keith Callard, *Political Forces in Pakistan* (New York: Institute of Pacific Relations, 1959), pp. 69–71. Ali, *Pakistan: Military Role,* pp. 81–82. Gupta, *Eclipse,* pp. 31–36, 299–345, and 360–363, concerning the Republican party split with Suhrawardy. *New York Times,* October 11–14, 1957.

8. Turmoil in East Pakistan. Callard, *Political Forces,* pp. 9–26. See also *New York Times,* September 21 and 26, 1958.

9. Ayub's regime. Lawrence Ziring, *The Ayub Khan Era: Politics in Pakistan 1958–69* (Syracuse, N.Y.: Syracuse University Press, 1971); emphasizes the administrative weaknesses of the Pakistani civil service and its involvement in the fall of Ayub. An enthusiastic account of the first five years of Ayub's term of office will be found in Karl Von Vorys, *Political Development in Pakistan.* Other accounts of Ayub's ascendancy and decline are contained in M. Rashiduzzaman, *Pakistan: A Study of Government and Politics* (Dacca: Ideal Library, 1967); Rounaq Jahan, *Pakistan: Failure in National Integration* (New York: Columbia University Press, 1972); Herbert Feldman, *Revolution in Pakistan: A Study of the Martial Law Administration* (New York: Oxford

University Press, 1967) and *From Crisis to Crisis, 1962–1969* (London: Oxford University Press, 1972). An admiring presentation of President Ayub is contained in a volume that includes the speeches of the president, Rais Ahmed Jafi, ed., *Ayub, Soldier and Statesman, Speeches and Statements, 1958–1965* (Lahore: Mohammad Ali Academy, 1966). See also Ayub's autobiography, *Friends Not Masters* (London: Oxford University Press, 1967), and I. H. Quershi, "The Development of Pakistan," in Guy S. Metraux and Francois Crouset, eds., *The New Asia* (New York: Mentor, 1965), pp. 232–274; Quershi was vice-chancellor of the University of Karachi.

10. Martial law. Feldman, *Revolution in Pakistan.* Von Vorys, *Political Development,* pp. 63 and 143. Stephens, *Pakistan: Old Country,* pp. 300–311. Callard, *Political Forces,* pp. 27–48. In *Friends Not Masters* Ayub Khan refers to his takeover as a "revolution," pp. 70 ff.

11. Basic Democracy. Stephens, *Pakistan: Old Country,* pp. 314–316. Choudhury, *Constitutional Development,* pp. 158 and 160–161. Edgar Owens, "Democratic Development in East Pakistan" (Washington, D.C.: Information Divison of the Embassy of Pakistan, June 1966). Von Vorys, *Political Development,* pp. 196–207 and 220–222. Rashiduzzaman, *Pakistan: A Study,* pp. 248–253. Jahan, *Pakistan: Failure,* pp. 109–126. Richard V. Weekes, *Pakistan, Birth and Growth of a Muslim Nation* (Princeton, N.J.: Princeton University Press, 1965), pp. 110–123. A.T.R. Rahman, "Rural Institutions in India and Pakistan," *Asian Survey* 8, no. 9 (September 1968), pp. 110–123.

12. Ayub's attitude toward the Bangalis is advanced in his *Friends Not Masters.* For his appraisal of the history of this "down-trodden race" and the proper way to regard and treat its people, see pp. 189–191. See also Richard S. Wheeler, *Politics of Pakistan* (Ithaca, N.Y.: Cornell University Press, 1970), pp. 234–236.

13. Muslim family law ordinance. Ayub Khan, *Friends Not Masters,* pp. 106–107. Donald E. Smith, ed., *South Asian Politics and Religion,* pp. 44–45, and Fazlur Rahman's contribution, pp. 414–427. Re family life see Stephens, *Pakistan: Old Country,* pp. 72–77, and Wilber, *Pakistan: Its People,* pp. 132–136.

14. Constitution of 1962. *Report of the Constitution Commission, Pakistan, 1961* (Karachi: Government of Pakistan Press, 1962). *The Constitution of the Republic of Pakistan, 1962* (Karachi: Government of Pakistan Press, 1962). Choudhury, *Constitutional Development;* Choudhury was an honorary adviser to the commission. The story of the drafting of the Constitution and the constitutional debate is told in Edgar A. and Kathryn R. Schuler, *Public Opinion and Constitution-Making in Pakistan, 1958–1962* (East Lansing: Michigan State University Press, 1967).

15. Rebellion and communal riots are summarized in *Keesing's Contemporary Archives,* July 15–25, 1964, p. 20185.

16. Emigrations. *Influx—Infiltration from East Pakistan* (Delhi: Ministry of Information and Broadcasting for the Ministry of External Affairs, August 1963); a pamphlet.

17. The report claimed that there had been forced mass evictions of Muslims from Tripura and Assam for many years. *Report of the Commission of Enquiry*

on the Refugee Problem Arising Out of the Expulsion of a Large Number of Muslims from Tripura State and Assam, vol. 1, part 1 (Dacca: East Pakistan Government Press, 1962) p. 15.

18. The elections of 1965 are discussed by Ayub in *Friends Not Masters,* pp. 232–239. Khalid B. Sayeed, "1965—An Epochmaking Year in Pakistan: General Elections and War with India," *Asian Survey* 6, no. 2 (February 1966), pp. 76–88.

CHAPTER 6: THE STRUGGLE FOR BANGALI AUTONOMY, 1965–71

General Sources: (a) Analyses of conditions in Pakistan that brought Ayub to yield power: Robert La Forte, Jr., "Succession in Pakistan: Continuity and Change in a Garrison State," *Asian Survey* 9, no. 11 (November 1969), pp. 842–861. Wayne Wilcox, "Pakistan: A Decade of Ayub," *Asian Survey* 9, no. 2 (February 1969), pp. 87–93. Khalid B. Sayeed, "The Capabilities of Pakistan's Political System," *Asian Survey* 7, no. 2 (February 1967), pp. 102–110. G. W. Choudhury, *The Last Days of United Pakistan* (Bloomington: Indiana University Press, 1974), pp. 13–45. Richard S. Wheeler, *Politics of Pakistan* (Ithaca, N.Y.: Cornell University Press, 1970), especially chapters 4 through 8. John E. Owen, "East Pakistan, 1947–71," *Contemporary Review* 221, no. 1278 (July 1972), pp. 23–28. (b) The Indo-Pakistan war: Charles B. Marshall, "India and Pakistan at War," *The New Republic,* September 25, 1965, pp. 19–21.

1. Economic disparity. Edward S. Mason, *Economic Development in India and Pakistan,* Occasional Paper on International Affairs no. 13 (Cambridge: Center for International Affairs, Harvard University, 1966). James P. Grant and Susan Sammartane, "Growth with Justice: A New Partnership," in Overseas Development Council, *Communiqué on Development Issues* (Washington, D.C.: Overseas Development Council, January 1973). Mahbub Ul Haq, *The Strategy of Economic Planning* (Karachi: Oxford University Press, 1963); includes an indictment of economic discriminations against East Pakistan. Rehman Sobhan, "Cost of a Strong Center," *Forum* (Dacca) (January 3, 1970), pp. 15–16. Azizur Rahman Khan, "A New Look at Disparity," ibid., pp. 8–9. Arthur McEwan, *Development Alternatives in Pakistan* (Cambridge: Harvard University Press, 1970). Rounaq Jahan, *Pakistan: Failure in National Integration* (New York: Columbia University Press, 1972), pp. 30–38 and 68–89. W. H. Morris-Jones, "Pakistan Post-Mortem and the Roots of Bangladesh," *Political Quarterly* 43, no. 2 (April–June 1972), pp. 191–192. *Economist,* November 4, 1972, pp. 59–70. M. Azizur Rahman, "East Pakistan: The Roots of Estrangement," *South Asian Review* 3, no. 3 (April 1970), pp. 235–239.

2. Other disparities. (a) Bureaucratic: S. J. Burki, "Twenty Years of the Civil Service, A Re-evaluation," *Asian Survey* 9, no. 4 (April 1969), pp. 239–254; M. Rashiduzzaman, *Pakistan: A Study of Government and Politics* (Dacca: Ideal Library, 1967), pp. 202–211. Lawrence Ziring, *The Ayub Khan Era: Politics in Pakistan 1958–69* (Syracuse, N.Y.: Syracuse University Press, 1971), pp. 114–

141. Frank Goodnow, *The Civil Service of Pakistan* (New Haven, Conn.: Yale University Press, 1966). (b) Military: Morris-Jones, "Pakistan Post-Mortem," pp. 192–194. Major General F. M. Muqueen Khan, *The Story of the Pakistan Army* (London: Oxford University Press, 1963).

3. Six-point manifesto. The text of Mujib's short 1966 political manifesto is cited by Jahan, *Pakistan: Failure*, p. 167; her comments on the document, pp. 167–171, are insightful. The text of the manifesto is in Robert Jackson, *South Asia Crisis: India, Pakistan, and Bangladesh* (London: Chatto and Windus, 1975), pp. 166–167.

4. Riot of 1966. *New York Times*, June 8 and 9, 1966.

5. Pakistan Democratic Movement. Rashiduzzaman, *Pakistan: A Study*, pp. 277–278. Jahan, *Pakistan: Failure*, pp. 170–171.

6. Ayub's moves. Khalid B. Sayeed, "Pakistan's New Challenge to the Political System," *Asian Survey* 8, no. 2 (February 1968), pp. 97–104. Re the effect of Ayub's illness on his activities, see Choudhury, *Last Days*, p. 27.

7. Arrests and unrest. (a) Agartala case: *New York Times*, August 5 and 6, 1968. Jahan, *Pakistan: Failure*, pp. 106n, 171n, and 173. Choudhury, *Last Days*, pp. 22–27. (b) 1968 riots: *New York Times*, December 6, 8, 9, 14, and 15, 1968. (c) Release of Sheikh Mujib Rahman and others: *New York Times*, February 23, 1969. Ziring, *The Ayub Khan Era*, pp. 90–92. See also the explanation of Choudhury, *Last Days*, pp. 36–37.

8. Fall of Ayub. Choudhury, *Last Days of United Pakistan*, pp. 13–45. S. J. Burki, "Ayub's Fall," *Asian Survey* 10, no. 3 (March 1970), pp. 201–212; *New York Times*, January 18–30, February 23, and March 20 and 22, 1969. Re Bhutto's and Mujib's role in East Pakistan see *New York Times*, February 24, 1969.

9. Yahya years. (a) Biography of Yahya Khan: *Current Biography* (January 1971), pp. 45–47. M. A. Akhya, "Pakistan: The Way Ahead for Martial Law," *South Asian Review* 3, no. 1 (October 1969), pp. 23–30. (b) President Yahya Khan's regime: Choudhury, *Last Days*, pp. 46–129; Choudhury, professor of political science at Dacca University, served as a minister in Yahya's cabinet and as an adviser at the March 1971 talks in Dacca. L. F. Rushbrook Williams, *The East Pakistan Tragedy* (London: Tom Stacey, 1972); highly critical of the "rebel" Bangalis.

10. Bangalis in Yahya's cabinet. *New York Times*, May 7, 1969.

11. Mujib and Yahya. Jackson, *South Asia Crisis*, pp. 24–28; gives a background analysis of their relationship. *New York Times*, July 20, 1969.

12. The year 1970. *New York Times*, March 29, April 1 and 6, May 7 and 10, June 7, August 16, and November 17, 1970.

13. Legal Framework Order. Herbert Feldman, *The End and the Beginning, 1969–1971* (London: Oxford University Press, 1978), pp. 62–75. G. W. Choudhury, "Last Days of United Pakistan," *International Relations* 4, no. 2 (April 1973), pp. 47–51. The text of the order is in *Bangla Desh Documents* (New Delhi: Ministry of External Affairs, 1971), pp. 49–64, as is President Yahya's address to the nation on March 28, 1970, pp. 44–49.

14. Awami League manifesto. The text of the manifesto of April 1970 is in *Bangla Desh Documents*, pp. 66–81, and *Morning News* (Dacca), June 8, 1970.

S. R. Chowdhury, *Genesis of Bangladesh* (New York: Asia Publishing House, 1972), pp. 50–57. M. Azizur Rahman, "East Pakistan: The Roots of Estrangement," *South Asian Review* 3, no. 3 (April 1970), pp. 235–239. Jahan, *Pakistan: Failure,* pp. 166–171.

15. The cyclone was reported extensively in the *New York Times* and *Chicago Tribune* from November 15, 1970, to the end of the year, and in other world press reports. A poignant report about the cyclone was written by Dom P. Moraes, "East Pakistan: The Wave," for the *New York Times Magazine,* January 10, 1971, pp. 26–27 and 71–76; see also his *The Tempest Within* (New Delhi: Vikas Publications, 1971).

16. U.S. relief efforts. Letter of Robert Murphy, *Saturday Review of Literature,* January 9, 1971, p. 22. In July 1971 Archer Blood, the American consul general in Dacca, received the Christian A. Herter Award from Secretary of State William P. Rogers. His reporting not only reflected "a sensitive understanding of forces at work in East Pakistan but demanded . . . great discretion." He was also commended for his direction of relief following the 1970 cyclone.

17. Elections of 1970. *New York Times,* December 8, 10, 13, 14, and 18, 1970. Choudhury, *Last Days,* pp. 106–131. Craig Baxter, "Pakistan Votes—1970," *Asian Survey* 11, no. 3 (March 1971), pp. 197–218; Sharif Mujahid, "Pakistan: The First General Election," *Asian Survey* 11, no. 2 (February 1971), pp. 159–171.

18. Cabinet dismissal. *New York Times,* February 22, 1971.

19. Negotiations and separation, 1971. *New York Times,* March 16–24, 1971. David Dunbar, "Pakistan: The Failure of Political Negotiations," *Asian Survey* 12, no. 5 (May 1972), pp. 444–461. Anthony Mascarenhas, *The Rape of Bangladesh* (New Delhi: Vikas Publications, 1971), pp. 63–81. Zulfikar Bhutto, *The Great Tragedy* (Karachi: Pakistan People's Party, 1971). Sidney H. Schonberg, "Pakistan Divided," *Foreign Affairs* 41 (October 1971), pp. 125–135. Rehman Sobhan, "Negotiating from Bangladesh: A Participant's View," *South Asian Review* 4, no. 4 (July 1971), pp. 315–326. The texts of several public documents on the negotiations are printed in *Bangla Desh Documents,* pp. 188–220 and passim; Choudhury, *Last Days,* pp. 201–212; Feldman, *End and Beginning,* pp. 114–126.

CHAPTER 7: THE BIRTH OF BANGLADESH, 1971

General Sources: See especially Robert Jackson, *South Asia Crisis: India, Pakistan and Bangladesh* (London: Chatto and Windus, 1975).

1. (a) Pakistani army massacre: David Loshak, *Pakistan Crisis* (New York: McGraw-Hill, 1971), pp. 88–126. Anthony Mascarenhas, *The Rape of Bangladesh* (New Delhi: Vikas Publications, 1971), pp. 115–125. *New York Times,* March 26–April 1, 1971. Robert Payne, *Massacre* (New York: Macmillan, 1973). *Economist,* April 3, 1971, pp. 29–30. *Newsweek,* "The Murder of a People," August 2, 1971. *Time,* "Pakistan's Agony," August 9, 1971, pp. 24–29, and August 16, 1971, p. 30. (b) Zia broadcast: Talukder Maniruzzaman, *The Bangladesh*

Revolution and Its Aftermath (Dacca: Books International, 1980), pp. 87 and 105–106, n. 30.

2. Pakistani views. *Federal Intervention in Pakistan, Background Reports 2 and 4* (Washington, D.C.: Pakistan Embassy, n.d.). Yahya interview, *Newsweek,* November 8, 1971, p. 53. Khalida Quershi, "An overview of the East Pakistan Situation," *Pakistan Horizon* 24, no. 4 (third quarter 1971), pp. 32–49. *Summary of the White Paper on the Crisis in East Pakistan* (Islamabad: Ministry of Information, Government of Pakistan, 1972). W. H. Morris-Jones, "Pakistan Postmortem and the Roots of Bangladesh," *Political Quarterly* 43, no. 2 (April–June 1972), pp. 187–200.

3. Refugees. *Bangla Desh Documents* (New Delhi: Ministry of External Affairs, 1971), pp. 446–501. *Economist,* April 1, 1972, pp. 30–39. Paul Dreyfus, *Du Pakistan au Bangladesh* (Paris: Arthaud, 1972), pp. 177–189.

4. Provisional government of Bangladesh. M. Rashiduzzaman, "Leadership, Organization, Strategies and Tactics of the Bangla Desh Movement," *Asian Survey* 12, no. 3 (March 1973), pp. 185–200. For the text of the April speech of Tajuddin Ahmed, prime minister of the provisional government, see *United Asia* 25, no. 3 (May–June 1971), pp. 125–134; this issue is entirely devoted to articles about the government and events in Bangladesh.

5. Mrs. Gandhi. *Washington Post,* May 8, 1971.

6. Guerrillas. Loshak, *Pakistan Crisis;* one of the best journalistic accounts. Payne, *Massacre,* pp. 44–60 and 100–111. Major General D.K. Palit, *The Lightning Campaign: The Indo-Pakistan War* (Salisbury: Compton Press, 1972), pp. 45–53. A Soviet account of the role of the Mukti Bahini is in *New Times* (Moscow), January 1972, pp. 6–8. See also Rounaq Jahan, *Pakistan: Failure in National Integration* (New York: Columbia University Press, 1972), pp. 198–204; Dreyfus, *Du Pakistan au Bangladesh,* pp. 201–214; Mohammad Ayoob and K. Subrahmanyan, *The Liberation War* (New Delhi: S. Chand and Company, 1972).

7. Provisional government and world opinion. *Bangla Desh Documents,* pp. 288–344.

8. Propaganda war. *Washington Post,* June 1 and 18, August 12 and 13, 1971. *New York Times,* July 20, 1971. *Time,* August 16, 1971, p. 30.

9. Indian-Soviet treaty. *Yearbook of the United Nations 1971,* vol. 25, 1974, pp. 145–146. *Washington Post,* August 11, 1971. Jackson, *South Asia Crisis,* pp. 69–74.

10. Refugees. The refugee problem received worldwide press attention from May through December 1971. John C. Haughey, "Pakistan Relief: Compound of Hope and Tragedy," *America,* November 20, 1971, pp. 420–423; see also editorial and list of relief agencies, pp. 413–415.

11. War fever. *Washington Post,* October 17, 1971. *Newsweek,* November 8, 1971.

12. War readiness. *New York Times,* November 4–7, 1971.

13. Intervention and the war. *Economist,* editorial, December 18, 1971, pp. 27–28. Palit, *Lightning Campaign.* Brigadier Cyril N. Barclay, "A Soldier Looks at the Indo-Pakistan War," *Army* (May 1972). Ravi Rikhye, "The Day India Won the 14 Day War," *Armed Forces Journal* (April 1972), pp. 38–40. The

armed forces casualties for India were about 10,000 killed and wounded, and for Pakistan 17,000, according to the International Institute for Strategic Studies as reported in the *Hindustan Times,* May 27, 1972. For a Pakistani account of the war see Fazal Muqueen Khan, *Pakistan's Crisis in Leadership* (Islamabad: National Book Foundation, 1973). For the Pakistani army attack on Dacca see Grant Parr, "Bangladesh and East Bengal," *Foreign Service Journal* 57, no. 1 (January 1980), pp. 19–22 and 36–37. Jackson, *South Asia Crisis,* pp. 106–145. See *New York Times* extensive coverage of the war from March 26, 1971, to Pakistan's surrender.

14. United Nations debates on Indian intervention. Jackson, *South Asia Crisis,* pp. 123–129. See also note 5, chapter 10, this volume.

15. The debate over the cease-fire in the U.N. Security Council and the General Assembly is summarized in the *Yearbook of the United Nations 1971,* pp. 146–159. Questions concerning the morality of the Pakistani war in East Pakistan are discussed in chapter 10, this volume.

CHAPTER 8: THE NEW NATION SETS ITS COURSE, 1972

1. Sheikh Mujibur Rahman. *Current Biography* 24, no. 1 (January 1973), pp. 41–44. *New York Times,* August 16, 1975. *New Times* (Moscow), February 1972, pp. 8–9. *Bangladesh Observer,* January 27, 1975. David Frost interview with Mujib, January 18, 1972 (New York: Radio TV Reports, Inc., The David Frost Show, Westinghouse Broadcasting Company, 1972). K. A. Kamal, *Sheikh Mujibur Rahman: Man and Politician* (Dacca: Kazi Giasuddin Ahmed, 1970). *Keesing's Contemporary Archives,* February 19–26, 1972, p. 20112.

2. Mujib in charge. *Washington Post,* January 10, 11, 13, 14, and 18, 1972. *New York Times,* January 9, 1972. *Chicago Tribune,* January 17 and 18, 1972. *Newsweek,* January 24, 1972, pp. 28–29. Lawrence Leamer, "Bangladesh in the Morning," *Harper's* magazine, August 1972, pp. 84–98; a richly colored account of Mujib's return, the background of the revolt, the events of March 25, the civil war, and the plight of the Biharis. Howard Wriggins, "One Year Later: India, Pakistan and Bangladesh," *Worldview* 16, no. 5 (May 1973); re Bangladesh, pp. 11–13.

3. Provisional Constitutional Order. *Bangla Desh Documents,* pp. 281–282. *Hindustan Standard* (Calcutta), January 13, 1972.

4. Constitution of 1972. *Constitution of the People's Republic of Bangladesh,* authorized English translation (Dacca: Government of Bangladesh Press, 1972), pp. viii–110. Albert P. Blaustein and Gilbert H. Glanz, *Constitutions of the Countries of the World,* vol. 2 (Dobbs Ferry, N.Y.: Oceana Publications, 1977), pagination same as above; this edition also includes the first nine amendments. Zillur Rahman Khan and A.T.R. Rahman, *Provincial Autonomy and Constitution Making: The Case of Bangladesh* (Dacca: Green Book House, 1973). Donald E. Smith, "Secularization in Bangladesh," *Worldview* 16, no. 4 (April 1973), pp. 11–16.

5. Economic conditions. Rounaq Jahan, "Bangladesh in 1972: Nation Building in a New State," *Asian Survey* 13, no. 2 (February 1973), pp. 208–209. *New*

York Times, October 4 and 8 (editorial), 1972, and January 21, 1973. *Far Eastern Economic Review,* February 26, 1973, p. 16.

6. (a) Emergency relief: *Statesman* (Calcutta), January 1, 1972. Handout no. 705, press information (Dacca: Government of People's Republic of Bangladesh, May 22, 1972). (b) Refugees: *June 7 Speech of Sheikh Mujibur Rahman* (Dacca: Ministry of Foreign Affairs, 1972).

7. Transportation. *Bangladesh* 2, no. 26 (December 29, 1972); includes a report of the *London Financial Times,* December 14, 1972, on the rebuilding of Bangali transportation.

8. Foreign relief. Lawrence A. Burley, "Disaster Relief Administration in the Third World," *International Development Review* 15, no. 1 (1973). *Humanitarian Assistance for Bangladesh* (Washington, D.C.: Department of State, Bureau of Public Affairs, 1972). *Washington Post,* August 3, 1972. John C. Haughey, "Rebuilding in Bangladesh," *America,* June 3, 1972, pp. 587–589. *War on Hunger* (Washington, D.C.: AID, September 1975), pp. 13–14; lists 46 American nongovernmental agencies operating relief and development programs in Bangladesh. *CORR of Bangladesh* 80, no. 1 (1972); CORR, a group of religious agencies, American, European, Catholic, and Protestant, reported it spent over $30 million in 1972, nearly $10 million in housing.

9. Guerrillas. (a) Disarming the Mukti Bahini: *Keesing's,* February 19–26, 1972, p. 25109. (b) Opposition killings: *Asian Recorder,* July 22–28, 1972, pp. 10885–86. Jahan, "Bangladesh in 1972," pp. 206–207.

10. Hoarding and black marketing. Jahan, ibid., pp. 208–209. *Keesing's,* April 9–15, 1973, p. 25822. *June 7 Speech of Sheikh Mujib* re border trade and smuggling. *Asian Recorder,* October 21–27, 1972, p. 11042.

CHAPTER 9: ECONOMIC POLICIES AND PROGRAMS, 1972

General Sources: Azizur Rahman Khan, *The Economy of Bangladesh* (London: Macmillan, 1972). Nurul Islam, *Development Planning in Bangladesh: A Study in Political Economy* (New York: St. Martin's Press, 1977) and *Development Strategy of Bangladesh* (New York: Pergamon Press, 1978); Islam was director of the planning commission in Dacca until 1974, when he left for England.

1. Socialism. The principles of socialism were laid down in the Awami League manifesto of 1970, an updated version of the 1966 manifesto. *Bangla Desh Documents* (New Delhi: Ministry of External Affairs, 1971), pp. 7–82. Tario Ali, *Pakistan: Military Rule or People's Power* (New York: Morrow, 1970), pp. 239–243, proposed a plan similar to the 1970 Awami manifesto that was more clearly Marxist in its political implications.

2. Pakistan and the economy. Gustav Papanek, *Pakistan's Development: Social Goals and Private Incentives* (Cambridge: Harvard University Press, 1972), p. 51; elsewhere (pp. 126–127) Papanek doubted the economic efficiency of corruption. In *Economic Development in East Pakistan: The Role of the Central Government* (Karachi: Department of Films and Publications, Government of Pakistan, June 1971) the Yahya regime justified its economic policies in East Pakistan.

3. Nationalization. Texts of the nationalization orders of March and April 1972 were published in press releases by the government of Bangladesh, public information office, Dacca. *Chicago Tribune,* March 27, 1972. W. Freedman and J. F. Garner, *Government Enterprise* (New York: Columbia University Press, 1970) discuss British experience with public corporations that were the models for Bangali nationalized industries. Irwin J. Roth, "Government and the Development of Industry in Pakistan," *Asian Survey* 11, no. 6 (June 1971), pp. 570–581. Guthrie S. Birkhead, *Administrative Problems in Pakistan* (Syracuse, N.Y.: Syracuse University Press, 1966), discusses WAPDA, a government corporation established in West Pakistan, on pp. 119–149; it was also set up in East Pakistan.

4. (a) Private industry: *Bangladesh,* August 1, 1974. (b) Private foreign investment: *Bangladesh Observer,* February 1, 1975.

5. Economic planning. *The Annual Plan 1972–73* (Dacca: Planning Commission, 1972); a summary of the plan appears in the *Times of India,* July 10, 1972. See also a brief analysis of the plan in K. U. Ahmed, "New Priorities and Old Biases," *South Asian Review* 6, no. 1 (October 1972), pp. 1–6. (a) The annual plan for 1973–74: see *Bangladesh Observer,* June 22, 29, 1973, and July 16, 1974. (b) The first five-year plan: *Bangladesh,* December 1, 1972, contains the text of the introduction to the plan; a summary is reported in the *Bangladesh Observer,* June 28, 1973. See also A.M.A. Rahim, "An Analysis of Planning Strategy in Bangladesh," *Asian Survey* 15, no. 5 (May 1975), pp. 383–393. See especially the books of Nurul Islam cited in General Sources, above.

6. Labor. *Bangladesh,* October 20, 1972. Rounaq Jahan, *Pakistan: Failure in National Integration* (New York: Columbia University Press, 1972). Islam, *Development Planning,* pp. 208–213.

7. Foreign trade. Nurul Islam, "What Price Exports?" *Forum* (Dacca), January 3, 1970, p. 10. Khan, *Economy of Bangladesh,* pp. 91–97.

8. Foreign assistance. International Development Association (IDA) *Press Releases* summarize IDA credits to Bangladesh. (The press releases can be obtained from the World Bank, 1818 H Street N.W., Washington, D.C. 20433.) See also World Bank *Annual Reports* (Washington, D.C.: World Bank). Lord Ritchie Calder, "Bangladesh Need Not Be a Basket Case," *Center Report* 5, no. 2 (April 1972), pp. 8–9 (Santa Barbara, Calif.: Center for the Study of Democratic Institutions).

9. Landownership. Ali, *Pakistan: Military Rule,* pp. 233–235. *New York Times,* January 25, 1976. Khan, *Economy of Bangladesh,* pp. 39–43 and 128–150. *Bangladesh,* October 6, 1972, summarizes plans for the redistribution of public land. "Taxing the Peasant," *Forum* (Dacca), January 3, 1970, pp. 5–6, contends that in Pakistan the arrears of land taxes were due mainly from larger landholders. Azizur Rahman Khan, "Bangladesh Economic Policies Since Independence," *South Asian Review* 8, no. 1 (October 1974), pp. 13–16 and 20–24. M. A. Zaman, "Bangladesh: The Case for Further Land Reform," *South Asian Review* 8, no. 2 (January 1975), pp. 97–115.

10. Cooperatives. *Bangladesh Observer,* May 12, 1975. A.M.A. Muhith, "Rural Development in Bangladesh," unpublished paper, n.d.

11. Rural public works. John Woodward Thomas, "Work for the Poor of East Pakistan," *South Asian Review* 2, no. 1 (October 1968), pp. 45–52. Rehman Sobhan, "The Rural Poor of East Pakistan: A Reply to John Thomas," *South Asian Review* 2, no. 2 (January 1969), pp. 136–147. Extensive studies of the operations of rural public works are included in Comilla Academy Publications, Comilla, Bangladesh. Edward V. Gilbert, "The Works Program in East Pakistan," *International Labor Review* 89, no. 3 (March 1964), pp. 213–226. Muhith's "Rural Development in Bangladesh" analyzes the history and problems of the rural public works program; he held out great hopes for it.

12. Water resources. (a) Ganges-Kobadak project: Richard S. Wheeler, *Politics of Pakistan* (Ithaca, N.Y.: Cornell University Press, 1970), pp. 56–57. (b) The Farraka Barrage and the Joint Rivers Commission: *Indian and Foreign Review* (July 15, 1972), p. 5. The 1976 issues of *Bangladesh* and *Indian News* published numerous articles on the Farraka Barrage controversy. David Winder, *Christian Science Monitor,* November 9, 1972, refers to a U.N. survey of the issue. See chapter 1, note 4, and chapter 16, notes 9 and 12.

CHAPTER 10: FOREIGN RELATIONS WITHIN THE SUBCONTINENT, 1971–75

1. South Asian Triangle. Phillips Talbot, "The Subcontinent: Menage à Trois," *Foreign Affairs* 50, no. 4 (July 1972), pp. 698–710.

2. Bangali neutralism. Louis M. Simon, "Bangladesh To Be Nonaligned," *Washington Post,* January 15, 1972. Peter Lyon, "Bangladesh: Fashioning a Foreign Policy," *South Asian Review* 5, no. 3 (April 1972), pp. 231–236. Howard Wriggins, "One Year Later: India, Pakistan, and Bangladesh," *Worldview* (May 1973), pp. 6–13. G. W. Choudhury, *India, Pakistan, Bangladesh and the Major Powers* (New York: The Free Press, 1975), pp. 197–217.

3. Bhutto. *Christian Science Monitor,* March 20, 1972. *Chicago Sun-Times,* March 19, 1972.

4. The Simla accord. *Christian Science Monitor,* June 20, 1972. *Washington Post,* June 28 and 29 and July 3, 1972. See also E. I. Tepper, "Pakistan and the Consequences of Bangladesh," *Pacific Affairs* 45 (winter 1972–73), pp. 573–581. *Pakistan Horizon* 25 (November 3, 1972).

5. (a) Indian reaction: *New York Times,* July 3, 1972. *Hindustan Times* (New Delhi), July 4, 1972. (b) Reaction in Bangladesh: *Christian Science Monitor,* July 5, 1972. (c) American reaction: *Washington Post,* July 8, 1972. *Chicago Sun-Times,* July 6, 1972 (editorial).

6. Bangalis and Biharis. (a) With respect to the Bangali intellectuals see *New York Times,* January 24, 1972; *Washington Post,* May 18, 1972; *Statesman* (Calcutta), July 17, 1972. (b) Biharis: *New York Times,* December 19, 1971. *Chicago Tribune,* December 24, 1971. *Economist,* May 13, 1972, pp. 14–15.

7. Bangalis in Pakistan. *Bangladesh,* November 3 and November 17, 1972, and February 8, 1973. *Economist,* April 28, 1973, pp. 29–30.

8. War trials. *Chicago Sun-Times,* January 17, 1972.

9. Pakistani recognition. *New York Times,* February 23, 1974. Talukder Maniruzzaman, "Bangladesh in 1974: Economic Crisis and Political Polarization," *Asian Survey* 15, no. 2 (February 1975), p. 126.

10. Bhutto's visit. *New York Times,* June 28–30, 1974. *Newsweek,* July 8, 1974. *Bangladesh Observer,* June 30, 1974.

11. Debt sharing. *Far Eastern Economic Review,* July 8, 1974, pp. 12–13. *Economist,* July 6, 1974, pp. 38, 49.

12. Text of the Bangladesh-India Treaty of Friendship and Peace was published in *Bangladesh,* March 24, 1972. See also *Washington Post,* March 20, 1972; *Time,* April 3, 1972.

13. Boundaries. For the joint declaration of May 16, 1974 and the demarcation agreement see *Indian and Foreign Review* 11, no. 16 (June 1, 1974), pp. 5–8.

14. India and Pakistan. *New York Times,* April 20, 1976. *Le Monde,* April 21, 1976. G. W. Choudhury, *Pakistan's Relations with India* (New York: Praeger, 1968), and other Choudhury books cited above. Indian literature on the subject is voluminous.

CHAPTER 11: RELATIONS WITH THE GREAT POWERS, 1971–74

General Source: Barbara Ward, *Spaceship Earth* (New York: Columbia University Press, 1966), p. 33.

1. The United States and Bangladesh. George J. Lerski, "The Pakistan-American Alliance: A Reevaluation of the Past Decade," *Asian Survey* 8, no. 5 (May 1968), pp. 400–415. *Chicago Sun-Times,* January 24, 1972. Zillar R. Khan, "Multipolar Politics and Emergence of Bangladesh," *Asian Forum* 6, no. 3 (July–September 1974), pp. 45–61. *Bangladesh,* January 2, 1973. "Remarks of the American Ambassador to the United Nations," *Department of State Bulletin* 66, no. 1699 (January 17, 1972), pp. 67–71. "U.S. Statement at Security Council," ibid. 65, no. 1696 (December 27, 1971), pp. 721–729. Lawrence Stern, "Stance of India Baffles U.S. Officials on the Scene," *Washington Post,* January 6, 1972. *Time,* November 15, 1971, pp. 32, 34. *United States Foreign Policy for the 70's: The Emerging Structure of Peace* (Washington, D.C.: Government Printing Office, 1972), re Bangladesh and South Asia, pp. 143–149. Pakistani Ambassador Hilaly's views, *Washington Post,* August 27 and 30, 1971.

2. Senator Kennedy. *Washington Post,* August 27 and 30, 1971.

3. Edgar Snow, *The Long Revolution* (New York: Random House, 1977), p. 12.

4. Anderson papers. For a partial text of the papers see *Chicago Sun-Times,* January 5 and 7, 1972, and Robert Jackson, *South Asia Crisis: India, Pakistan and Bangladesh* (London: Chatto and Windus, 1975), pp. 212–229. Jack Anderson with George Gifford, *The Anderson Papers* (New York: Random House, 1973). See also Henry Brandon, *The Retreat of American Power* (New York: Doubleday, 1970), p. 247, re Yahya's role in helping the United States reestablish relations with Peking.

5. Marvin and Bernard Kalb, *Kissinger* (Boston: Little, Brown, 1974), pp. 256 and 265.

6. Kissinger and Anderson. Anderson, *The Anderson Papers,* pp. 205–269. *Washington Post,* editorial, January 6, 1972.

7. Henry Kissinger, *White House Years* (Boston: Little, Brown, 1979), pp. 842–918.

8. (a)Arms embargo: *Chicago Sun-Times,* January 31, 1973. *New York Times,* February 3, 1972. (b) Nixon and Bangladesh: *Chicago Sun-Times,* April 15, 1975.

9. Issue of recognition. *Washington Post,* January 11, 1972. *New York Times,* February 3, 1972.

10. Refugee subcommittee. *Chicago Sun-Times,* January 31, 1972.

11. President Nixon and Bangladesh. *New York Times,* February 11, 1972. *Department of State Bulletin* 66, no. 1709 (March 27, 1972), pp. 488–490.

12. Recognition nears. Flora Lewis, *Chicago Sun-Times,* March 21, 1972. *United States Foreign Policy, 1971: A Report of the Secretary of State,* General Foreign Policy Series 260 (Washington, D.C.: Government Printing Office, 1972), pp. 110–115, used the term *Bangladesh* for the first time.

13. U.S. recognizes Bangladesh. *Department of State Bulletin* 66, no. 1713 (April 24, 1972), p. 597.

14. Great Britain and Bangladesh. *Bangladesh Documents* 2, no. 1 (July–September 1973), pp. 13–15.

15. Europe and Bangladesh. *International Herald Tribune,* September 8, 1974. *Le Monde,* September 6, 1974. *Daily American* (Rome), December 5, 1974.

16. USSR. William J. Barnds, "Moscow and South Asia," *Problems of Communism* 30, no. 3 (May-June 1972), pp. 12–31; Podgorny letter, *New York Times,* April 6 and 7, 1971.

17. Russian recognition and agreements. *New York Times,* January 25, 1972. M. S. Rajan, "Bangladesh and After," *Pacific Affairs* 45, no. 2 (summer 1972), pp. 191–205, says Bangladesh came into existence with the support of Moscow. See also V. S. Budhaj, "Moscow and the Birth of Bangladesh," *Asian Survey* 13, no. 5 (May 1973), pp. 482–495, and *Problems of Communism* 23 (July-August 1974), pp. 62–63.

18. Summary of USSR-Bangladesh agreements. *New York Times,* March 2 and 3, 1972.

19. Soviet influence. *Washington Post,* March 9, 1972. G. W. Choudhury, "Moscow's Influence in the Indian Subcontinent," *World Today* 28, no. 7 (July 1972), pp. 304–311.

20. Soviet influence. *Newsweek,* July 24, 1972. Mary Soderberg, "The Soviet Presence in Bangladesh," *Commonweal,* November 17, 1972, pp. 149–150. KGB in Bangladesh. *Far Eastern Economic Review,* December 31, 1976, p. 31.

21. China and Bangladesh. *International Herald Tribune,* November 22, 1974. (a) Chou En-lai in Dacca: Donald Wilber, *Pakistan: Its People, Its Society, Its Culture* (New Haven, Conn.: HRAF Press, 1964), p. 319. M. A. Chaudri, *Emergence of Pakistan,* pp. 81–83. (b) Chinese-Indian war, 1962: Wayne

Wilcox, *India, Pakistan and the Rise of China* (New York: Walker Co., 1964), pp. 62–76. Neville Maxwell, *India's China War* (New York: Pantheon, 1971). Edward Friedman, "China, Pakistan and Bangladesh," *Bulletin of Concerned Asian Scholars* (Winter 1972), pp. 99–106; a Maoist point of view. *Le Monde,* September 6, 1974. S. Viswan, *The Statesman* (New Delhi), August 10, 1972.

22. Other Asian nations and Bangladesh. *Hindustan Times,* June 17, 1972. *Bangladesh,* August 25, 1972. *Bangladesh Documents* 2, nos. 1 and 2 (July and December 1973).

23. United Nations. Donel E. Connery, "Mission in Dacca," *Vista* 8, no. 2 (September–October 1972), pp. 18–23. Ibid., pp. 47–48.

24. Bhutto. *Washington Post,* August 11, 1972. *Statesman* (Calcutta), August 22, 1972.

25. Bangladesh and the United Nations. *Chicago Sun-Times,* August 20, 1972 (editorial), and August 26, 1972. *New York Times,* August 27 and 29, 1972. *Department of State Bulletin* 71, no. 1828 (July 8, 1974), pp. 73–74.

26. Admission of Bangladesh into the United Nations. *Yearbook of the United Nations 1974,* vol. 28, p. 296.

CHAPTER 12: INTERNAL STRIFE, 1972–74

1. Awami League. M. Rashiduzzaman, "The Awami League in the Political Development of Pakistan," *Asian Survey* 10, no. 7 (July 1970), pp. 574–587. Leonard Binder, *Religion and Politics in Pakistan* (Berkeley: University of California Press, 1963), p. 379; Rounaq Jahan, *Pakistan: Failure in National Integration* (New York: Columbia University Press, 1972), pp. 118–140, and her article "Bangladesh in 1972: Nation Building in a New State," *Asian Survey* 13, no. 2 (February 1973), pp. 199–210. *Bangladesh Observer,* "History of the Awami League," supplement, January 18, 1974. Zillur Rahman Khan, "Leadership, Parties and Politics in Bangladesh," *Western Political Quarterly* 29, no. 1 (March 1976), pp. 102–125.

2. Communists. Bureau of Intelligence and Research, Department of State, *World Strength of the Communist Party Organizations, 25th Annual Report* (Washington, D.C.: Government Printing Office, 1973), pp. 100–102. Bangladesh Communist party. Marcus F. Franda, "Communists in East Pakistan," *Asian Survey* 10, no. 7 (July 1970), pp. 588–606. J. M. Van Der Kroef, "India, Peking and Bangladesh," *Studies in Comparative Communism* 5, nos. 2 and 3 (Summer-Autumn 1972), pp. 127–162. *Far Eastern Economic Review,* December 5, 1975, p. 28.

3. Anthony Mascarenhas, "Mujib Is Menaced by a Summer of Tigers," *The Times* (London), June 11, 1972.

4. Opposition. (a) National Awami party: *New York Times,* April 11, 1972. M. Rashiduzzaman, "The National Awami Party of Pakistan: Leftist Politics in Crisis," *Pacific Affairs* 43 (Fall 1970), pp. 394–409. Jahan, *Pakistan,* pp. 135–138. (b) Bhashani's death notice: *The Times* (London), November 24, 1976. (c) Naxalists: Dom Moraes, "Indian Revolutionaries with a Chinese Accent—The Naxalites," *New York Times Magazine,* November 8, 1970, p. 30 ff.

5. *Times of India,* July 7, 1972. *Bangladesh Observer* (editorial), December 20, 1973, on the death of Ahmed. *New York Times,* September 18, 1972, re Bhashani protesters.

6. National Socialist party. *Far Eastern Economic Review,* December 5, 1975, pp. 28 and 31, and December 19, 1975, p. 18. Bernard Lévy, *Bangladesh: Nationalisme dans la revolution* (Paris: Maspero, 1973). Sirajul Hussain Khan, "National Democratic Revolution in Bangladesh," *Journal of Contemporary Asia* 3, no. 2 (1973), pp. 181–191. See also ibid., vol. 3, no. 1 (1973), pp. 111–118, for an interview with Enayetullah, editor of the leftist *Holiday,* held in September 1972.

7. Elections of 1973. *New York Times,* March 9, 1973. Rounaq Jahan, "Bangladesh in 1973: Management of Factional Politics," *Asian Survey* 14, no. 2 (February 1974), pp. 127–128. Walter Schwarz, "One Party Democracy in Bangladesh," *Guardian Weekly,* March 17, 1973, p. 7. *Economist,* March 10, 1973, p. 36. Re the reelection of President Chowdhury: *Chicago Sun-Times,* December 25, 1973. *Bangladesh,* January 11, 1974. Anne Lopatto, *Christian Science Monitor,* January 31, 1974.

8. More discontents. See especially the pessimistic accounts of Richard Critchfield, *Christian Science Monitor,* October 31 and November 1 and 6, 1973; the November 6 article is titled "Bangladesh Teetering on the Brink of Revolution." In the same vein is Donald Kirk's *Chicago Tribune* report of June 21, 1973; Daniel Sutherland's article in the *Christian Science Monitor,* December 27, 1973; and a story in the *Economist,* September 28, 1974, pp. 40–41. The drive against the political opponents of the regime was reported in the *Bangladesh Observer,* July 11 and September 16 and 25, 1973. See also Claire Sterling, "Bangladesh," *Atlantic,* September 1974, pp. 4, 6–14, and 16.

9. Bureaucracy. Richard S. Wheeler, *Politics of Pakistan* (Ithaca, N.Y.: Cornell University Press, 1970), pp. 128–133; *Bangladesh Observer,* July 13, 1973; A.T.R. Rahim, "Administration and Its Political Environment in Bangladesh," *Pacific Affairs* 47, no. 2 (summer 1974), pp. 171–191. See Mujib's speech on bureaucracy in *Bangabandhu Speaks* (Dacca: Ministry of Foreign Affairs, Government of Bangladesh, 1972), pp. 28–29. Najmul Abedin, *Local Administration and Politics in Modernizing Societies: Bangladesh and Pakistan* (New York: Oxford University Press, 1973).

10. Military. Werner Adams, "Bangladesh: Bitter Fruits of Freedom," *Atlas and World Press Review,* November 1974, pp. 40–41. Richard F. Nyrop et al., *Area Handbook for Bangladesh* (Washington, D.C.: Government Printing Office, 1975), pp. 275–305, for an extended discussion of the military, police, and national security under Mujib.

11. For an analysis of the Awami League's difficulties, see Jahan's *Asian Survey* article "Bangladesh in 1973," pp. 126–135.

12. For Mujib's December 16 speech see *Bangladesh,* January 11, 1974.

CHAPTER 13: THE END OF THE MUJIB REGIME, 1974–75

1. Daniel Sutherland, *Christian Science Monitor,* January 7, 1974. Zillur Rahman, *General Secretary Report,* Bangladesh Awami League Biennial Council

Session, January 18, 19, and 20, 1974 (Dacca: Awami League, 1974). *Bangladesh Observer,* January 21, 1974. Talukder Maniruzzaman, "Bangladesh in 1974," *Asian Survey* 15, no. 2 (February 1975), pp. 117–128. Maniruzzaman, "Bangladesh in 1975: The Fall of the Mujib Regime and Its Aftermath," *Asian Survey* 16, no. 2 (February 1976), pp. 119–129.

2. Mujib in Moscow. *Bangladesh,* April 12, 1974.

3. The second amendment to the 1972 Constitution. Albert P. Blaustein and Gisbert H. Flanz, *Constitutions of the Countries of the World,* vol. 2, pp. 85–89.

4. Emergency decrees. *Bangladesh Observer,* April 26, 1974. Maniruzzaman, "Bangladesh in 1974," p. 122. *New York Times,* April 26, 1974. *Asian Recorder,* May 14–20, 1974, p. 11997. *Far Eastern Economic Review,* January 10, 1975, p. 10.

5. Summer floods. The *Bangladesh Observer* carried daily stories of the floods during July and August, 1974. *Economist,* August 17, 1974, pp. 33–34. *New York Times,* August 10 and 18, October 18, and November 24, 1974.

6. Plight of Dacca. *International Herald Tribune,* October 25 and November 13, 1974. *Le Monde,* October 23, 1974. *The Times* (London), November 1, 1974.

7. Search for flood aid. Sheikh Mujib's address at the Asia Society, *International Herald Tribune,* September 24, 1974. His speech to the United Nations, *Bangladesh Today* 4, no. 3 (1974). *Yearbook of the United Nations 1974,* pp. 582, 586–587, and 592–593.

8. Kissinger in Dacca. *New York Times,* October 31, 1974; see also October 1, 2, and 18, 1974.

9. A bad year. *Far Eastern Economic Review,* October 23, 1974, pp. 28–29; November 8, 1974, p. 26; and December 20, 1974, pp. 24–25. *Keesing's Contemporary Archives,* September 2–8, 1974, pp. 26693–94.

10. Mujib and civil rights. Rounaq Jahan, "Bangabandhu and After," *Round Table,* no. 261 (January 1976), p. 78. Jonathan Dimbley, "The Tragedy of Bangladesh," *New Statesman,* September 27, 1974, pp. 405–406. Re JSD revolt, see *Far Eastern Economic Review,* November 15, 1974, pp. 33–34, and *Keesing's,* January 20–26, 1975, p. 26925.

11. Dismissal of Tajuddin Ahmed. *Economist,* November 2, 1974, p. 35. *Observer* (London), November 18, 1974, article by Walter Schwarz. *Far Eastern Economic Review,* November 16, 1974, pp. 33–34, and December 13, 1974, pp. 24–25.

12. Youth organizations. Talukder Maniruzzaman, "Bangladesh in 1974," *Asian Survey,* pp. 124–125.

13. Bhashani and the United Front. *Economist,* September 23, 1974, pp. 40–41. *Bangladesh Observer,* September 23 and November 18, 1974.

14. The underground. Maniruzzaman, "Bangladesh in 1974," pp. 121–122. *Bangladesh Observer,* November 17 and 18, 1974.

15. Third birthday. *International Herald Tribune,* December 16, 1974.

16. Emergency decrees. *Bangladesh Observer,* December 29, 1974; its January 5, 1975, issue carried the text of the proclamation.

17. Government action against saboteurs. *New York Times,* January 15, 1975. *Bangladesh Observer,* January 7 and July 20, 1975.

18. Evacuation of Dacca. *New York Times,* January 15, 1975. *Bangladesh Observer,* February 7, 1975.

19. Press reactions. *Observer* (London), December 29, 1974. *Telegraph* (London), December 2 and 29, 1974. *New York Times,* December 30, 1974. *Wall Street Journal,* December 20, 1974.

20. End of 1974. Jack Cahill, "Ride on a Death Truck," *Toronto Star,* November 26, 1974. *Telegraph* (London), article by Peter Gill, January 5, 1975. *Far Eastern Economic Review,* November 22, 1974, p. 11. *Croissance des Jeunes Nations* (Paris), February 1975, pp. 17–18.

21. Presidential rule. *World Constitutions,* vol. 2, January 25, 1975, pp. 96–110. *Bangladesh* 5, no. 3 (February 1, 1975). *New York Times* (editorial), January 30, 1975. *Economist,* February 1, 1975, p. 16. *Observer* (London), January 26, 1975.

22. BAKSAL. *Bangladesh Observer,* February 25, 1975. *International Herald Tribune,* February 24, March 4 (editorial), and April 6, 1975. Re Maulana Bhashani see *Bangladesh Observer,* March 9, 1975.

23. Speech of Sheikh Mujib. *Bangladesh Observer,* March 30, 1975; editorial in same issue favored compulsory cooperatives.

24. Press controls. Text of newspaper ordinance and list of exempted newspapers, *Bangladesh Observer,* June 17, 1975, pp. 1 and 8.

25. Local government and compulsory cooperatives. *Bangladesh Observer,* June 20, 1975.

26. Assassination of Sheikh Mujibur Rahman. *New York Times,* August 15, 18, 21, 23, and 25, 1975. *Economist,* August 13 and 30, 1975. *Le Figaro,* August 16 and 17, 1975. *Christian Science Monitor,* August 20 and 26, 1975. Editorial reactions: *Editorials on File* 6, no. 17, September 1–15, 1975, pp. 1080–1083. Marcus F. Franda, "The Bangladesh Coup," *Field Staff Reports* 19, no. 15, South Asia Series, pp. 1–15 (Hanover, N.H.: American Universities Field Staff); discusses the political personalities and forces behind the assassination. Rounaq Jahan, "Bangabandhu and After," *Round Table,* no. 261 (January 1976), pp. 73–84; also discusses the many factors that led to the assassinations and later coups. Maniruzzaman, "Bangladesh in 1975," pp. 121–124.

CHAPTER 14: UNSTEADY PROGRESS, 1975–81

1. Government of Moshtaque Ahmed. Rounaq Jahan, "Bangabandhu and After," *Round Table,* no. 261 (January 1976), pp. 73–84; Talukder Maniruzzaman, "Bangladesh in 1975: The Fall of the Mujib Regime and Its Aftermath," *Asian Survey* 16, no. 2 (February 1976), pp. 119–129; includes an account of the brief life of the Ahmed government. Marcus F. Franda, "The Bangladesh Coup," *American Universities Field Services Staff Report,* South Asian Series 19, no. 15 (1975), pp. 5–15. Stephen Oren, "After the Bangladesh Coups," *World Today* 32, no. 1 (January 1976), pp. 18–24. Lawrence Lifschultz and Kai Bird, "Kissinger's Bangladesh Sideshow," *The Nation,* June 21, 1980, pp. 747–751; discusses the background of the coup during which Mujib was assassinated and Moshtaque Ahmed came to power. The authors suggest that Kissinger and others were behind the coup.

2. *Chicago Tribune,* August 16, 1975. *Washington Post,* August 15 and 16, 1975.

3. Mujib buried. *New York Times,* August 17, 1975.

4. Martial law. *New York Times,* August 23, 1975. *Bangladesh Observer,* September 2, 1975. *Globe and Mail* (Toronto), August 25, 1975.

5. Army. *Bangladesh Observer,* September 2, 1975.

6. Amnesty. Ibid., September 7 and 8, 1975.

7. Promise of reforms. Ibid., October 6, 11, and 15, 1975. *Economist,* October 11, 1975, p. 64. *Far Eastern Economic Review,* October 3, 1975, pp. 36 and 37.

8. Military appointments. *Economist,* October 11, 1975, p. 64.

9. JSD. *Far Eastern Economic Review,* December 5, 1975, pp. 29–34. *Washington Post,* November 19, 1975.

10. "August majors," *Bangladesh Observer,* November 4, 1975.

11. Second coup. *New York Times,* November 5, 1975. *Asian Recorder,* December 10–16, 1975, p. 21914.

12. Assassins' flight. *Bangladesh* 5, no. 21 (November 15, 1975). *Far Eastern Economic Review,* November 7, 1975, pp. 18 and 20.

13. Mujibists' protest. *Bangladesh Observer,* November 4, 1975.

14. Ahmed and Sayem. *Asian Recorder,* December 10–16, 1975, pp. 21914–45. *New York Times,* November 6, 1975. *Bangladesh Observer,* November 4, 1975. *Economist,* November 15, 1975, p. 68.

15. Third coup and JSD revolt. *Economist,* November 15, 1975, p. 68. *Far Eastern Economic Review,* November 14, 1975, pp. 10–11, and December 5, 1975, pp. 28–31. *Bangladesh Observer,* November 9, 1975. *Time,* November 17, 1975. Maniruzzaman, "Bangladesh in 1975," pp. 125–127. *New York Times,* November 7, 1975. G. W. Choudhury, "Bangladesh Coups and Counter Coups: International Complications," *Orbis* 19 (winter 1976), pp. 1181–91.

16. Martial law. *Bangladesh Observer,* November 9, 1975.

17. General Zia's address. *Bangladesh Observer,* November 12, 1975.

18. National Economic Council. *Bangladesh Observer,* November 7 and 12, 1975. Re civilian on the council see ibid., November 16 and 25, 1975.

19. JSD revolutionaries. *Far Eastern Economic Review,* December 5, 1975, pp. 28–31, and December 19, 1975, p. 18. *Bangladesh Observer,* November 16, 1975. Talukder Maniruzzaman, "Bangladesh in 1976: Struggle for Survival as an Independent State," *Asian Survey* 17, no. 2 (February 1977), pp. 194–197. M. Rashiduzzaman, "Changing Political Patterns in Bangladesh: Internal Controversies and External Fears," *Asian Survey* 17, no. 9 (September 1977), pp. 793–808. Robert S. Anderson, "Impressions of Bangladesh: The Role of the Awami League and the Politics of Exhortation," *Pacific Affairs* 49, no. 3 (fall 1976), pp. 443–475; discusses events between November 1975 and May 1976.

20. Martial law operations. Maniruzzaman, "Bangladesh in 1976," pp. 195–197. *Far Eastern Economic Review,* December 19, 1975, p. 18, and July 2, 1976, pp. 16 and 18; *Keesing's Contemporary Archives,* October 1, 1976, p. 27990. *Bangladesh Observer,* August 11, 1976.

21. Preparation for elections. *Keesing's,* October 15, 1976, p. 27978. *Far Eastern Economic Review,* October 1, 1976, pp. 31–32. Maniruzzaman, "Ban-

gladesh in 1976," pp. 197–198. The *Bangladesh Observer* during the summer and fall of 1976 carried columns entitled "Parlour Politics," describing party activities.

22. General Zia, martial law administrator. *New York Times,* December 1, 1976. *Far Eastern Economic Review,* December 17, 1976, p. 28. *Asian Recorder,* January 28–February 4, 1977, p. 13565.

23. Local elections. M. Rashiduzzaman, "Bangladesh in 1977: Dilemmas of Military Rulers," *Asian Survey* 18, no. 2 (February 1978), pp. 127–128.

24. Sayem resigns presidency. *New York Times,* April 22, 1977.

25. Biography of President Ziaur Rahman. *New York Times,* June 7, 1978. *Le Monde,* June 6, 1978. *Internationalist* (London), March 1977. Kevin Rafferty, "The Other General Zia," *New Statesman,* January 6, 1978, pp. 8–9. I. Guest, "New Strongman of Bangladesh," *New Statesman,* March 16, 1977, pp. 343–344. *Current Biography* (New York: H. W. Wilson, 1981), pp. 450–453.

26. Popular referendum. *Guardian,* May 31, 1977. *International Herald Tribune,* May 30, 1977. *Chicago Tribune,* May 31, 1977.

27. Constitutional issues. *Asian Recorder,* June 18–24, 1977, p. 13789.

28. Municipal elections. Rashiduzzaman, "Bangladesh in 1977," pp. 127–128. *Keesing's,* February 24, 1978, p. 28845.

29. Mutinies and hijacking. *The Times* (London) October 3–4, 1977. *New York Times,* October 2, 3, and 28, 1977. Kai Bird, "Mutiny in Bangladesh," *The Nation,* December 17, 1977, pp. 650–653. *Economist,* October 8, 1977, p. 70.

30. Zia and his opposition. *Keesing's,* February 24, 1978, pp. 28845. M. Rashiduzzaman, "Bangladesh in 1978: Search for a Political Party," *Asian Survey* 19, no. 2 (February 1979), pp. 191–194. *New York Times,* October 15, 1977.

31. Prepresidential campaign. *Economist,* March 11, 1978, pp. 62 and 64.

32. The campaign. *Far Eastern Economic Review,* May 12, 1978, pp. 10–11. *Economist,* June 3, 1978, p. 79.

33. Election of President Zia. *Guardian,* June 5, 1978. *Le Monde,* June 6, 1978. *New York Times,* June 4 and 5, 1978.

34. Cabinet. *Keesing's,* September 15, 1978, p. 29197. *Far Eastern Economic Review,* July 21, 1978, p. 34. Re aftermath of election see Maniruzzaman, "Bangladesh in 1975," pp. 192–194.

35. Maneuvers before parliamentary elections. *Far Eastern Economic Review,* January 26, 1979, p. 28, and February 16, 1979, p. 39. *Keesing's,* November 15, 1978, p. 29197. *Bangladesh* (Dacca), February 1, 1979.

36. Parliamentary campaign and elections. *Bangladesh,* March 2, 1979, pp. 26–27. *Le Monde,* February 21, 1979. *New York Times,* February 19, 20, and 22, 1979 (editorials). *Far Eastern Economic Review,* March 2, 1979, pp. 26–27. *Economist,* February 24, 1979, p. 64. *Statesman Weekly* (Calcutta) March 3, 1979 (editorial). Azizul Haque, "Bangladesh in 1979: Cry for a Sovereign Parliament," *Asian Survey* 20, no. 2 (February 1980), pp. 218–219. Mohammad M. Khan and Habib M. Zafarulla, "The 1979 Parliamentary Elections in Bangladesh," *Asian Survey* 19, no. 10 (October 1979), pp. 1023–1036.

37. Shah Azizur Rahman. *Far Eastern Economic Review,* April 13, 1979, pp. 30–31. *Bangladesh,* April 15, 1979.

38. Fifth Constitutional Amendment Bill, 1979. *Bangladesh,* ibid. Haque, "Bangladesh in 1979," pp. 219–221. Parliament. *Far Eastern Economic Review,* April 27, 1979, p. 17.

39. End of martial law. *Asian Recorder,* May 21–27, 1979, p. 14891. *Bangladesh,* April 15, 1979.

40. Cabinet. *Keesing's,* August 10, 1979, p. 29770.

41. Bureaucracy. Jahan, "Bangabandhu and After," pp. 75–77. Emajuddin Ahamed, "Dominant Bureaucratic Elites in Bangladesh," *Indian Political Science Review* 13, no. 1 (January 1977), especially pp. 43–48. Haque, "Bangladesh in 1979," pp. 221–222.

42. Bangladesh Nationalist party. *Patriot* (New Delhi), July 13, 1979. *Keesing's,* August 10, 1979, p. 29769. *Far Eastern Economic Review,* March 23, 1980, p. 25, and July 18, 1980, pp. 20–21.

43. Nationalist party committees. *Far Eastern Economic Review,* September 14, 1979, p. 44.

44. Muslim League. *Statesman Weekly* (Calcutta), May 5, 1979. *Keesing's,* August 10, 1979, p. 29790. *Far Eastern Economic Review,* April 13, 1979, p. 31.

45. Awami League and the left. Haque, "Bangladesh in 1979," p. 220. *Far Eastern Economic Review,* April 13, 1979, p. 30; July 27, 1979, p. 33; and August 31, 1979, p. 14. *Statesman Weekly* (Calcutta), May 24, 1980.

46. Student organizations. *Far Eastern Economic Review,* August 10, 1979. Haque, "Bangladesh in 1979," p. 217.

47. Parliamentary boycott. *Statesman Weekly* (Calcutta), June 14, 1980. *Far Eastern Economic Review,* March 7, 1980, p. 28. *Economist,* February 15, 1980, p. 47, and March 7, 1980, p. 28. *Asian Recorder,* January 29–February 4, 1980, p. 15292, and March 25–31, 1980, p. 15375.

48. Political prisoners released. *Chicago Tribune,* March 28, 1980. *Far Eastern Economic Review,* April 4, 1980, p. 30, and May 30, 1980, p. 6.

49. Strikes. *Far Eastern Economic Review,* July 25, 1980, pp. 26–27. *Statesman Weekly* (Calcutta), June 14, 1980. Azizul Haque, "Bangladesh in 1980: Strains and Stresses: Opposition in the Doldrums," *Asian Survey* 21, no. 2 (February 1981), pp. 189–190 and 193–194.

50. Aborted coup. Haque, "Bangladesh in 1980," p. 191. *Keesing's,* January 9, 1981, pp. 30657–58.

51. Political violence. *Far Eastern Economic Review,* May 30, 1980, p. 6; July 25, 1980, pp. 26–27; and May 13, 1981, p. 6.

52. Bureaucratic strikes and reorganization. *Asian Recorder,* November 25–December 1, 1980, p. 15759; *Far Eastern Economic Review,* March 28, 1980, p. 22; April 4, 1980, p. 6; September 19, 1980, p. 32; and September 18, 1981. Haque, "Bangladesh in 1980," pp. 191–192.

53. Cabinet. *Keesing's,* January 7, 1981, p. 30657. *Far Eastern Economic Review,* May 9, 1980, p. 40, and July 18, 1980, pp. 20–21. *Asian Recorder,* July 1–7, 1980, p. 15528.

54. Tenth anniversary. *Far Eastern Economic Review,* June 6, 1980, p. 28; June 20, 1980, p. 41; July 18, 1980, pp. 20–21; and April 24, 1981, p. 31. Haque, "Bangladesh in 1980," p. 192.

55. Hasina. *Statesman Weekly* (Calcutta), March 7, 1981. *Economist,* May 30, 1981, p. 36. *Far Eastern Economic Review,* March 6, 1981, pp. 18–19.

56. Zia's warning. *The Times* (London), May 19, 1981.

CHAPTER 15: ECONOMIC POLICIES AND PROGRESS, 1975–81

1. The economy, 1975–81. *World Bank Annual Reports* from 1975 through 1981 (Washington, D.C.: World Bank). *Far Eastern Economic Review,* July 27, 1979, pp. 31–33; June 20, 1980, pp. 40–42; and September 5, 1980, p. 75. *Bangladesh,* July 15, 1979. Azizul Haque, "Bangladesh in 1979: Cry for a Sovereign Parliament," *Asian Survey* 20, no. 2 (February 1980), pp. 225–227, and "Bangladesh in 1980, Strains and Stresses: Opposition in the Doldrums," *Asian Survey* 21, no. 2 (February 1981), pp. 197–199. *Europa Year Book 1981,* vol 1. pp. 1601–1615; includes up-to-date economic statistics. *Chicago Tribune,* February 4, 1981.

2. Budgets. *Europa Year Book 1981,* vol. 1, pp. 1607–1608. *Asian Reader,* August 6–12, 1979, p. 15015. *Bangladesh,* June 15, 1979. *Far Eastern Economic Review,* June 20, 1980, pp. 40–42, and April 24, 1981, p. 30. The largest single current expenditures in recent years have been for defense. *The Military Balance, 1978–79* (London: International Institute for Strategic Studies, 1978), reports on the armed forces of Bangladesh.

3. Two- and five-year plans. *Far Eastern Economic Review,* June 20, 1980, pp. 40–42, and April 24, 1981, p. 30. *Keesing's Contemporary Archives,* October 9, 1981, p. 31128.

4. Private and public industries. *Bangladesh Observer,* December 28, 1975. *Keesing's,* October 15, 1976, p. 27992. *New York Times,* April 9, 1979. *Bangladesh,* June 15, 1979. *Far Eastern Economic Review,* June 20, 1980, pp. 40–42; September 19, 1980, p. 129; and April 3, 1981, p. 6.

5. Public sector. *Bangladesh,* February 1, 1979, and May 15, 1979. Nurul Islam, *Development Planning in Bangladesh: A Study in Political Economy* (New York: St. Martin's Press, 1977), pp. 173–174 and 262. Emajuddin Ahamed, "Development Strategy in Bangladesh," *Asian Survey* 18, no. 11 (November 1978), pp. 1168–1180. A.M.A. Rahim, "A Review of Industrial Development Policy in Bangladesh, 1971–1972," *Asian Survey* 18, no. 11 (November 1978), pp. 1181–1190.

6. Labor unions. U.S., Department of State, *Country Reports on Human Rights 1979,* report submitted to the Committee on International Relations, U.S. House of Representatives, and the Committee on Foreign Relations, U.S. Senate, February 4, 1980 (Washington, D.C.: Government Printing Office, 1980), p. 728.

7. International aid for agriculture. *World Bank Annual Report 1980* (Washington, D.C.: World Bank, 1980), p. 121; *Far Eastern Economic Review,* February 27, 1981, pp. 64–65.

8. Self-reliance and rural areas. (a) Zia's manifesto: *Asian Recorder,* January 8–14, 1978, p. 14110. (b) Aid to northwest Bangladesh: *Bangladesh,* August 1978. (c) Rural development: *Economist,* December 8, 1979, p. 56. *Far Eastern*

Economic Review, May 19, 1978, pp. 30–35; June 22, 1979, pp. 86 and 88; and January 18, 1980, p. 26. *Bangladesh,* March 15, 1979, and May 1, 1979. See also Just Faaland and J. R. Parkinson, *Bangladesh: The Test Case of Development* (Boulder, Colo.: Westview Press, 1976), for an excellent analysis of the nation's agricultural problems and early programs.

9. Population growth and control. *World Bank Annual Report 1980,* p. 48. *Bangladesh,* May 15, 1979.

10. Rural industries. *Bangladesh,* April 15, 1979. *Far Eastern Economic Review,* June 22, 1979, p. 88.

11. Canal digging. *Economist,* December 8, 1979, p. 56. *Far Eastern Economic Review,* January 18, 1980, pp. 26–27. *Statesman Weekly,* May 3, 1980.

12. Food for Work program. Ian Quest, "Food for Work in Bangladesh," *Contemporary Review* 23, no. 1342 (November 1977), pp. 242–244. *Far Eastern Economic Review,* May 19, 1978, pp. 35–36.

13. Export policy. *Bangladesh,* June 15, 1979, and July 15, 1979. *Europa Year Book 1981,* vol. 1, p. 1610. *Far Eastern Economic Review,* August 24, 1979, pp. 44–45; August 31, 1979, pp. 85–86; February 1, 1980, p. 43; June 20, 1980, p. 41; July 11, 1980, p. 43; July 18, 1980, p. 51; and December 12, 1980, p. 50.

14. Bangladesh Aid Group. *New York Times,* May 21 and 29, 1976. *Agenda* 2, no. 3 (April 1979), p. 9 (Washington, D.C.: Agency for International Development).

15. McNamara's visit to Dacca. *Bangladesh Observer,* November 4, 1976. *Far Eastern Economic Review,* December 31, 1976, p. 54, and May 2, 1980, pp. 27–28.

16. Local government. *Far Eastern Economic Review,* June 24, 1977, pp. 26–29.

17. International economic aid. *New York Times,* October 10, 1977 (editorial). *Far Eastern Economic Review,* May 19, 1978, pp. 30–31, 36, and 37; August 31, 1979, pp. 85–86; and June 20, 1980, p. 42. *World Bank Annual Report 1980,* pp. 97–125. Re external public debt see ibid., p. 135.

CHAPTER 16: FOREIGN RELATIONS, 1975–81

1. Death of Mujib. *Keesing's Contemporary Archives,* October 13–19, 1975, p. 27383. *Far Eastern Economic Review,* August 29, 1975, pp. 10–13.

2. Bhutto recognizes Ahmed regime. *Economist,* October 11, 1974, p. 64.

3. Mujibist guerrillas. *The Times* (London), April 21, 1976. *New York Times,* April 22, 1976. *Keesing's Contemporary Archives,* October 15, 1976, p. 27990. M. Rashiduzzaman, "Changing Political Patterns in Bangladesh: Internal Controversies and External Fears," *Asian Survey* 17, no. 9 (September 1977), p. 807; *Far Eastern Economic Review,* May 8, 1981, p. 8.

4. Agreements with India. (a) Land boundary demarcation: *India News* (Washington, D.C.), April 17, 1978. (b) Trade: *Far Eastern Economic Review,* April 17, 1981, p. 52.

5. Ganges talks. *New York Times,* May 18, 1976. *Keesing's,* July 29, 1977, pp. 28480–81. *Asian Recorder,* December 10–16, 1977, pp. 14065–66. M. Rash-

iduzzaman, "Bangladesh in 1977: Dilemmas of Military Rulers," *Asian Survey* 18, no. 2 (February 1978), pp. 131–132. K. P. Misra, "The Farraka Accord," *World Today* 34, no. 2 (February 1978), pp. 41–44.

6. Regional water problem. *Asian Recorder,* September 3–9, 1978, p. 14485. *India News* (Washington, D.C.), January 30, 1978. *Far Eastern Economic Review,* October 13, 1978, p. 34, and March 21, 1980, p. 24. *Keesing's,* September 18, 1981, p. 31091.

7. Bangladesh and India. For a general view of subcontinental relations see Archer Blood, "Détente and South Asia," *Foreign Service Journal* 53, no. 1 (January 1976), pp. 14–18 and 24–25. *Statesman Weekly* (Calcutta), March 24, 1979, p. 6. *India Express,* April 28, 1979. *Hindustan Times,* July 6, 1979. *Far Eastern Economic Review,* July 20, 1979, pp. 32–33, and January 25, 1980, p. 27. *Economist,* August 9, 1980, pp. 33–34.

8. Zia and Desai. *New York Times,* April 19, 1979. *Asian Recorder,* May 28–June 3, 1979, p. 14903. *Bangladesh,* May 1, 1979, contains the text of their joint communiqué. *Indian Express,* June 28, 1979.

9. Joint Rivers Commission. *Bangladesh,* May 15, 1979.

10. Migrations. (a) Bangalis: See chapter 5, notes 16 and 17 this volume. Marcus F. Franda, "Refugees and Migrants, Patterns in Northeastern India," *Field Staff Reports* 16, no. 3, South Asia Series, pp. 1–14 (Hanover, N.H.: American Universities Field Staff). (b) Biharis: *Economist,* August 18, 1979, p. 50, and December 8, 1979, pp. 55–56. U.S., Department of State, *Country Reports on Human Rights Practices 1979,* report submitted to the Committee on International Relations, U.S. House of Representatives, and the Committee on Foreign Relations, U.S. Senate, February 4, 1980 (Washington, D.C.: 1980), p. 729. *Economic and Political Weekly* (Bombay), April 21, 1979, pp. 718–719. *Statesman Weekly* (Calcutta), June 28, 1979.

11. Return of Mrs. Gandhi. *Chicago Tribune,* January 8, 1980. *New York Times,* January 8–9, 1980. *Far Eastern Economic Review,* January 25, 1980, p. 27.

12. Ganges agreement. *Economist,* January 17, 1981, p. 37. *Far Eastern Economic Review,* March 21, 1980, p. 24; April 4, 1980, pp. 30–31; and July 25, 1980, p. 24. *Asian Recorder,* February 19–25, 1981, p. 15891.

13. New island. *Economist,* August 9, 1980, pp. 33–34. *Far Eastern Economic Review,* December 26, 1980, p. 6. *Keesing's,* September 18, 1981, pp. 31090–91.

14. Assam. *Indian Express,* June 28, 1979. *Hindustan Times,* July 6, 1979. *Economist,* December 8, 1979, pp. 55–56. *Chicago Tribune,* June 17, 1980. *Far Eastern Economic Review,* April 4, 1980, pp. 30–31, and August 1, 1980, pp. 23–24. *New York Times,* April 2, 6, 8, and 10, June 16, and July 27, 1980. *Statesman Weekly* (Calcutta), June 14, 1980. *Time,* June 30, 1980, p. 33.

15. Chittagong Hill Tracts. *The Nation,* December 15, 1979, pp. 614 and 616. *Statesman Weekly* (Calcutta), May 17, 1980. *Far Eastern Economic Review,* May 2, 1980, pp. 30–31, and May 23, 1980, p. 34. *New York Times,* September 17, 1980.

16. Other neighbors. (a) Nepal: *Asian Recorder,* April 22–28, 1976, p. 13121. *Far Eastern Economic Review,* October 13, 1978, pp. 32–33. (b) Bhutan: ibid., January 25, 1980, p. 27.

17. Pakistan. *New York Times,* February 2, 1976, and December 23 and 27, 1978. *Economist,* March 27, 1976, p. 59. *Christian Science Monitor,* January 21, 1976. *Keesing's,* July 29, 1977, p. 28481. *Pakistan Affairs* (Washington, D.C.) 32 (May 16 and June 11, 1979). *Asian Recorder,* January 8–14, 1978, p. 14109–10.

18. Regionalism. *Far Eastern Economic Review,* August 8, 1980, p. 32, September 12, 1980, p. 25, and December 5, 1980, p. 38.

19. Other Muslim nations. *Asian Recorder,* October 22–28, 1977, p. 13987, and June 29–July 4, 1981, p. 15860. *New York Times,* January 11, 1978. *Bangladesh,* February 1, 1979, and March 15, 1979. Re OPEC see *Washington Star,* August 27, 1980.

20. Burma. *Washington Post,* April 27, 1978. *The Times* (London), May 26 and 31 and June 13, 1978. *New York Times,* June 5, 1978, and March 2, 1979. *Economist,* June 10, 1978, p. 77–78. *Keesing's,* October 6, 1978, pp. 29238–39. *Bangladesh,* April 15 and June 15, 1979. *Far Eastern Economic Review,* May 19, 1978, p. 36.

21. Southeast Asia. *Bangladesh,* April 15, 1979.

22. China. *New York Times,* January 3, 1977. *Bangladesh,* January 15, 1977. *Asian Recorder,* February 5–11, 1977, pp. 13577–78. *Far Eastern Economic Review,* April 11, 1980, p. 52.

23. Japan. *Far Eastern Economic Review,* July 11, 1980, p. 47.

24. Soviets. *New York Times,* August 18, 1975. *Far Eastern Economic Review,* August 31, 1979, p. 31, and September 7, 1979, pp. 49–50.

25. Soviet invasion of Afghanistan. *Far Eastern Economic Review,* March 14, 1980, p. 36.

26. Bangladesh, the West, and the United Nations. (a) Western aid: *Bangladesh,* March 15, 1979. Azizul Haque, "Bangladesh in 1981: Cry for a Sovereign Parliament," *Asian Survey* 20, no. 2 (February 1980), p. 199. *Washington Post,* August 28, 1980. (b) Group of 77: *Washington Post,* October 26, 1982. (c) Bangladesh in the U.N. Security Council: *Bangladesh,* April 1, 1979. (d) Vote on Iran: *New York Times,* January 10, 1980. *Economist,* January 19, 1980, p. 52. (e) Vote on Afghanistan. *New York Times,* January 19, 1980. See also "Soviet Invasion Attacked in U.N.," January 6, 1980, *Current Policy* no. 124, p. 3 (Washington, D.C.: Department of State, Bureau of Public Affairs); contains the text of the U.N. resolution.

27. UNCTAD. *Bangladesh,* May 15, 1979. Re Manila meeting of UNCTAD see Roger D. Hansen, *Can the North-South Impasse Be Overcome?* Development Paper 23 (Washington, D.C.: Overseas Development Council, 1979). Stephen Taylor, "UNCTAD, Part of the Long Haul," *World Today* 35, no. 8 (August 1978), pp. 311–314. United Nations. *Washington Star,* August 27, 1980. Re President Zia's U.N. speech see *Far Eastern Economic Review,* September 12, 1980, pp. 24–25, and *Washington Star,* August 28, 1980.

28. Human rights. U.S., Department of State, *Human Rights Report,* submitted to the Subcommittee on Foreign Assistance of the Committee on Foreign

Relations, U.S. Senate, March 1977 (Washington, D.C.: Government Printing Office, 1977), pp. 28–29. U.S., Department of State, *Country Reports on Human Rights,* report submitted to the Committee on International Relations, U.S. House of Representatives, and the Committee on Foreign Relations, U.S. Senate, February 4, 1980, pp. 723–729; February 7, 1981, pp. 948–58; February, 1981, pp. 941–952; and February, 1983, pp. 1097–1107. *Chicago Tribune,* February 11, 1979. *Far Eastern Economic Review,* April 8, 1977, pp. 23–28. *Amnesty International* annual reports, London.

29. *Report of Amnesty International Mission to Bangladesh* (London: Amnesty International, 1978).

CHAPTER 17: TRANSITION AND REORGANIZATION, 1981–83

1. Violence. *Keesing's Contemporary Archives,* October 9, 1981, p. 31127. *Far Eastern Economic Review,* June 19, 1981, pp. 21–22.

2. Assassination of Zia. *The Times* (London), *New York Times, Washington Post, Chicago Tribune, Guardian,* and *Le Monde* of May 31, 1981, gave accounts of the assassination and evaluations of Zia, followed by other reports on June 1, 2, 3, and 5. *Far Eastern Economic Review,* June 5, 1981, pp. 10–14; June 12, 1981, p. 10; and July 10, 1981, pp. 22–23. *Keesing's,* October 9, pp. 31126–27. Kai Bird, "The Unknown Zia," *The Nation,* June 13, 1981, pp. 216–217; a highly critical view of Zia. Re Manzur and Zia see *Far Eastern Economic Review,* June 19, 1981, pp. 21–22.

3. Rebel broadcast. *Washington Post,* May 31, 1981. *New York Times,* June 1, 1981. *Keesing's,* October 9, 1981, p. 31126.

4. Sattar. *Keesing's,* ibid. *New York Times,* May 31, 1981. *Guardian,* June 5, 1981. *Far Eastern Economic Review,* June 5, 1981, p. 11.

5. Manzur's demands. *Washington Post,* May 31, 1981. *The Times* (London), June 2, 1981.

6. Government action. *New York Times,* June 2, 3, and 5, 1981. *Washington Post,* June 3, 1981. Re military tribunal see *Far Eastern Economic Review,* July 17, 1981, pp. 18–19, and July 24, 1981, pp. 26–27.

7. White paper. *Far Eastern Economic Review,* ibid. *Keesing's,* October 9, 1981, pp. 31126–27.

8. Opposition objections. *Far Eastern Economic Review,* August 14, 1981, p. 23.

9. Manzur's motives. *Le Monde,* June 5, 1981. *Far Eastern Economic Review,* June 5, 1981, pp. 11–12; June 19, 1981, p. 22; and July 10, 1981, pp. 22–23.

10. South Asia's reaction. (a) India: *Le Monde,* May 31–June 1, 1981. *Washington Post,* May 31, 1981. *New York Times,* June 8, 1981 (editorial and article). (b) Pakistan: *Pakistan Affairs,* no. 12 (June 16, 1981) (Washington, D.C.). *Far Eastern Economic Review,* June 5, 1981, pp. 13–14.

11. World press reaction. *The Times* (London) June 1, 1981. *New York Times,* June 12, 1981 (editorial). *Economist,* June 6, 1981, pp. 41–42. *Le Monde,* June 3 and 5, 1981. *Christian Science Monitor,* June 1, 1981 (editorial).

12. Sattar administration. *Washington Post,* June 8, 1981. *Far Eastern Economic Review,* July 3, 1981, p. 26, and July 17, 1981, p. 18. For critical comments see *New York Times,* June 5, 1981.

13. Election announced. *New York Times,* June 17, 1981. *Christian Science Monitor,* June 17, 1981. *Far Eastern Economic Review,* June 19, 1981, p. 6.

14. Candidates. *Far Eastern Economic Review,* June 12, 1981, pp. 10–11; July 3, 1981, pp. 26–27; July 17, 1981, pp. 18–19.

15. Sattar candidacy and biography. *Guardian,* November 16, 1981. *Los Angeles Times,* November 19, 1981.

16. Cabinet dismissals. *Far Eastern Economic Review,* July 3, 1981, pp. 26–27; July 17, 1981, pp. 18–19; and July 31, 1981, pp. 38–39.

17. Party coalitions. Ibid.

18. Trial of assassins. *The Times* (London), March 16, 1981. *New York Times,* June 4 and September 24, 1981. *Far Eastern Economic Review,* July 24, 1981, p. 26; August 14, 1981, p. 23; and September 18, 1981, p. 46.

19. Kitchen cabinet. *Far Eastern Economic Review,* July 17, 1981, pp. 18–19.

20. Opposition maneuvers. *Far Eastern Economic Review,* September 4, 1981, pp. 38–39; September 18, 1981, p. 46; and October 2, 1981, pp. 22–23.

21. Awami League demands. *Far Eastern Economic Review,* September 18, 1981, p. 46.

22. Bureaucrats. *Far Eastern Economic Review,* September 18, 1981, p. 48, and October 2, 1981, pp. 22–23.

23. Sattar campaign. *Washington Post,* November 15, 1981. *Le Monde,* November 14 and 16, 1981. *New York Times,* November 14, 1981. *Far Eastern Economic Review,* October 2, 1981, p. 22; October 23, 1981, p. 23; November 6, 1981, p. 30.

24. General Ershad. Quote in *Far Eastern Economic Review,* October 2, 1981, p. 23. See also ibid., July 3, 1981, pp. 26–27, and October 30, 1981, p. 22. *New York Times,* November 14, 1981.

25. Awami campaign. *Guardian,* November 12, 1981. *New York Times,* November 14, 1981. *Washington Post,* November 15, 1981. *Le Monde,* November 16, 1981. *Far Eastern Economic Review,* October 2, 1981, pp. 22–23; October 23, 1981, p. 23; November 6, 1981, p. 30; and November 13, 1981, pp. 13–14.

26. Election. *New York Times,* November 16, 18, and 22, 1981. *Washington Post,* November 14–16, 1981. *The Times* (London), November 16 and 25, 1981. *Chicago Tribune,* November 21, 1981. *Economist,* November 21, 1981, pp. 41–42. *Guardian,* November 16 and 17, 1981. *Far Eastern Economic Review,* November 20, 1981, pp. 17–18.

27. Sattar government. (a) Inaugural: *Chicago Tribune,* November 21, 1981. (b) Biography of Sattar: *New York Times,* November 22, 1981. (c) Political problems: *New York Times,* November 17, 1981. *Guardian,* November 17, 1981. *Far Eastern Economic Review,* November 27, 1981, pp. 10–11; December 4, 1981, pp. 10–11; January 8, 1982, p. 9; January 15, 1982, p. 14; February 12, 1982, p. 14; February 19, 1982, pp. 7–9. *The Times* (London), November 21 and 25, 1981. (d) Strength of armed forces: N. Dupuy et al., *The Almanac of*

World Military Power, 4th ed. (San Rafael, Calif.: Presidio Press, 1980), pp. 66–67. John Keegan, *World Armies* (New York: Facts on File, 1979), pp. 44–54. Keegan estimated the army to consist of 65,000 men plus 20,000 Bangladesh Rifles (border guards), the navy 3,500, and the air force 2,500, for a total of 71,000 men, an increase of 200 percent since 1974. See also *Le Monde,* November 14, 1981, for an analysis of the military.

28. Economic problems. (a) IMF: *Far Eastern Economic Review,* September 18, 1981, p. 51; October 9, 1981, pp. 60–61; and November 27, 1981, pp. 52–53. *Washington Post,* November 21, 1981. *New York Times,* October 30, 1981. *Economist,* November 21, 1981, p. 41. (b) Other issues: *Far Eastern Economic Review,* June 5, 1981, pp. 46–47; June 19, 1981, pp. 59–60; September 11, 1981, pp. 51–52; January 15, 1982, p. 57; January 22, 1982, p. 8; March 5, 1982, p. 62; March 26, 1982, pp. 105–106.

29. Private enterprise. *Far Eastern Economic Review,* July 24, 1981, pp. 52 and 55, and December 18, 1981, p. 44.

30. Bangali-Indian relations. (a) New Moore and other problems: *Far Eastern Economic Review,* August 28, 1981, pp. 20–21, and September 18, 1981, p. 8. *Economist,* August 9, 1980, pp. 33–34. (b) Hill Tracts: *Economist,* October 17, 1981, pp. 42–43. *Le Monde,* November 10, 1981. *Far Eastern Economic Review,* October 16, 1981, pp. 11–13. *Keesing's,* October 9, 1981, p. 31128.

31. Human rights. U.S., Department of State, *Country Reports on Human Rights 1981* (Washington, D.C.: Government Printing Office), pp. 941–950.

32. U.N. General Assembly elections. *New York Times,* September 16, 1981. *Far Eastern Economic Review,* September 4, 1981, p. 8.

33. Warning of coup. *Far Eastern Economic Review,* March 19, 1982, pp. 12–13.

34. March 24 coup. (a) Background: Craig Baxter, "Bangladesh," *The Washington Quarterly* 5, no. 2 (spring 1982), pp. 189–193. Mohammad Ataur Rahman, "Bangladesh in 1982: Beginnings of the Second Decade," *Asian Survey* 23, no. 2 (February 1983), p. 151. (b) Coup: *New York Times,* March 25, 1982. *The Times* (London) March 25, 1982. *China Daily* (Hong Kong), March 26, 1982. *Le Monde,* March 25, 1982. *Economist,* March 27, 1982, p. 26.

35. Biography of General Ershad. *Le Monde,* March 25 and 30, 1982. *Guardian,* March 25 and April 13, 1982. *New York Times,* March 25, 1982. *Economist,* March 27, 1982, p. 26. See also note 24, this chapter.

36. Reaction to coup. (a) General: *Guardian,* March 26 and April 10, 1982. *The Times* (London), April 11, 1982. *Le Monde,* March 29, 1982. (b) Awami League: *Le Monde,* March 26, 1982. *Guardian,* March 27, 1982. (c) Foreign governments: *Chicago Tribune,* March 24, 1982. *New York Times,* March 29 and April 1, 1982. *The Times* (London), March 25, 1982. *Le Monde,* March 25, 1982. *Washington Post,* March 30, 1982; reprinted *Guardian* editorial.

37. Martial law. *Guardian,* March 26, 1982. *The Times* (London), March 26 and 27 and April 4, 1982. *New York Times,* March 26, 1982. *Le Monde,* March 30, 1982. *China Daily* (Hong Kong), March 30, 1982. *Far Eastern Economic Review,* April 2, 1982, p. 22; April 9, 1982, p. 29; and December 24, 1982, p. 28. Rahman, "Bangladesh in 1982," pp. 151–152.

38. Arrests. *Far Eastern Economic Review,* April 9, 1982, p. 7; May 21, 1982, p. 6; June 18, 1982, p. 9; September 10, 1982, p. 11; November 5, 1982, pp. 42–43; and May 28, 1983, p. 13.

39. Reactions to martial law. *New York Times,* March 29, 1982.

40. Government reorganization. (a) Council of advisers: *Far Eastern Economic Review,* July 2, 1982, pp. 22–23. *Guardian,* March 31, 1982. (b) Ombudsmen: *New York Times,* March 27, 1982. *The Times* (London), April 14, 1982. (c) President Choudhury: *New York Times,* March 27, 1982. (d) Decentralization: Rahman, "Bangladesh in 1982," pp. 152–153. *Far Eastern Economic Review,* April 16, 1982, pp. 20–22; May 7, 1982, p. 35; June 11, 1982, pp. 10–11; July 30, 1982, pp. 31–32; October 22, 1982, p. 24; and December 24, 1982, p. 26.

41. Food shortages. *The Times* (London), April 4, 1982. *Guardian,* April 13, 1982.

42. Private and public sectors. (a) General: Rahman, "Bangladesh in 1982," pp. 153–154. *Far Eastern Economic Review,* January 1, 1982, p. 6; February 5, 1982, pp. 98–99; and June 18, 1982, pp. 30 and 90–92. *Time,* August 2, 1982. *World Bank Annual Report 1982,* pp. 78–80.

43. Black money. *Far Eastern Economic Review,* May 14, 1982, p. 114, and September 10, 1982, p. 10.

44. Budgets. (a) 1982/83: *Europa Year Book 1983: A World Survey* (London: Europa Publications, 1983), p. 1599. *Far Eastern Economic Review,* July 8, 1982, p. 66. (b) 1983/84. *Far Eastern Economic Review,* July 14, 1983, pp. 49–50.

45. Land reform. Rahman, "Bangladesh in 1982," p. 153. Peter J. Bertocci, "Bangladesh in the Early 80's," pp. 1003–04.

46. The economy. *World Bank Annual Report 1982* (Washington, D.C.: World Bank, 1982), pp. 79–80. *World Bank Annual Report 1983,* p. 86.

47. Relations with India. (a) India and the world: *Far Eastern Economic Review,* March 5, 1982, pp. 24–25. (b) Ershad and India: *Far Eastern Economic Review,* April 23, 1982, p. 30, and May 28, 1982, p. 16. (c) Ershad and Mrs. Gandhi agree: *Asian Reader,* November 5–11, 1982, pp. 16871–72. *Keesing's,* November 5, 1982, p. 31796. *Far Eastern Economic Review,* October 15, 1982, pp. 28–29. Rahman, "Bangladesh in 1982," p. 155. (d) Assam: *New York Times,* January 7, 1983; February 13–15, 1983; February 19–22, 1983; March 4, 1983. *Far Eastern Economic Review,* February 3, 1983, p. 16; March 10, 1983, pp. 9–10; May 10, 1983, pp. 29–30; May 26, 1983, p. 12.

48. Saudis. *Far Eastern Economic Review,* April 9, 1982, p. 8, and May 14, 1982, p. 95. Re Pakistan see *Asian Recorder,* October 22–28 1982, p. 16847.

49. Other foreign relations. (a) Nepal: *Far Eastern Economic Review,* March 25, 1982, pp. 62–63. (b) Soviet Union: ibid., February 21, 1983. U.S., Department of State, *Background Notes: Bangladesh 1984* (Washington, D.C., 1984).

50. Aid from Western nations and United Nations. (a) Western aid: See *World Bank Annual Report 1982. Asian Recorder,* June 11–17, 1982, p. 16539. *Keesing's,* October 22, 1982, pp. 31771–72. (b) IMF: *Keesing's,* ibid. (c) Ershad at the United Nations: *New York Times,* June 18, 1983.

51. Ershad and democracy. (a) Promises of democracy: *International Herald Tribune,* March 29, 1982. *New York Times,* March 25, 1982. *Far Eastern Economic Review,* December 24, 1982, pp. 28–29. See also note 47, this chapter. (b) Law and order: *Le Monde,* March 30, 1982. *Washington Post,* March 25, 1982. *New York Times,* March 25, 1982. *Far Eastern Economic Review,* April 2, 1982, p. 22; April 23, 1982, p. 9; May 7, 1982, p. 9; and December 24, 1982, pp. 24–26. (c) Ershad's June 20 address: *Far Eastern Economic Review,* July 2, 1982, pp. 22–23. (d) Proposed constitution: *Far Eastern Economic Review,* August 20, 1982, p. 16. *Asian Recorder,* October 8–14, 1982, p. 16827.

52. (a) Reforms: *Far Eastern Economic Review,* April 23, 1982, p. 8; May 7, 1982, p. 35; July 30, 1982, pp. 31–32; and December 24, 1982, p. 261. *Asian Recorder,* October 29–November 4, 1982, p. 16859. *Keesing's,* October 22, 1982, p. 31770. (b) Ershad's new title: *Asian Recorder,* December 10–16, 1982, p. 16982, and December 17–23, 1982, p. 16937. (c) Courts: *Far Eastern Economic Review,* October 15, 1982, p. 9, and November 5, 1982, pp. 42–43. (d) Professors: *Asian Recorder,* December 17–23, 1982, p. 16937. *Far Eastern Economic Review,* February 24, 1983, p. 9.

53. (a) Islamic state: Background. *New York Times,* March 11, 1982. *Far Eastern Economic Review,* October 29, 1982, pp. 18–19, and April 7, 1983, pp. 16–17. Ershad's statements on Islamic state. *Far Eastern Economic Review,* December 24, 1982, pp. 16–17 and February 10, 1983, p. 22. (b) Martyr's Day: *Far Eastern Economic Review,* March 10, 1983, p. 30. *Economist,* February 26, 1983, p. 52. (c) Opposition: *Far Eastern Economic Review,* February 24, 1983, pp. 14–15. (d) Students: *Economist,* February 26, 1983, p. 52. *Far Eastern Economic Review,* February 17, 1983, p. 5; February 24, 1983, pp. 14–15; and March 31, 1983, p. 10.

54. (a) Dialogue: *Economist,* February 26, 1983, p. 52. *Far Eastern Economic Review,* March 10, 1983, p. 30; April 14, 1983, p. 10; and May 12, 1983, p. 12. (b) March 24 ceremony: *Economist,* April 2, 1983, p. 59. *Far Eastern Economic Review,* April 7, 1983, p. 18. (c) Coalitions: Ibid., April 21, 1983, pp. 8–9; June 16, 1983, p. 11; and June 23, 1983, p. 11.

55. (a) Ershad's 1983 decisions: *Far Eastern Economic Review,* September 1, 1983, pp. 21–25 and 27, and September 28, 1983, p. 14. (b) Promised elections: *Far Eastern Economic Review,* December 8, 1983, p. 38. (c) People's party: *Statesman Weekly* (Calcutta), December 3, 1983. *Far Eastern Economic Review,* December 8, 1983, p. 13. (d) Ershad names himself president: *New York Times,* December 12, 1983. *Chicago Tribune,* December 12, 1983. (e) Opposition: *New York Times,* December 14 and 18, 1983. *Far Eastern Economic Review,* December 8, 1983, p. 31; January 19, 1984, p. 34; and February 9, 1984, p. 24.

EPILOGUE

1. Carl J. Friedrich, *The Pathology of Politics* (New York: Harper and Row, 1977), pp. 127–169.

A Select Bibliography

BIBLIOGRAPHIC SOURCES

Bertocci, Peter, ed. *Bangladesh, History, Society and Culture*. Occasional Paper no. 22. East Lansing: Asian Studies Center, Michigan State University, 1973. Bibliography of secondary materials.

Kayastha, Ved P. *The Crisis in the Indian Subcontinent and the Birth of Bangladesh*, rev. ed. Ithaca, N.Y.: Cornell University, 1972. Selected reading list.

Satyaprakash, ed. *Bangladesh: A Select Bibliography*. Columbia, Mo.: South Asia Books, 1977.

Sharma, Prakash C. *Rural and Economic Development Planning in Bangladesh, 1950–1972*. Monticello, Ill.: Council of Planning Librarians, 1975. Selected research bibliography, 18 pages, mimeographed.

Sikhwal, B. L. *South Asia: A Systematic Geographic Bibliography*. Metuchen, N.J.: Scarecrow Press, 1974. Bangladesh, pp. 604–629.

U.S. Library of Congress. *Accession List, Bangladesh*. New Delhi: Library of Congress Office, vols. 1–2, 1972, through vol. 7, 1978.

DOCUMENTS AND OTHER SOURCES

Asian Recorder. New Delhi, India, 1971–1982. A weekly digest of Asian events arranged alphabetically by countries; its sources comprise journals, radio reports, and government statements, in addition to world newspapers.

Bangladesh. Planning Commission. *The Annual Plan, 1972–1973*. Dacca: Bangladesh Government Press, 1972.

Bangladesh Speaks. Dacca: Bangladesh Government Printing Office, 1972. A collection of speeches and statements by Sheikh Mujibur Rahman, March 7, 1971–March 26, 1972.

Bangla Desh Documents. New Delhi: Ministry of External Affairs, 1971.

Blaustein, A. P., and Flanz, G. H. *Constitutions of the Countries of the World*, vol. 2. Dobbs Ferry, N.Y.: Oceana Publishing Company, 1977.

Europa Year Book: A World Survey, vol. 1, 1972–1983. London: Europa Publications. Contains statistical data about individual countries.

Keesing's Contemporary Archives, vol. 18, 1971–vol. 28, 1982. London: Keesing's Publications.

Pakistan. *White Paper on the Crisis in East Pakistan.* Islamabad: August 1971.

Pakistan Horizon, vol. 25, nos. 1 and 3, 1972. Karachi: Pakistan Institute of International Affairs.

Singh, Sheelandra. *Bangladesh Documents,* 2 vols. New York: International Publications Service, 1974.

United Nations. International Bank for Reconstruction and Development and International Development Association. *Reconstructing the Economy of Bangladesh,* 2 vols. New York: United Nations, September 1972.

United Nations Yearbook, vol. 27, 1972–vol. 33, 1979. New York: United Nations.

United States. *U.S. Foreign Policy for the 70's: Building for Peace.* A Report to the Congress by Richard Nixon, President of the United States, February 25, 1971. Washington, D.C.: Government Printing Office, 1971. Pakistan and India, pp. 111–114.

United States. *U.S. Foreign Policy for the 70's: The Emerging Structure of Peace.* A Report to the Congress by Richard Nixon, President of the United States, February 9, 1972. Washington, D.C.: Government Printing Office, 1972. Bangladesh and South Asia, pp. 141–152.

United States. *U.S. Foreign Policy for the 70's: Shaping Durable Peace.* A Report to the Congress by Richard Nixon, President of the United States, May 3, 1973. Washington, D.C.: Government Printing Office, 1973. Bangladesh and South Asia, pp. 143–152.

U.S. Congress. Senate. Judiciary Committee. Subcommittee to Investigate Problems Connected with Refugees and Escapees. "Relief Problems in East Pakistan and India," *Hearings,* 92nd Cong., 1st sess., June 28–October 4, 1971, and "Relief Problems in Bangladesh," *Hearings,* 92nd Cong., 2nd sess., February 2, 1972. Washington, D.C.: Government Printing Office, 1971 and 1972.

U.S. Congress. Senate. Committee on Foreign Relations. "Recognition of Bangladesh," *Hearings,* 92nd Cong., 2nd sess., on various state resolutions, March 6 and 7, 1972. Washington, D.C.: Government Printing Office, 1972.

U.S. Department of State. *United States Foreign Policy, 1971, 1972 and 1973.* Reports of the Secretary of State. Washington, D.C.: Government Printing Office, 1972, 1973, and 1974.

Other Titles of Interest from Westview Press

Geography of Bangladesh, Haroun Er Rashid

Bangladesh: The Test Case for Development, Just Faaland and John Richard Parkinson

Agricultural Development in Bangladesh: Prospects for the Future, E. Boyd Wennergren, Morris D. Whitaker, and Charles Antholt

†*Southeast Asia: Realm of Contrasts,* edited by Ashok K. Dutt

PROFILES OF CONTEMPORARY ASIA:

Bangladesh: A New Nation in an Old Setting, Craig Baxter

Burma: A Socialist Nation of Southeast Asia, David I. Steinberg

Nepal: Profile of a Himalayan Kingdom, Leo E. Rose and John T. Scholz

Pakistan: A Nation in the Making, Shahid Javed Burki

Sri Lanka: An Island Republic, Tissa Fernando

†*The Philippines: A Singular and A Plural Place,* David Joel Steinberg

†*Vietnam: A Nation in Revolution,* William J. Duiker

†*Japan: Profile of a Postindustrial Power,* Second, Updated Edition, Ardath Burks

Indonesia, William Liddle

Thailand, Charles F. Keyes

South Korea, David I. Steinberg

†Available in hardcover and paperback.

About the Book and Author

Bangladesh: Biography of a Muslim Nation
Charles Peter O'Donnell

This is an up-to-date and comprehensive account of eight centuries of colonial rule over the Bangali people and of twelve event-filled, swift-paced years of Bangladesh's independence. Dr. O'Donnell analyzes the problems confronted by Bangladesh in its economic and political development, domestically and internationally, and underlines the role of the country in South Asian affairs, its place in the Third World, and the dual importance of economic self-reliance and interdependence. He portrays, as well, the geographic, social, linguistic, and religious background of a nation that, in the face of poverty, overpopulation, and seismic political upheavals among its civilian and military leaders, continues to struggle for survival and an improved way of life. Dr. O'Donnell draws on the work of contemporary scholars and journalists, public documents, and his personal experience and contacts with Bangali officials and others.

Charles Peter O'Donnell has taught and lectured on history, government, economics, political theory, and foreign policy at De Paul University, Catholic University of America, the Université Officielle du Congo, and Loyola University of Chicago and Loyola's Rome Center. He has been associate dean of Georgetown University School of Foreign Service, deputy director of the Foreign Service Institute, and coordinator of the Senior Seminar in Foreign Policy. He has served as a Foreign Service officer in Sri Lanka (then Ceylon), France, Switzerland, and Bangladesh (then East Pakistan).

Index